MW00785552

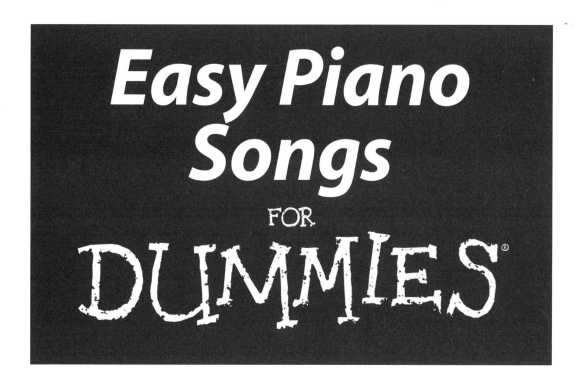

Easy Piano Songs FOR DUMMIES®

Performance Notes by Adam Perlmutter

ISBN 978-1-4803-5284-1

HAL•LEONARD® CORPORATION

7777 W. Bluemound Rd. P.O. Box 13819 Milwaukee, WI 53213

Visit Hal Leonard Online at
www.halleonard.com

Table of Contents

Introduction

Welcome to *Easy Piano Hits for Dummies.* Gathered in this collection are arrangements of 40 notable songs from the 1920s to the present day, ranging from pop and jazz standards like "The Way You Look Tonight" to the country-pop songs of the young singer-songwriter Taylor Swift. The music notation includes simplified piano arrangements with the lyrics notated between the treble and bass staves, along with chord symbols that a guitarist can use to follow along. Also included are performance notes that provide background for the artists and their tunes, as well as tips like technical suggestions and musical analysis — in other words, everything you need to make these great songs your own. Enjoy!

About This Book

For each song, I include a bit of background information to satisfy the historically curious. The information is followed by a variety of tidbits that struck me as I made my way through the teaching of these songs, including some of the following:

- A run-down of the parts you need to know.
- A breakdown of some of the chord progressions you need to navigate the sheet music.
- Some tips and shortcuts you can use to expedite the learning process.

In many cases, you may already know how to do a lot of this. If so, feel free to skip over those familiar bits.

How to Use This Book

The music contains lyrics, piano parts and guitar chords for each song. And included throughout are handy performance notes to help you learn how to play these songs and understand how they work. I recommend that you first play through the song, and then practice all the main sections and chords. From there, you can add the tricks and treats of each one — and there are many. Approach each song one section at a time and then assemble the sections together in a sequence. This technique helps to provide you with a greater understanding of how the song is structured, and enables you to play it through more quickly.

In order to follow the music and my performance notes, you need a basic understanding of scales and chords. But if you're not a wiz, don't worry. Just spend a little time with the nifty tome *Music Theory For Dummies* by Michael Pilhofer and Holly Day (Wiley), and with a little practice, you'll be on your way to entertaining family and friends.

Conventions Used in This Book

As you might expect, I use quite a few musical terms in this book. Some of these may be unfamiliar to you, so here are a few right off the bat that can help your understanding of basic playing principles:

- **Arpeggio:** Playing the notes of a chord one at a time rather than all together.
- **Bridge:** Part of the song that is different from the verse and the chorus, providing variety and connecting the other parts of the song to each other.
- **Coda:** The section at the end of the song, which is sometimes labeled with the word "coda."
- **Chorus:** The part of the song that is the same each time through, usually the most familiar section.
- **Hook:** A familiar, accessible, or sing-along melody, lick, or other section of the song.
- **Verse:** The part of the song that tells the story; each verse has different lyrics, and each song generally has between two and four of these.

Icons Used in This Book

In the margins of this book are several handy icons to help make following the performance notes easier:

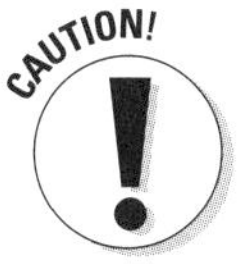

A reason to stop and review advice that can prevent personal injury to your fingers, your brain, or your ego.

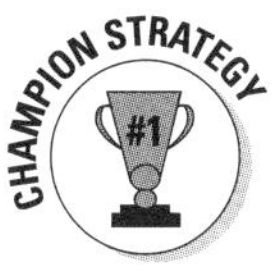

These are optional parts, or alternate approaches that those who'd like to find their way through the song with a distinctive flair can take. Often these are slightly more challenging routes, but encouraged nonetheless, because there's nothing like a good challenge!

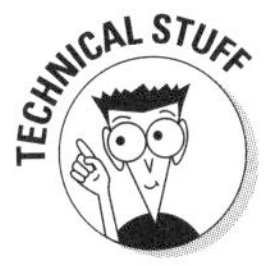

This is where you will find notes about specific musical concepts that are relevant but confusing to non-musical types — stuff that you wouldn't bring up, say, at a frat party or at your kid's soccer game.

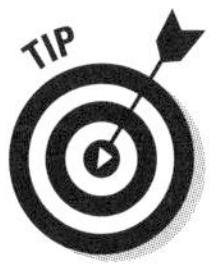

You get lots of these tips, because the more playing suggestions I can offer, the better you'll play. And isn't that what it's all about?

Back to December

Words and Music by
TAYLOR SWIFT

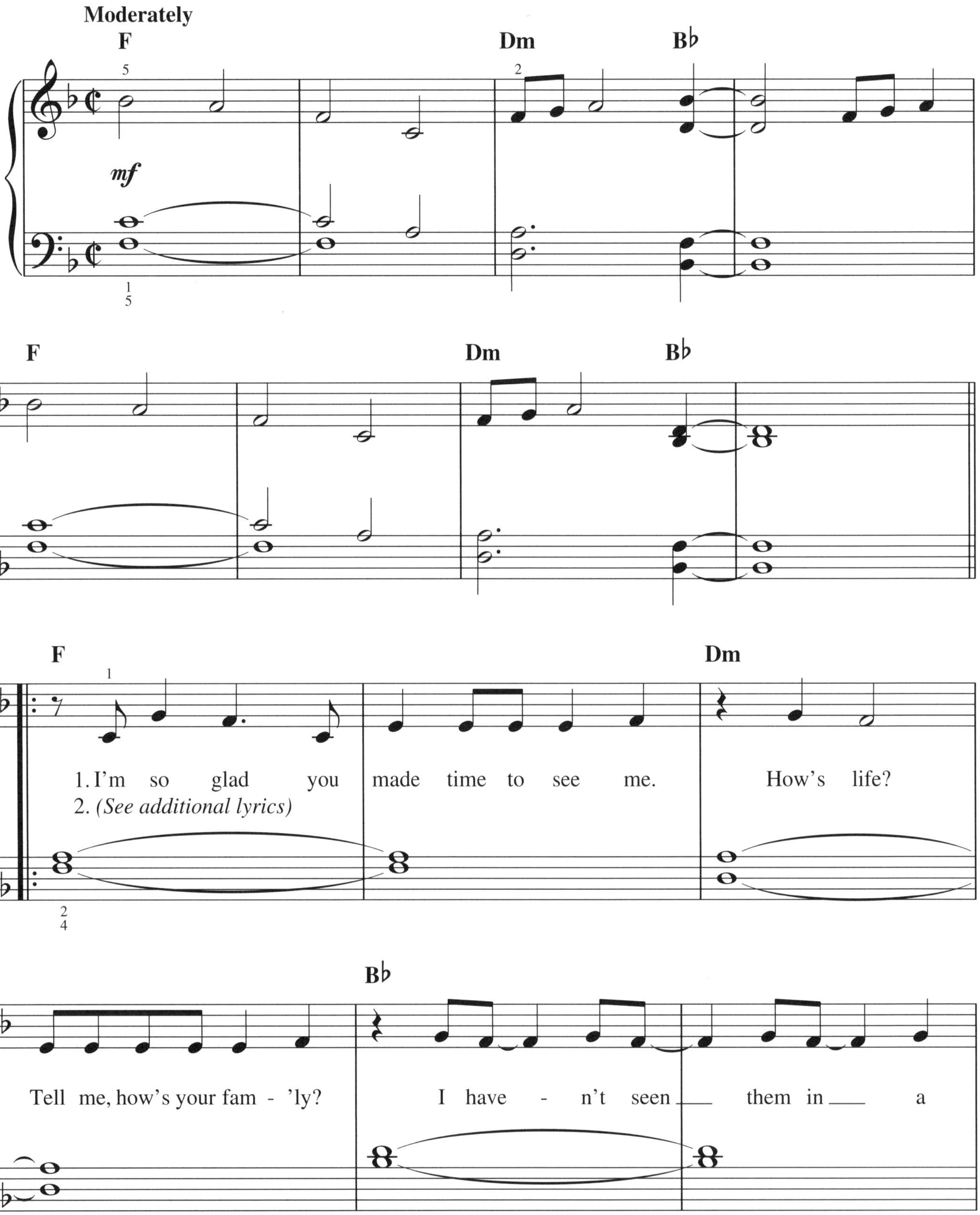

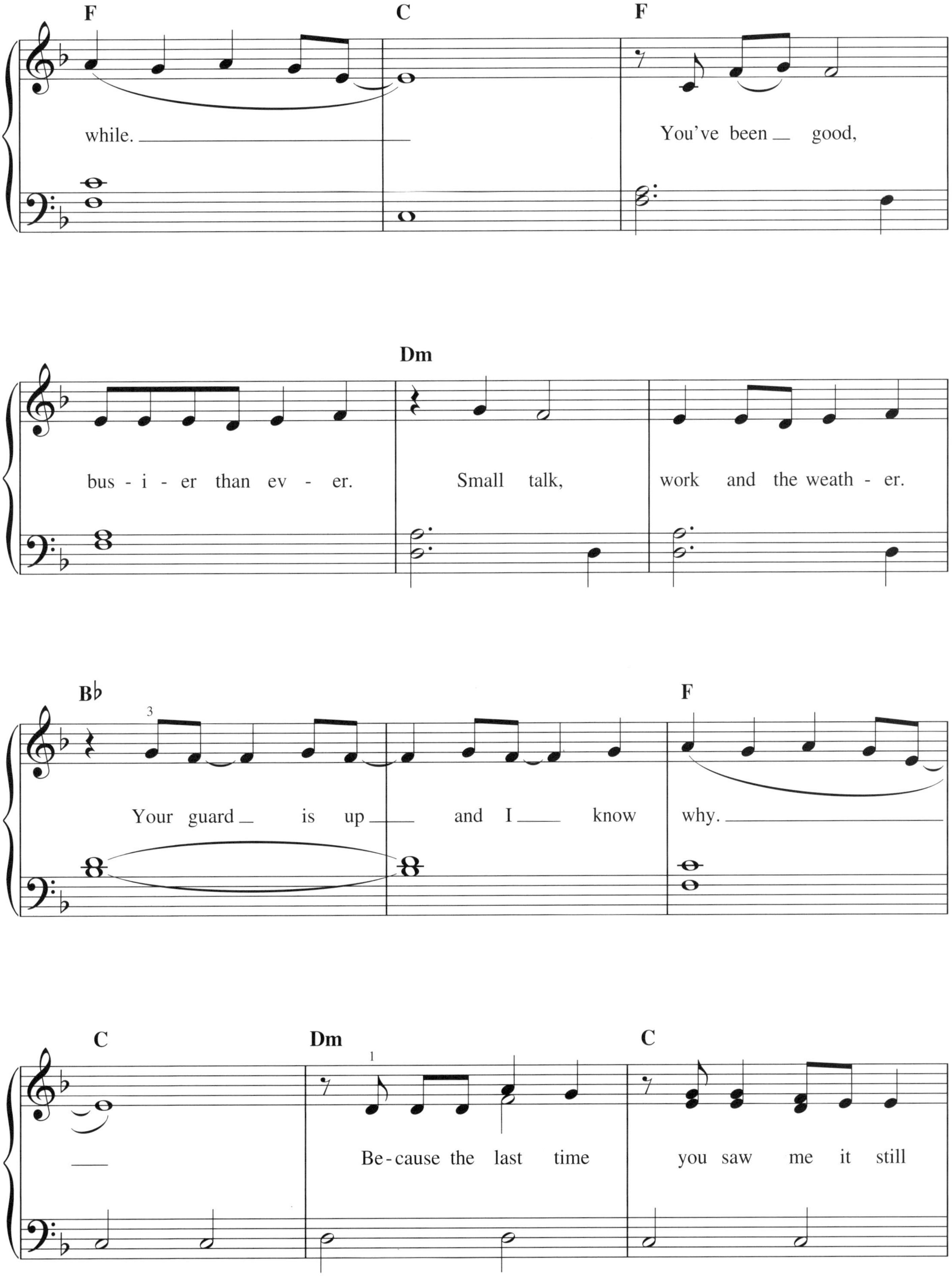
F C F
while.
You've been good,
Dm
bus - i - er than ev - er.
Small talk,
work and the weath - er.
B♭ F
3
Your guard is up and I know why.
C Dm C
1
Be - cause the last time you saw me it still

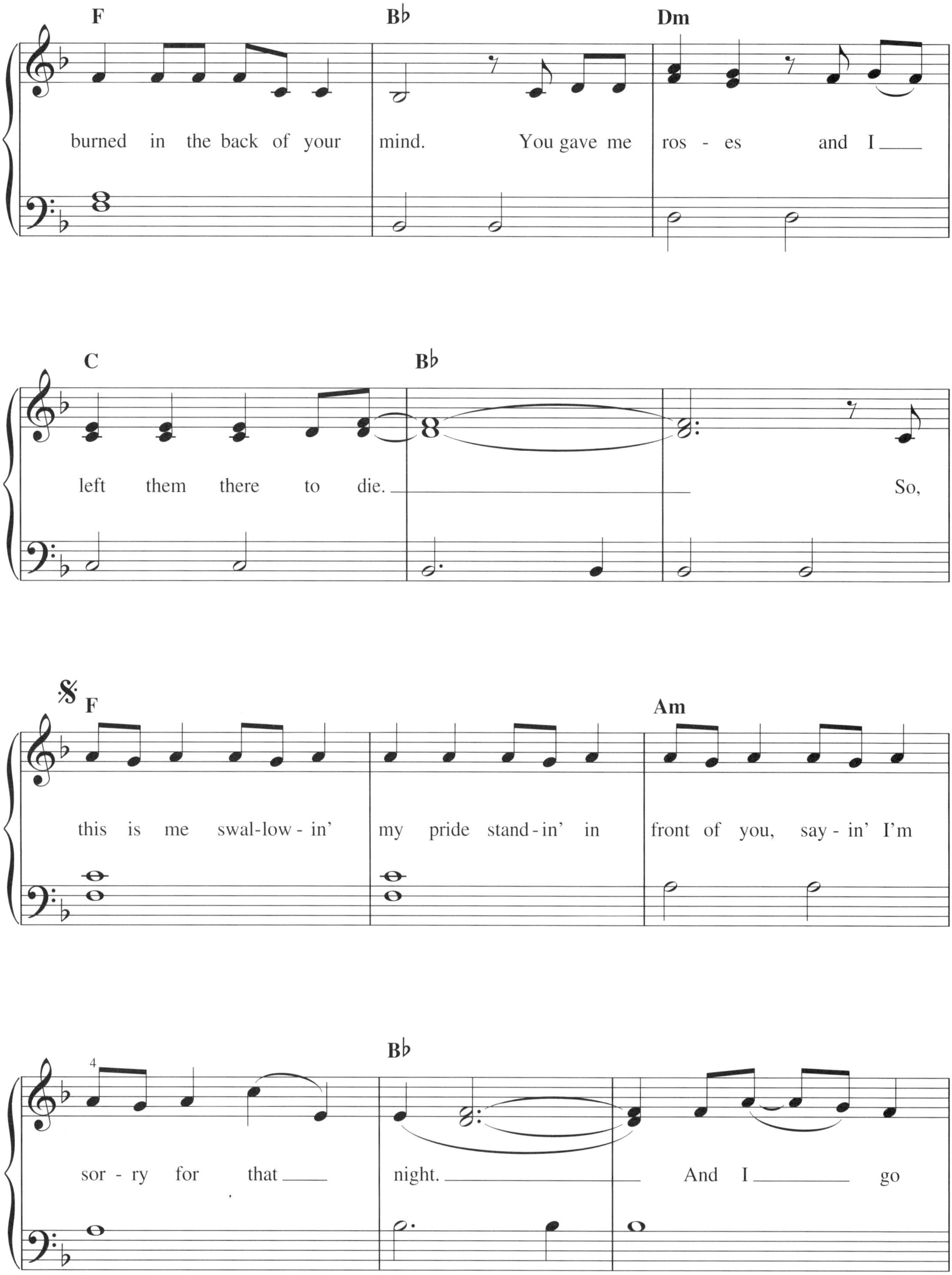
F
Bb
Dm
burned in the back of your mind. You gave me ros - es and I
C
Bb
left them there to die. So,
F
Am
this is me swal-low - in' my pride stand - in' in front of you, say - in' I'm
4
Bb
sor - ry for that night. And I go

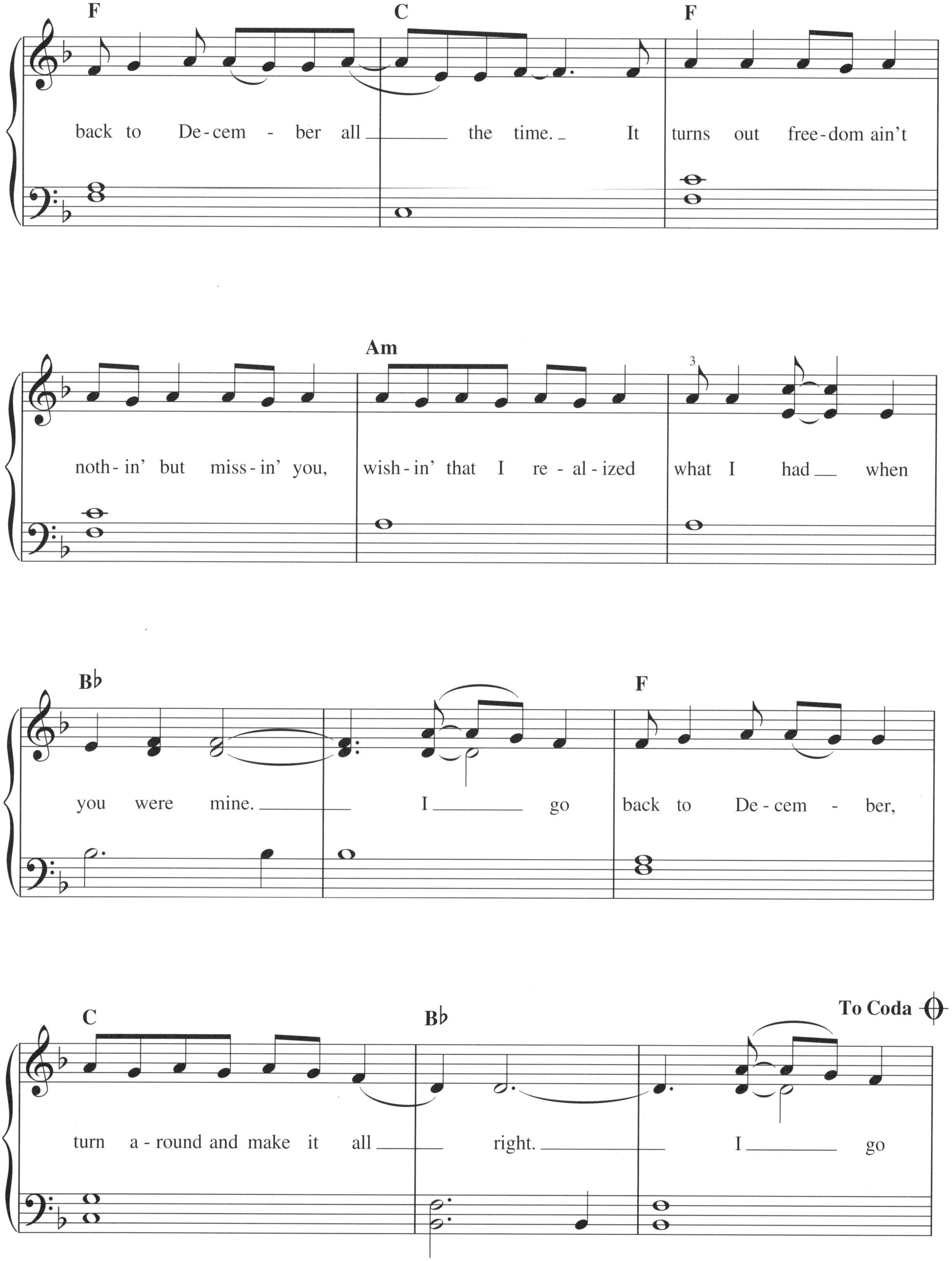
F
C
F
back to De-cem - ber all the time. It turns out free-dom ain't
Am
noth-in' but miss-in' you, wish-in' that I re - al-ized what I had when
B♭
F
you were mine. I go back to De-cem - ber,
C
B♭
To Coda
turn a-round and make it all right. I go

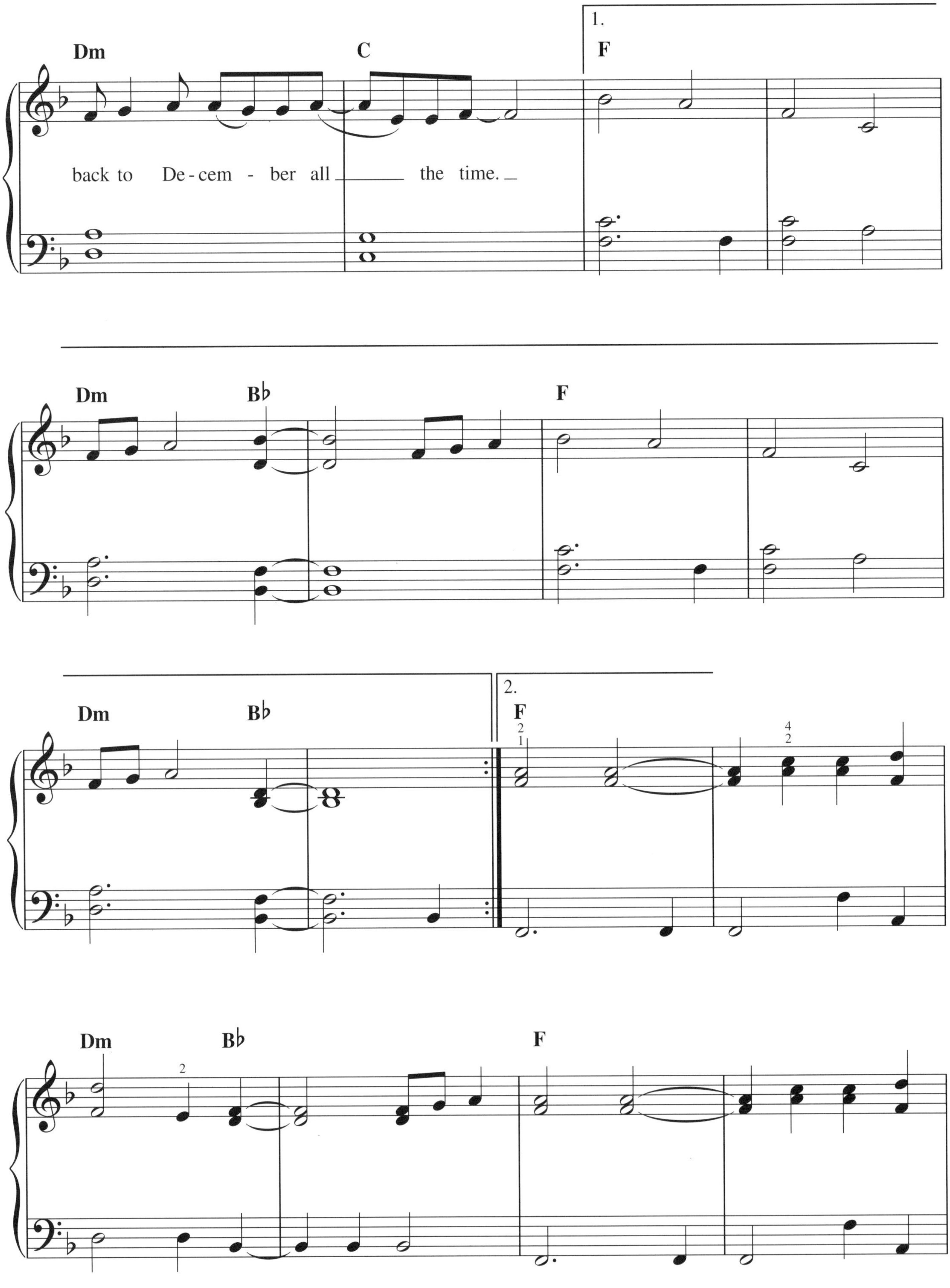
1.
Dm
C
F
back to De - cem - ber all the time.
Dm
B♭
F
Dm
B♭
2.
F
2
1
4
2
Dm
2
B♭
F

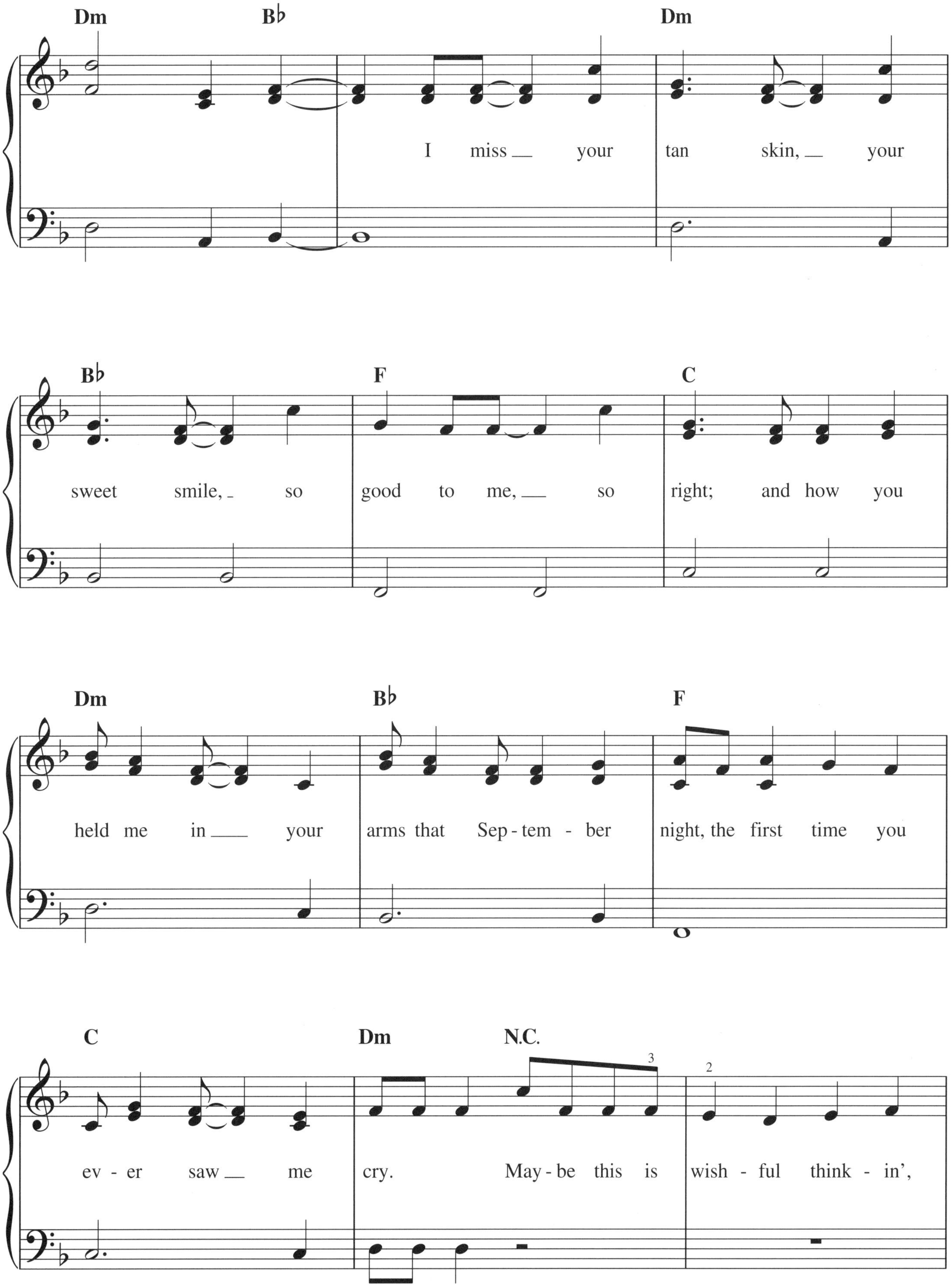
Dm
B♭
Dm
I miss your tan skin, your
B♭
F
C
sweet smile, so good to me, so right; and how you
Dm
B♭
F
held me in your arms that Sep - tem - ber night, the first time you
C
Dm
N.C.
ev - er saw me cry. May - be this is wish - ful think - in',
3
2

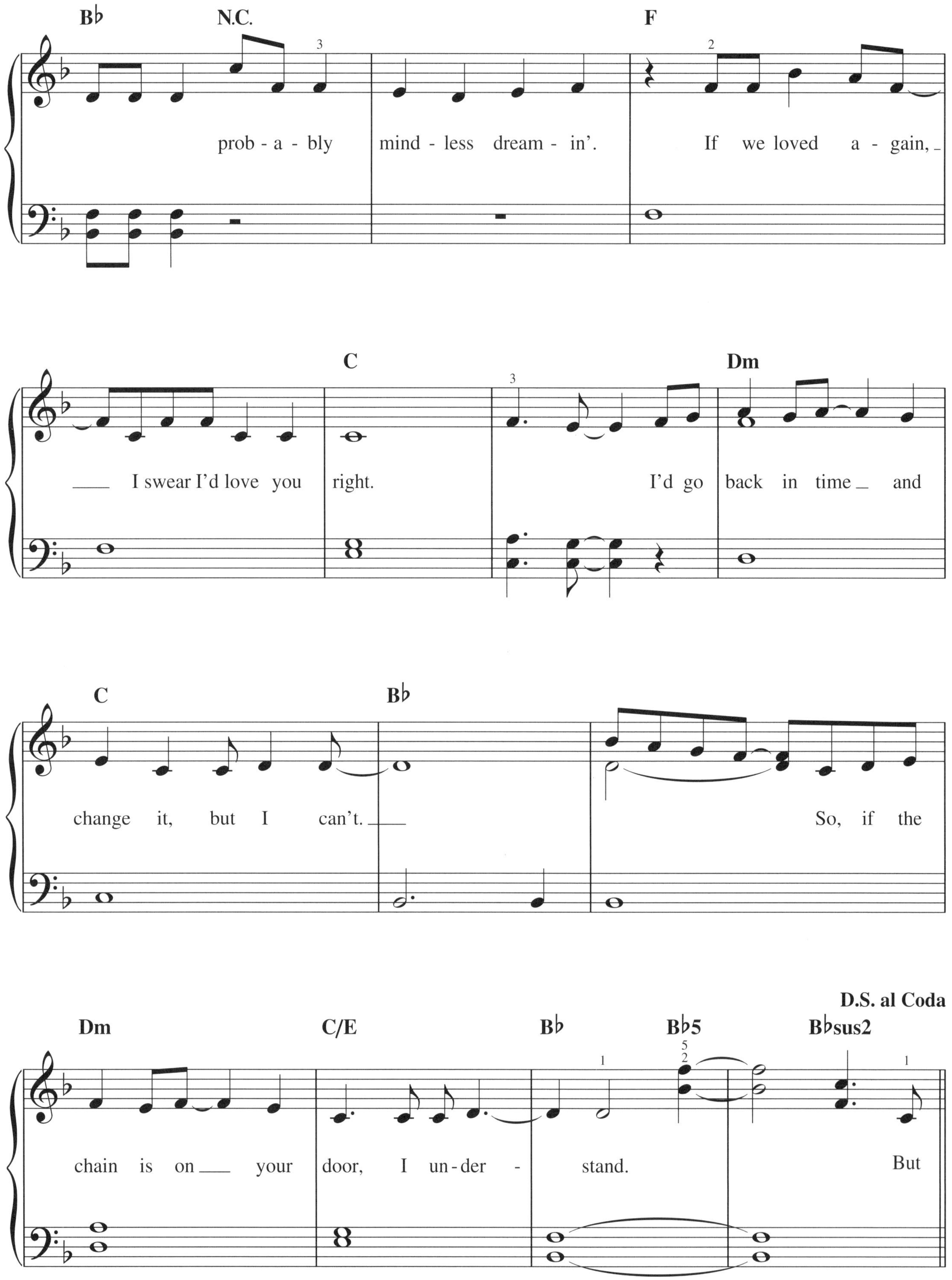
B♭ N.C. F
prob - a - bly mind - less dream - in'. If we loved a - gain,
C Dm
I swear I'd love you right. I'd go back in time and
C B♭
change it, but I can't. So, if the
D.S. al Coda
Dm C/E B♭ B♭5 B♭sus2
chain is on your door, I un-der - stand. But

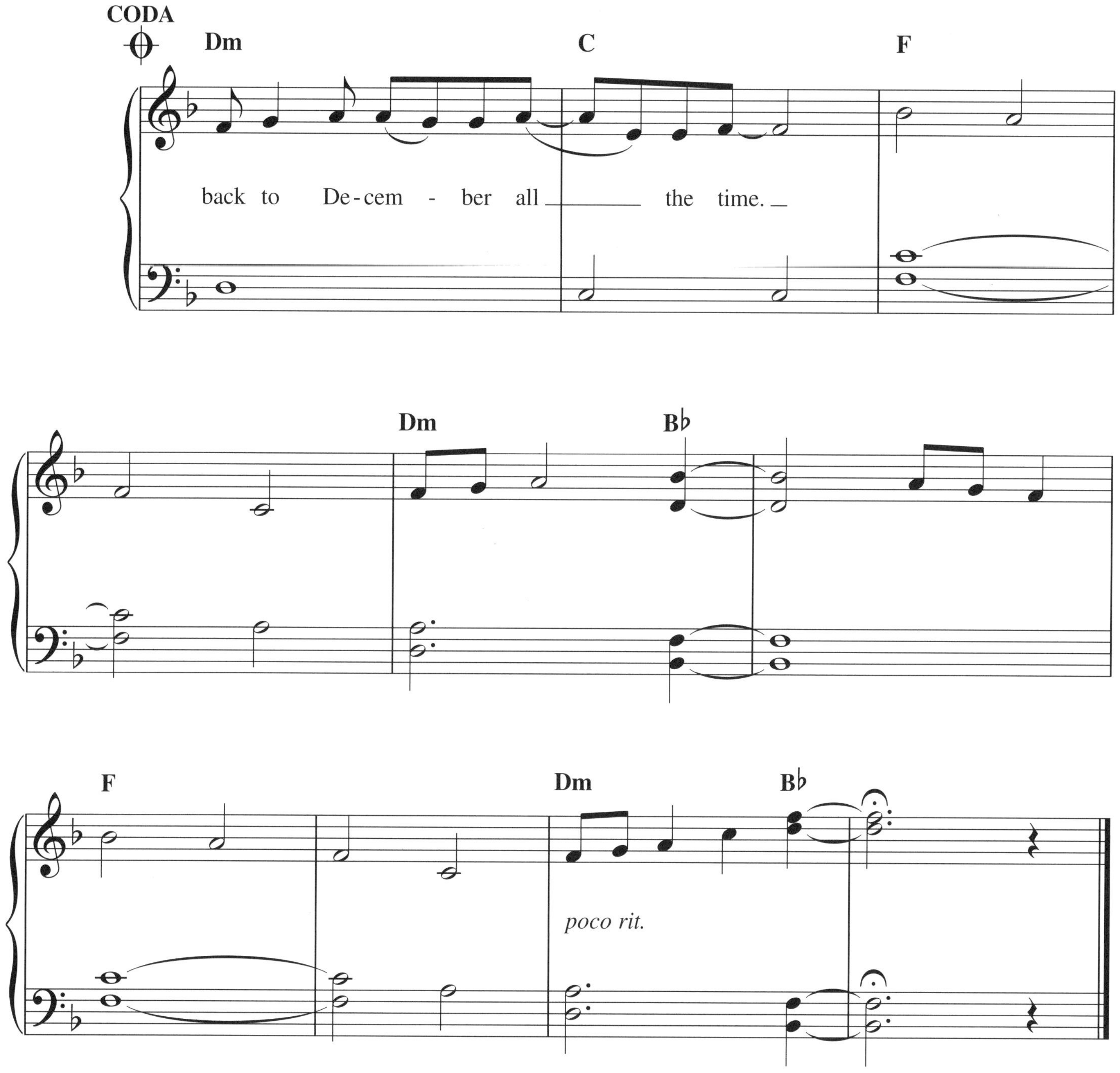

Additional Lyrics

2. These days I haven't been sleepin';
Stayin' up, playin' back myself leavin',
When your birthday passed and I didn't call.
Then I think about summer, all the beautiful times
I watched you laughin' from the passenger side
And realized I loved you in the fall.
And then the cold came, the dark days
When fear crept into my mind.
You gave me all your love and
All I gave you was goodbye.

So, this is me swallowin' my pride...

Blowin' in the Wind

Words and Music by
BOB DYLAN

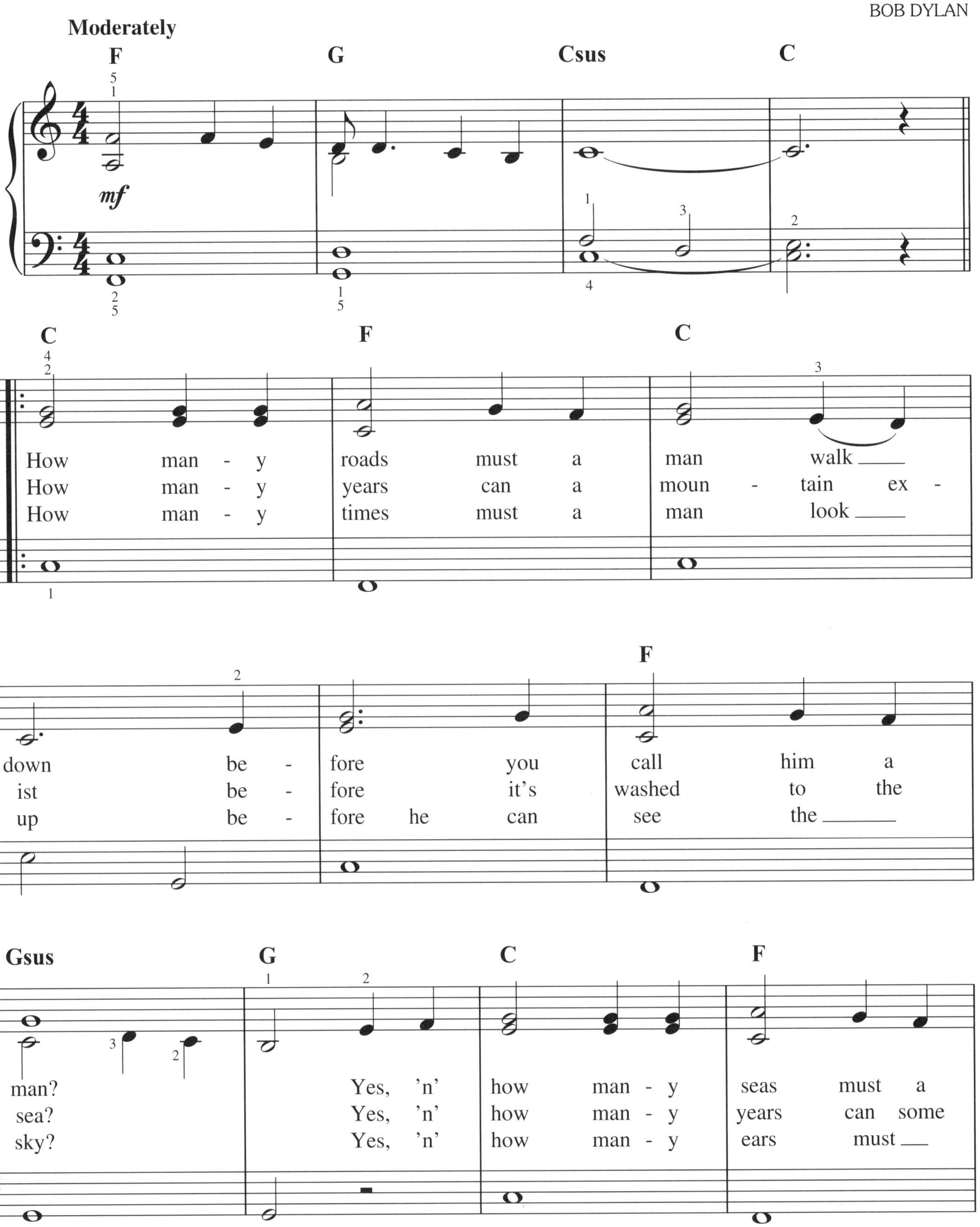

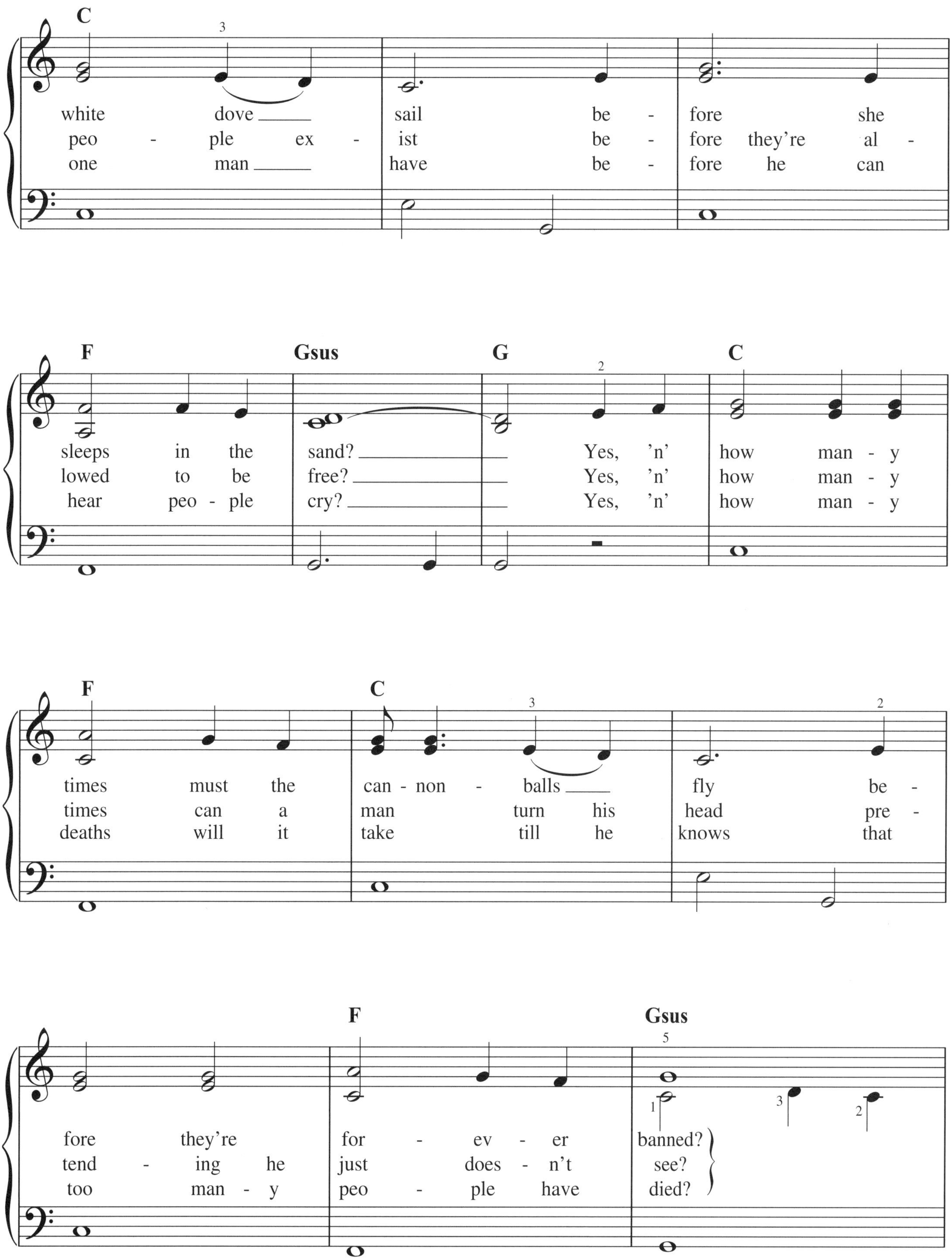
C
white dove sail be - fore she
peo - ple ex - ist be - fore they're al -
one man have be - fore he can
F Gsus G C
sleeps in the sand? Yes, 'n' how man - y
lowed to be free? Yes, 'n' how man - y
hear peo - ple cry? Yes, 'n' how man - y
F C
times must the can - non - balls fly be -
times can a man turn his head pre -
deaths will it take till he knows that
F Gsus
fore they're for - ev - er banned?
tend - ing he just does - n't see?
too man - y peo - ple have died?

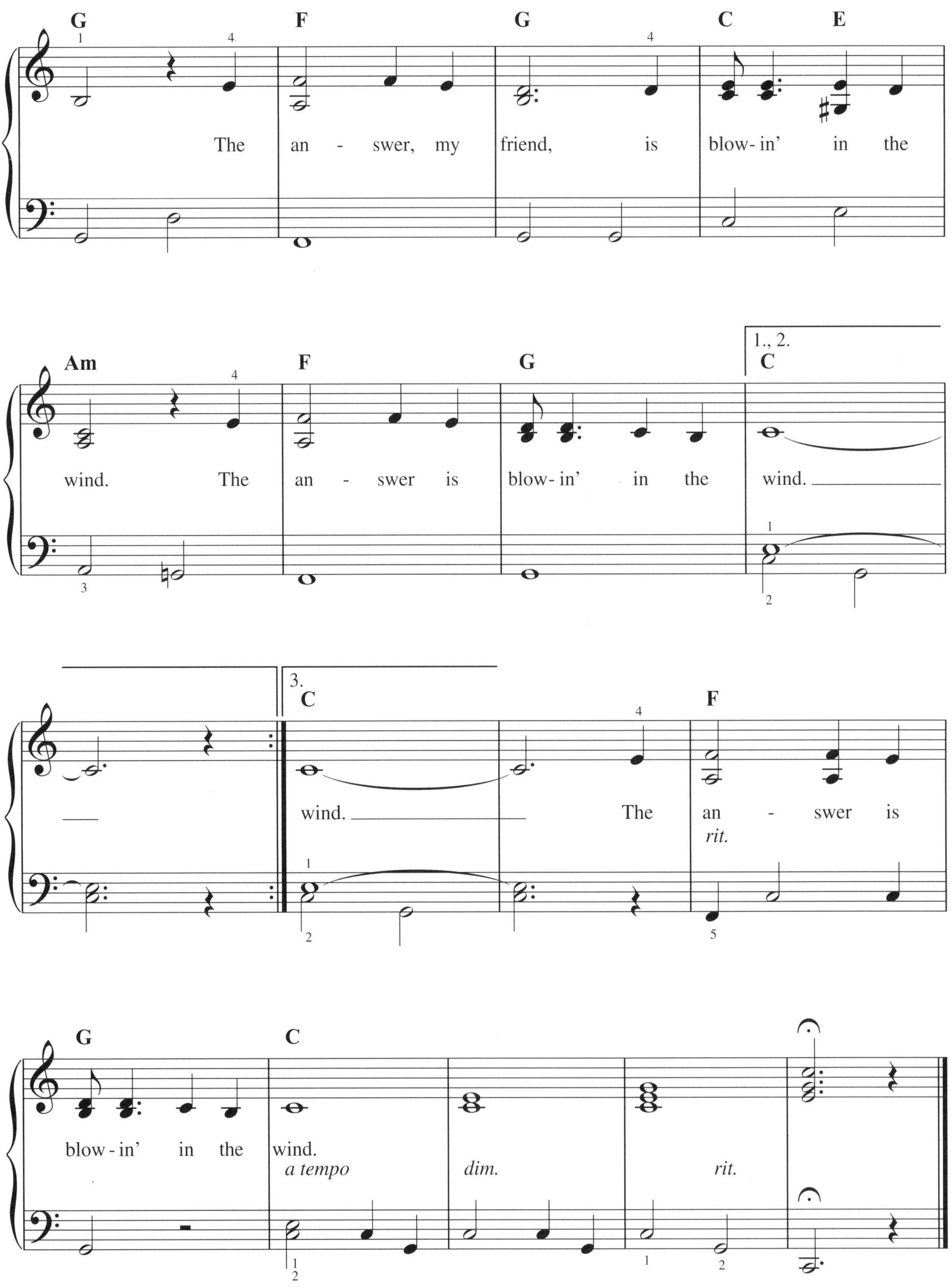
G F G C E
The an - swer, my friend, is blow- in' in the
Am F G
1., 2.
C
wind. The an - swer is blow- in' in the wind.
3.
C F
wind. The an - swer is
rit.
G C
blow - in' in the wind.
a tempo
dim.
rit.

Blue Skies

Words and Music by
IRVING BERLIN

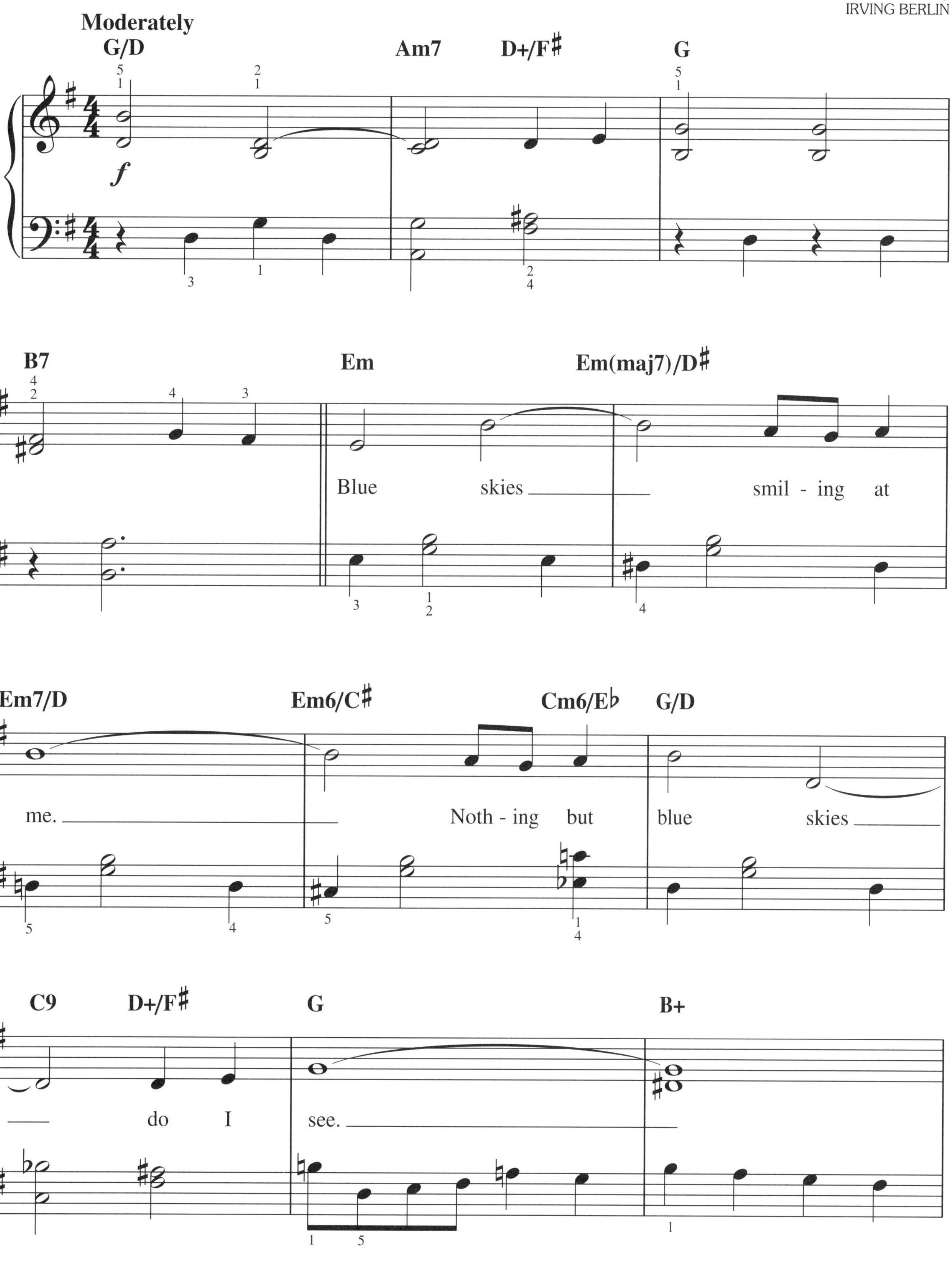

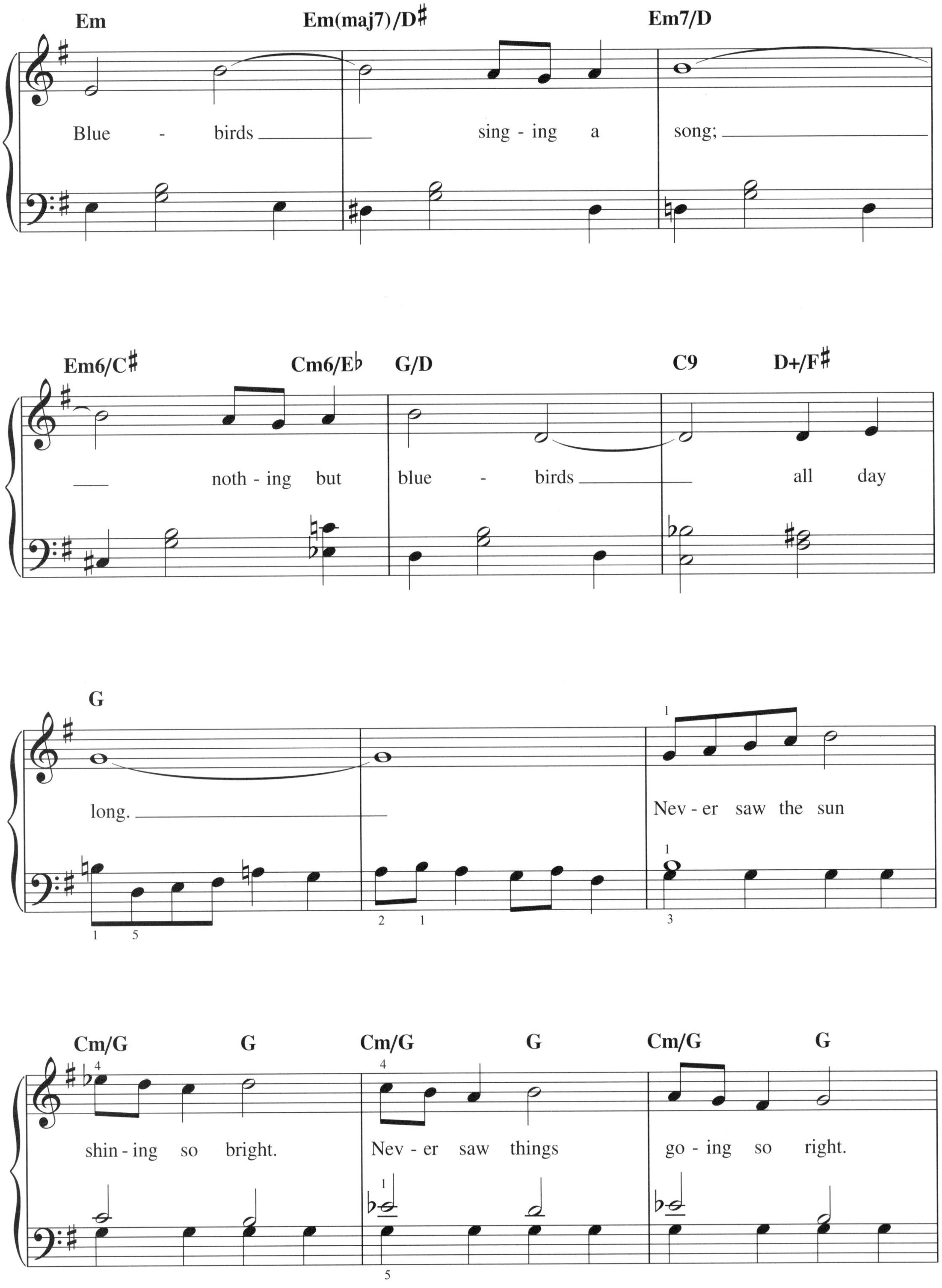
Em
Em(maj7)/D♯
Em7/D
Blue - birds singing - ing a song;
Em6/C♯
Cm6/E♭
G/D
C9
D+/F♯
nothing - ing but blue - birds all day
G
long.
Nev - er saw the sun
Cm/G
G
Cm/G
G
Cm/G
G
shin - ing so bright.
Nev - er saw things
go - ing so right.

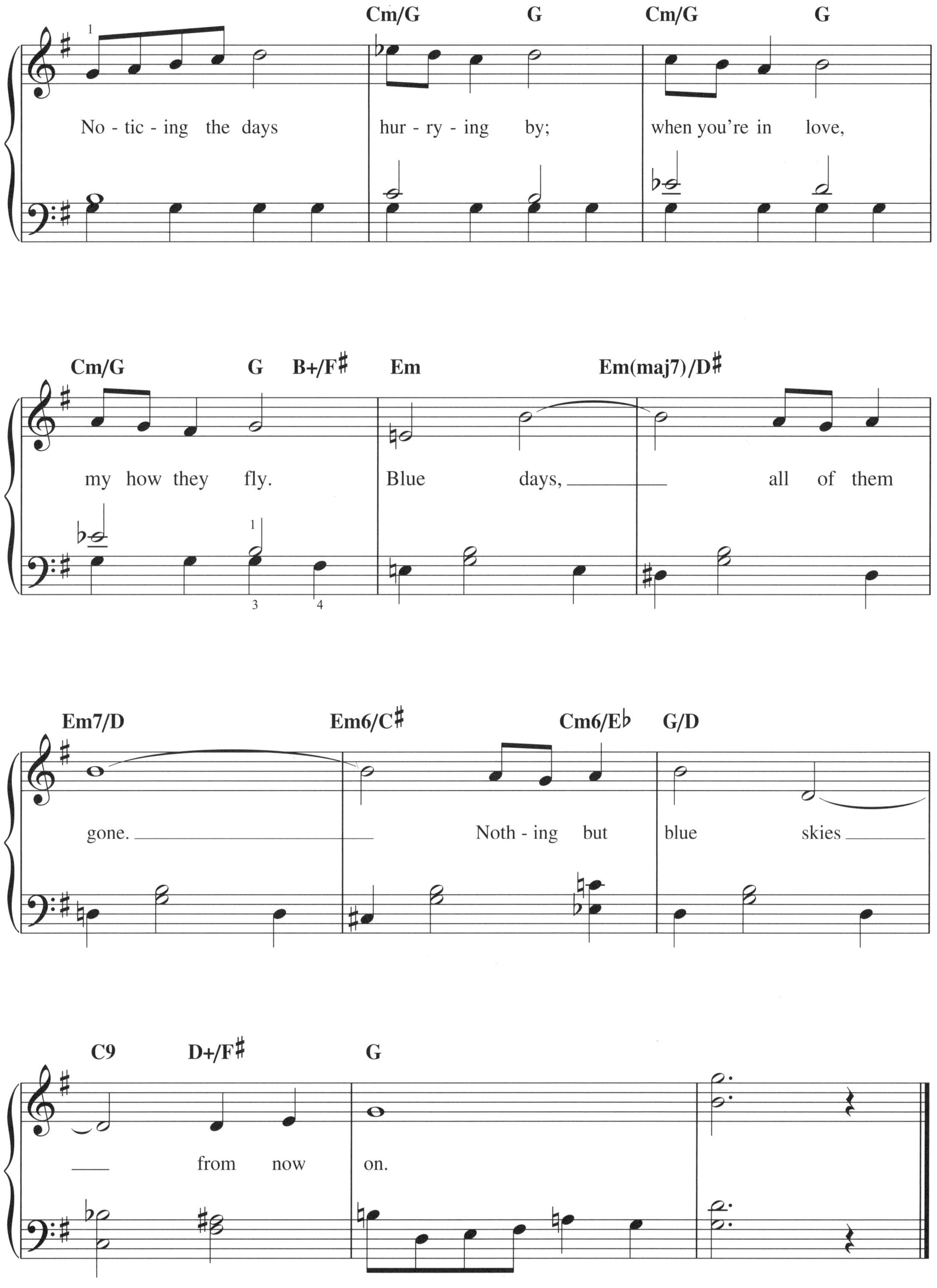
Cm/G G Cm/G G
No - tic - ing the days hur - ry - ing by; when you're in love,
Cm/G G B+/F♯ Em Em(maj7)/D♯
my how they fly. Blue days, all of them
Em7/D Em6/C♯ Cm6/E♭ G/D
gone. Noth - ing but blue skies
C9 D+/F♯ G
from now on.

California Girls

Words and Music by BRIAN WILSON
and MIKE LOVE

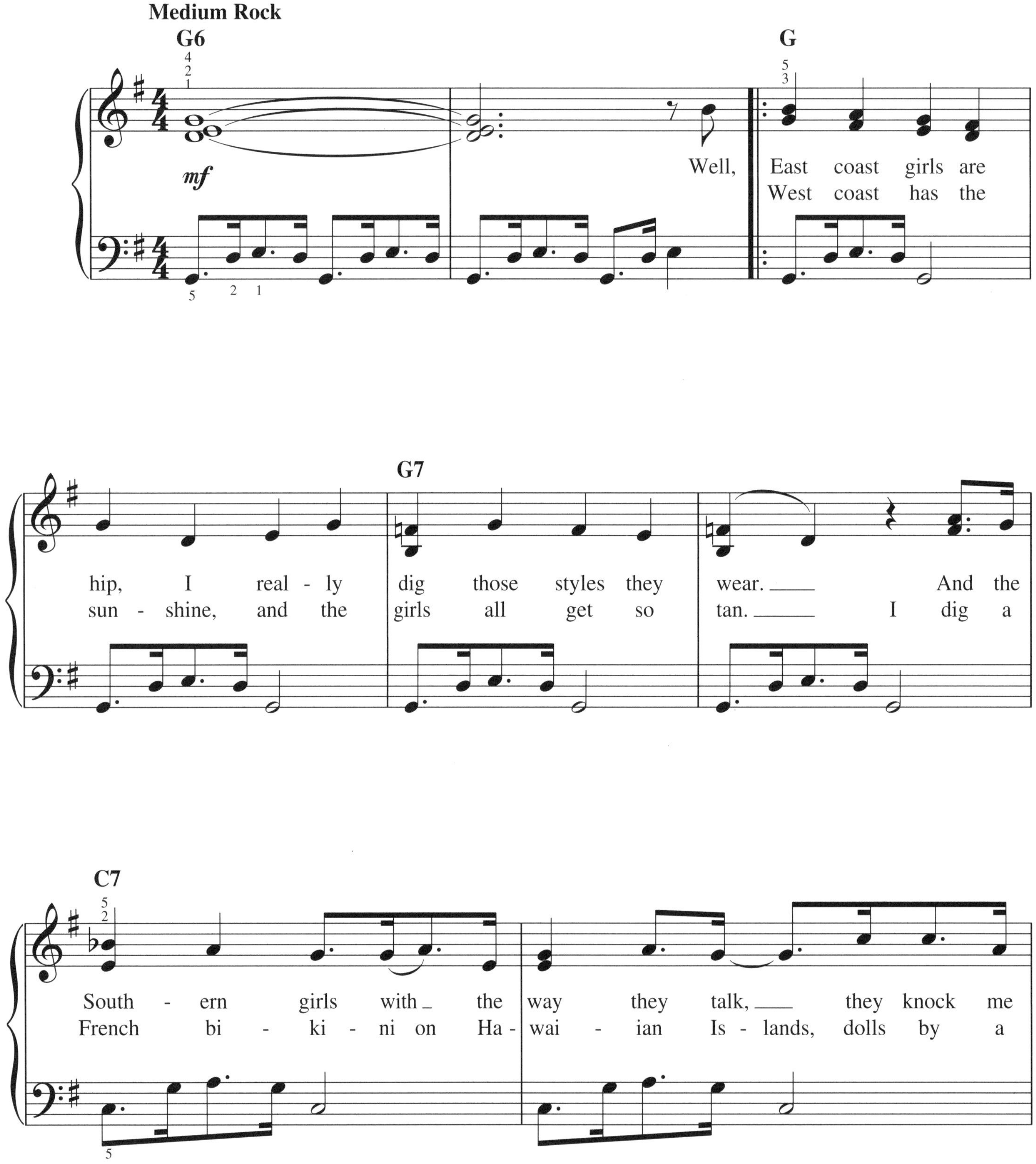
Medium Rock
G6
G
mf
Well,
East coast girls are
West coast has the
hip, I real - ly
sun - shine, and the
G7
dig those styles they
girls all get so
wear. And the
tan. I dig a
C7
South - ern girls with the
French bi - ki - ni on Ha -
way they talk, they knock me
wai - ian Is - lands, dolls by a

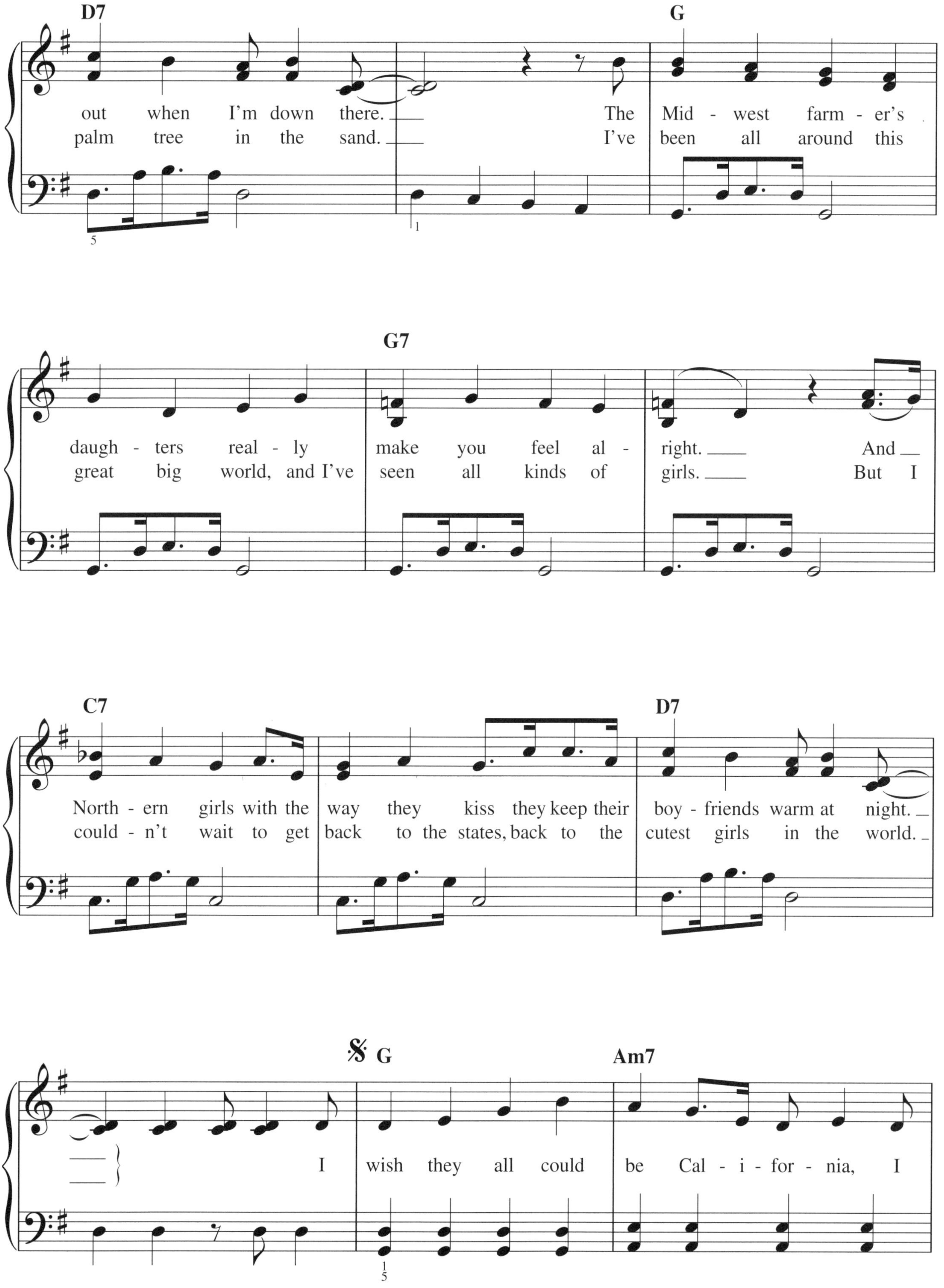
D7
out when I'm down there. The
palm tree in the sand. I've
G
Mid - west farm - er's
been all around this
G7
daugh - ters real - ly make you feel al - right. And
great big world, and I've seen all kinds of girls. But I
C7
North - ern girls with the way they kiss they keep their
could - n't wait to get back to the states, back to the
D7
boy - friends warm at night.
cutest girls in the world.
I
G
wish they all could
Am7
be Cal - i - for - nia, I

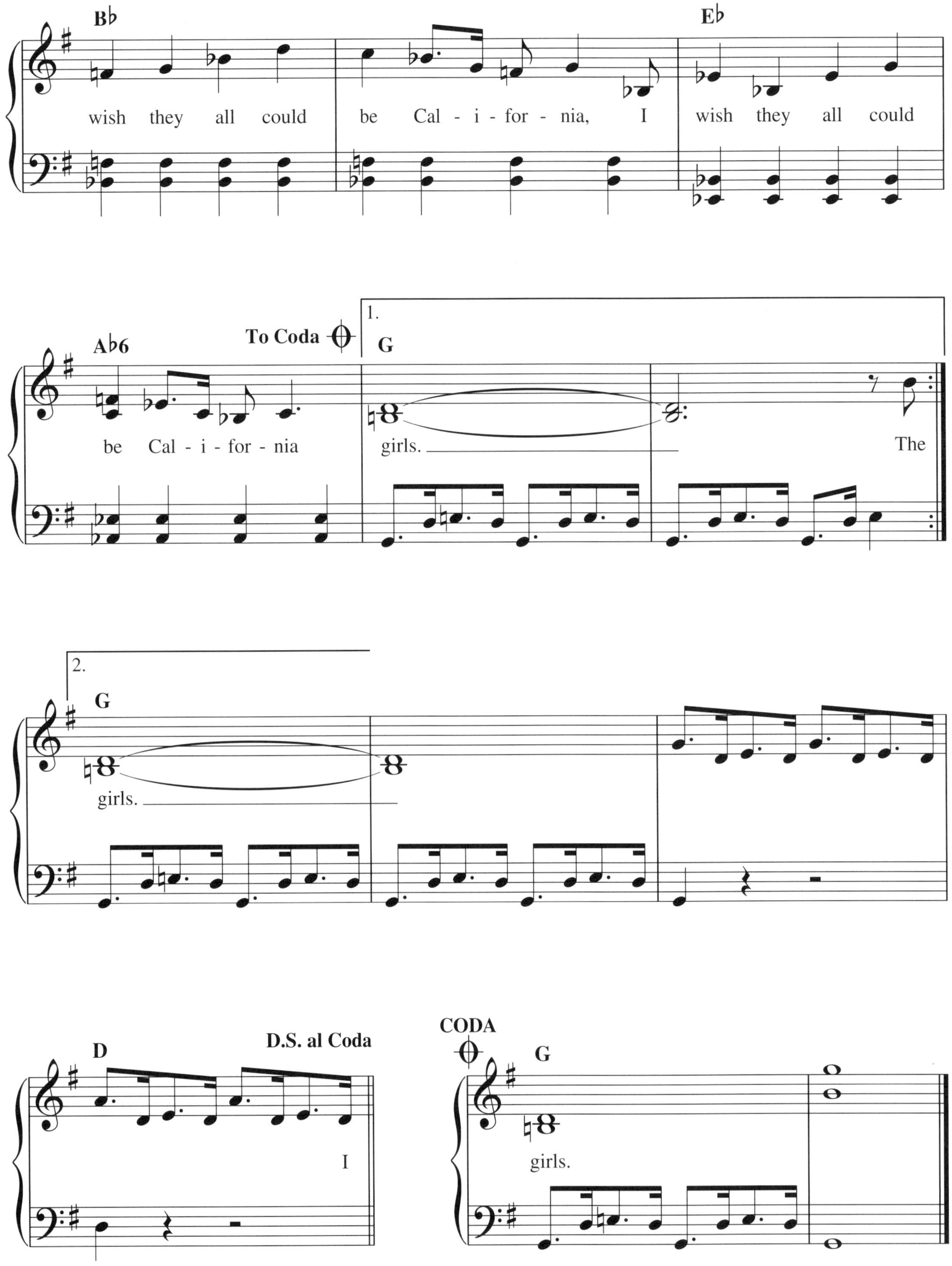
B♭
E♭
wish they all could be Cal - i - for - nia, I wish they all could
A♭6
To Coda
1.
G
be Cal - i - for - nia girls.
The
2.
G
girls.
D
D.S. al Coda
I
CODA
G
girls.

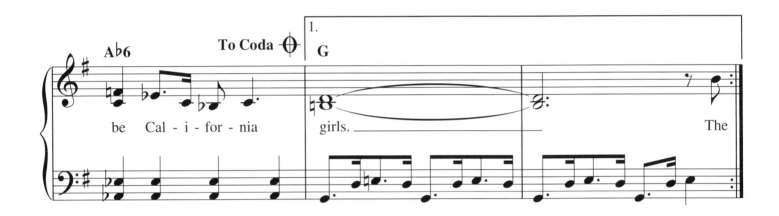

Bridge Over Troubled Water

Words and Music by
PAUL SIMON

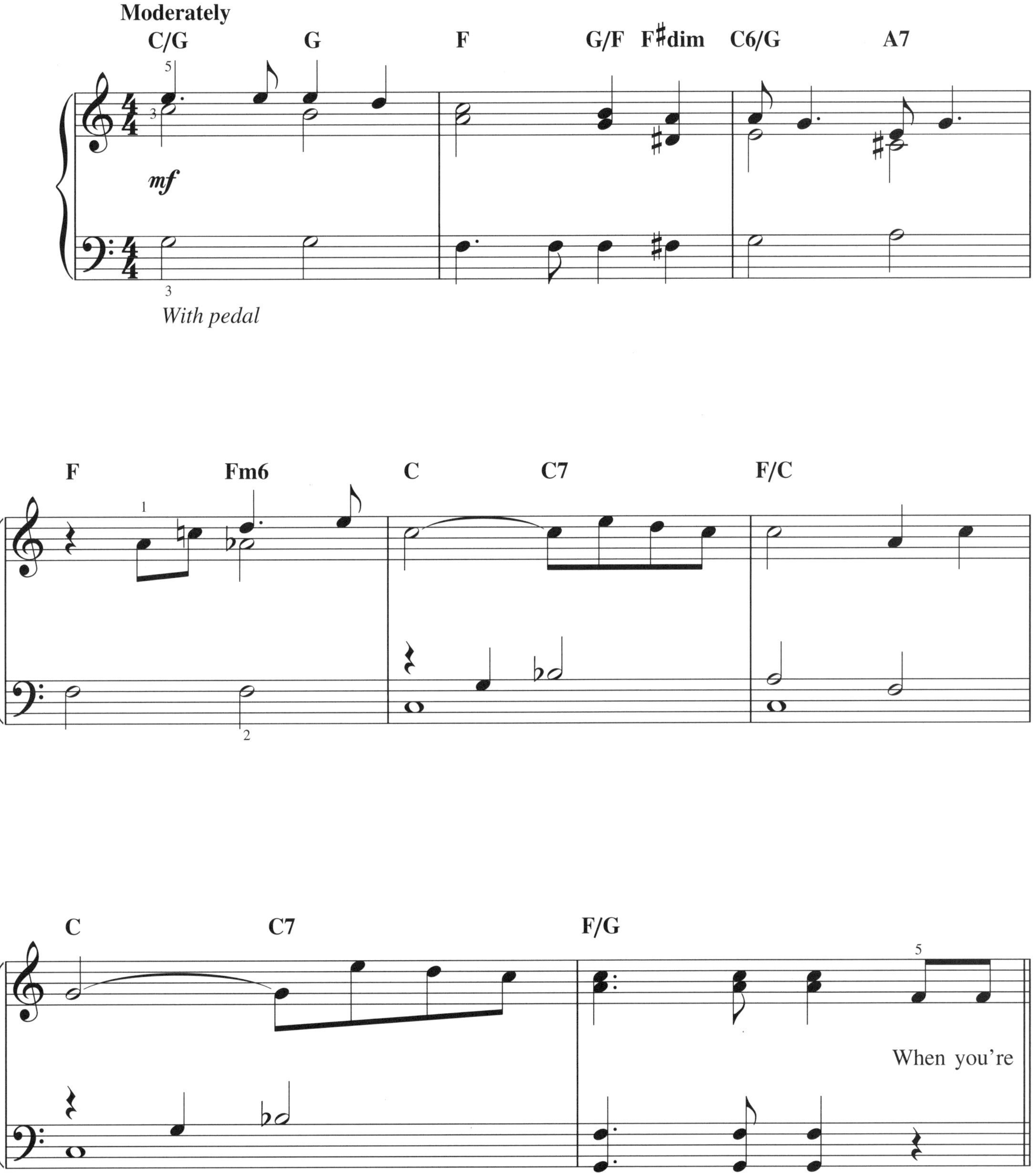

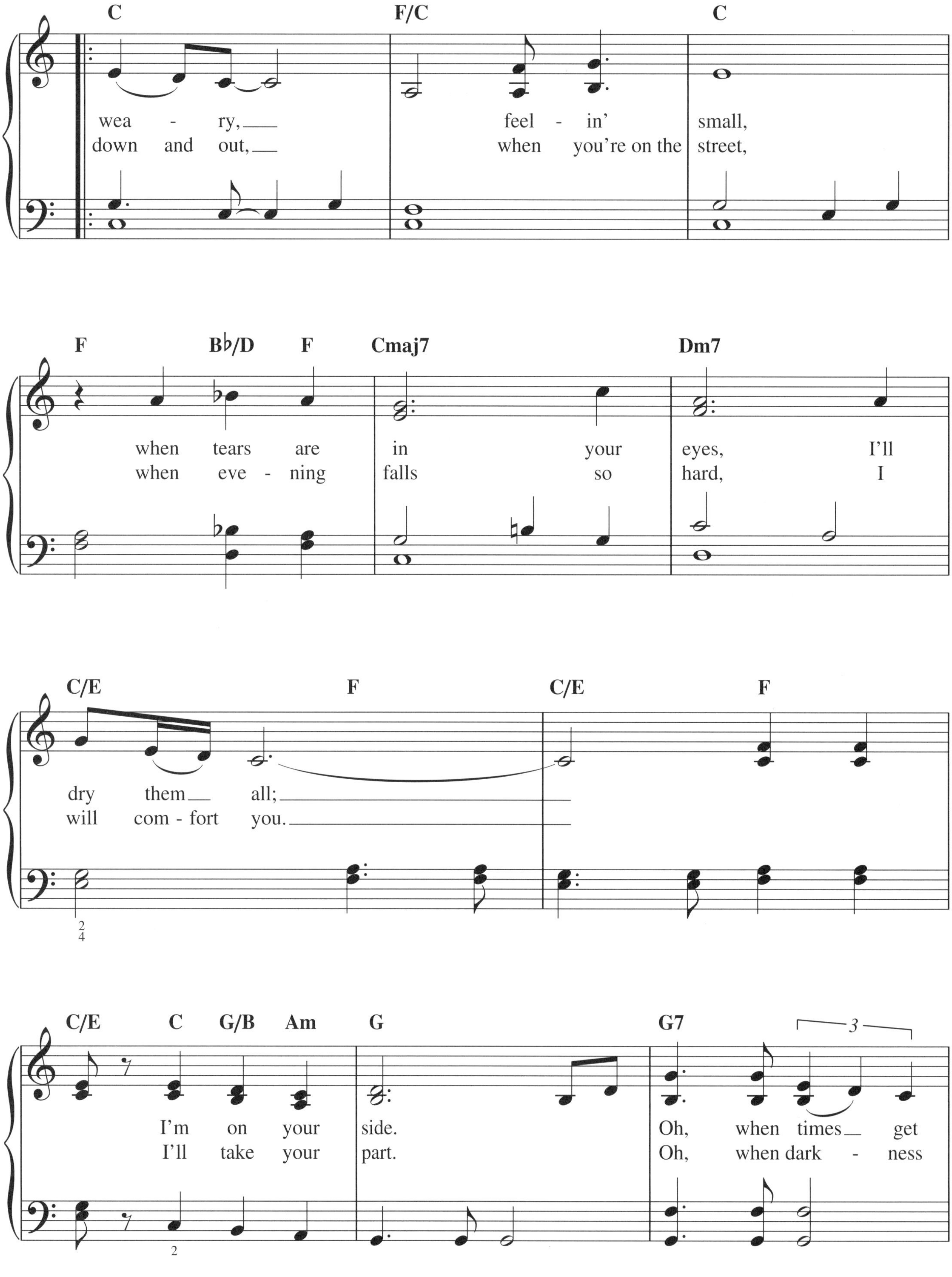
C F/C C
wea - ry, feel - in' small,
down and out, when you're on the street,
F B♭/D F Cmaj7 Dm7
when tears are in your eyes, I'll
when eve - ning falls so hard, I
C/E F C/E F
dry them all;
will com - fort you.
2
4
C/E C G/B Am G G7
3
I'm on your side. Oh, when times get
I'll take your part. Oh, when dark - ness
2

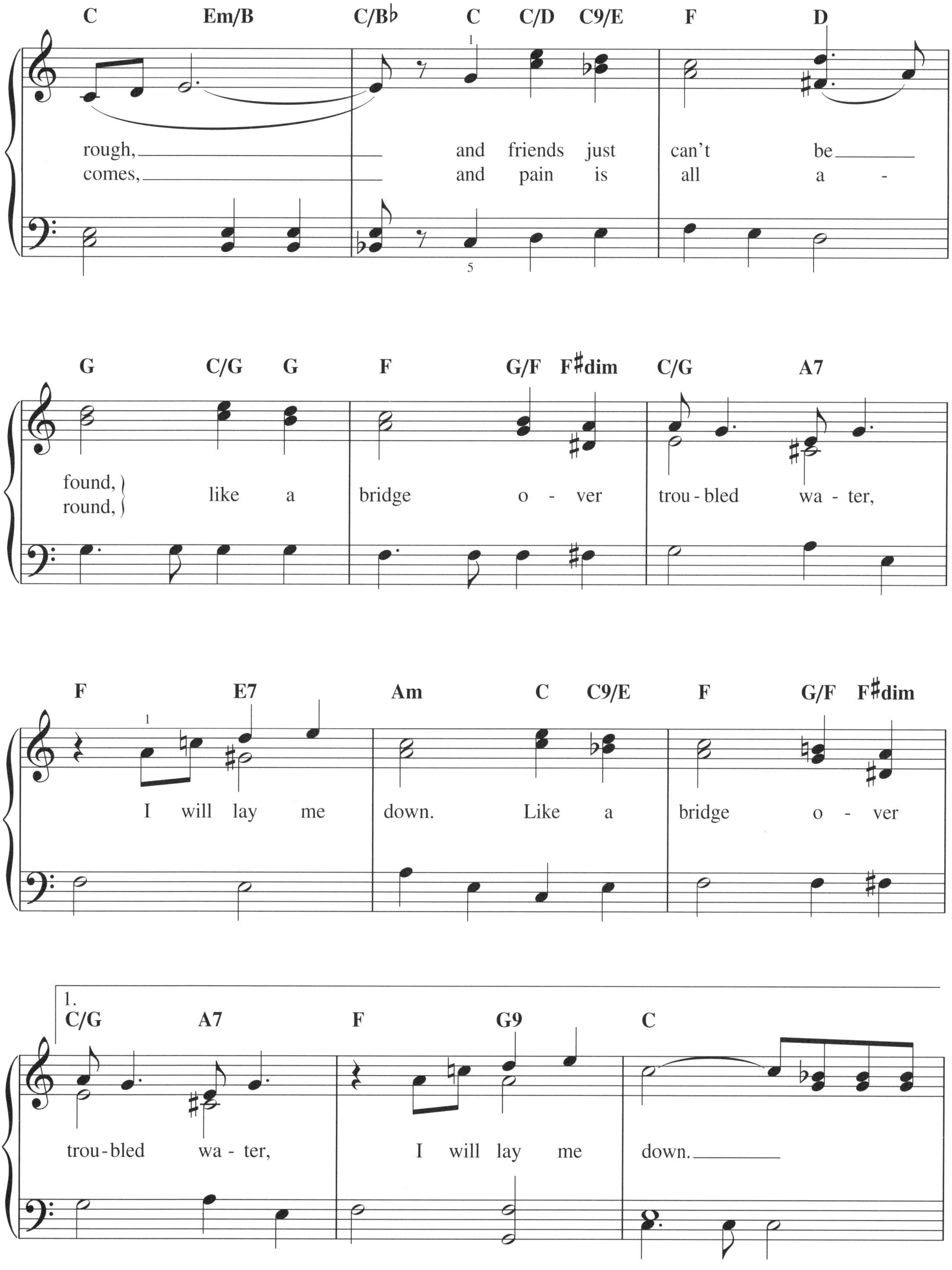
C Em/B C/B♭ C C/D C9/E F D
rough, and friends just can't be
comes, and pain is all a -
G C/G G F G/F F♯dim C/G A7
found, like a bridge o - ver trou - bled wa - ter,
round,
F E7 Am C C9/E F G/F F♯dim
I will lay me down. Like a bridge o - ver
1.
C/G A7 F G9 C
trou - bled wa - ter, I will lay me down.

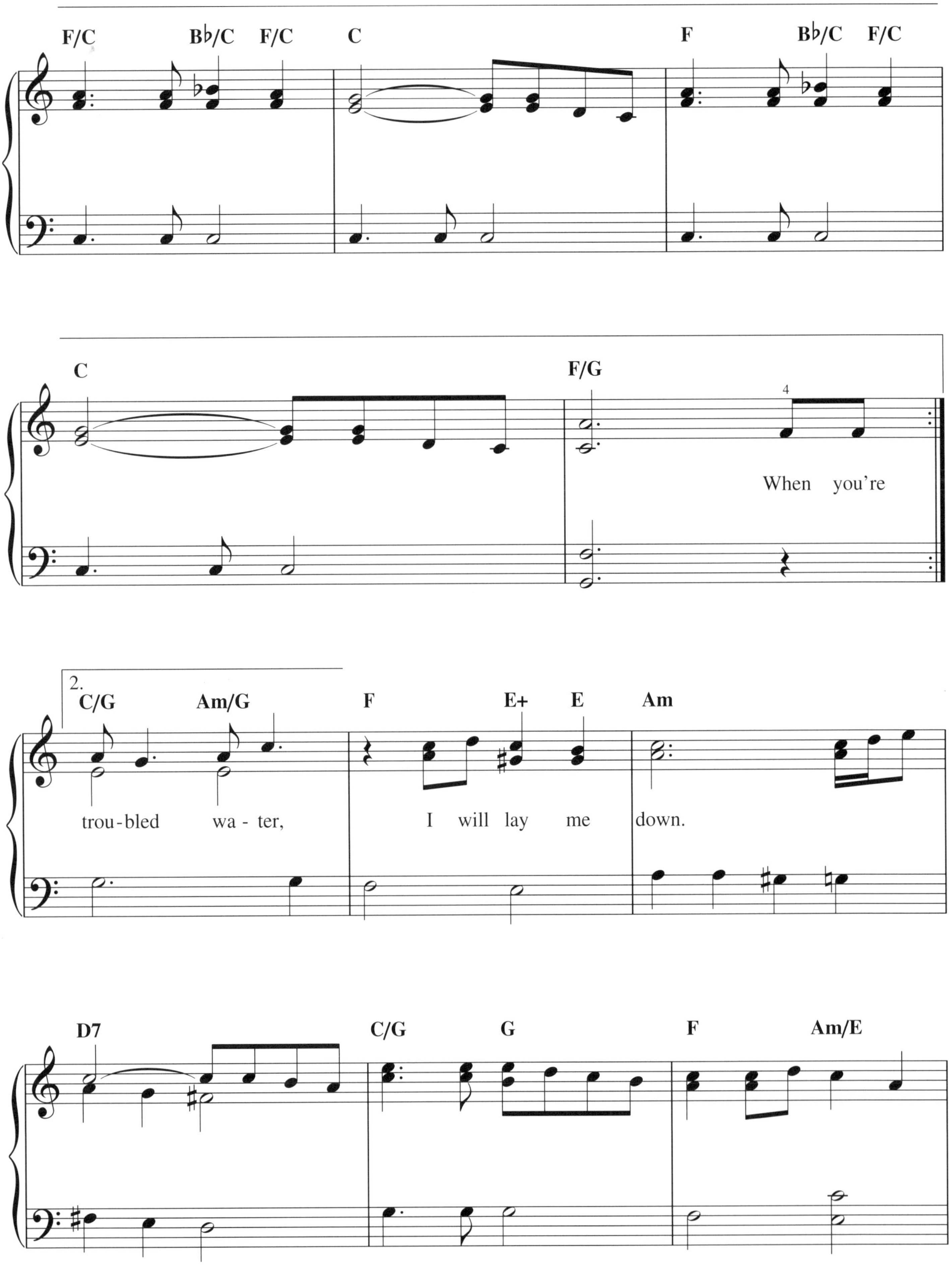
F/C
Bb/C
F/C
C
F
Bb/C
F/C
C
F/G
4
When you're
2.
C/G
Am/G
F
E+
E
Am
trou-bled wa - ter,
I will lay me down.
D7
C/G
G
F
Am/E

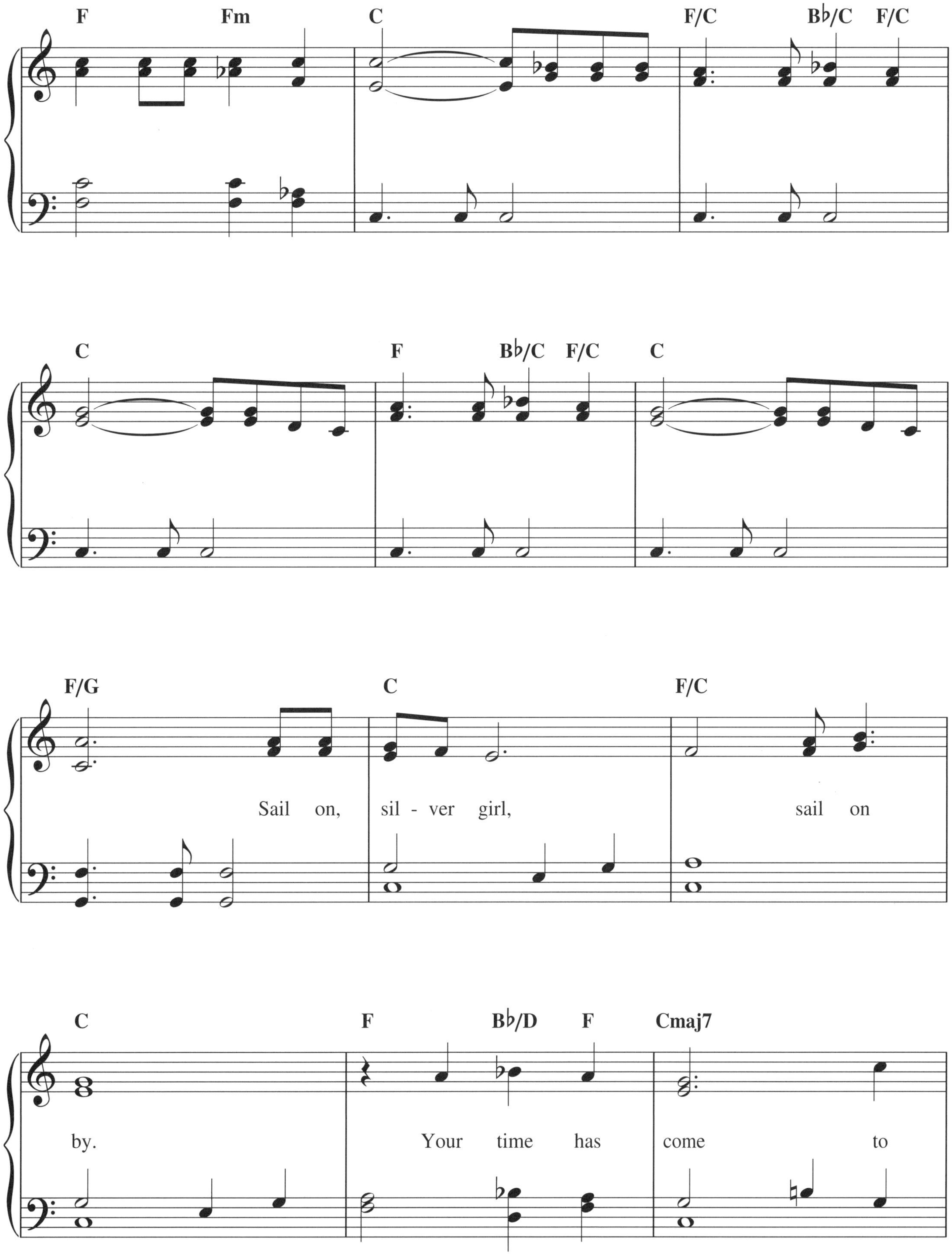
F Fm C F/C B♭/C F/C
C F B♭/C F/C C
F/G C F/C
Sail on, sil - ver girl, sail on
C F B♭/D F Cmaj7
by. Your time has come to

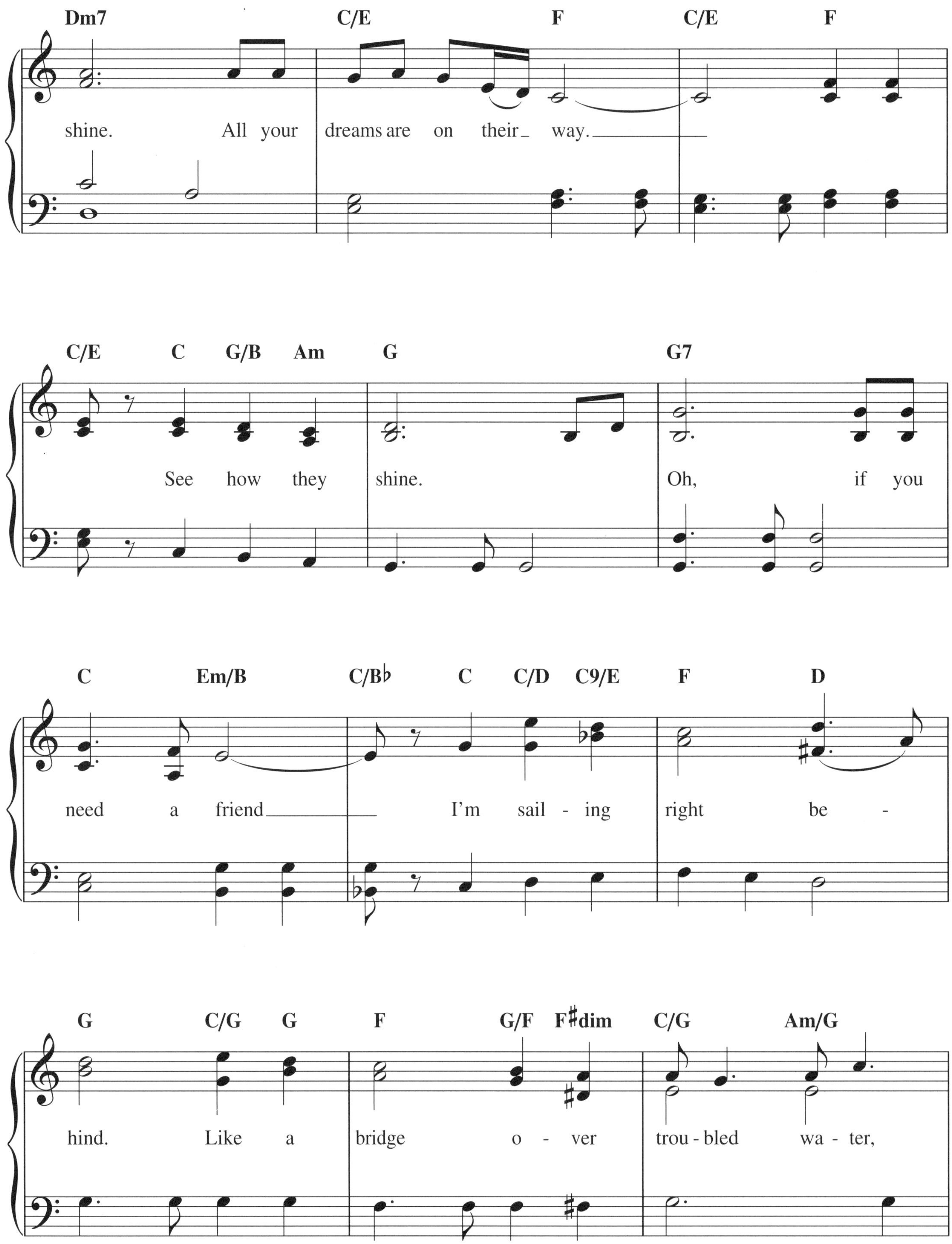
Dm7 C/E F C/E F
shine. All your dreams are on their way.
C/E C G/B Am G G7
See how they shine. Oh, if you
C Em/B C/B♭ C C/D C9/E F D
need a friend I'm sail - ing right be -
G C/G G F G/F F♯dim C/G Am/G
hind. Like a bridge o - ver trou - bled wa - ter,

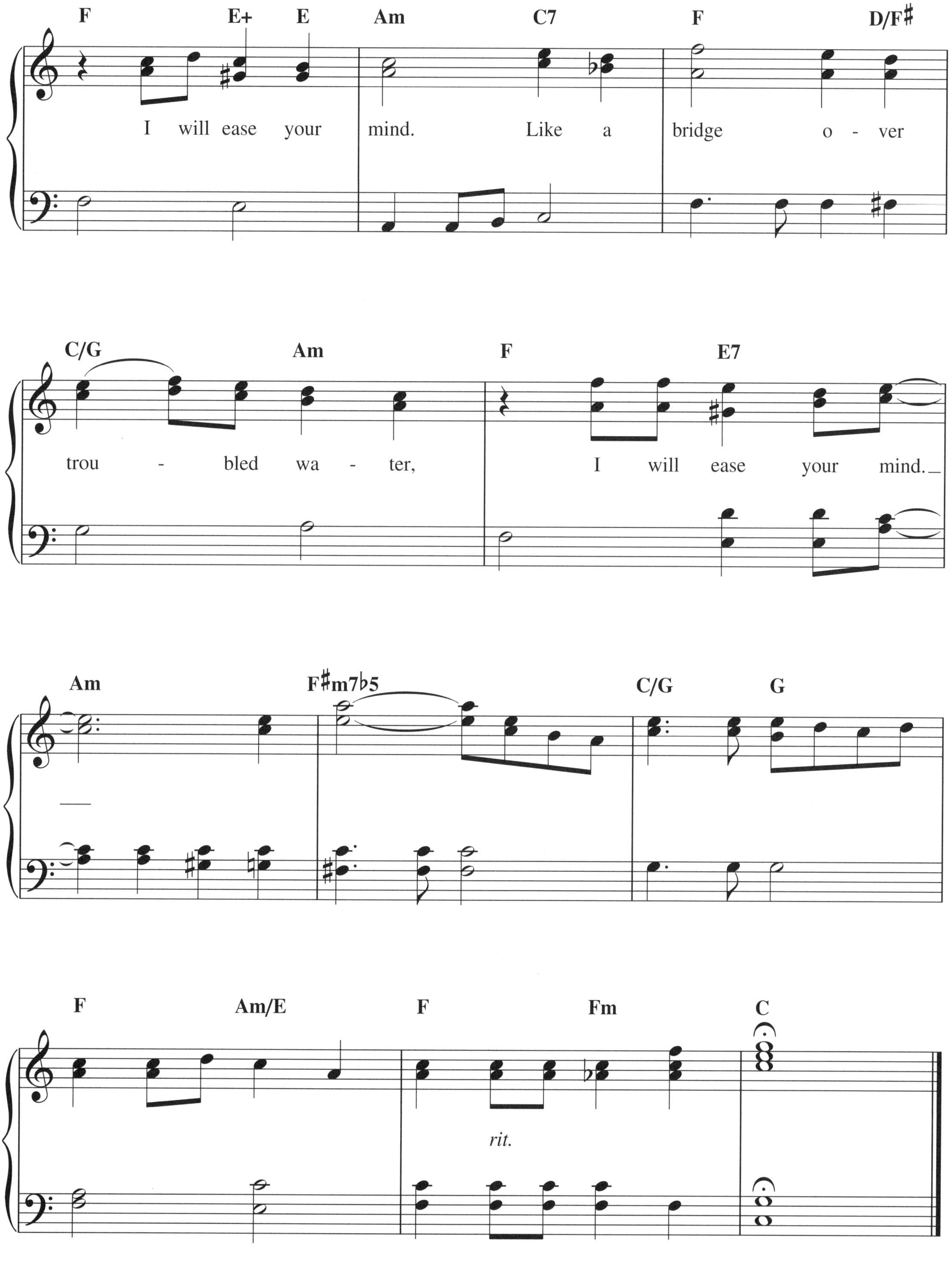
F E+ E Am C7 F D/F♯
I will ease your mind. Like a bridge o - ver
C/G Am F E7
trou - bled wa - ter, I will ease your mind.
Am F♯m7♭5 C/G G
F Am/E F Fm C
rit.

Can't Help Falling in Love

Words and Music by GEORGE DAVID WEISS,
HUGO PERETTI and LUIGI CREATORE

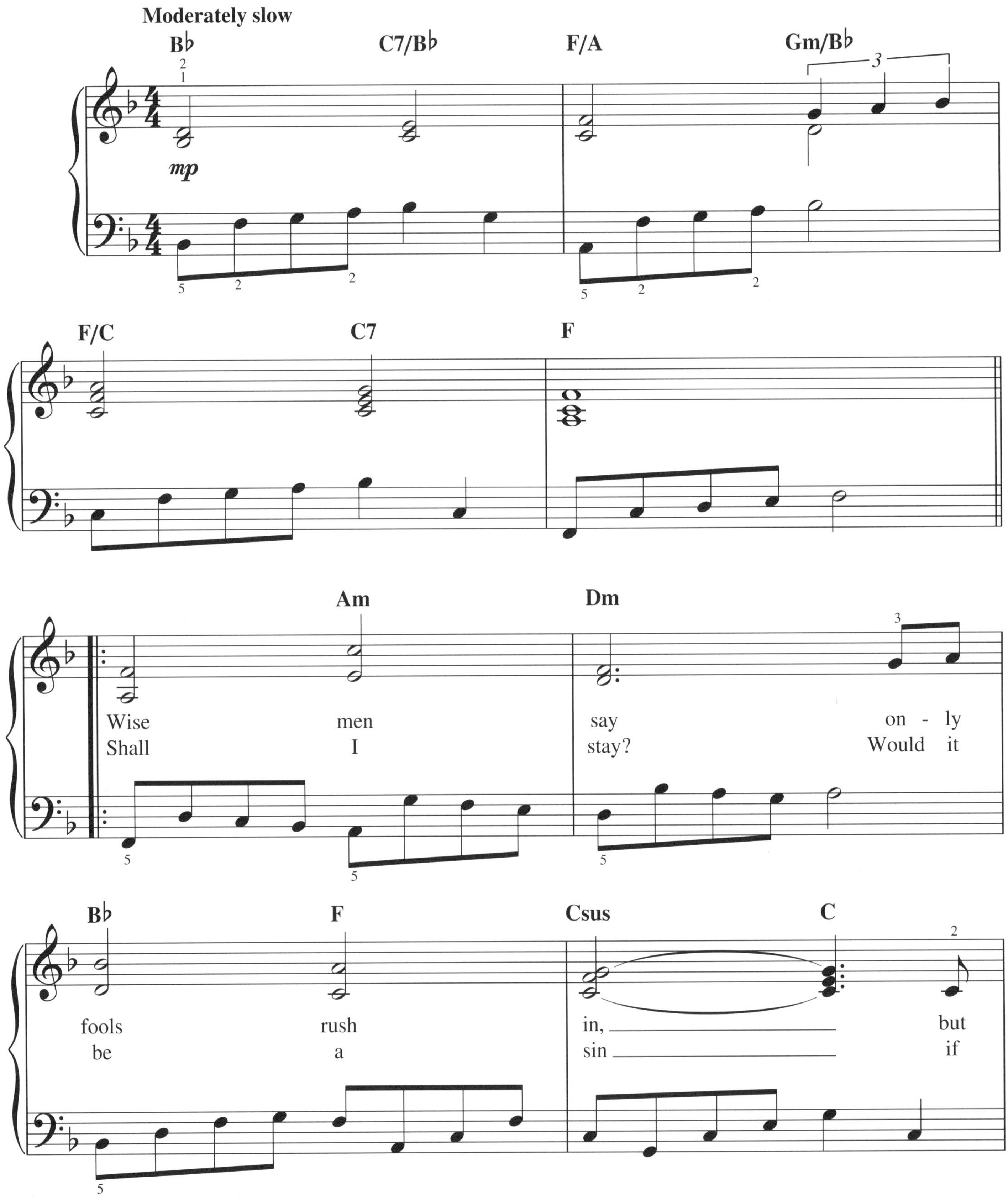

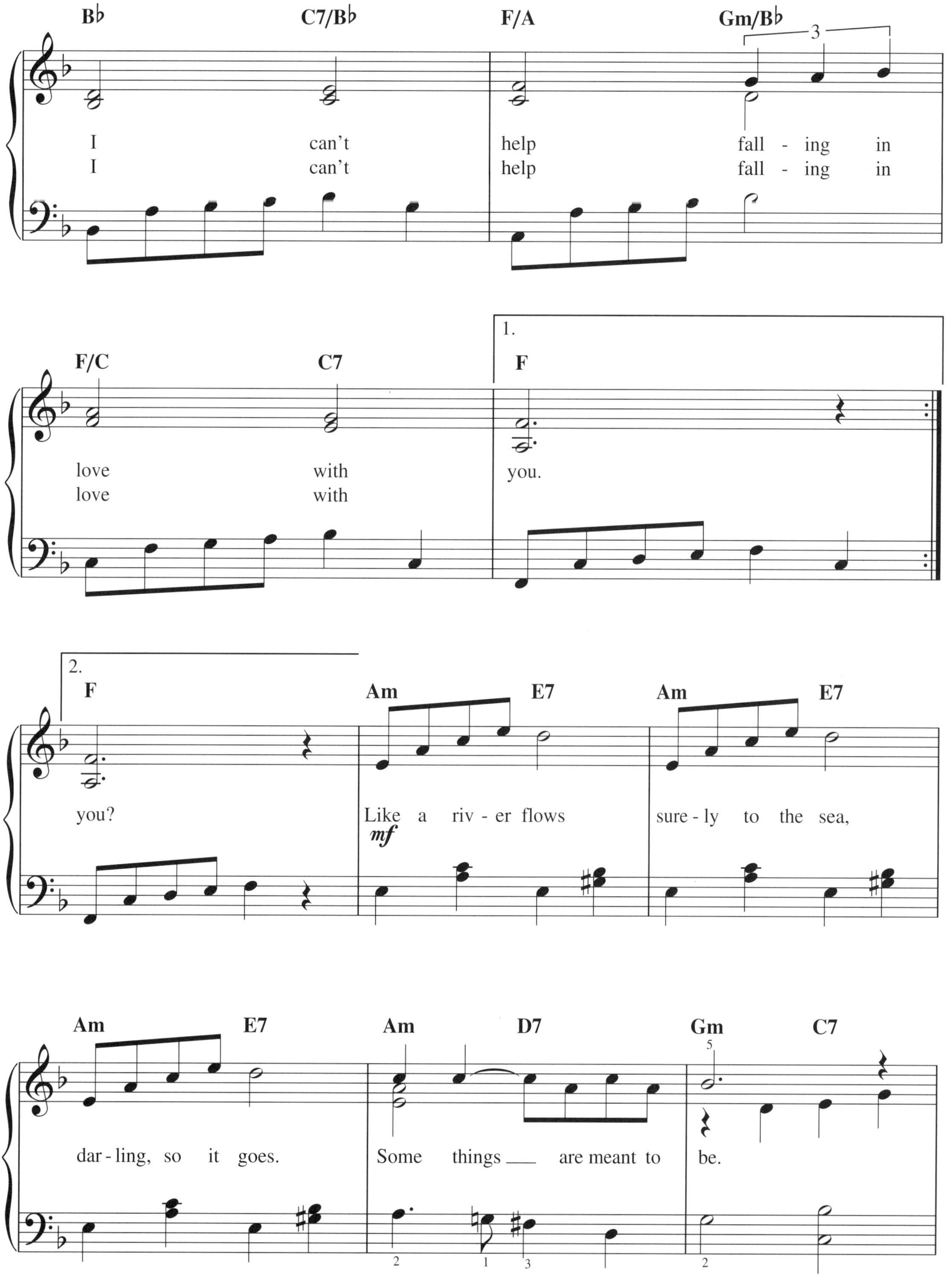
B♭ C7/B♭ F/A Gm/B♭
3
I can't help fall - ing in
I can't help fall - ing in
F/C C7
1.
F
love with you.
love with
2.
F Am E7 Am E7
you? Like a riv - er flows sure - ly to the sea,
mf
Am E7 Am D7 Gm C7
dar - ling, so it goes. Some things are meant to be.

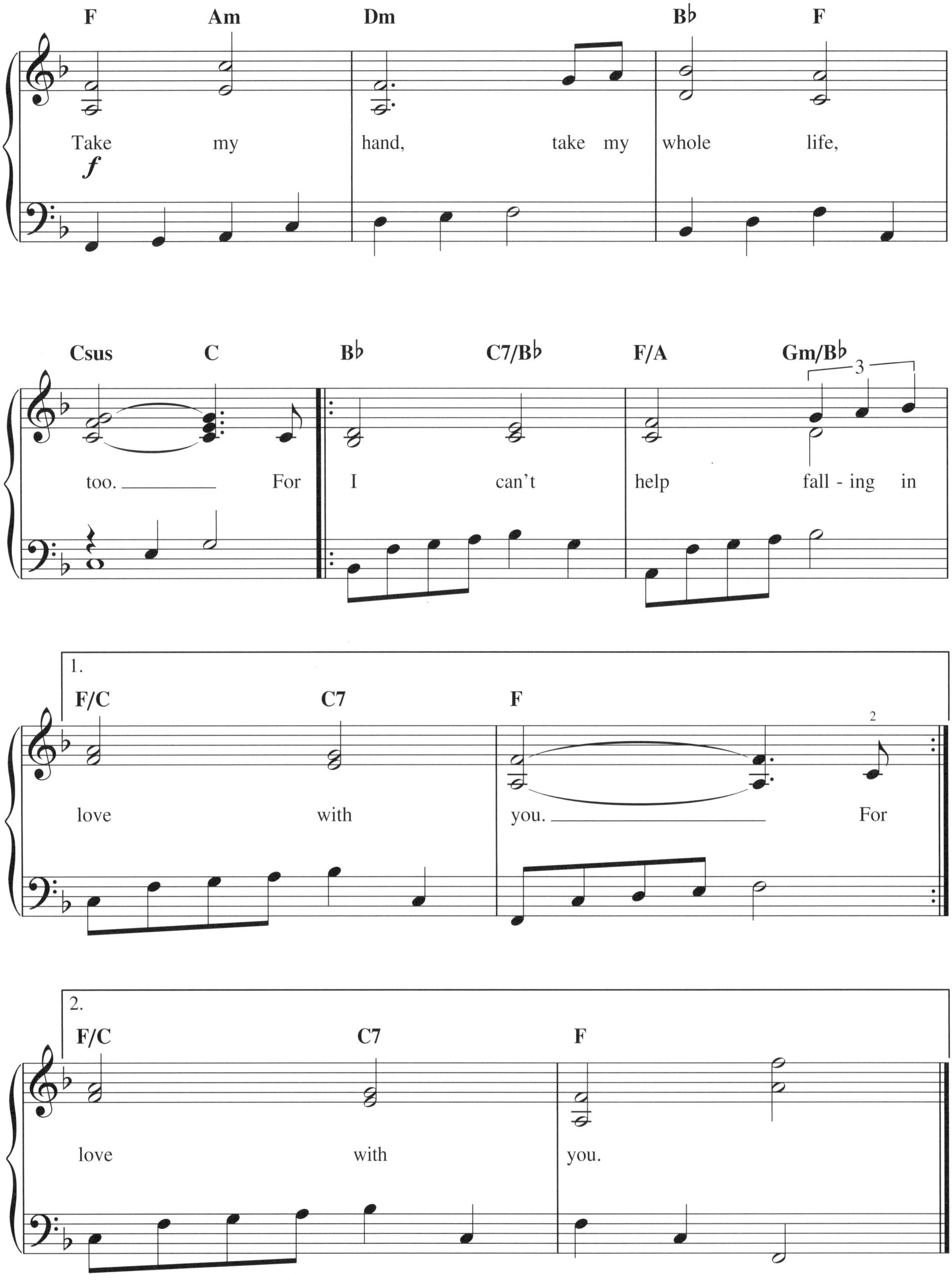
F Am Dm B♭ F
Take my hand, take my whole life,
f
Csus C B♭ C7/B♭ F/A Gm/B♭
too. For I can't help fall - ing in
3
1.
F/C C7 F
love with you. For
2
2.
F/C C7 F
love with you.

Candle in the Wind

Words and Music by ELTON JOHN
and BERNIE TAUPIN

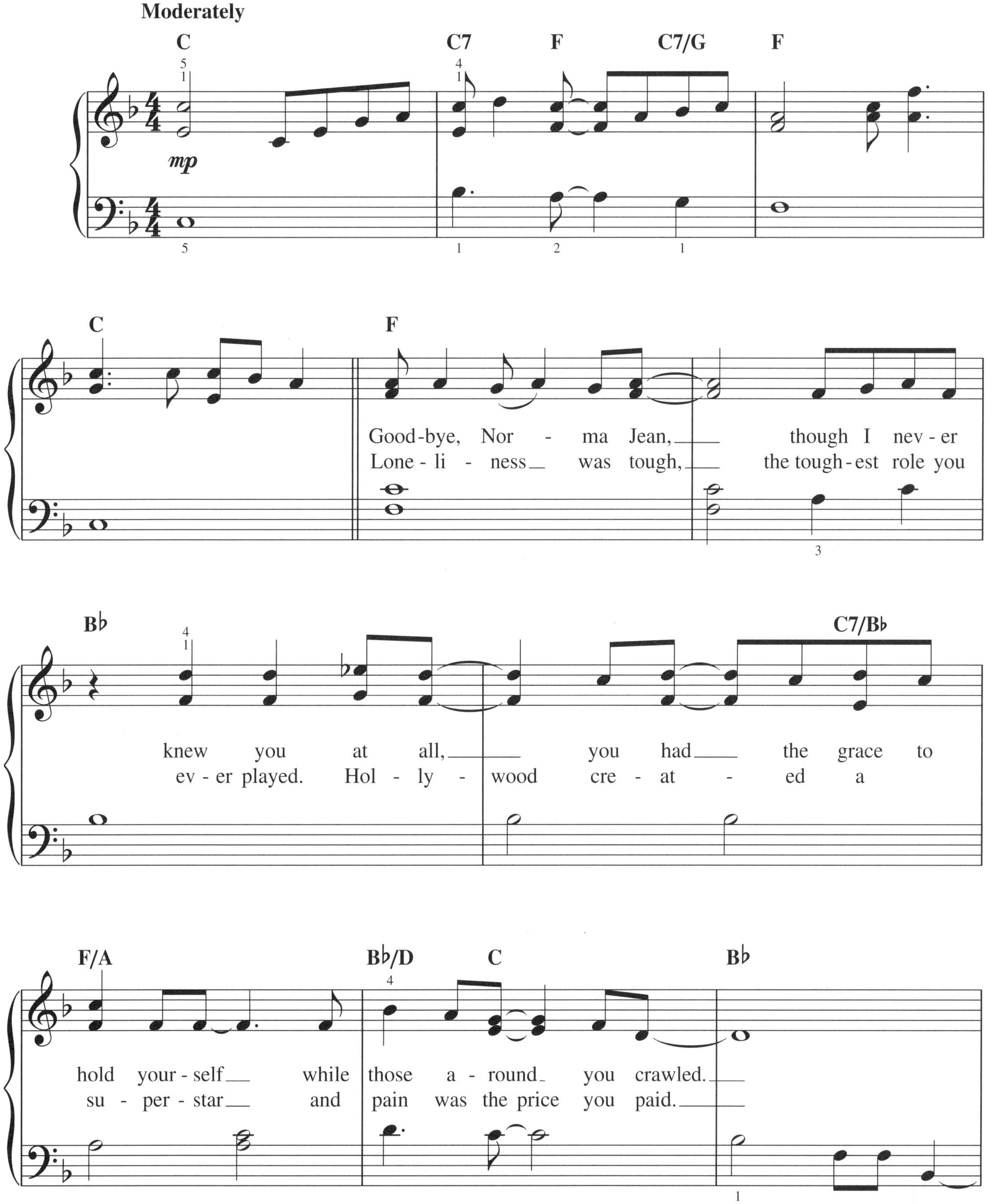

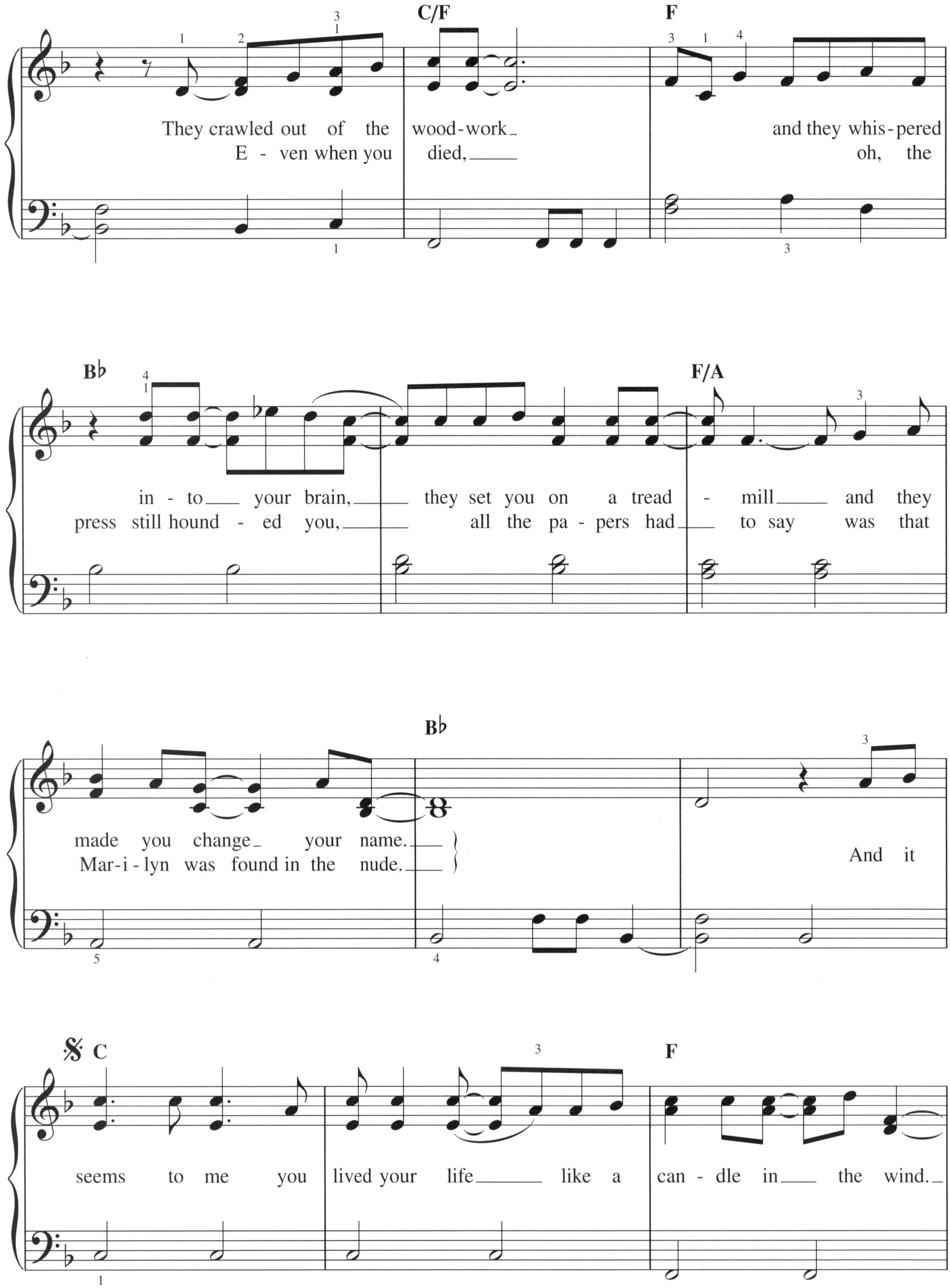
C/F
F
They crawled out of the wood-work and they whis-pered
E - ven when you died, oh, the
B♭
F/A
in - to your brain, they set you on a tread - mill and they
press still hound - ed you, all the pa - pers had to say was that
B♭
made you change your name.
Mar-i-lyn was found in the nude.
And it
C
F
seems to me you lived your life like a can - dle in the wind.

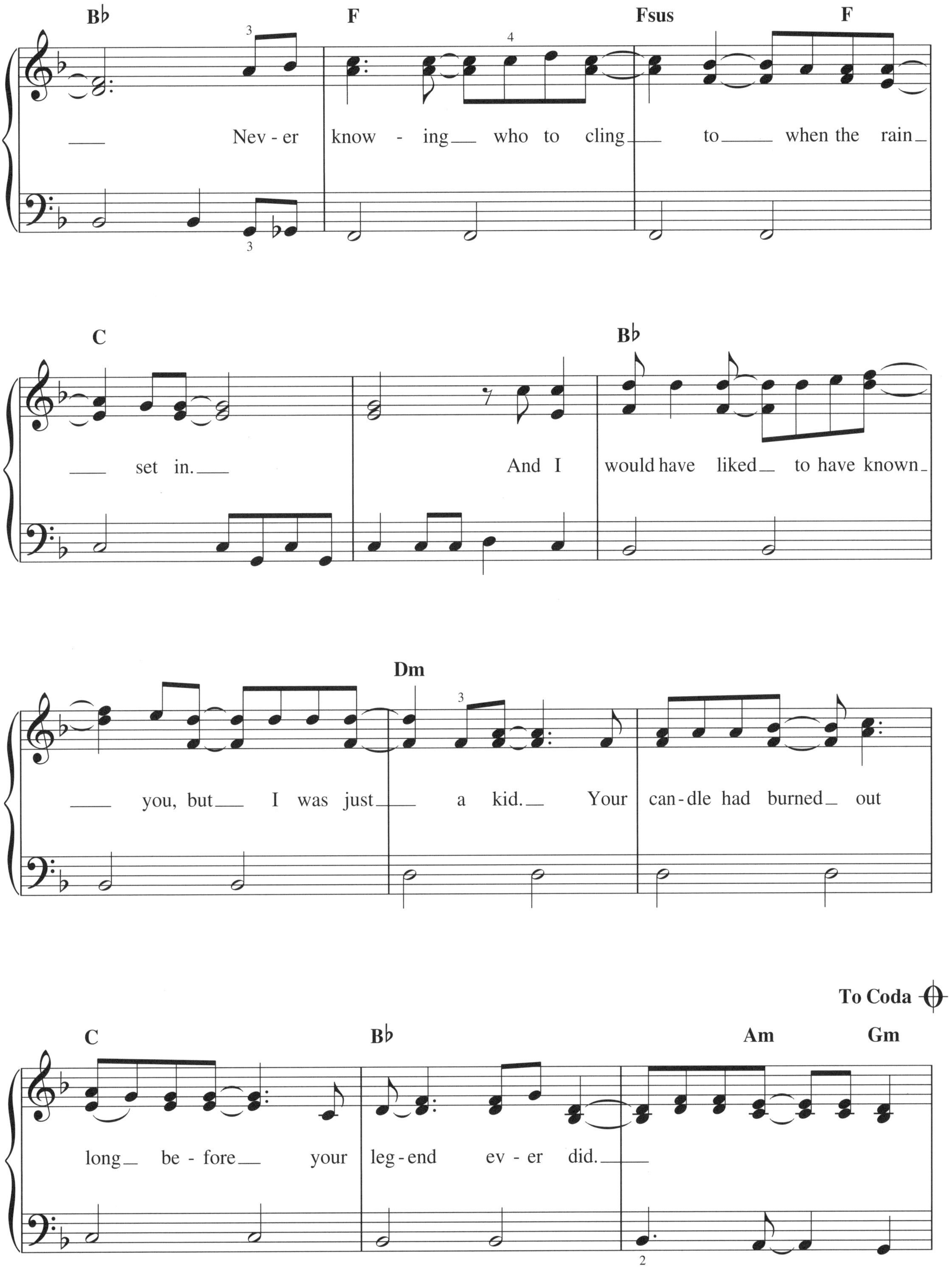
B♭
F
Fsus
F
Nev - er know - ing who to cling to when the rain
C
B♭
set in. And I would have liked to have known
Dm
you, but I was just a kid. Your can - dle had burned out
To Coda
C
B♭
Am
Gm
long be - fore your leg - end ev - er did.

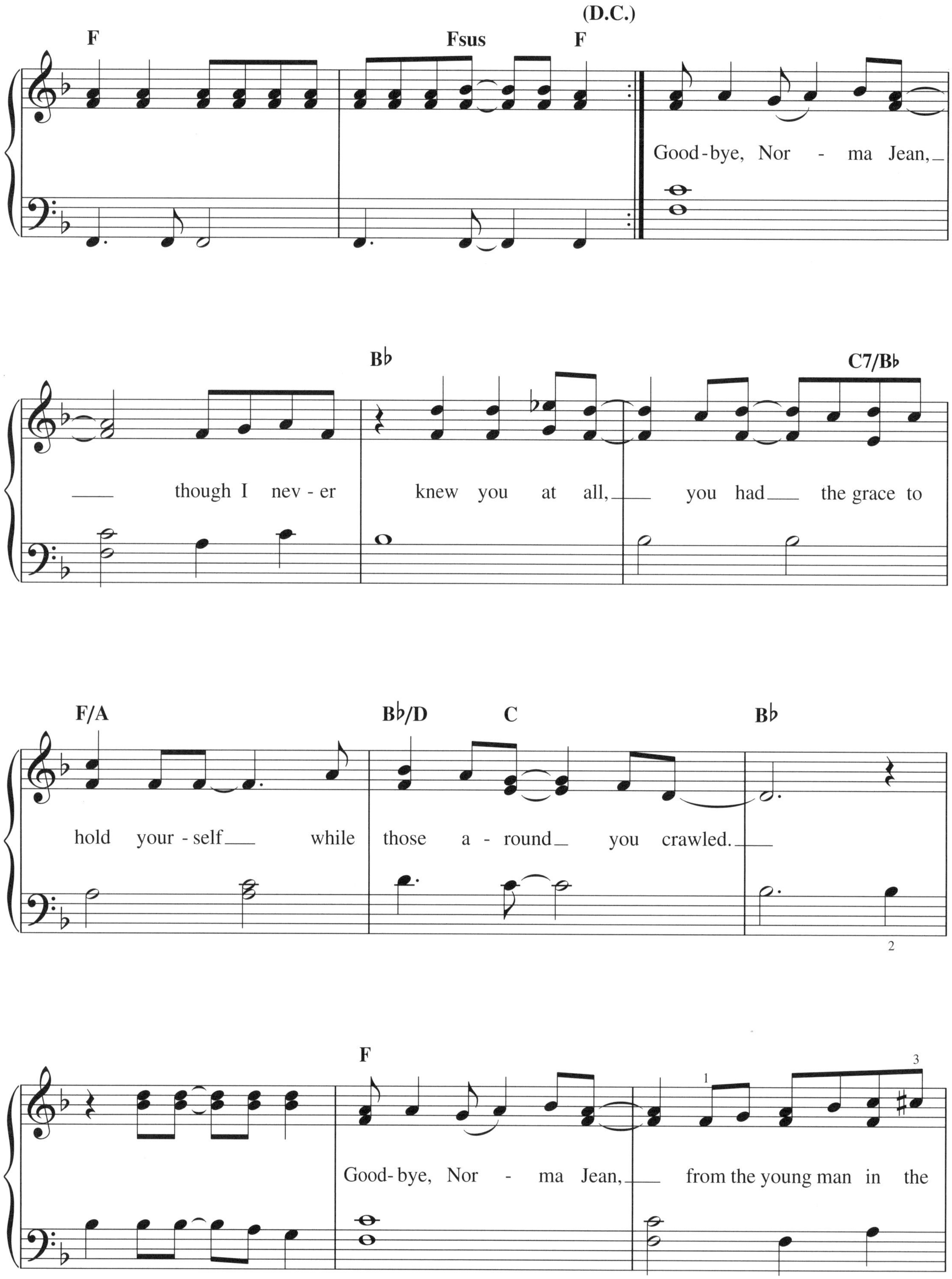
(D.C.)
F
Fsus
F
Good-bye, Nor - ma Jean,
B♭
C7/B♭
though I nev - er
knew you at all,
you had the grace to
F/A
B♭/D
C
B♭
hold your - self while
those a - round you crawled.
F
Good-bye, Nor - ma Jean,
from the young man in the

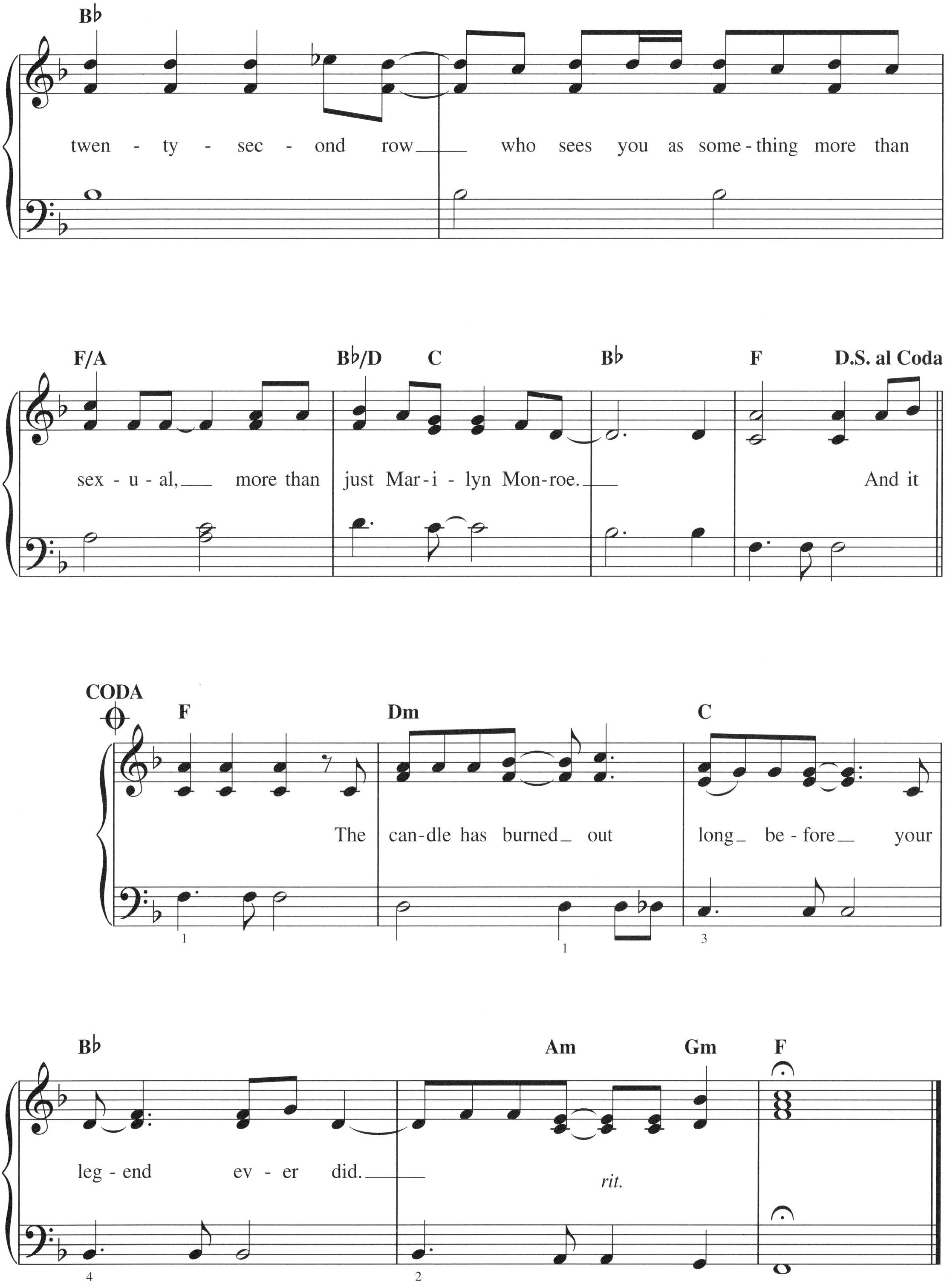
B♭
twen - ty - sec - ond row who sees you as some-thing more than
F/A B♭/D C B♭ F D.S. al Coda
sex - u - al, more than just Mar-i - lyn Mon-roe. And it
CODA
F Dm C
The can-dle has burned out long be-fore your
B♭ Am Gm F
leg - end ev - er did.
rit.

The Climb

Words and Music by JESSI ALEXANDER
and JON MABE

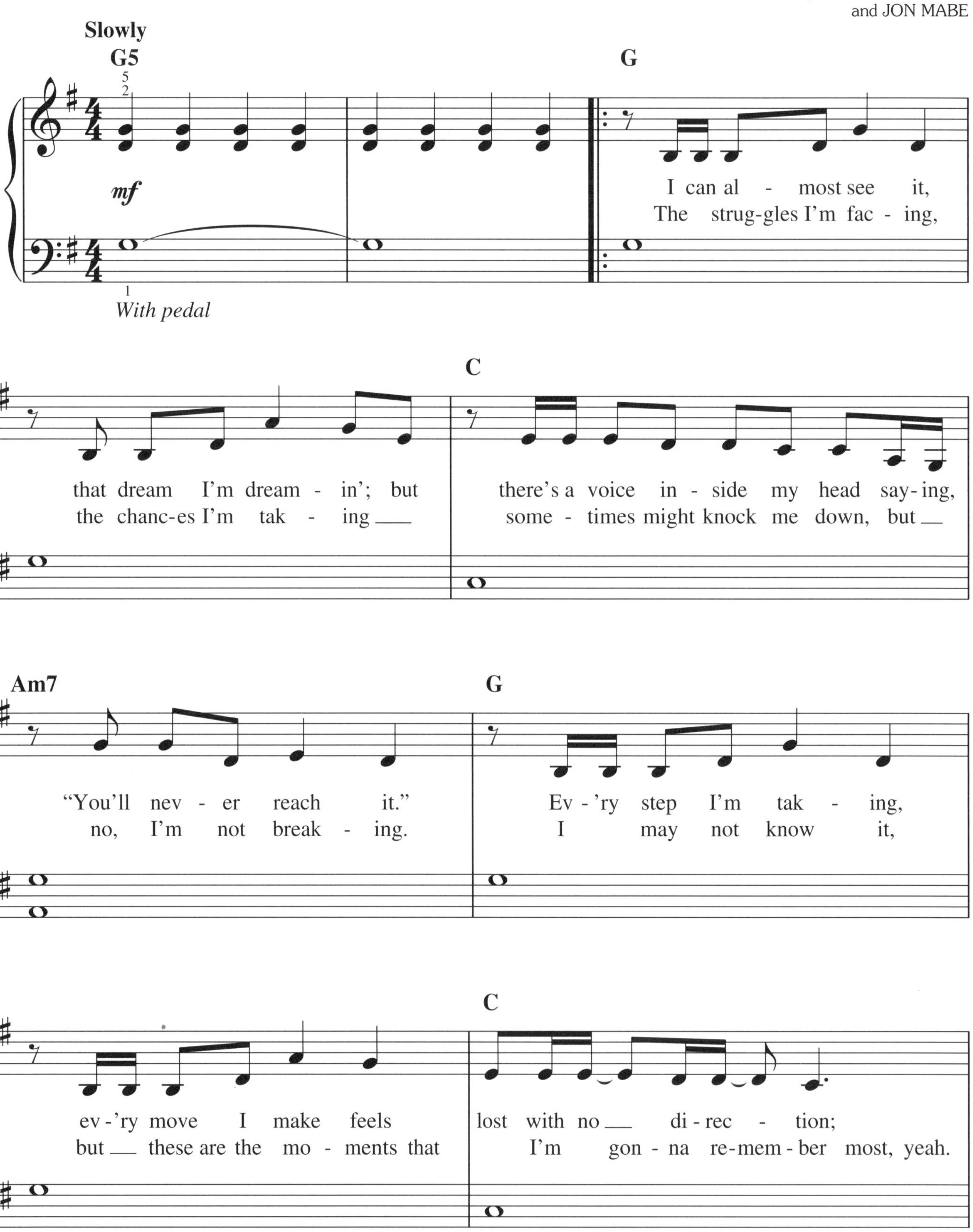

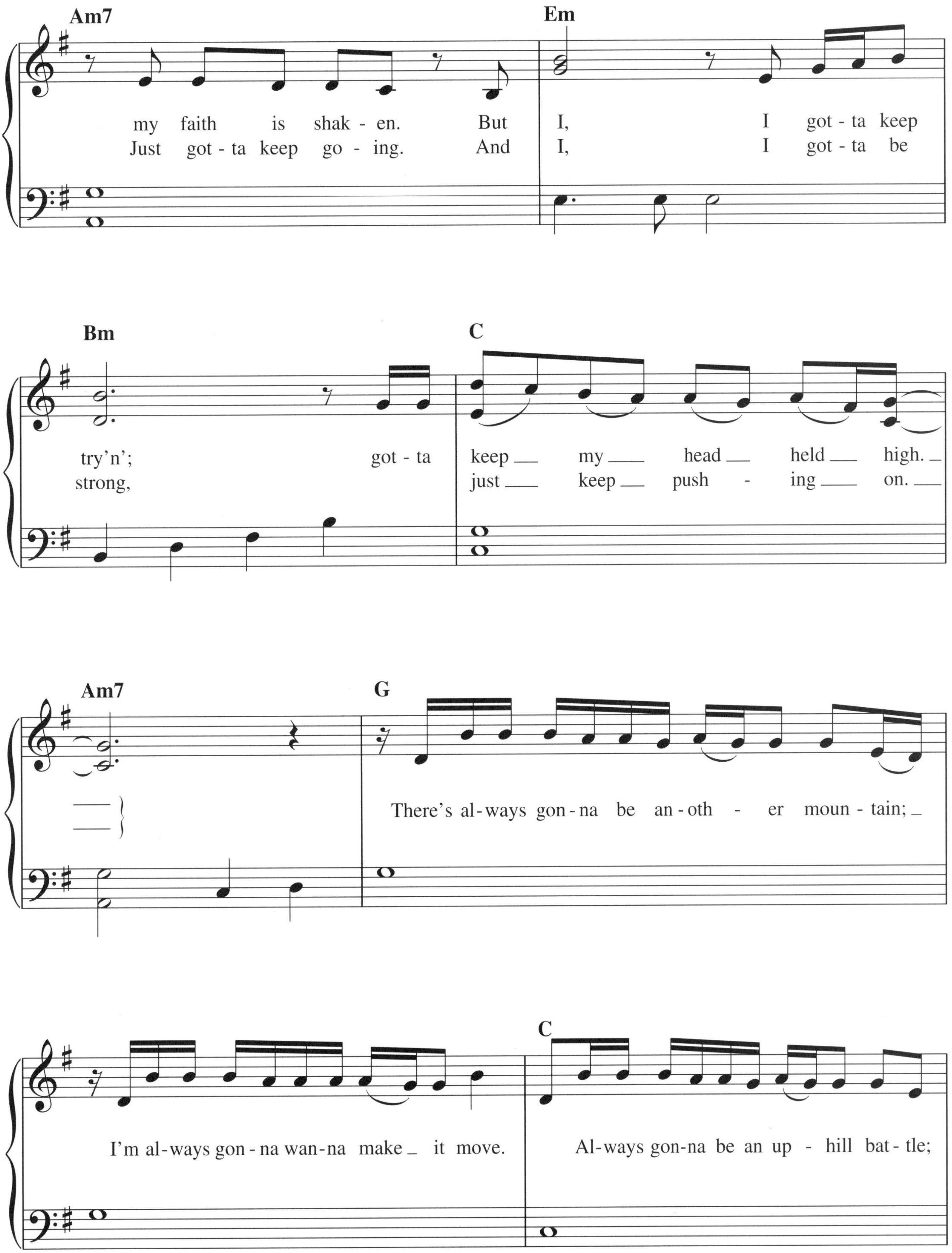
Am7
Em
my faith is shak - en. But I, I got - ta keep
Just got - ta keep go - ing. And I, I got - ta be
Bm
C
try'n'; got - ta keep my head held high.
strong, just keep push - ing on.
Am7
G
There's al - ways gon - na be an - oth - er moun - tain;
I'm al - ways gon - na wan - na make it move.
C
Al - ways gon - na be an up - hill bat - tle;

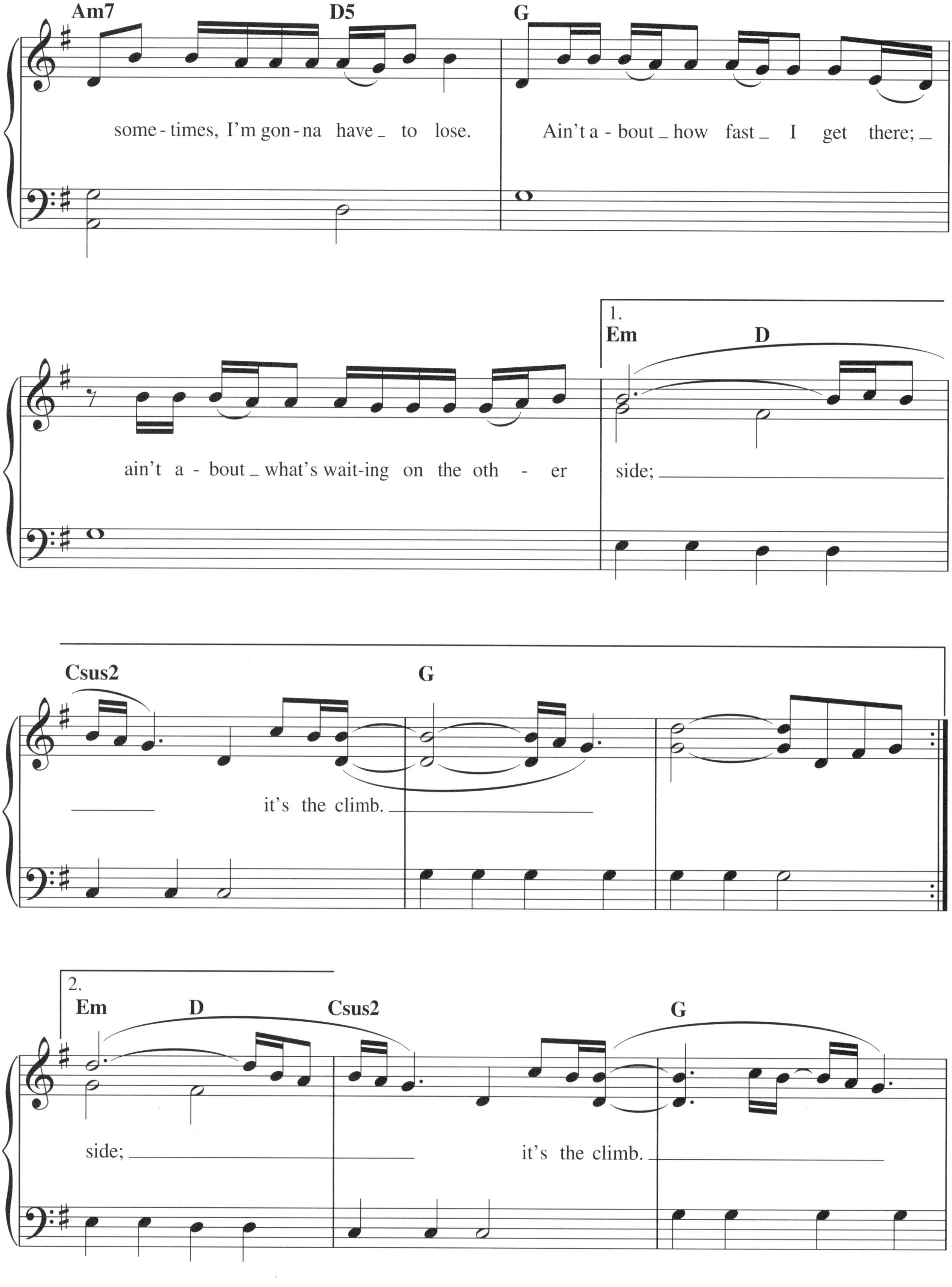
Am7
D5
G
some - times, I'm gon - na have _ to lose.
Ain't a - bout _ how fast _ I get there; _
1.
Em
D
ain't a - bout _ what's wait - ing on the oth - er
side; _
Csus2
G
it's the climb. _
2.
Em
D
Csus2
G
side; _
it's the climb. _

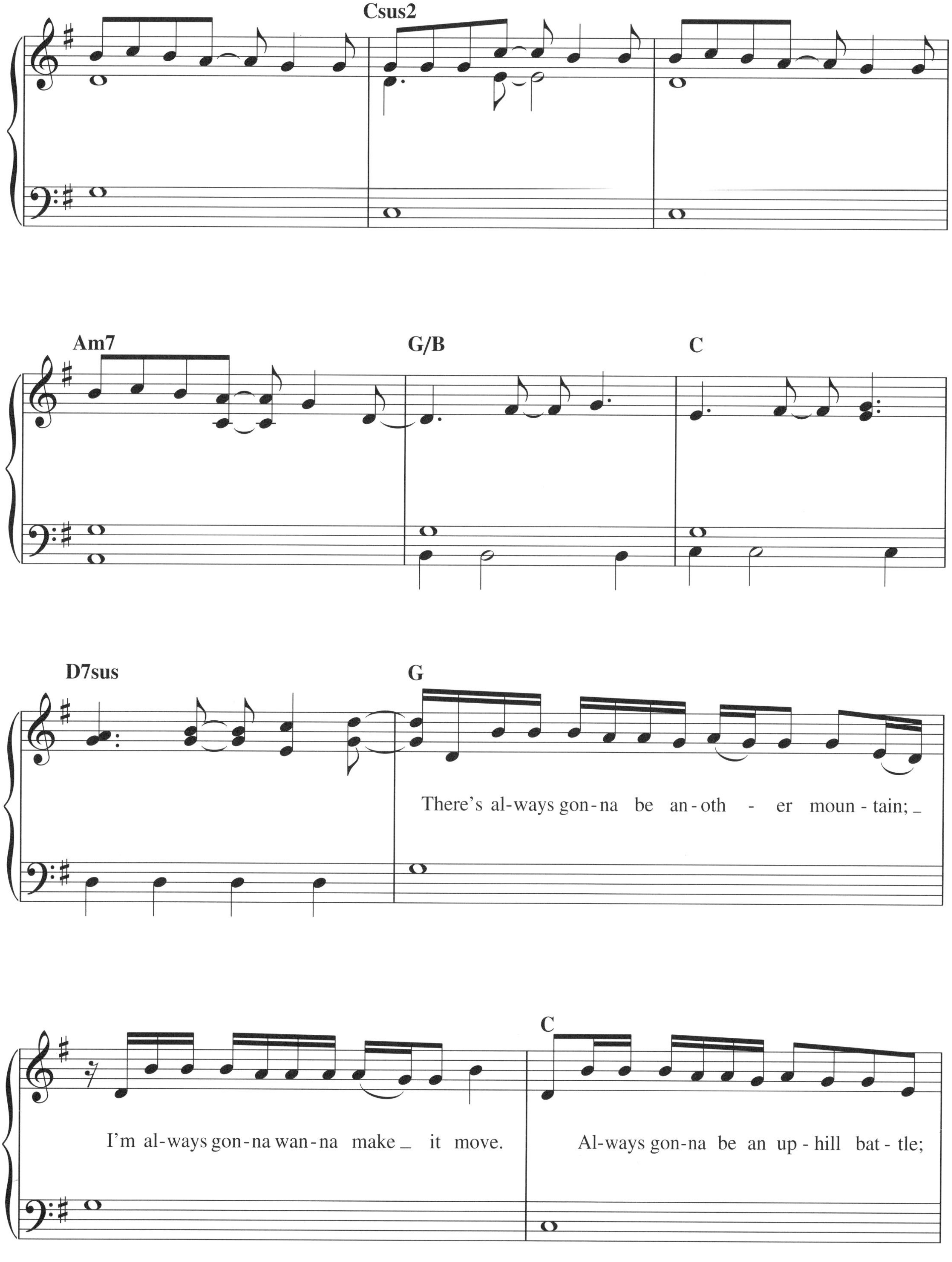
Csus2
Am7
G/B
C
D7sus
G
There's al-ways gon-na be an-oth - er moun-tain; _
I'm al-ways gon-na wan-na make _ it move.
C
Al-ways gon-na be an up-hill bat-tle;

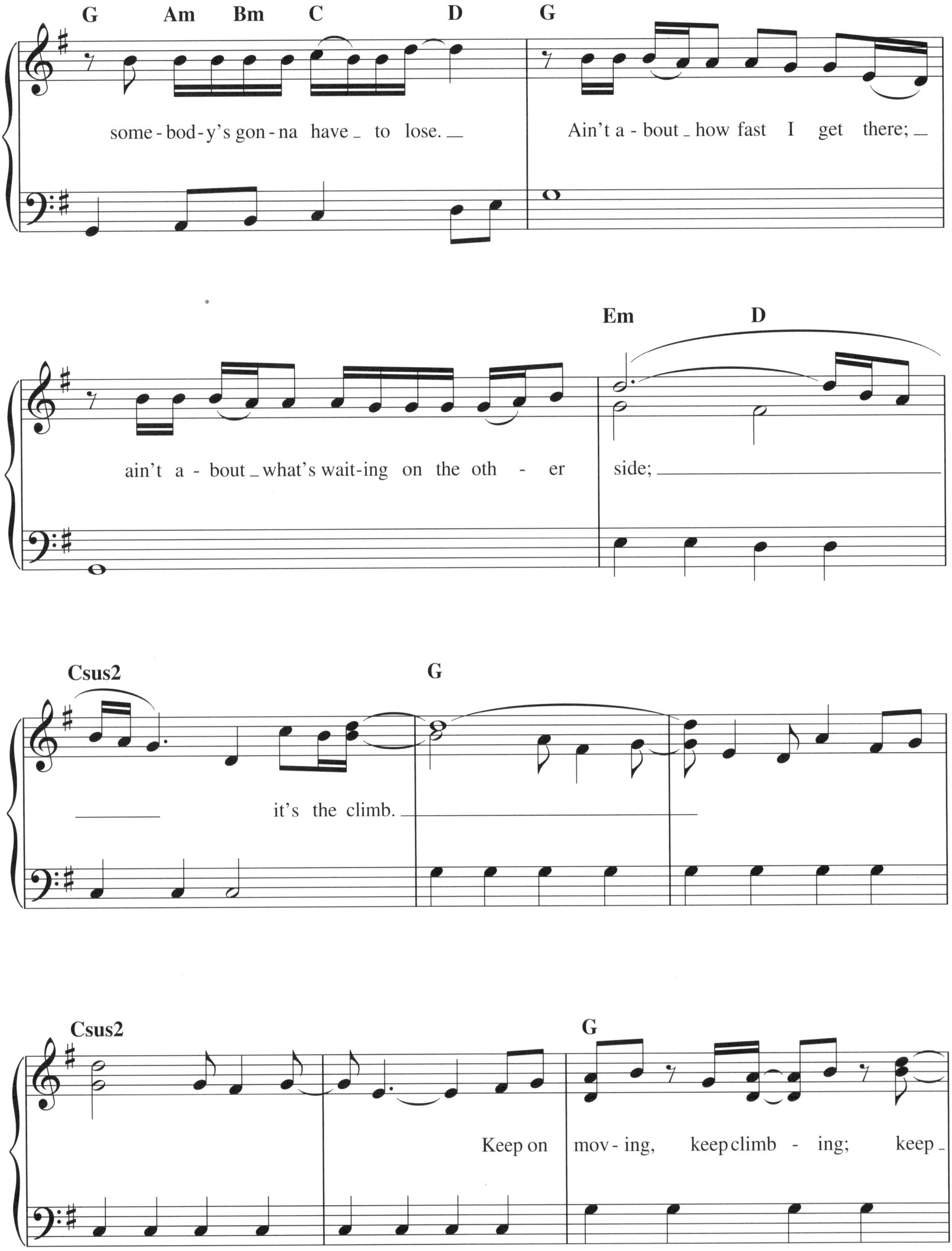
G Am Bm C D G
some - bod - y's gon - na have to lose.
Ain't a - bout how fast I get there;
ain't a - bout what's wait - ing on the oth - er
Em D
side;
Csus2 G
it's the climb.
Csus2 G
Keep on mov - ing, keep climb - ing; keep

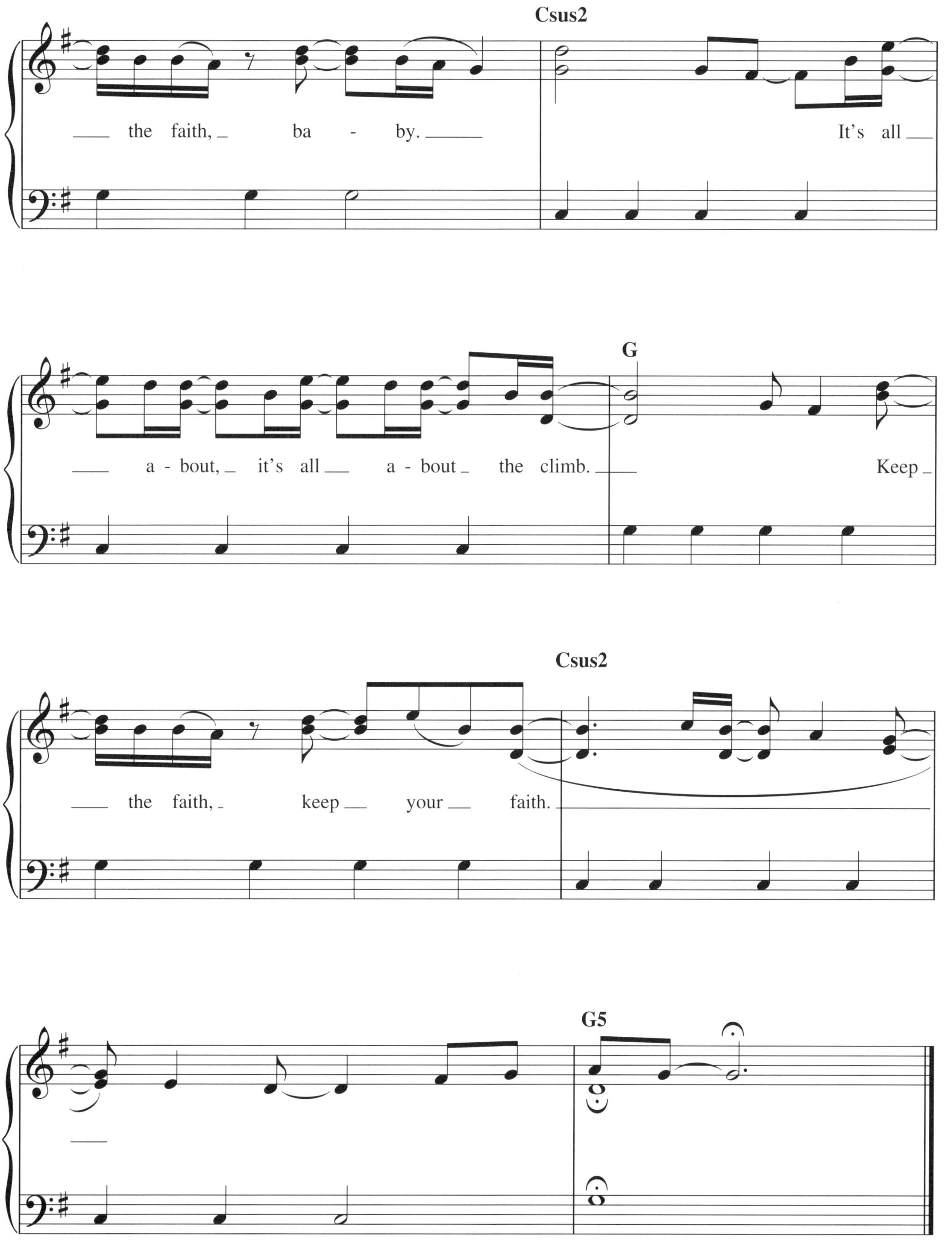
Csus2
the faith, ba - by.
It's all
a - bout, it's all a - bout the climb.
G
Keep
Csus2
the faith, keep your faith.
G5

Clocks

Words and Music by GUY BERRYMAN,
JON BUCKLAND, WILL CHAMPION
and CHRIS MARTIN

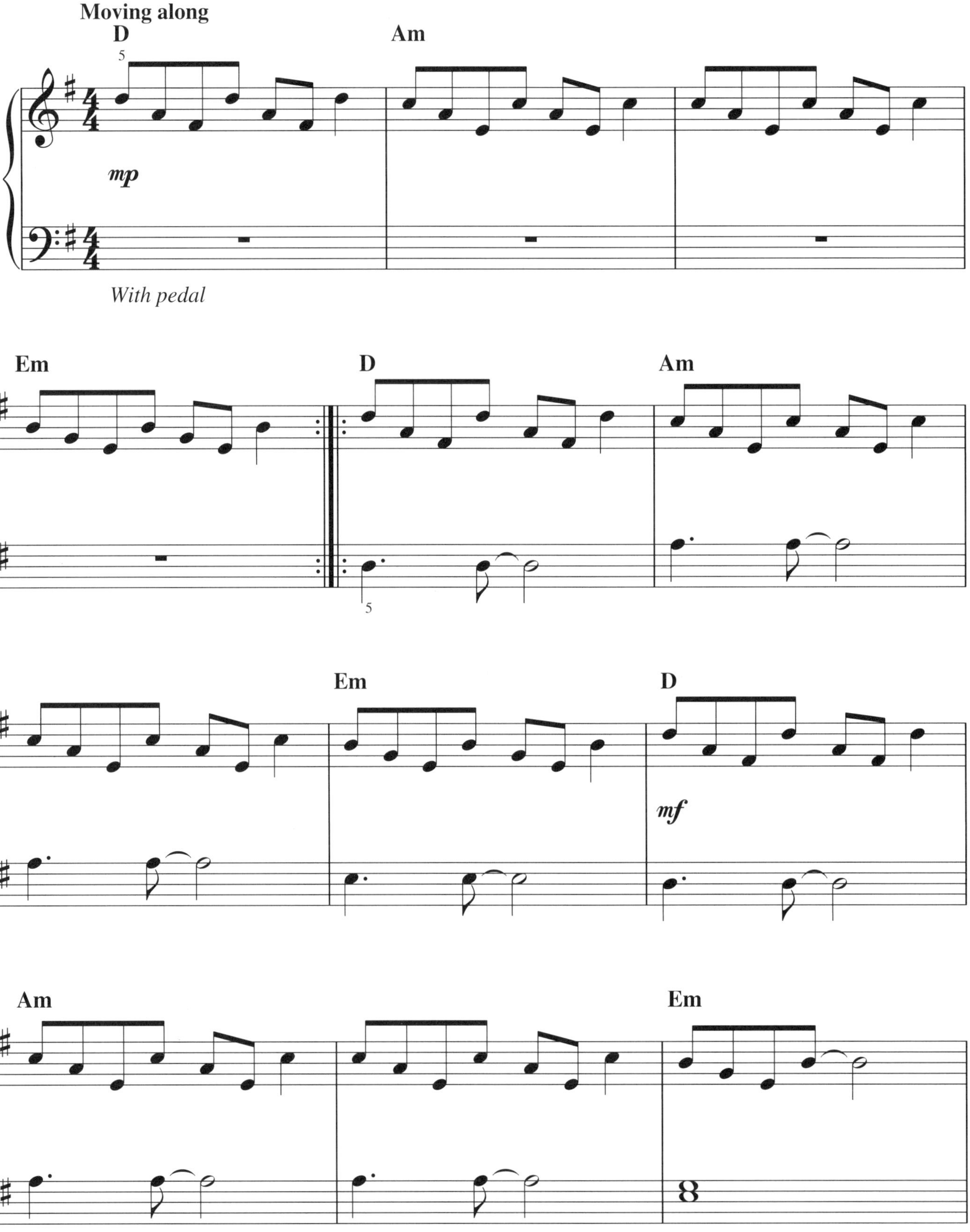

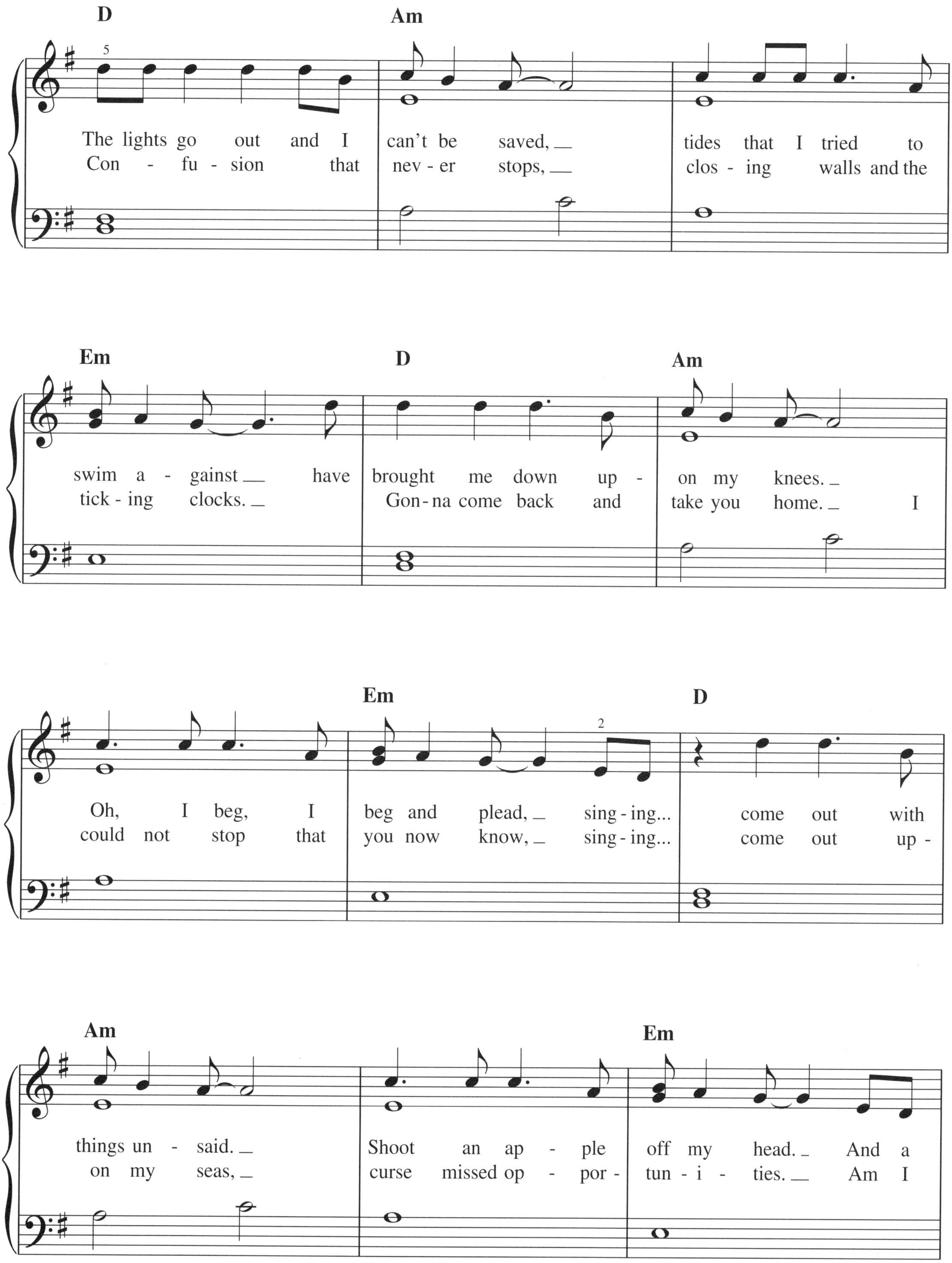
D
5
Am
The lights go out and I can't be saved, tides that I tried to
Con - fu - sion that nev - er stops, clos - ing walls and the
Em
D
Am
swim a - gainst have brought me down up - on my knees.
tick - ing clocks. Gon - na come back and take you home. I
Em
2
D
Oh, I beg, I beg and plead, sing - ing... come out with
could not stop that you now know, sing - ing... come out up -
Am
Em
things un - said. Shoot an ap - ple off my head. And a
on my seas, curse missed op - por - tun - i - ties. Am I

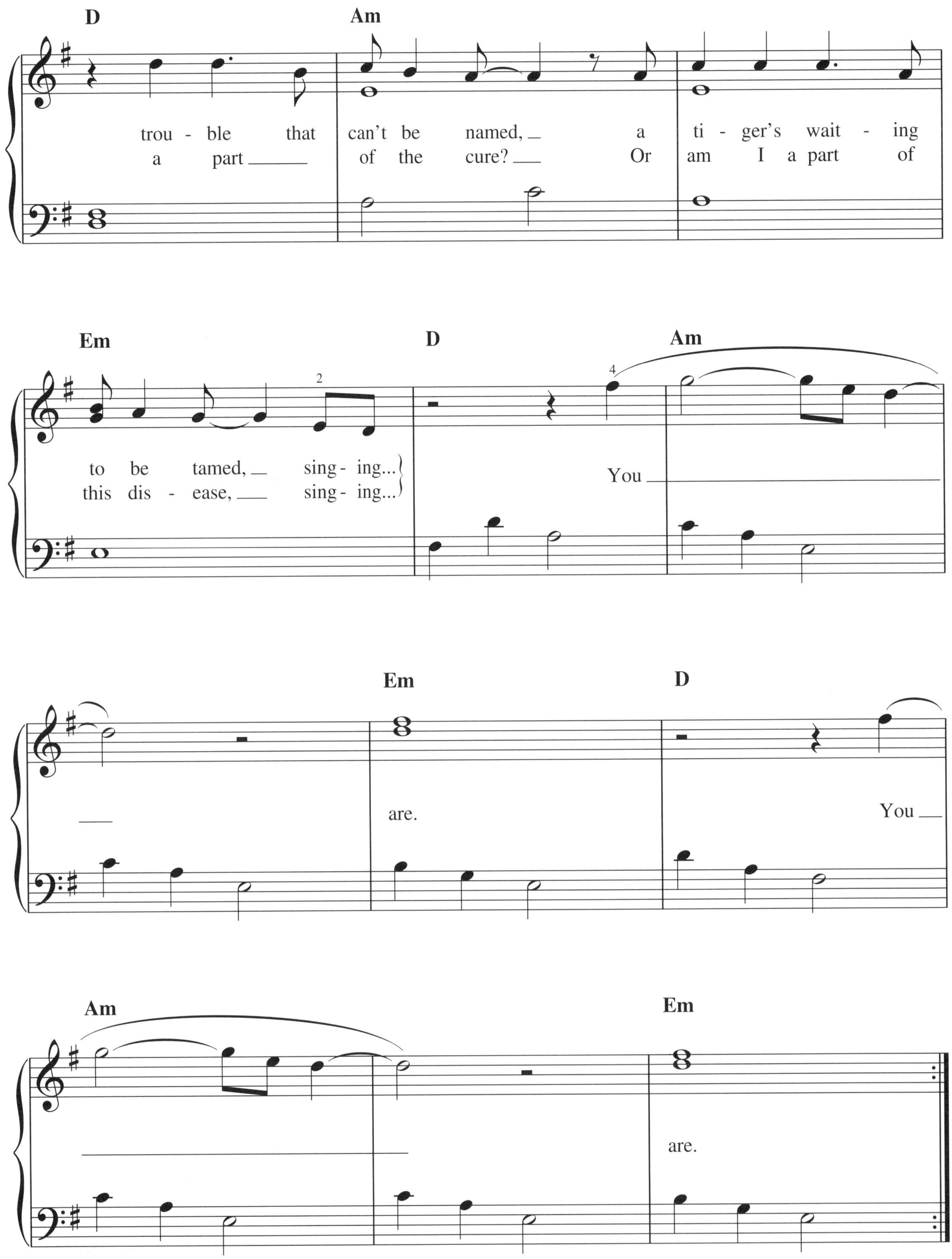
D
Am
trou - ble that can't be named, a ti - ger's wait - ing
a part of the cure? Or am I a part of
Em
D
Am
to be tamed, sing - ing...
this dis - ease, sing - ing...
You
Em
D
are.
You
Am
Em
are.

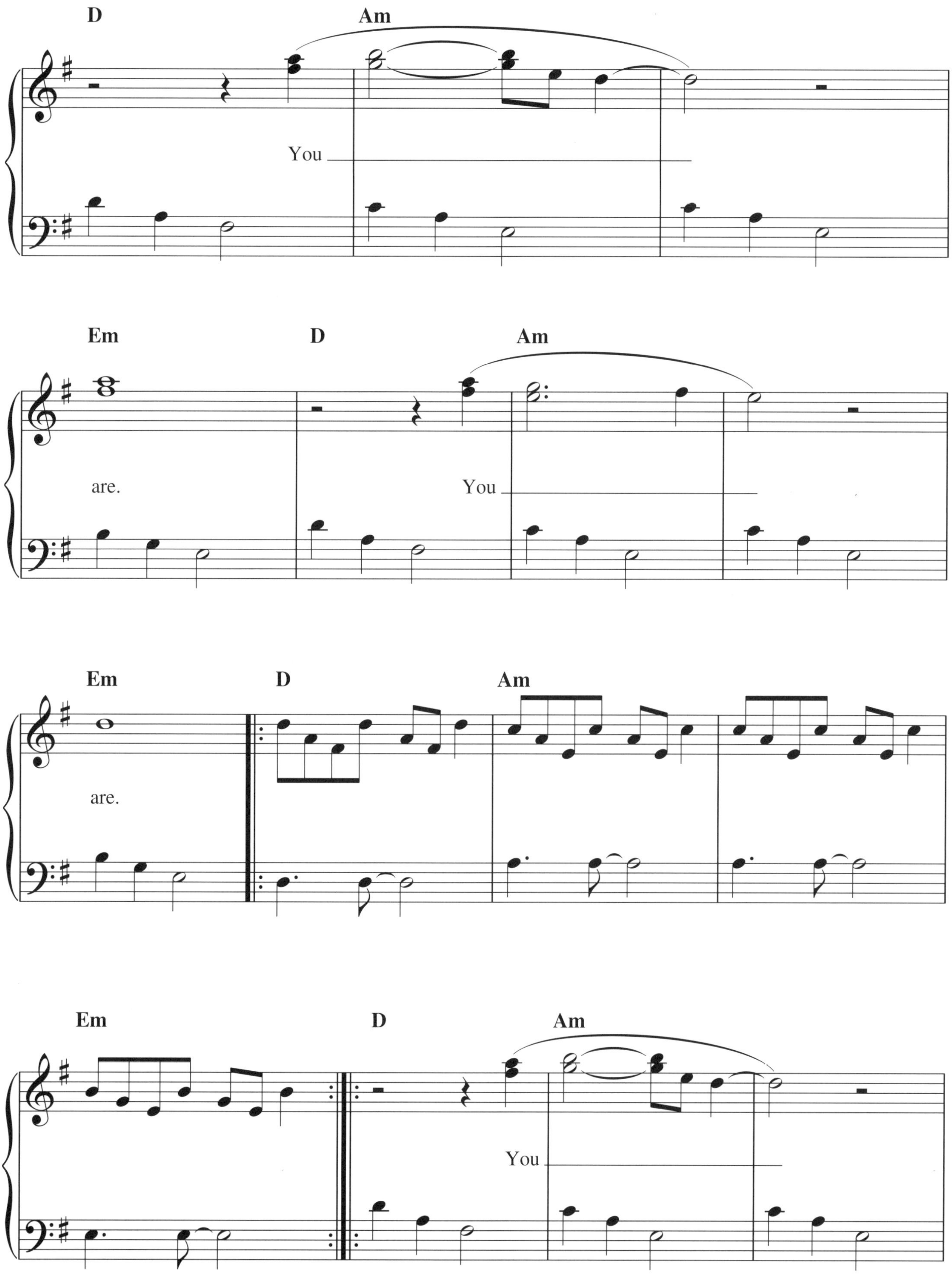
D
Am
You
Em
D
Am
are.
You
Em
D
Am
are.
Em
D
Am
You

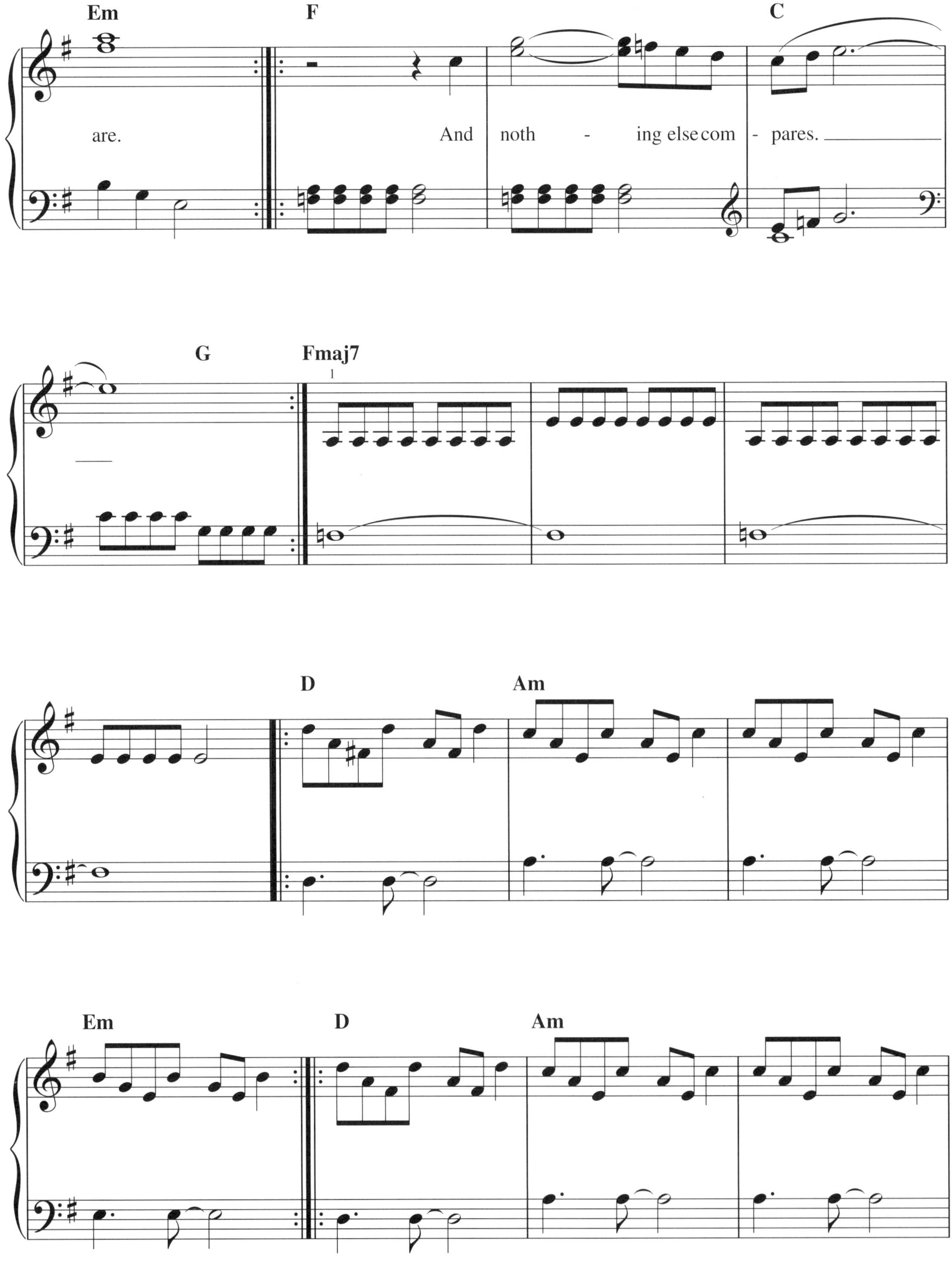
Em
F
C
are.
And
noth - ing else com - pares.
G
Fmaj7
D
Am
Em
D
Am

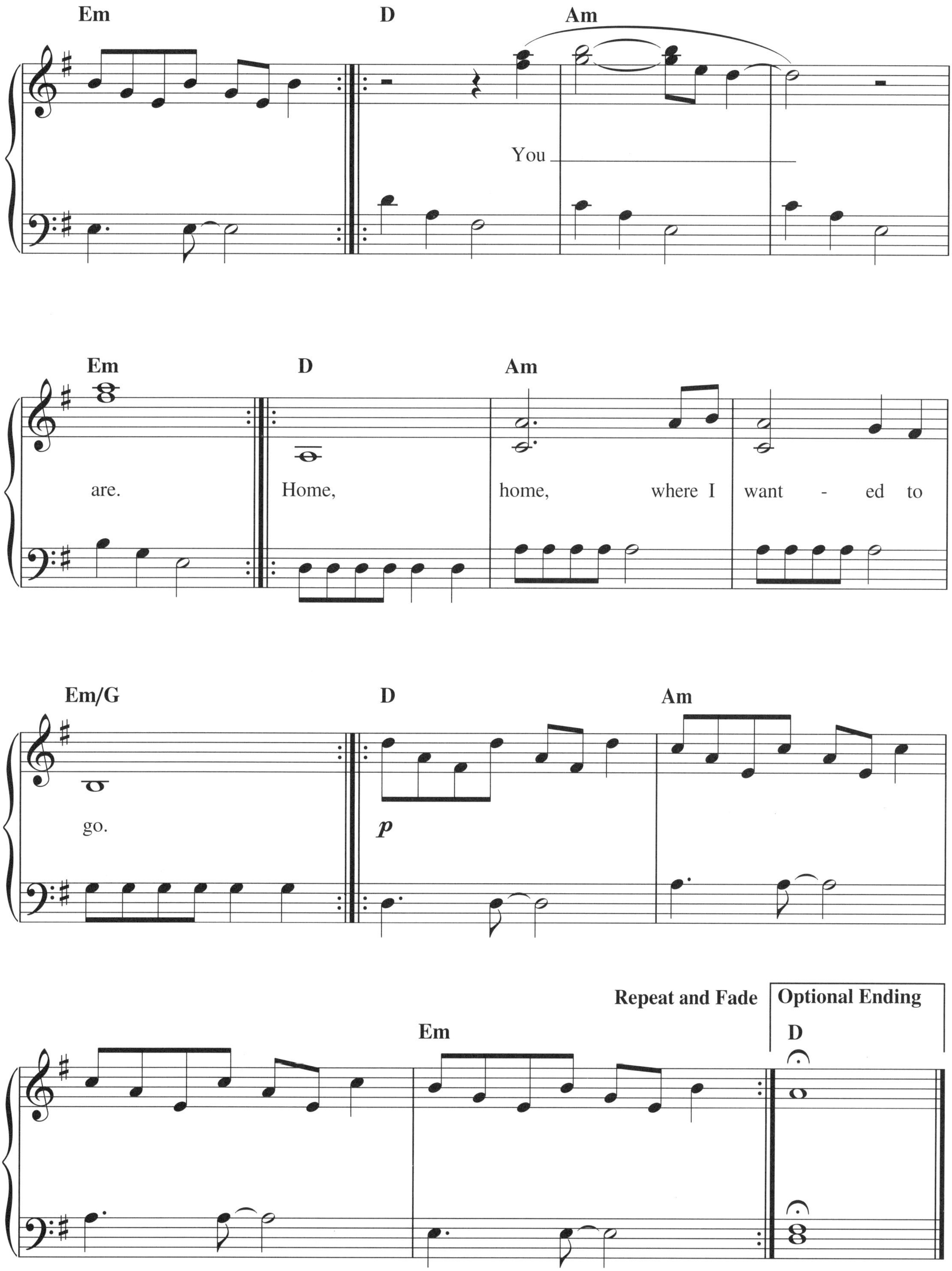
Em
D
Am
You
Em
D
Am
are.
Home,
home, where I want - ed to
Em/G
D
Am
go.
p
Repeat and Fade
Optional Ending
Em
D

Daniel

Words and Music by ELTON JOHN
and BERNIE TAUPIN

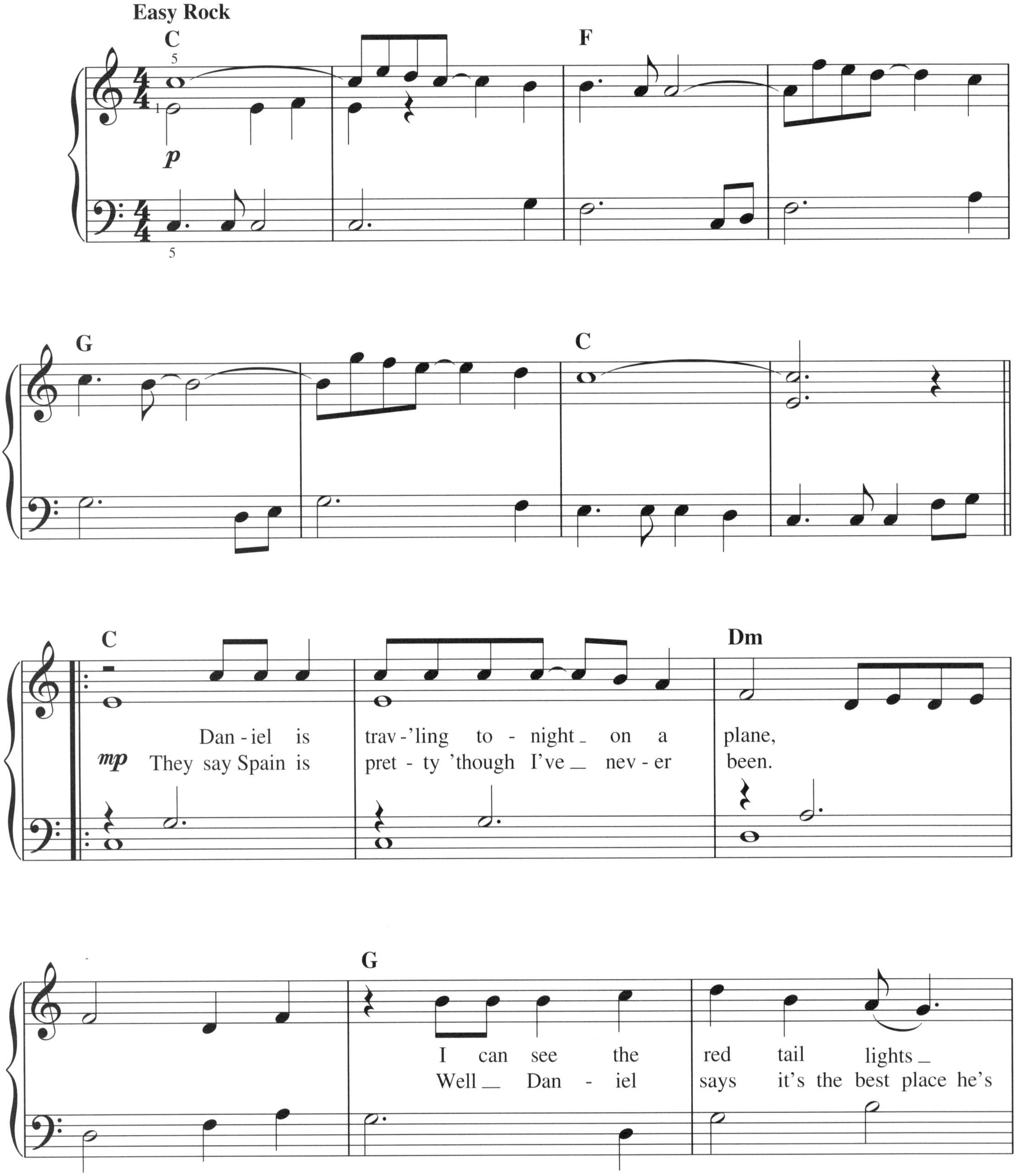
Easy Rock
C
F
p
G
C
C
Dm
mp
Dan - iel is trav - 'ling to - night on a plane,
They say Spain is pret - ty 'though I've never - er been.
G
I can see the red tail lights
Well Dan - iel says it's the best place he's

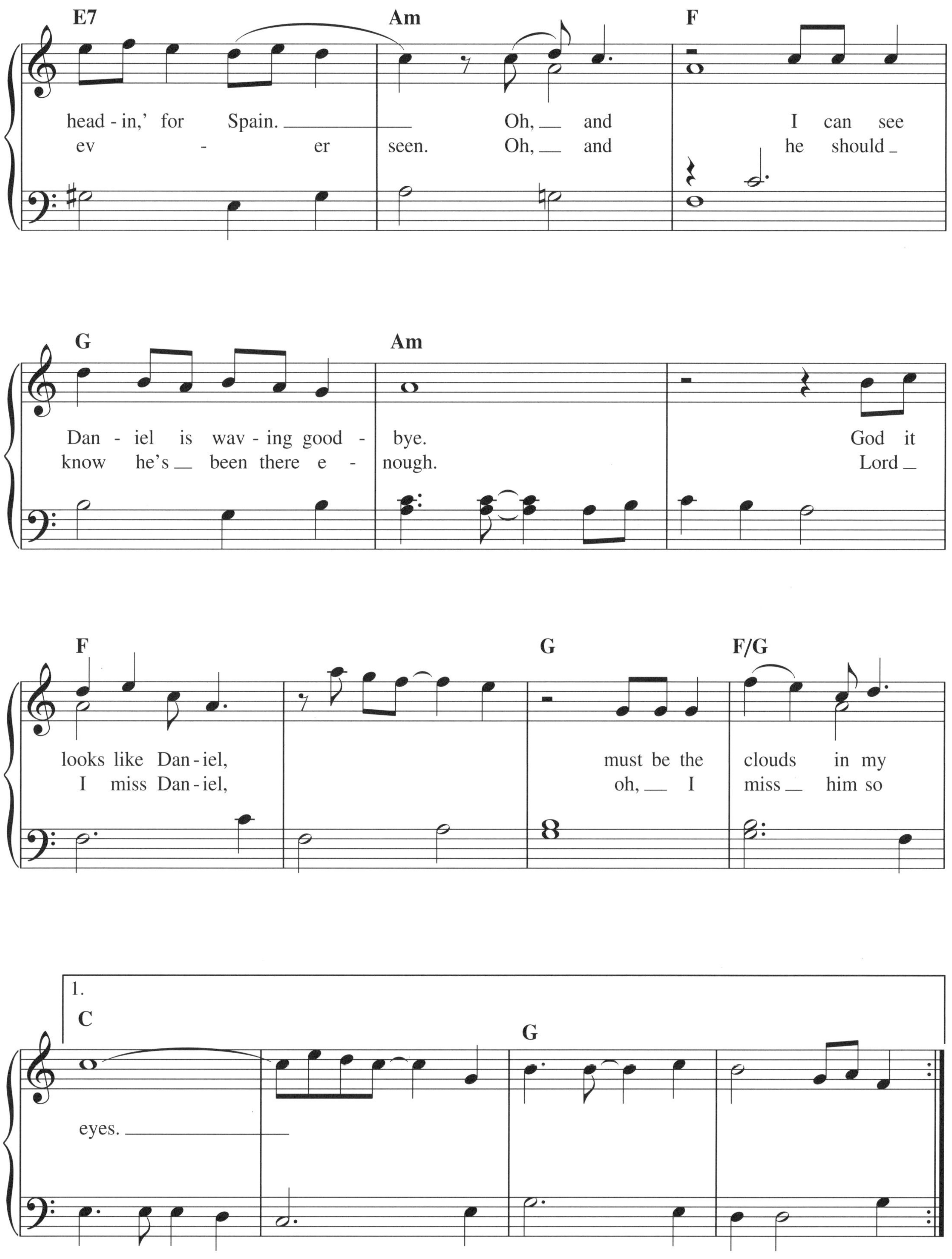
E7
Am
F
head - in,' for Spain. Oh, and I can see
ev - er seen. Oh, and he should
G
Am
Dan - iel is wav - ing good - bye. God it
know he's been there e - nough. Lord
F
G
F/G
looks like Dan - iel, must be the clouds in my
I miss Dan - iel, oh, I miss him so
1.
C
G
eyes.

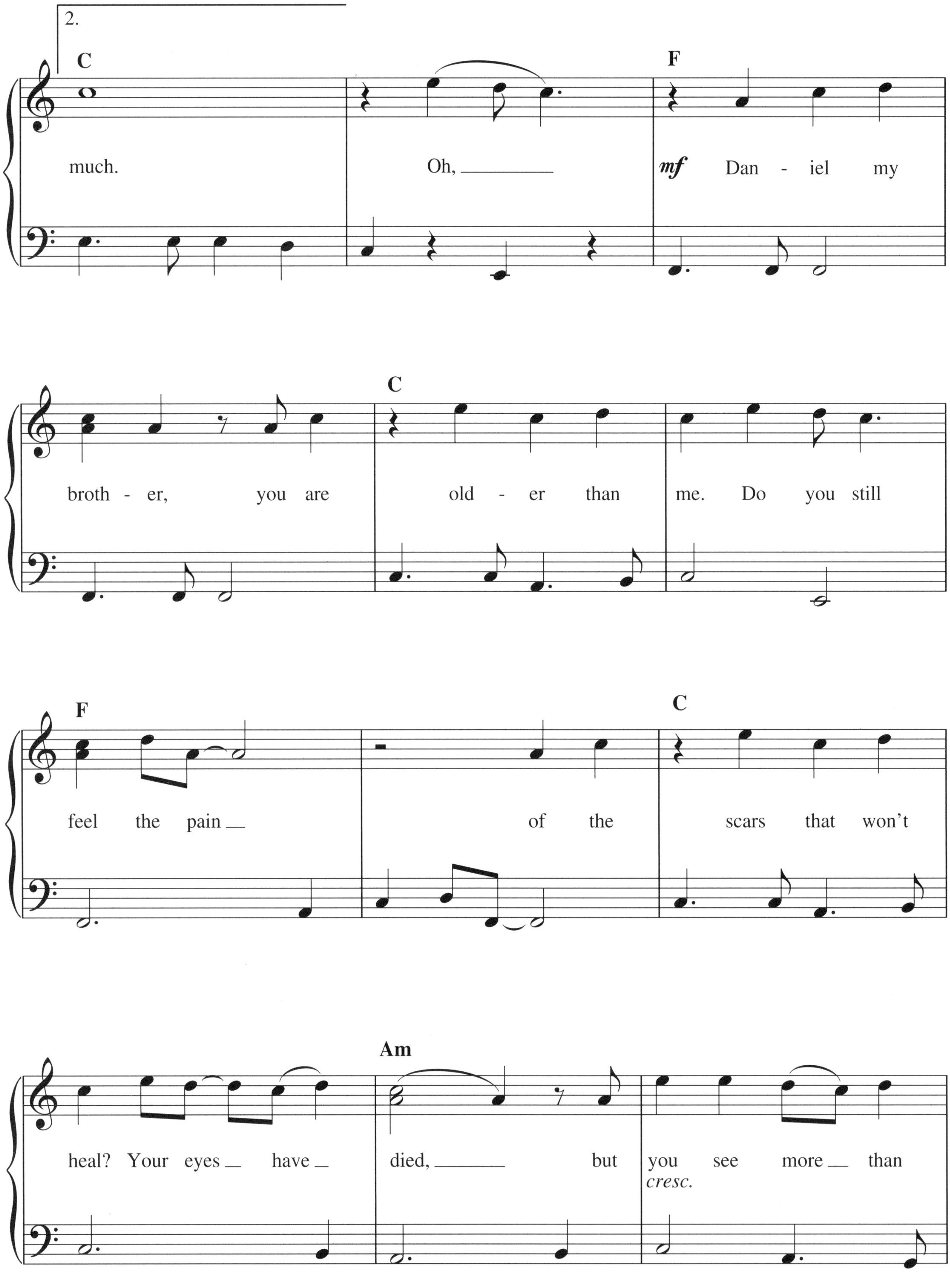
2.
C
F
much. Oh,
mf
Dan - iel my
C
broth - er, you are old - er than me. Do you still
F
C
feel the pain of the scars that won't
Am
heal? Your eyes have died, but you see more than
cresc.

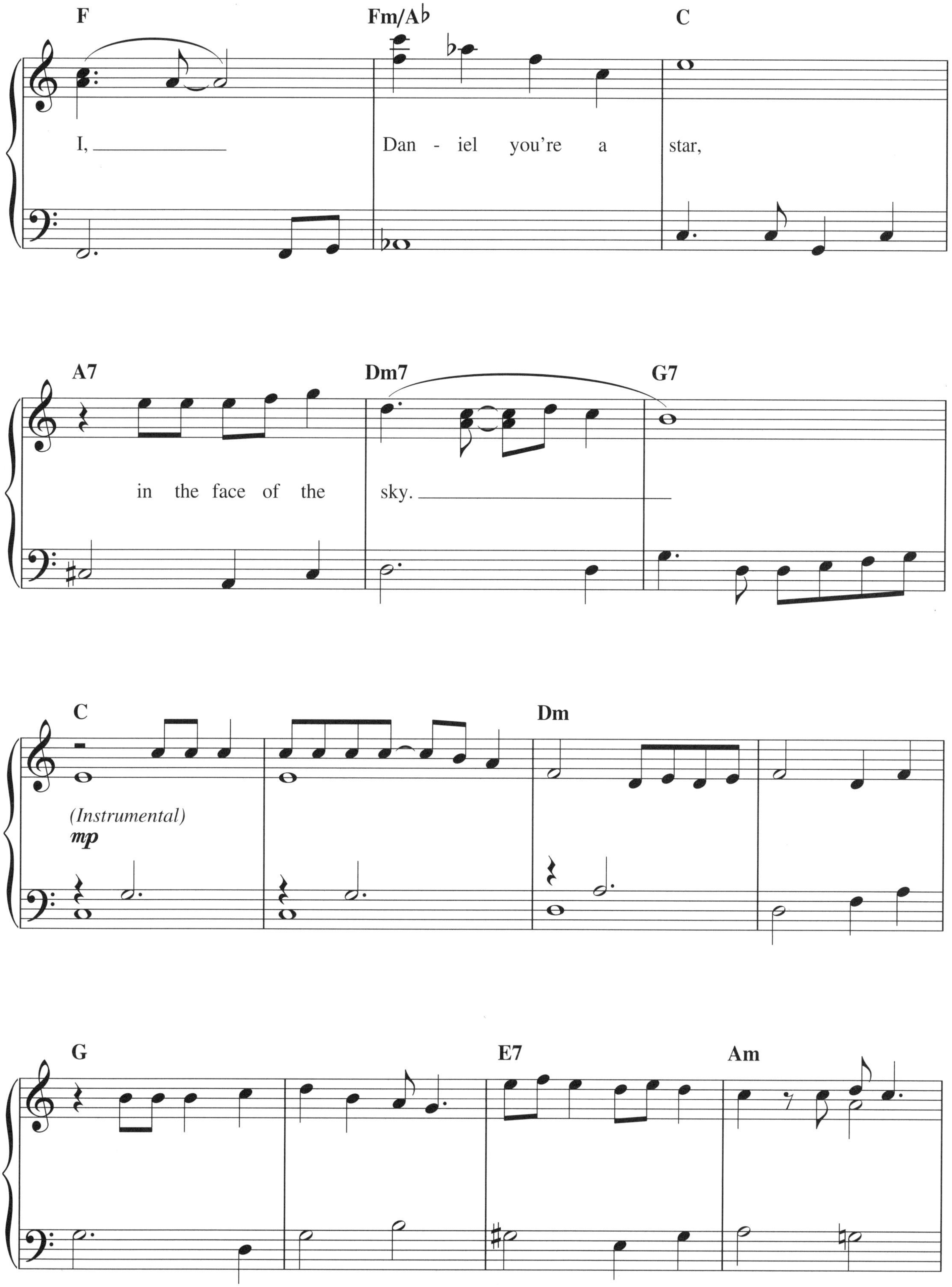
F
Fm/A♭
C
I, ___
Dan - iel you're a star,
A7
Dm7
G7
in the face of the sky. ___
C
Dm
(Instrumental)
mp
G
E7
Am

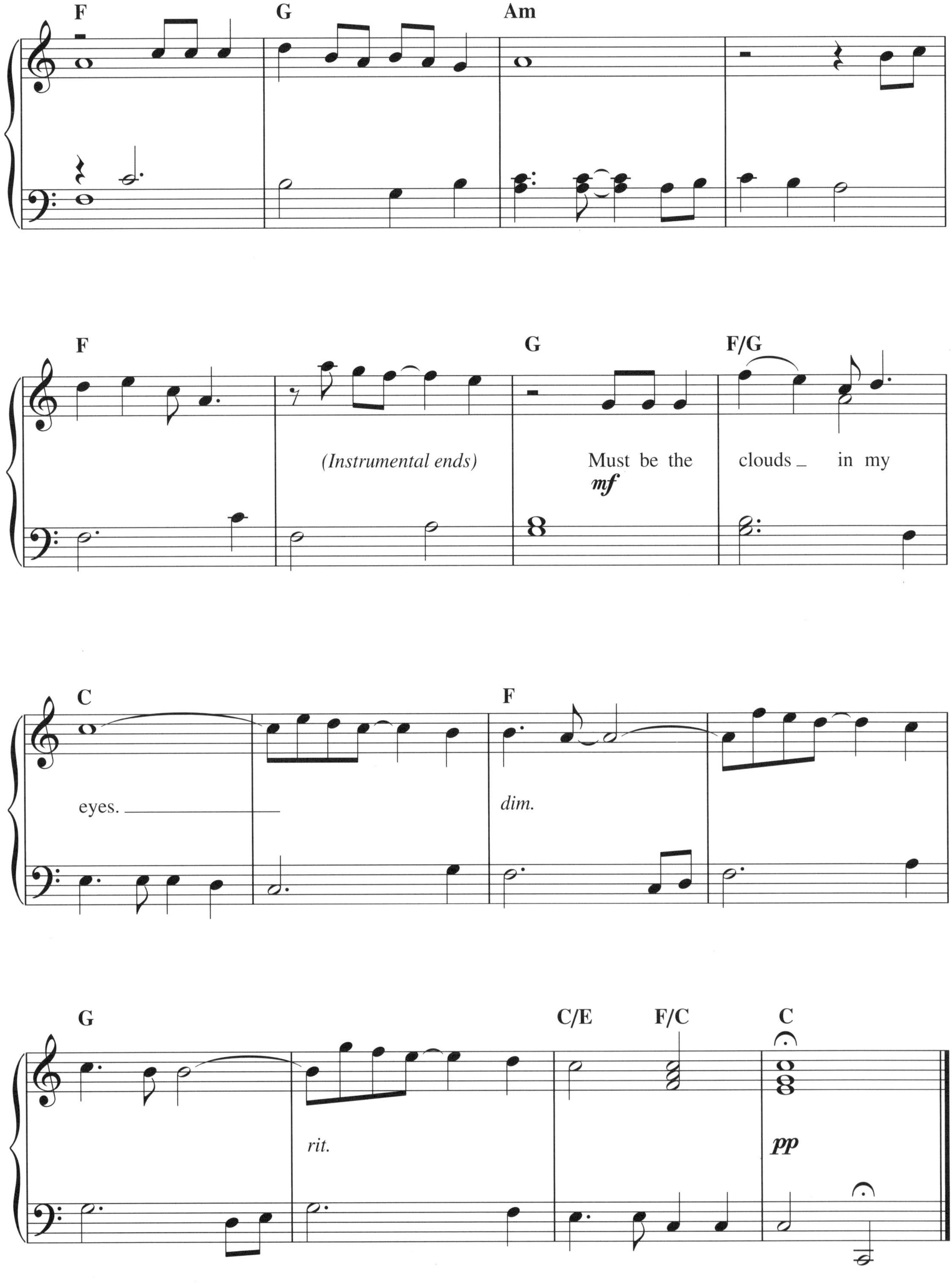
F
G
Am
F
G
F/G
(Instrumental ends)
Must be the
mf
clouds _ in my
C
F
eyes.
dim.
G
C/E
F/C
C
rit.
pp

Dancing Queen

Words and Music by BENNY ANDERSSON,
BJÖRN ULVAEUS and STIG ANDERSON

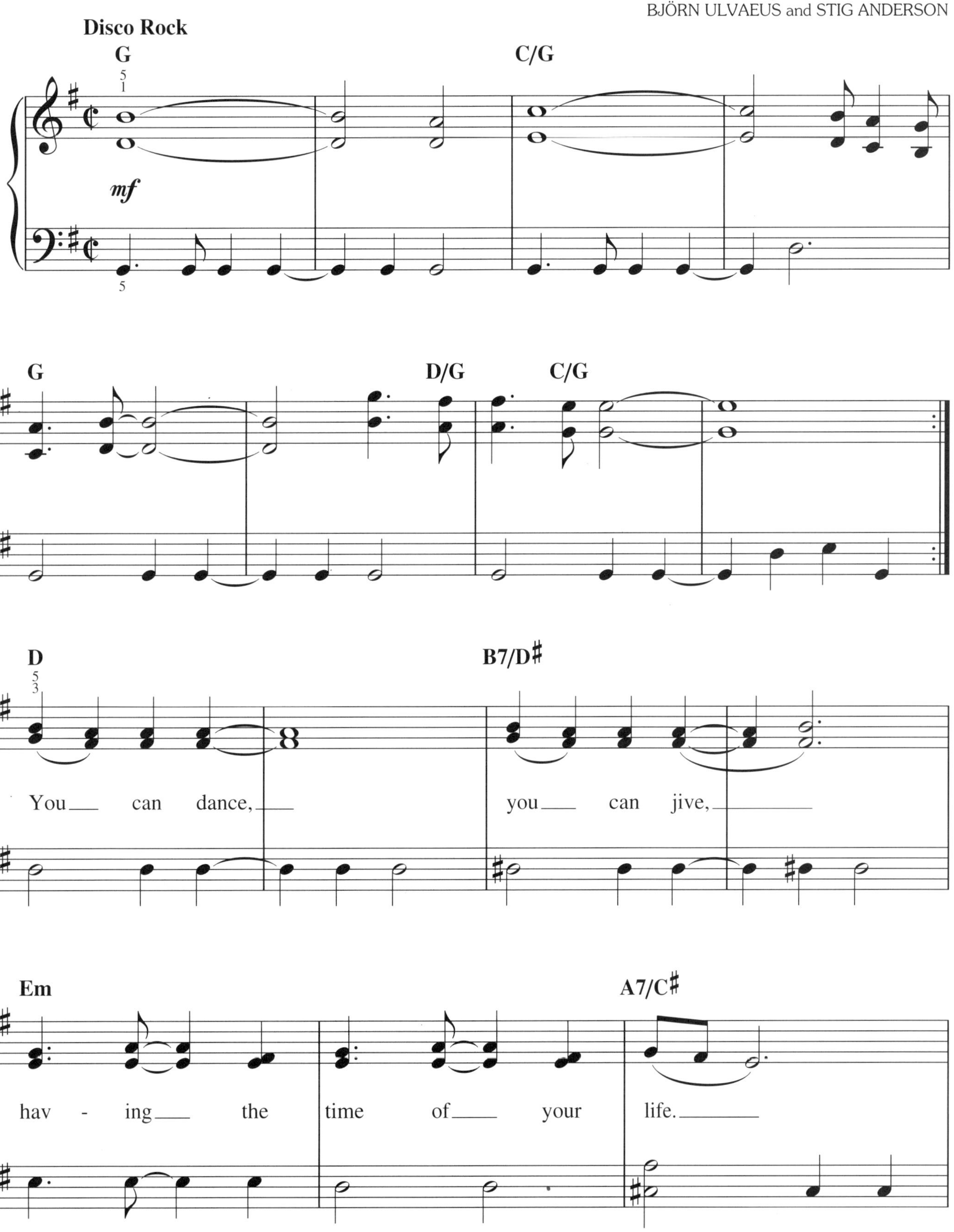

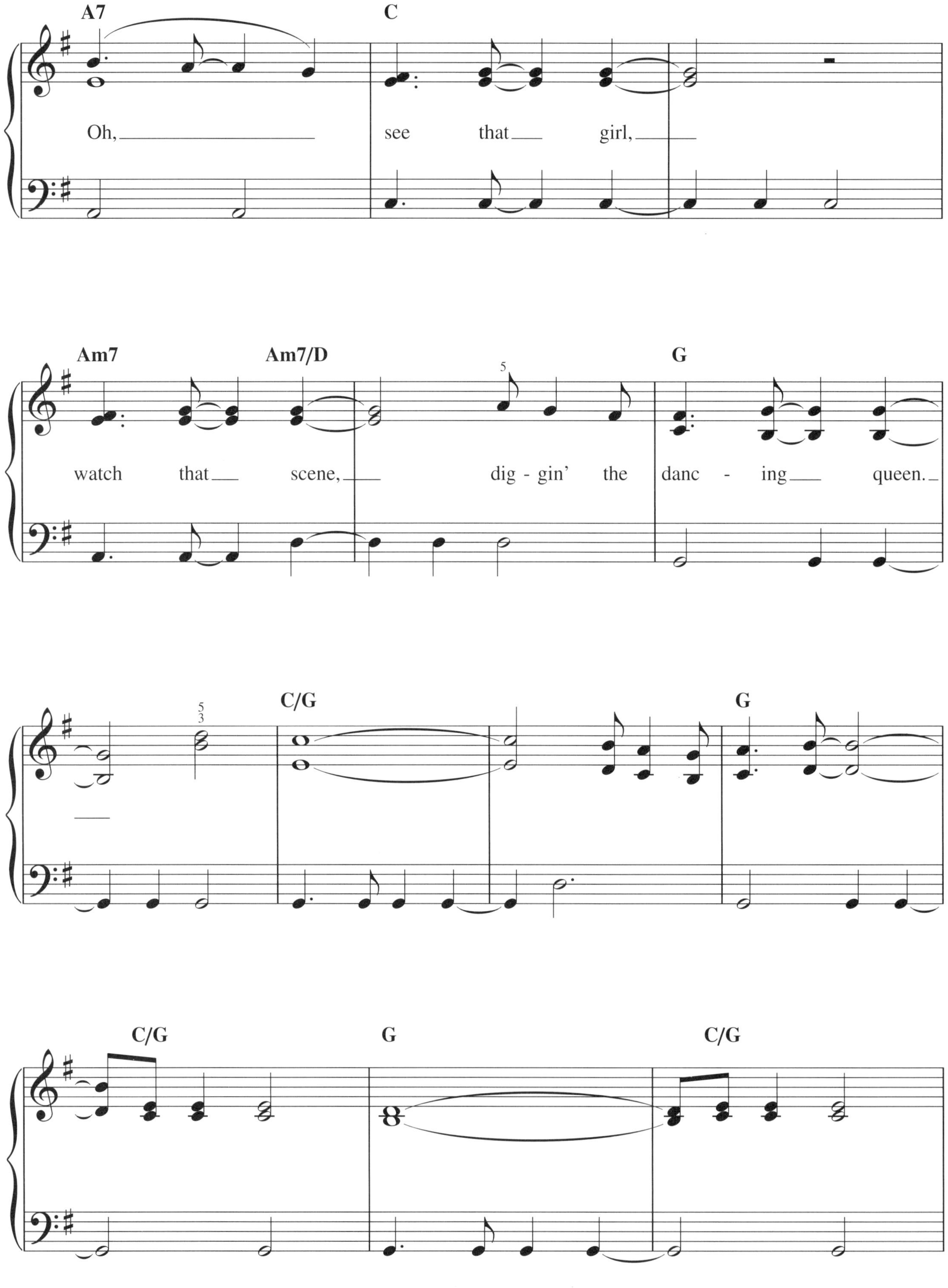
A7
C
Oh, see that girl,
Am7
Am7/D
G
watch that scene, dig - gin' the danc - ing queen.
C/G
G
C/G
G
C/G

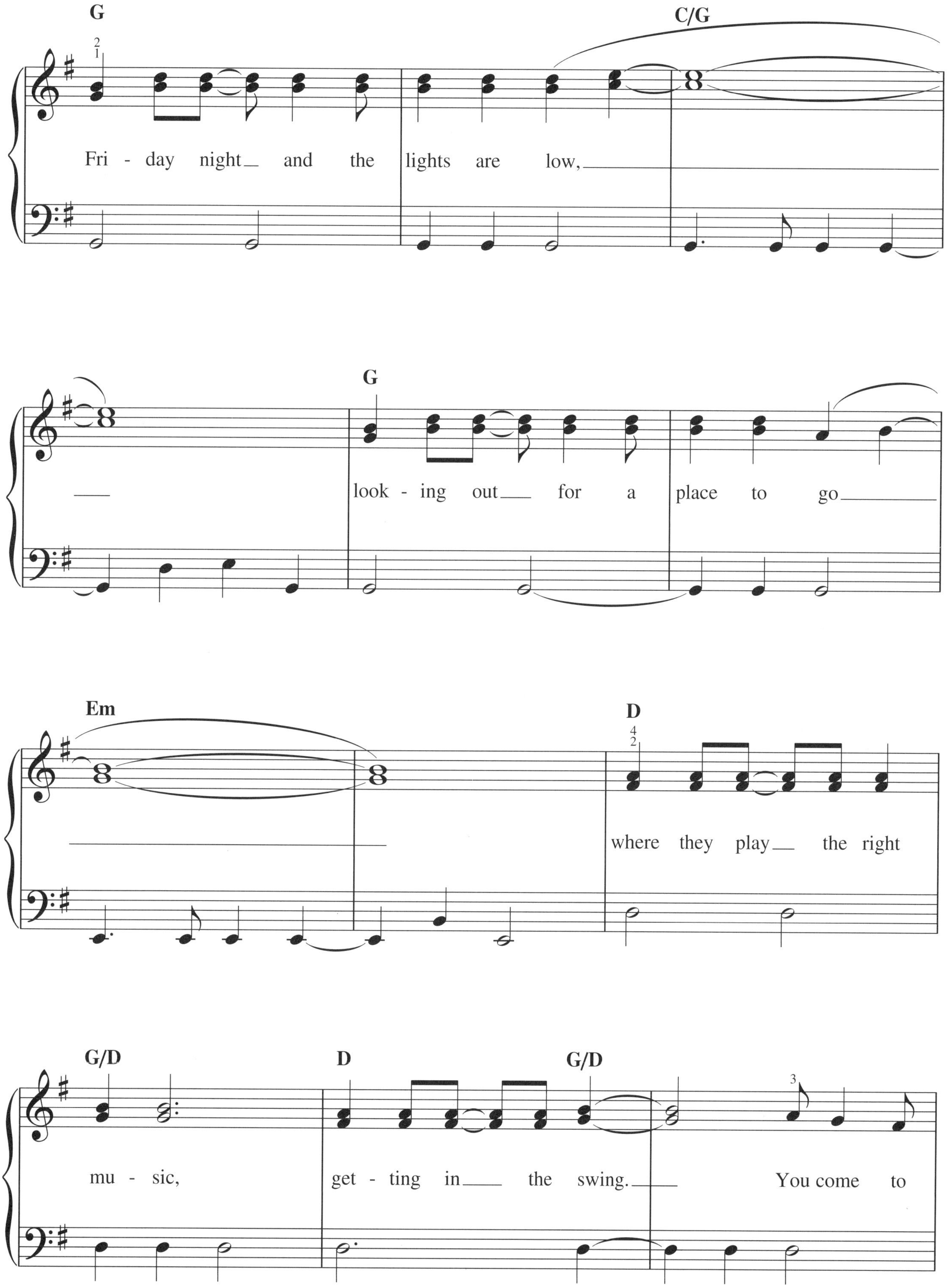
G
C/G
Fri - day night and the lights are low,
G
look - ing out for a place to go
Em
D
where they play the right
G/D
D
G/D
mu - sic,
get - ting in the swing.
You come to

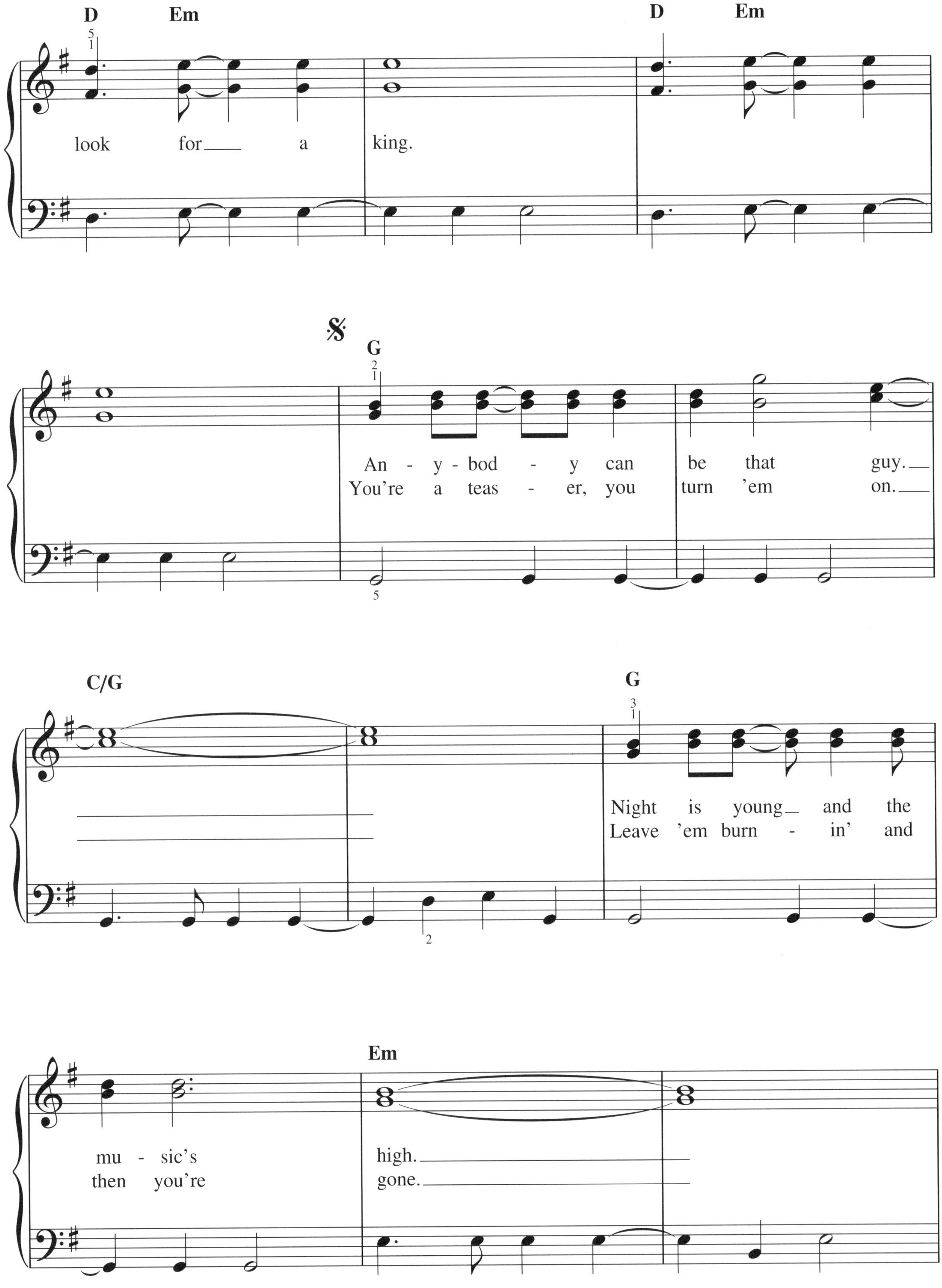
D Em D Em
look for a king.
G
An - y - bod - y can be that guy.
You're a teas - er, you turn 'em on.
C/G G
Night is young and the
Leave 'em burn - in' and
Em
mu - sic's high.
then you're gone.

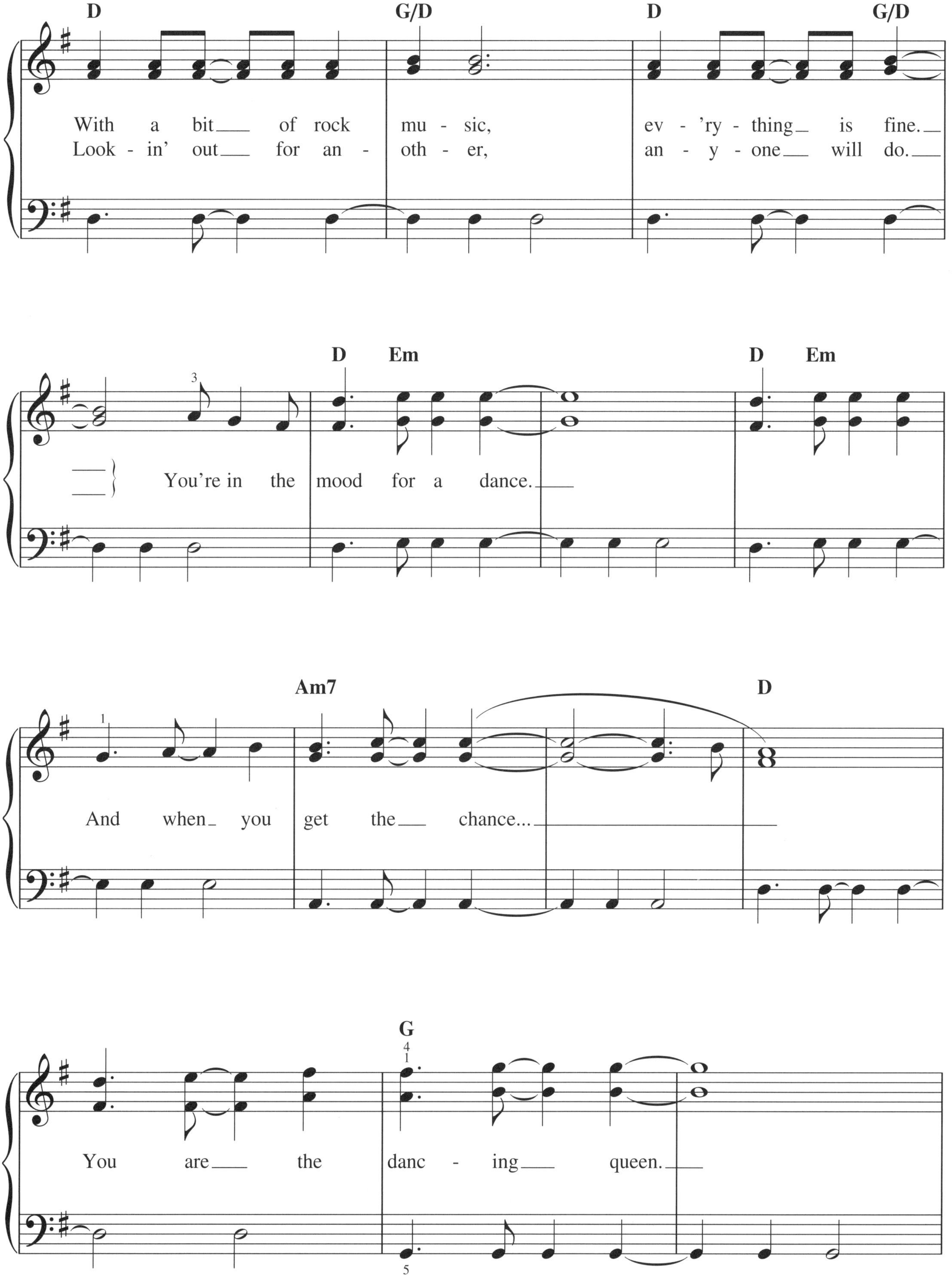
D
G/D
D
G/D
With a bit of rock mu - sic, ev - 'ry - thing is fine.
Look - in' out for an - oth - er, an - y - one will do.
3
D
Em
D
Em
You're in the mood for a dance.
1
Am7
D
And when you get the chance...
G
4
1
You are the danc - ing queen.
5

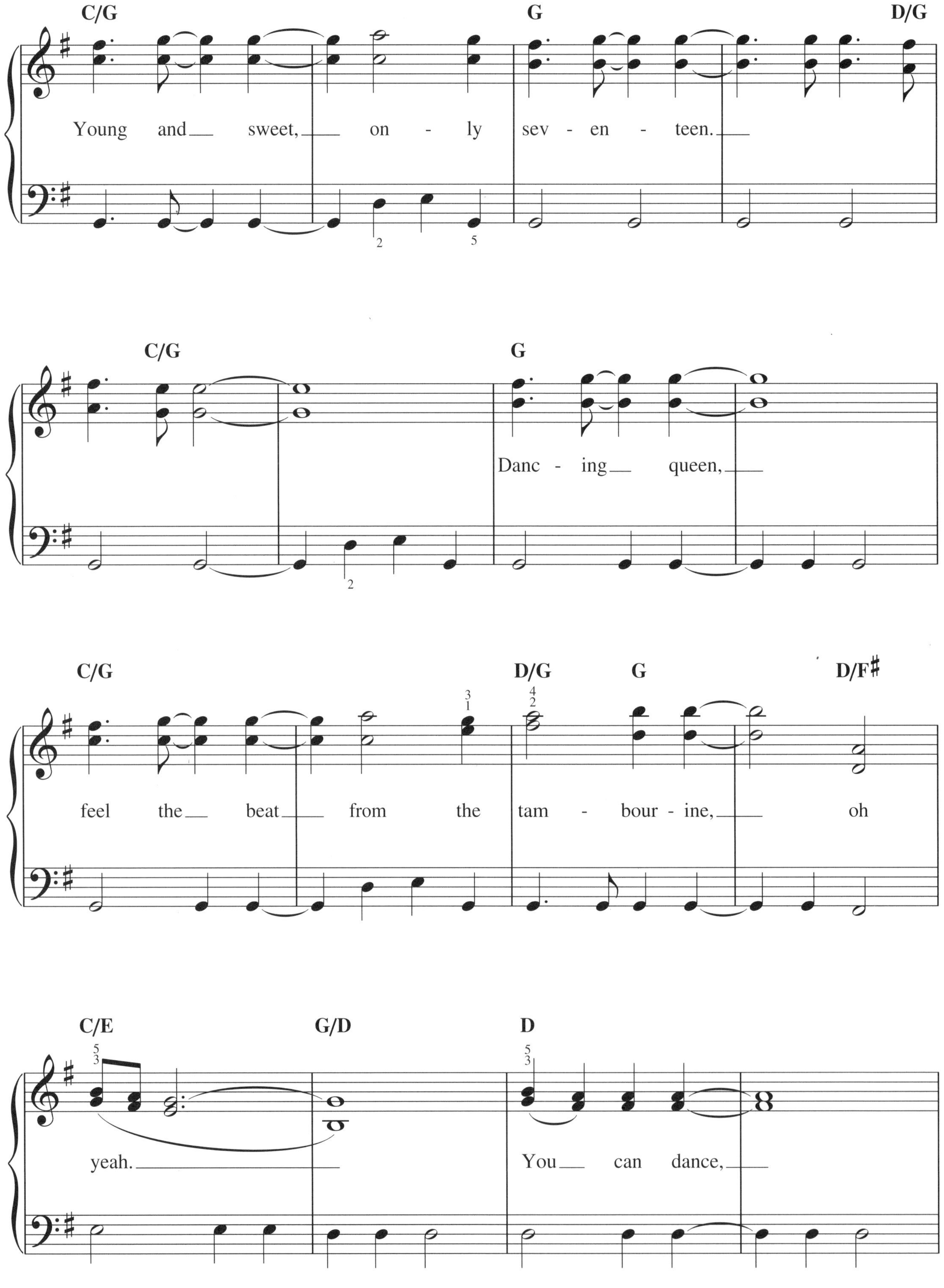
C/G
G
D/G
Young and sweet, on - ly sev - en - teen.
C/G
G
Danc - ing queen,
C/G
D/G
G
D/F#
feel the beat from the tam - bour - ine, oh
C/E
G/D
D
yeah.
You can dance,

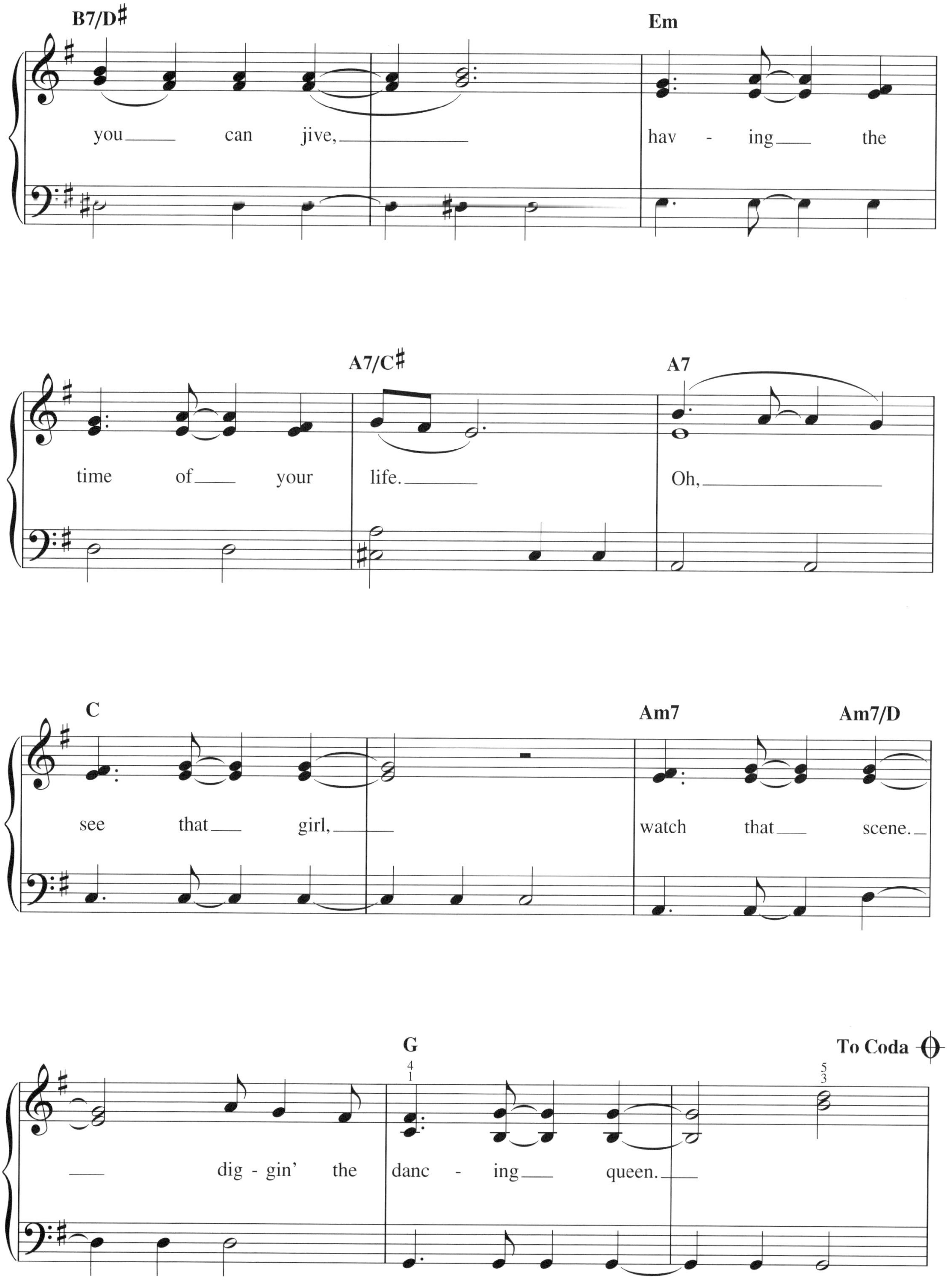
B7/D♯
you can jive,
Em
hav - ing the
time of your
A7/C♯
life.
A7
Oh,
C
see that girl,
Am7
watch that
Am7/D
scene.
dig - gin' the
G
4
1
danc - ing queen.
To Coda
5
3

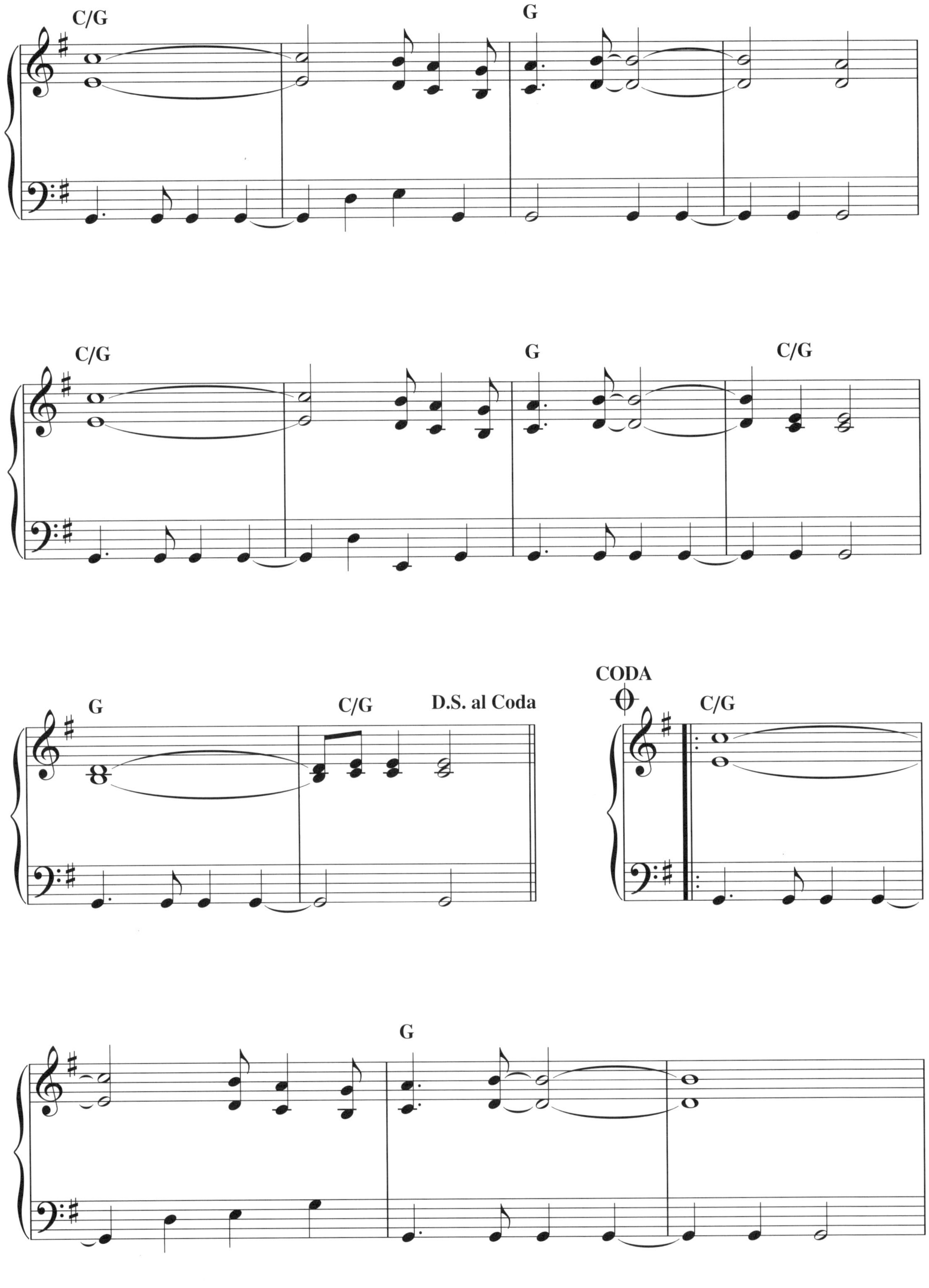
C/G
G
C/G
G
C/G
G
C/G
D.S. al Coda
CODA
C/G
G

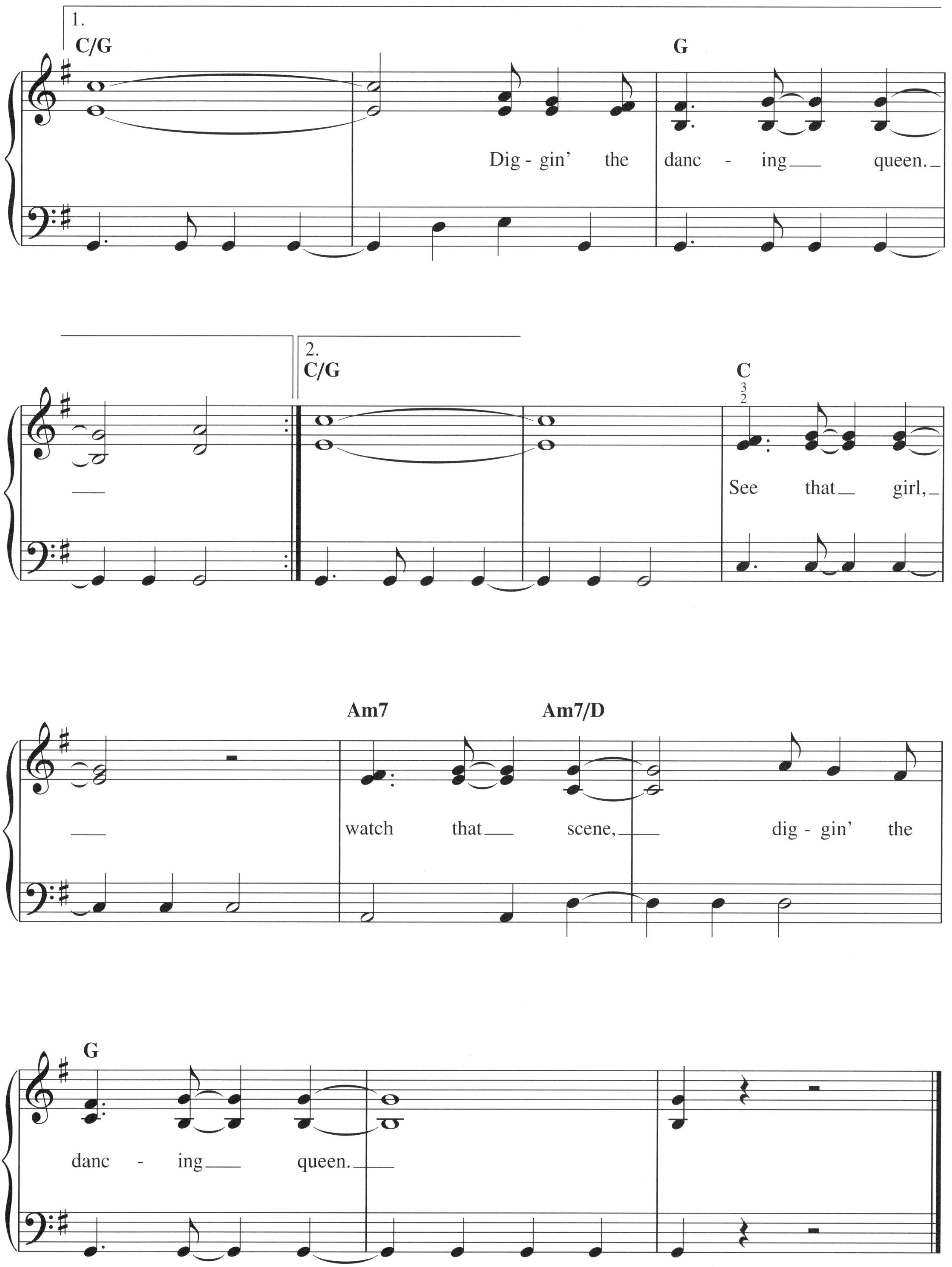
1.
C/G
G
Dig - gin' the danc - ing queen.
2.
C/G
C
3
2
See that girl,
Am7
Am7/D
watch that scene, dig - gin' the
G
danc - ing queen.

Defying Gravity

Music and Lyrics by
STEPHEN SCHWARTZ

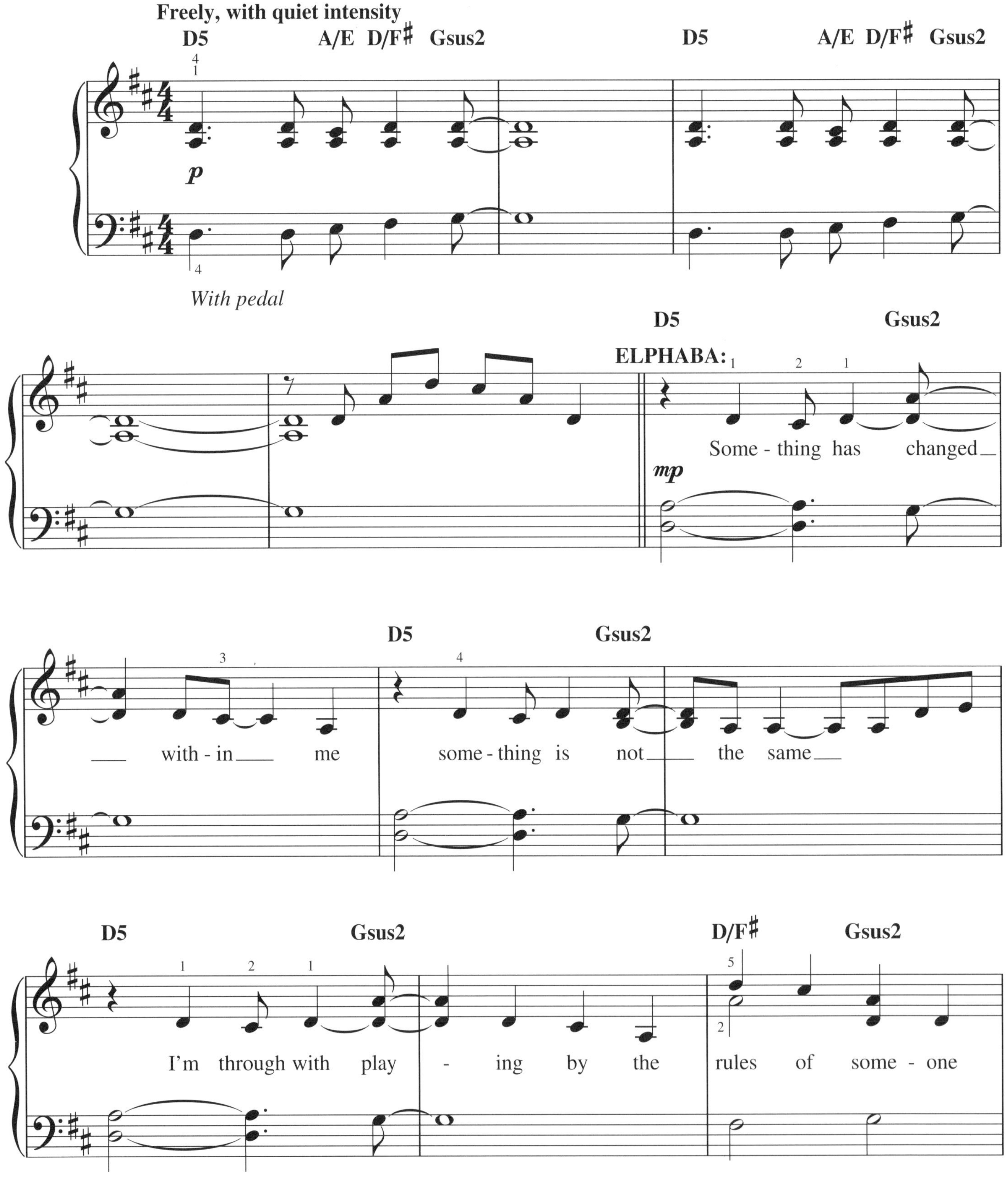

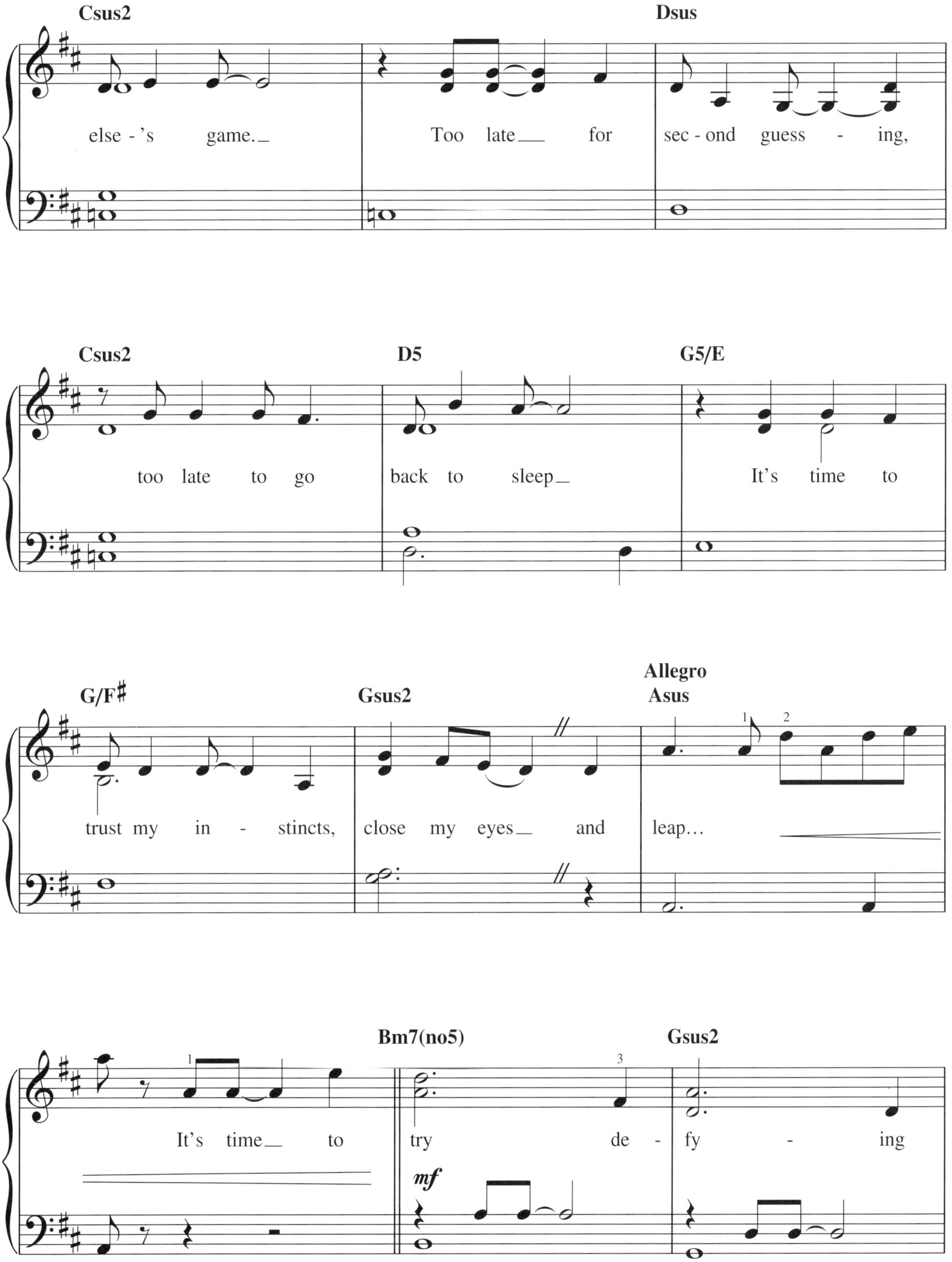
Csus2
Dsus
else - 's game.
Too late for sec - ond guess - ing,
Csus2
D5
G5/E
too late to go back to sleep
It's time to
G/F#
Gsus2
Allegro
Asus
trust my in - stincts, close my eyes and leap...
It's time to
Bm7(no5)
Gsus2
try de - fy - ing
mf

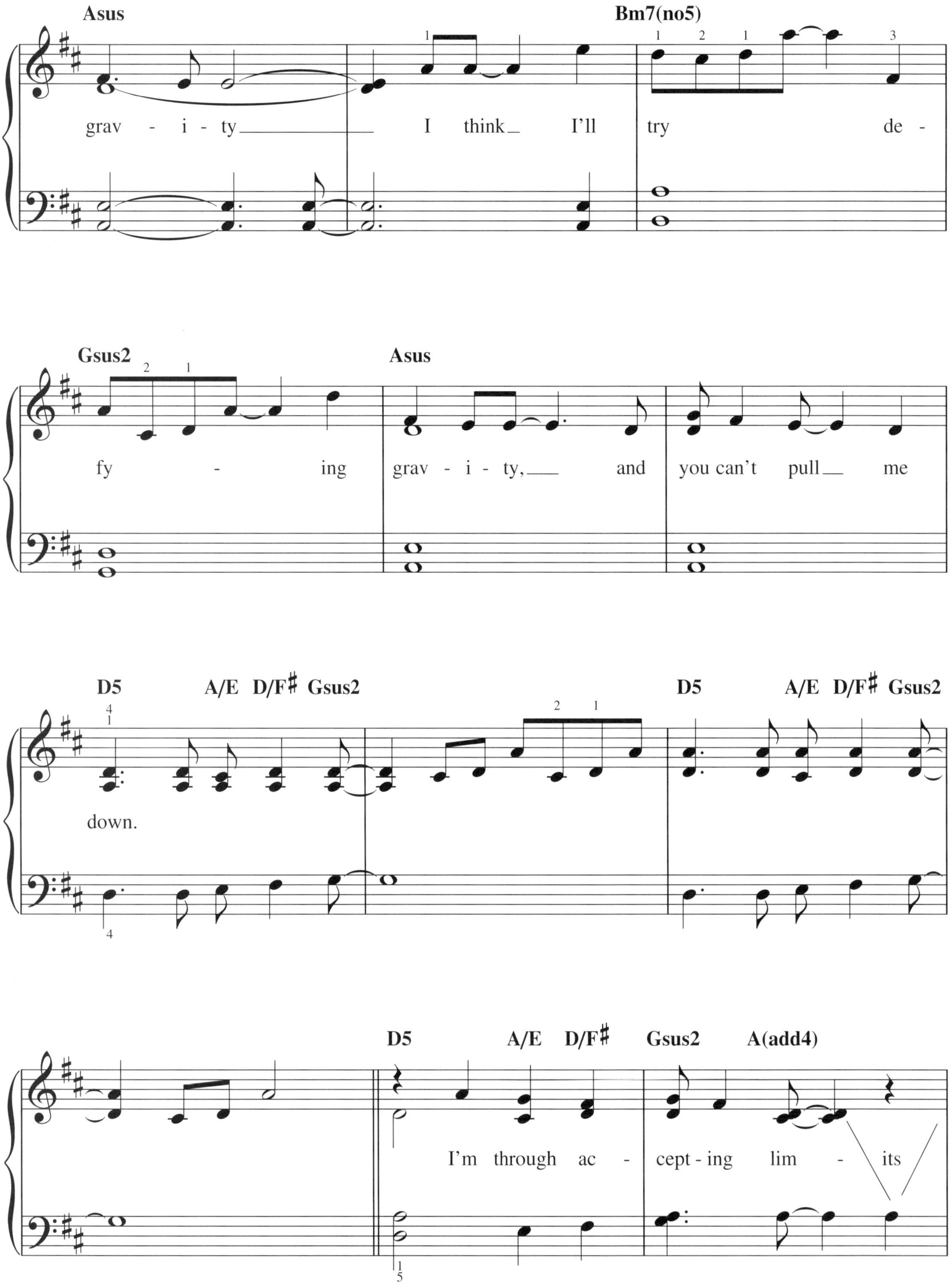
Asus
Bm7(no5)
grav - i - ty I think I'll try de -
Gsus2
Asus
fy - ing grav - i - ty, and you can't pull me
D5 A/E D/F♯ Gsus2
D5 A/E D/F♯ Gsus2
down.
D5 A/E D/F♯ Gsus2 A(add4)
I'm through ac - cept - ing lim - its

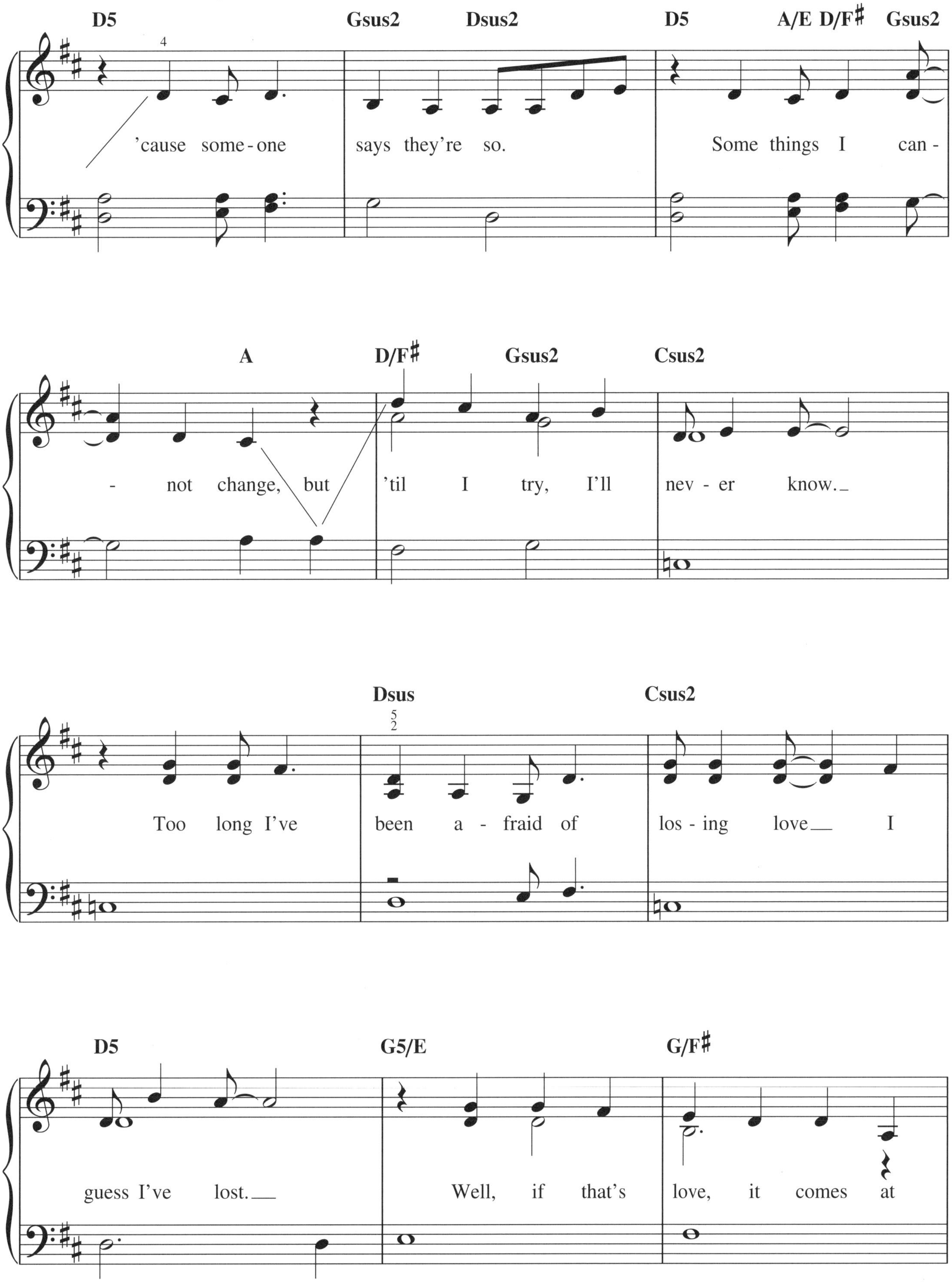
D5 Gsus2 Dsus2 D5 A/E D/F♯ Gsus2
'cause some-one says they're so. Some things I can -
A D/F♯ Gsus2 Csus2
- not change, but 'til I try, I'll nev - er know.
Dsus Csus2
Too long I've been a - fraid of los - ing love I
D5 G5/E G/F♯
guess I've lost. Well, if that's love, it comes at

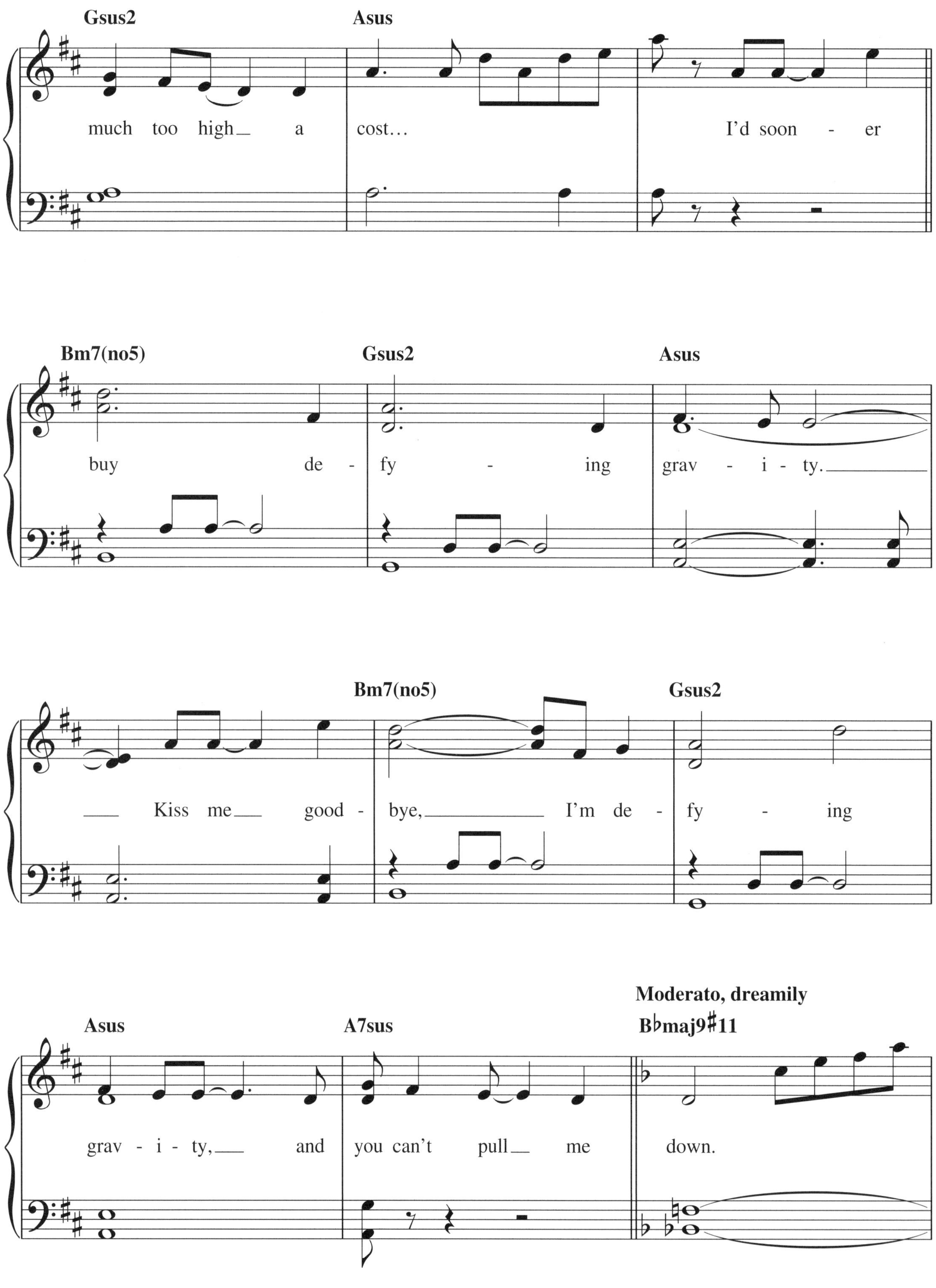
Gsus2
Asus
much too high a
cost…
I'd soon - er
Bm7(no5)
Gsus2
Asus
buy de - fy - ing grav - i - ty.
Kiss me good - bye, I'm de - fy - ing
Bm7(no5)
Gsus2
Moderato, dreamily
Asus
A7sus
B♭maj9♯11
grav - i - ty, and you can't pull me down.

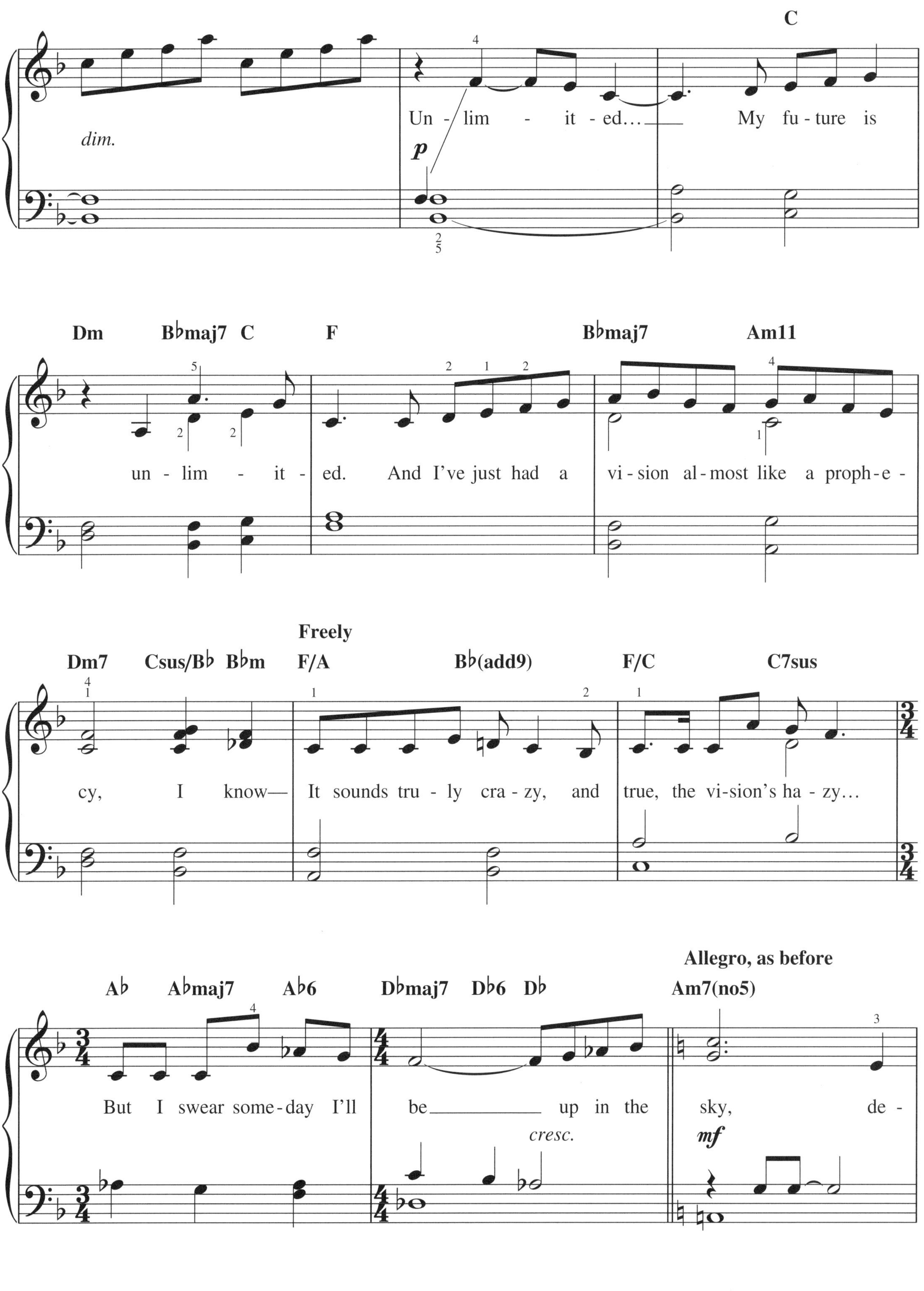
C
dim.
Un - lim - it - ed… My fu - ture is
p
Dm Bbmaj7 C F Bbmaj7 Am11
un - lim - it - ed. And I've just had a vi - sion al - most like a proph - e -
Freely
Dm7 Csus/Bb Bbm F/A Bb(add9) F/C C7sus
cy, I know— It sounds tru - ly cra - zy, and true, the vi - sion's ha - zy…
Allegro, as before
Ab Abmaj7 Ab6 Dbmaj7 Db6 Db Am7(no5)
But I swear some - day I'll be up in the sky, de -
cresc.
mf

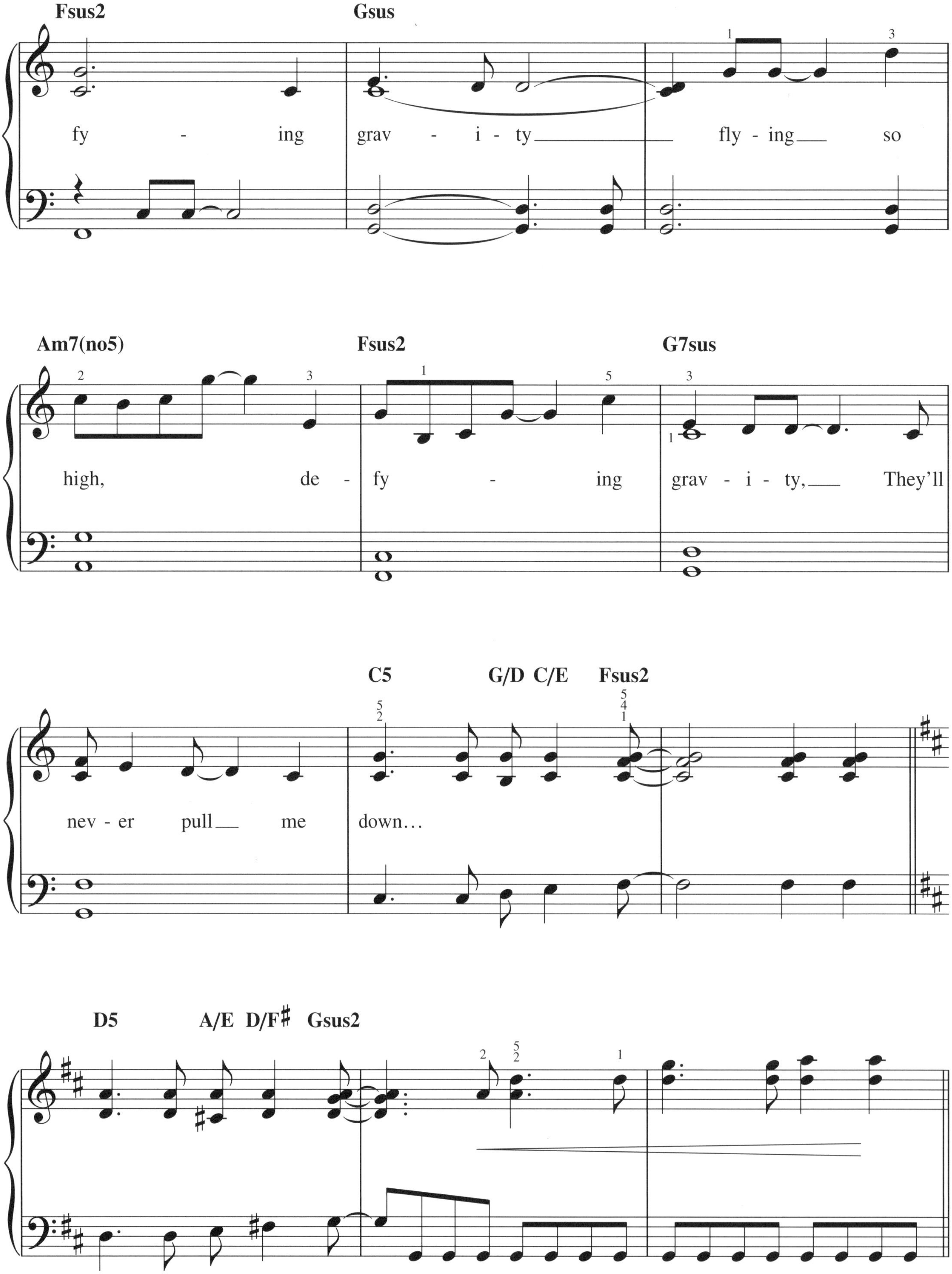
Fsus2
Gsus
fy - ing grav - i - ty fly - ing so
Am7(no5)
Fsus2
G7sus
high, de - fy - ing grav - i - ty, They'll
C5
G/D C/E
Fsus2
nev - er pull me down…
D5
A/E D/F♯ Gsus2

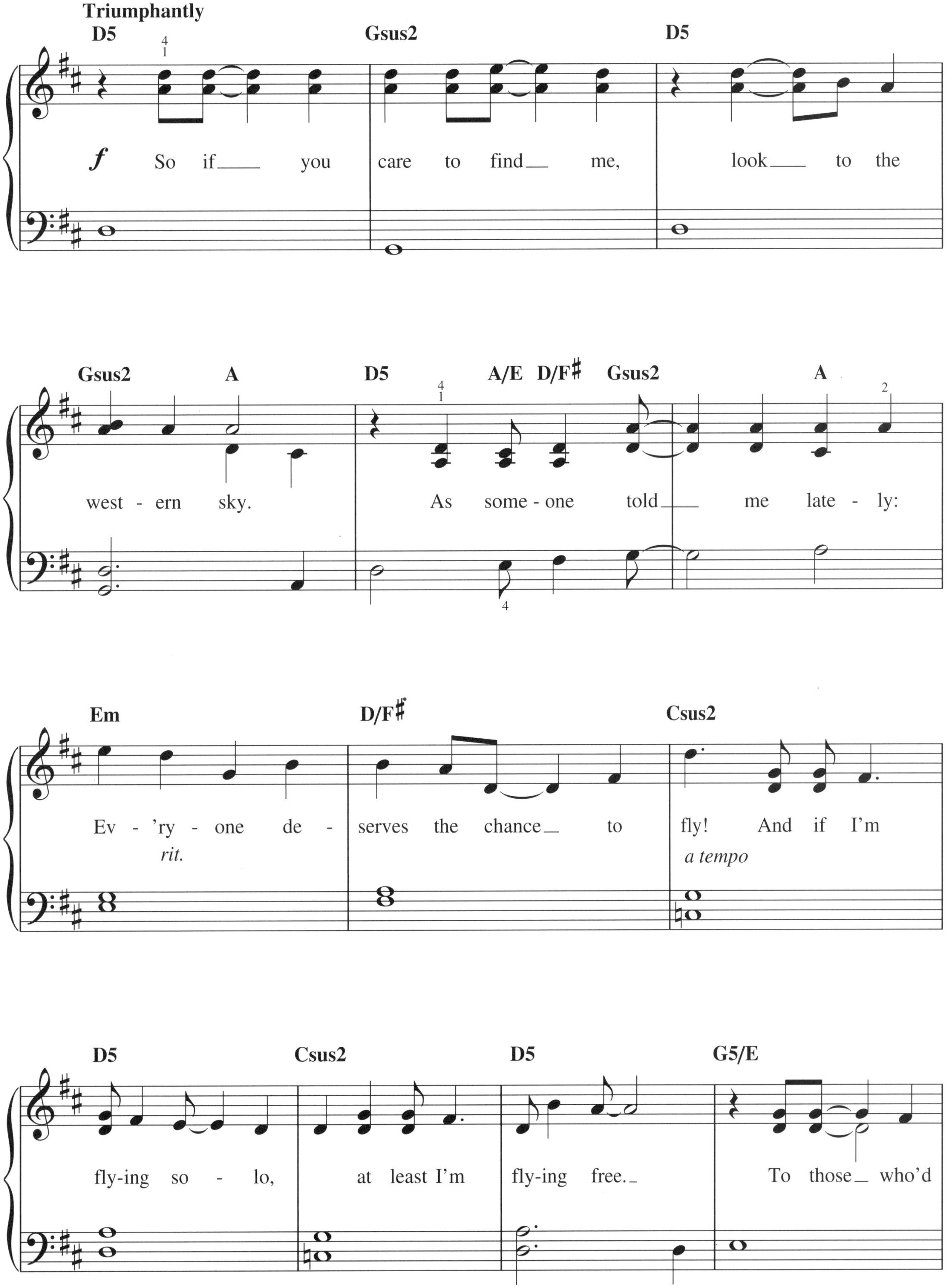
Triumphantly
D5 Gsus2 D5
So if you care to find me, look to the
Gsus2 A D5 A/E D/F♯ Gsus2 A
west - ern sky. As some - one told me late - ly:
Em D/F♯ Csus2
Ev - 'ry - one de - serves the chance to fly! And if I'm
rit.
a tempo
D5 Csus2 D5 G5/E
fly-ing so - lo, at least I'm fly-ing free. To those who'd

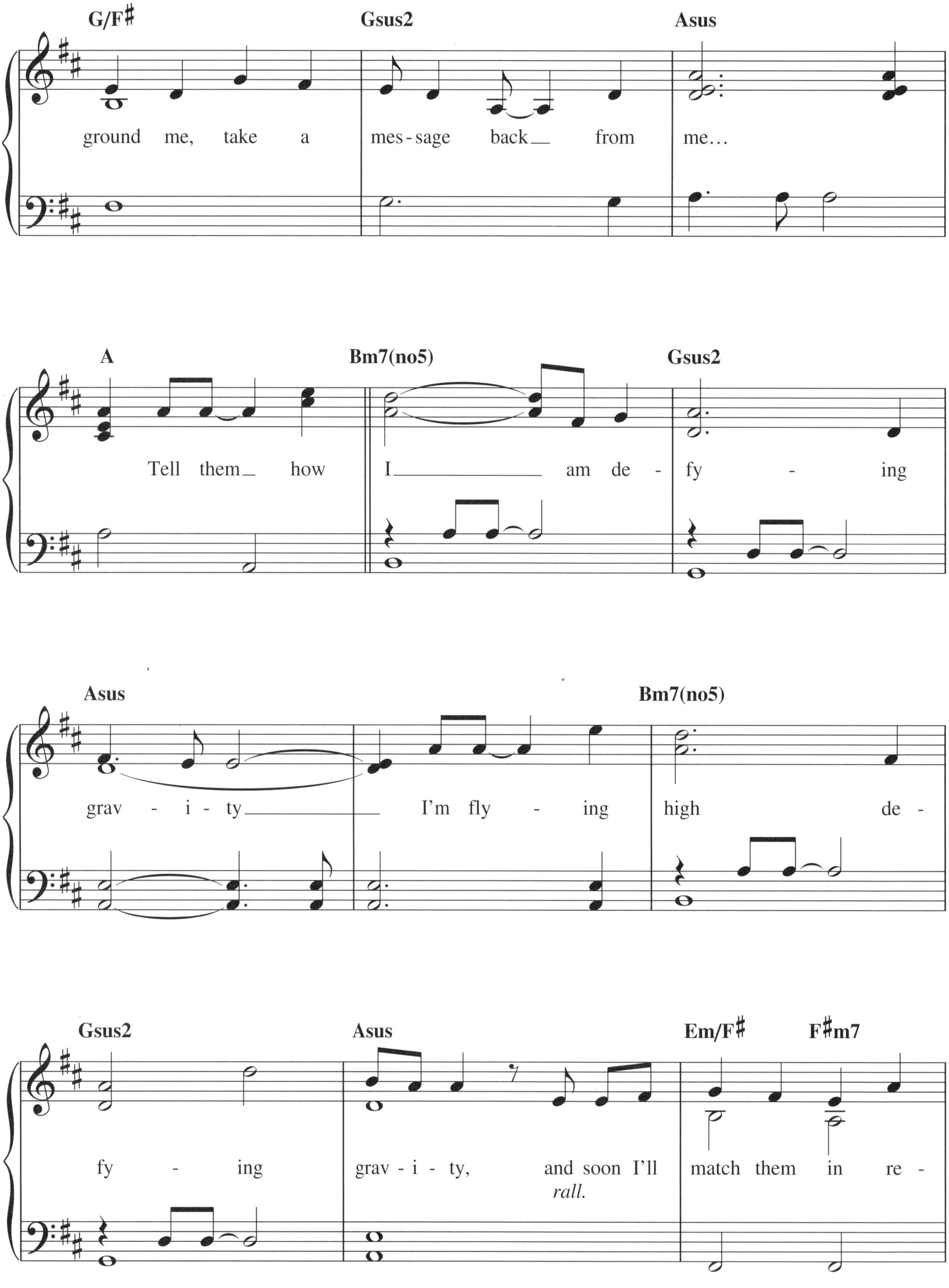
G/F♯
Gsus2
Asus
ground me, take a mes-sage back from me…
A
Bm7(no5)
Gsus2
Tell them how I am de - fy - ing
Asus
Bm7(no5)
grav - i - ty I'm fly - ing high de -
Gsus2
Asus
Em/F♯
F♯m7
fy - ing grav - i - ty, and soon I'll match them in re -
rall.

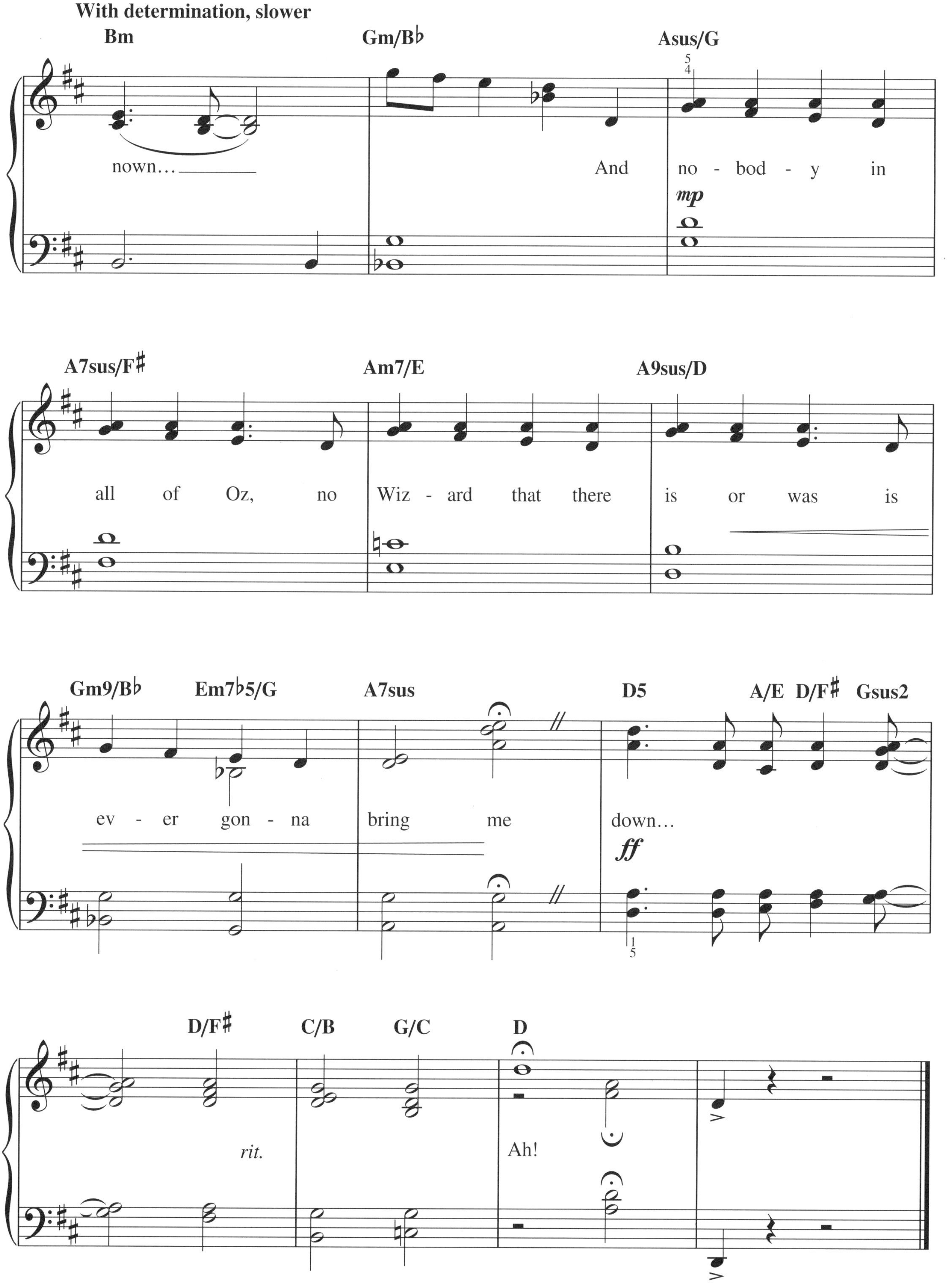
With determination, slower
Bm
Gm/B♭
Asus/G
now…
And
no - bod - y in
mp
A7sus/F♯
Am7/E
A9sus/D
all of Oz, no
Wiz - ard that there
is or was is
Gm9/B♭
Em7♭5/G
A7sus
D5
A/E
D/F♯
Gsus2
ev - er gon - na
bring me
down…
ff
D/F♯
C/B
G/C
D
rit.
Ah!

Fever

Words and Music by JOHN DAVENPORT
and EDDIE COOLEY

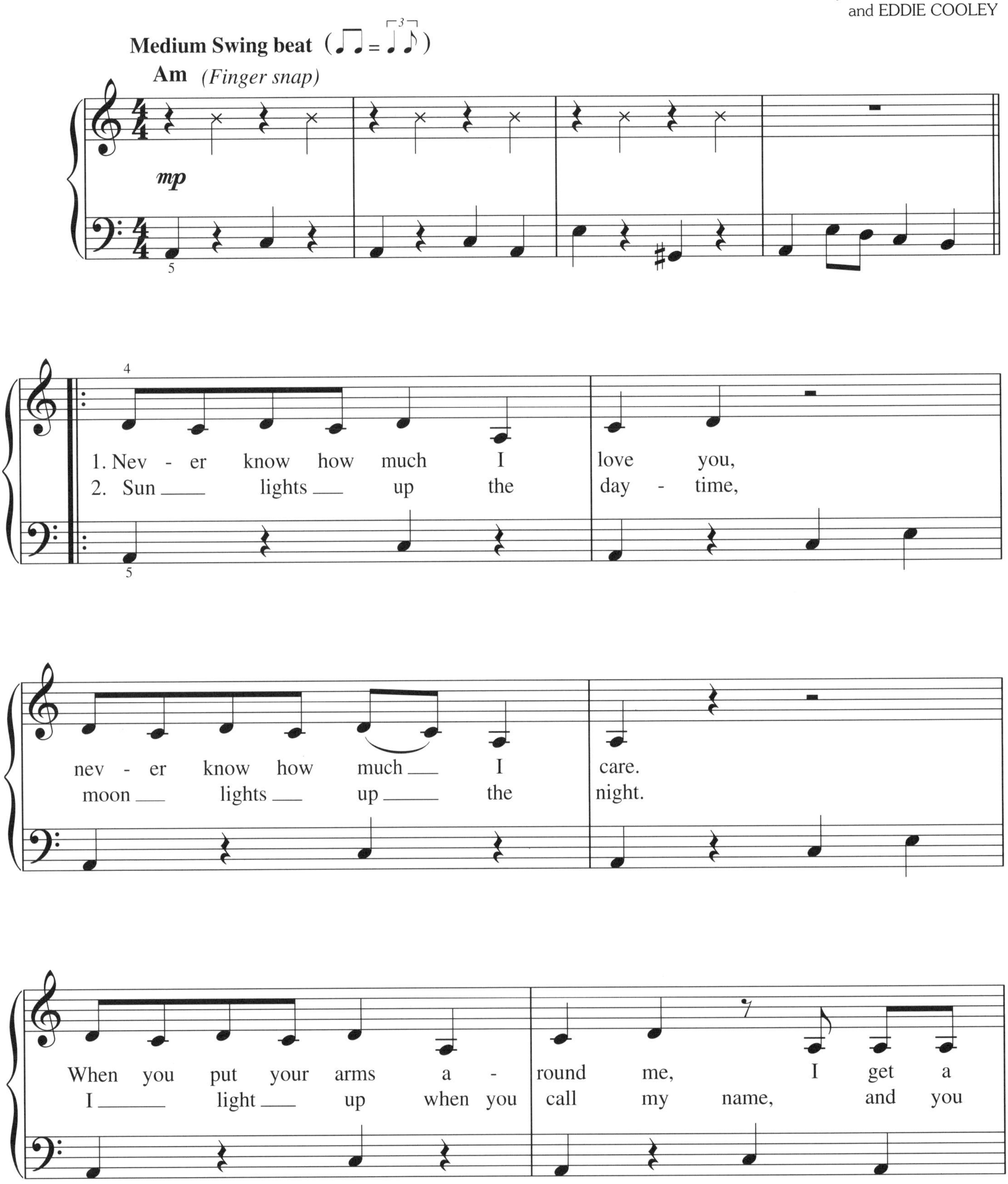

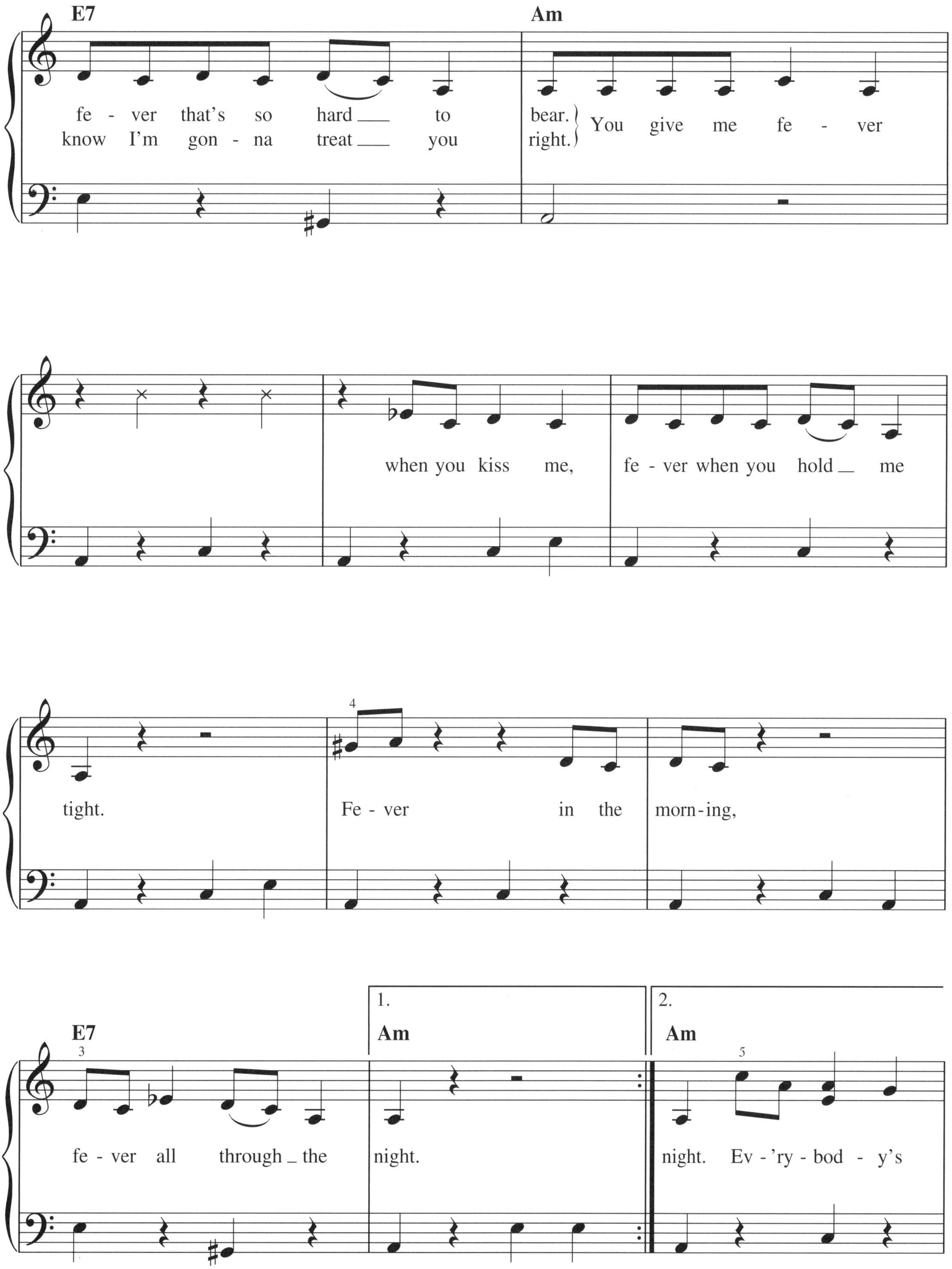
E7
Am
fe - ver that's so hard to
know I'm gon - na treat you
bear.
right.
You give me fe - ver
when you kiss me,
fe - ver when you hold me
tight.
Fe - ver in the
morn - ing,
E7
fe - ver all through the
1.
Am
night.
2.
Am
night. Ev - 'ry - bod - y's

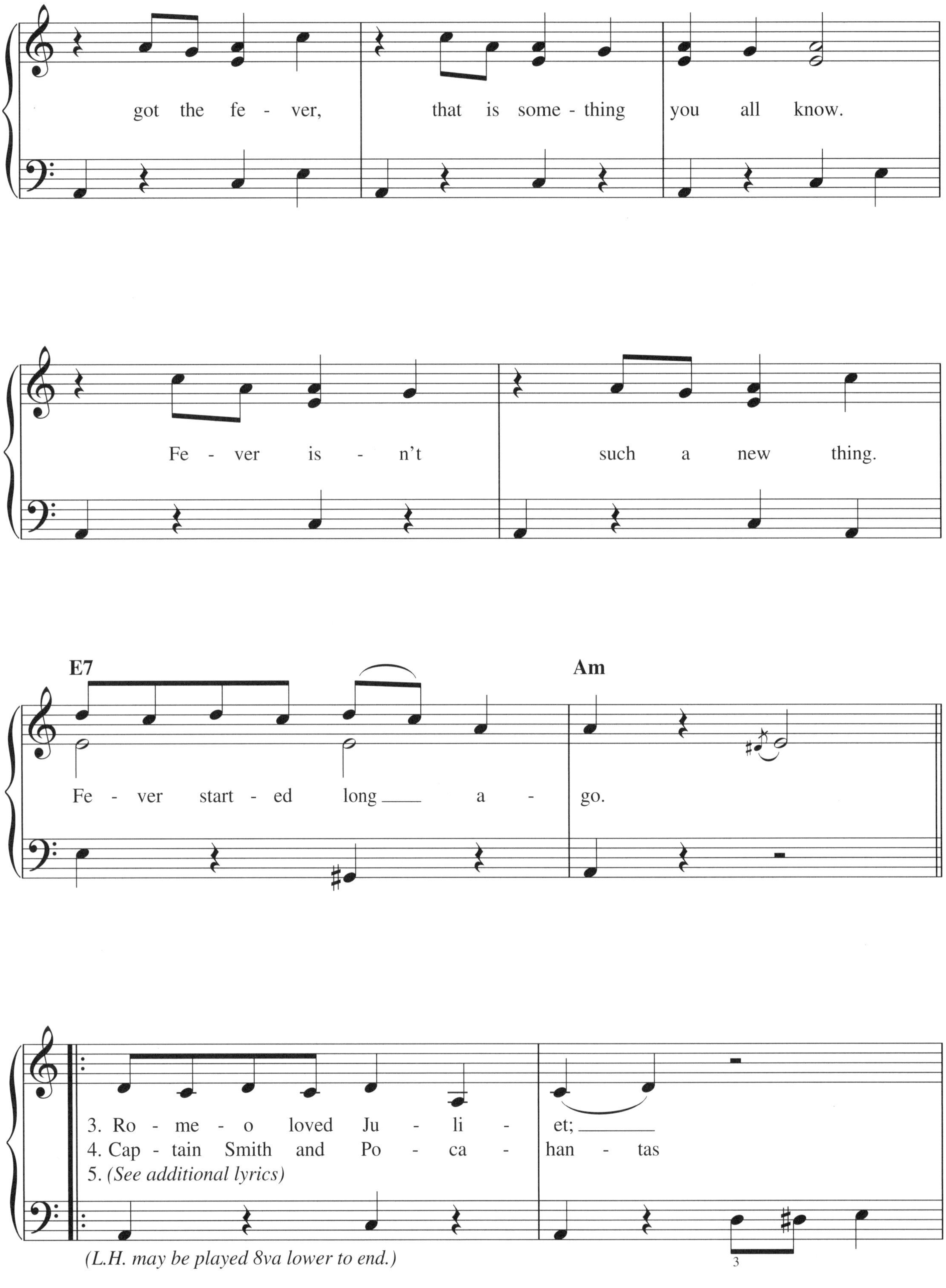
got the fe - ver, that is some - thing you all know.
Fe - ver is - n't such a new thing.
E7
Am
Fe - ver start - ed long a - go.
3. Ro - me - o loved Ju - li - et;
4. Cap - tain Smith and Po - ca - han - tas
5. (See additional lyrics)
(L.H. may be played 8va lower to end.)
3

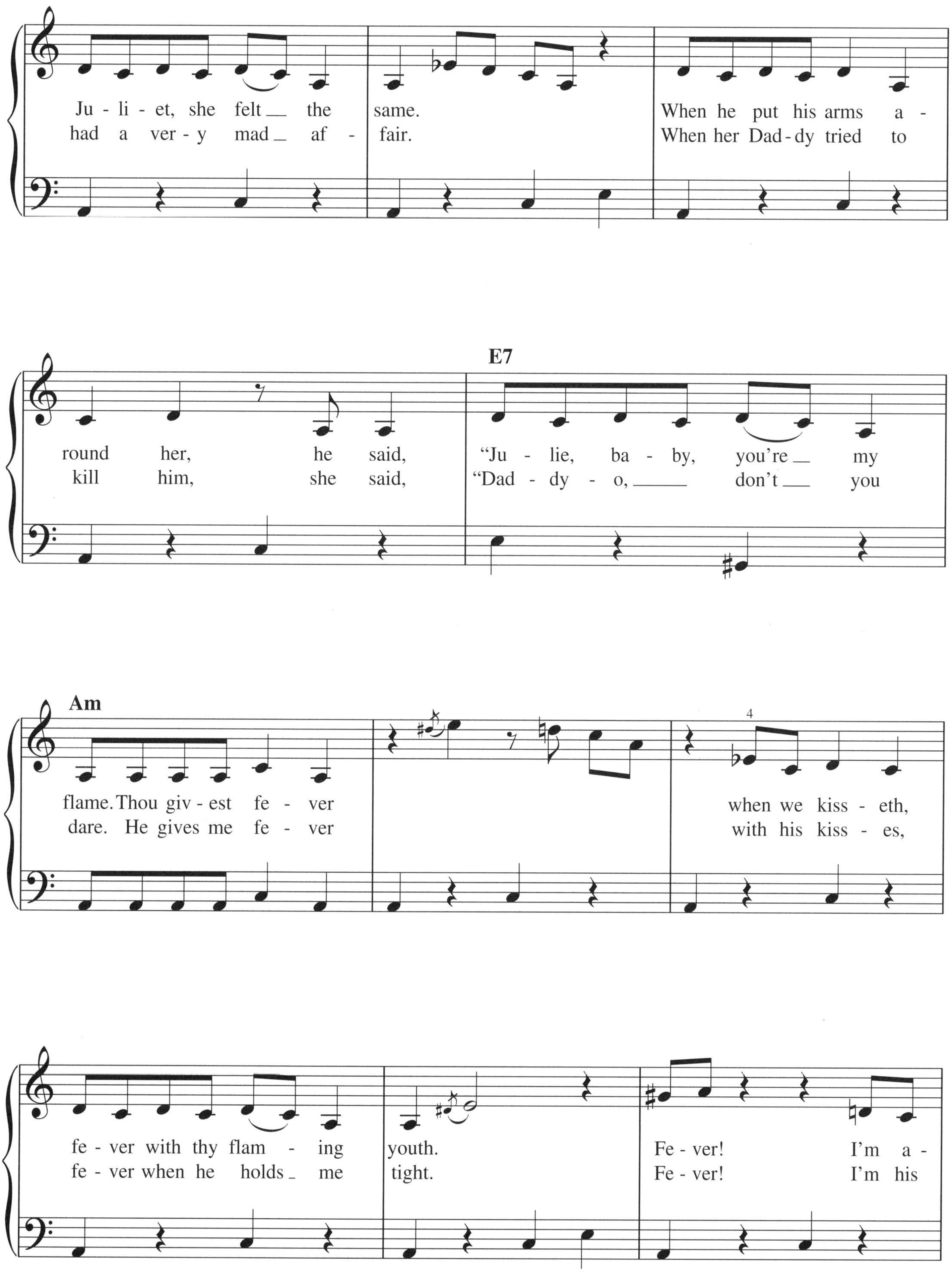
Ju - li - et, she felt the same.
had a ver - y mad af - fair.
When he put his arms a -
When her Dad - dy tried to
round her, he said,
kill him, she said,
E7
"Ju - lie, ba - by, you're my
"Dad - dy - o, don't you
Am
flame. Thou giv - est fe - ver
dare. He gives me fe - ver
4
when we kiss - eth,
with his kiss - es,
fe - ver with thy flam - ing youth.
fe - ver when he holds me tight.
Fe - ver! I'm a -
Fe - ver! I'm his

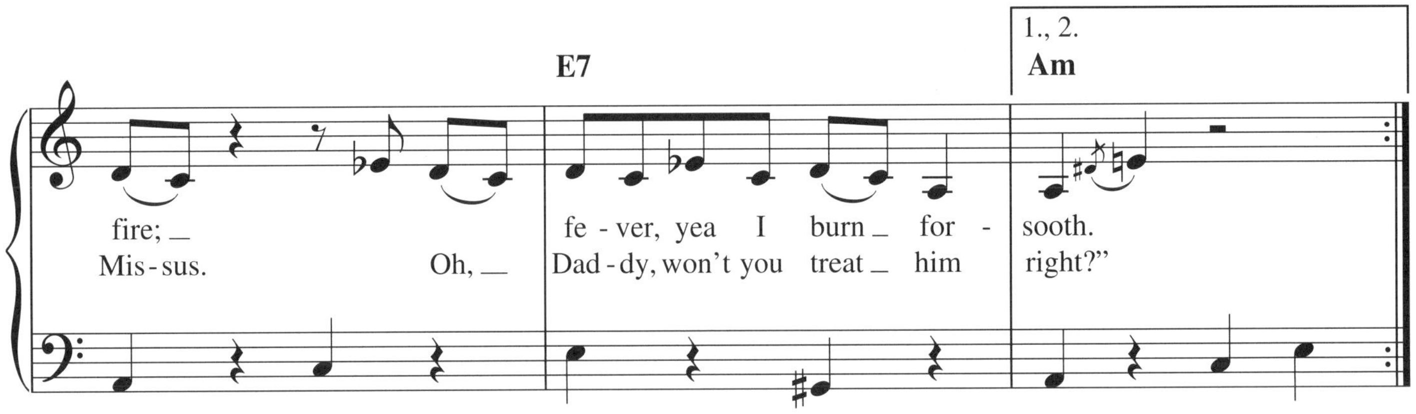

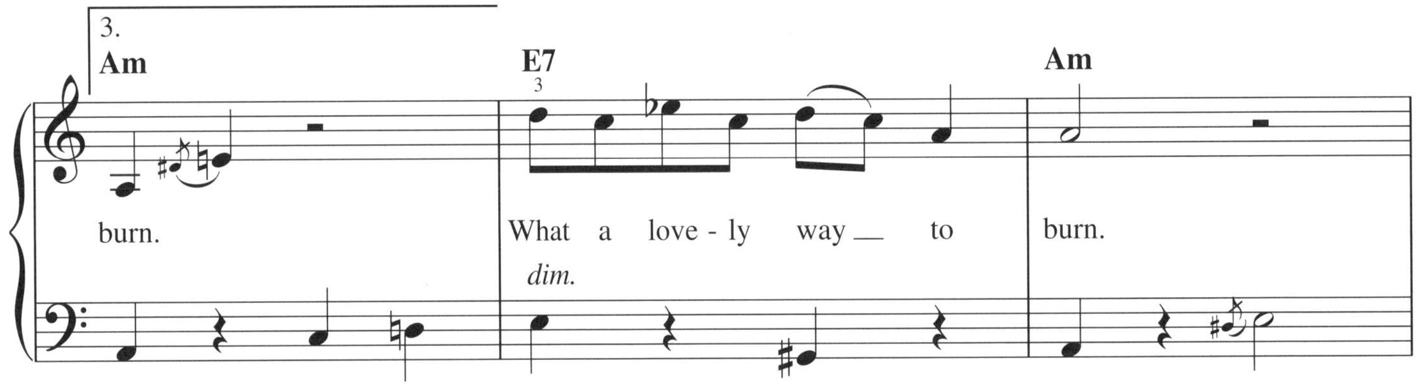

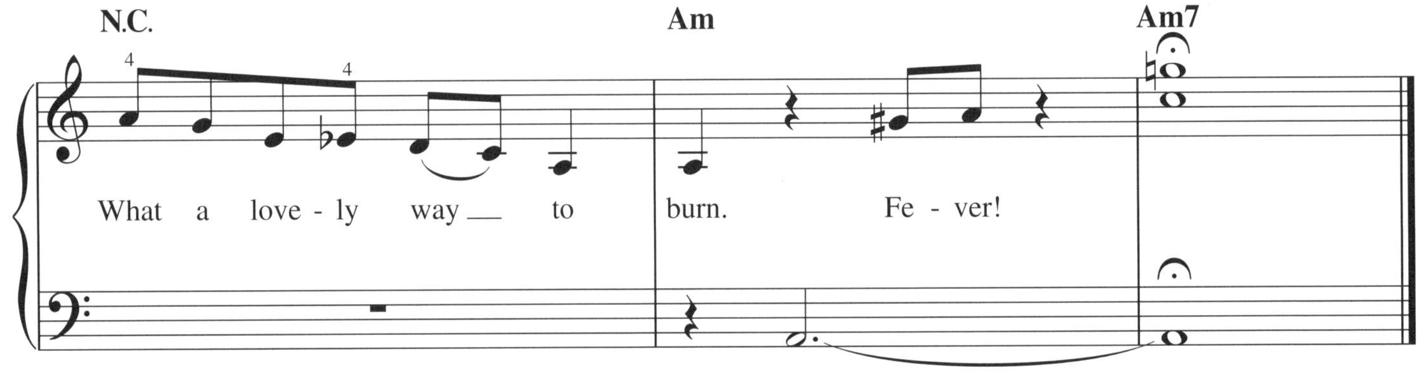

Additional Lyrics

5. Now you've listened to my story.
Here's the point that I have made:
Chicks were born to give you fever,
Be it fahrenheit or centigrade.

They give you fever when you kiss them,
Fever if you live and learn,
Fever till you sizzle:
What a lovely way to burn.

Georgia on My Mind

Words by STUART GORRELL
Music by HOAGY CARMICHAEL

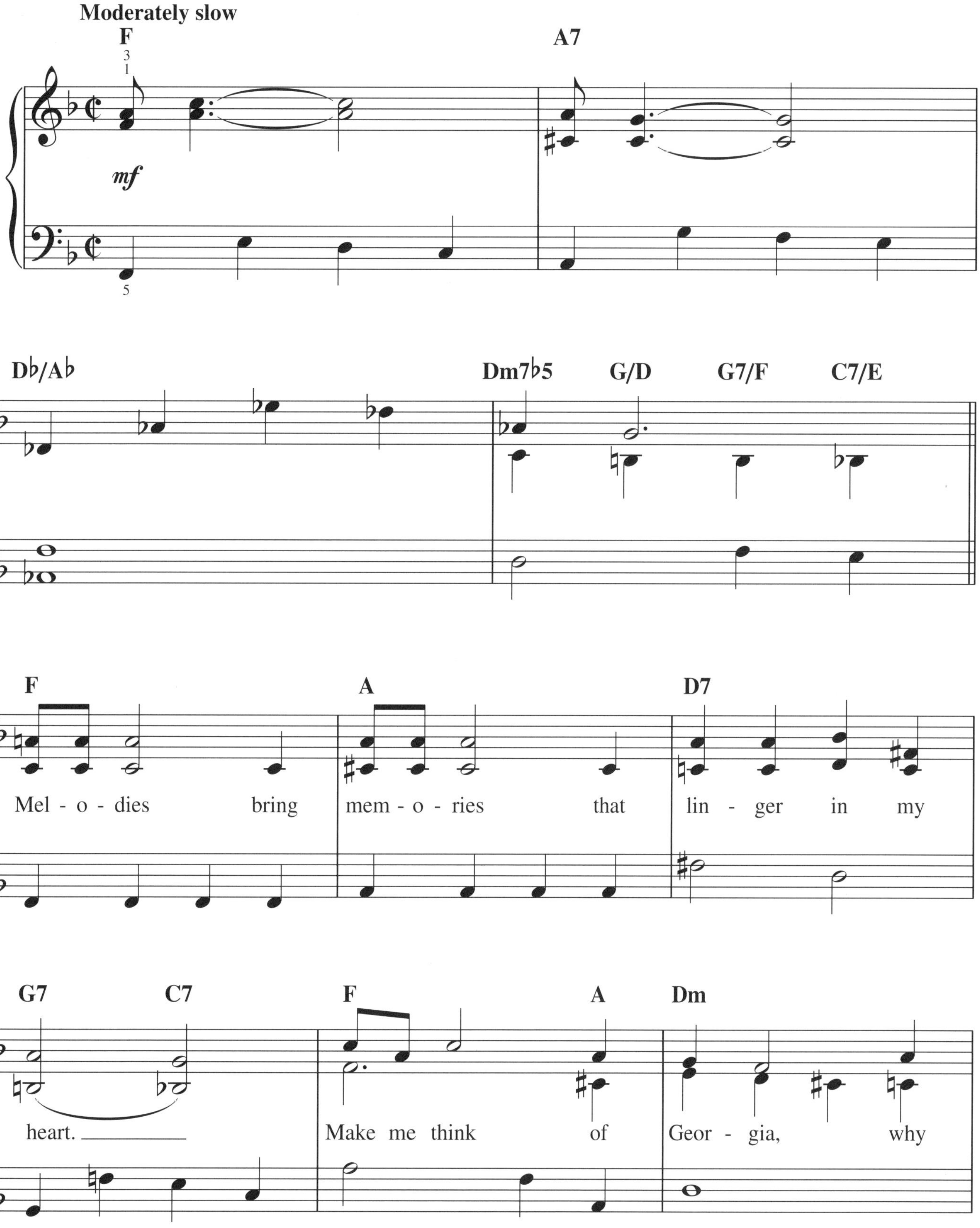

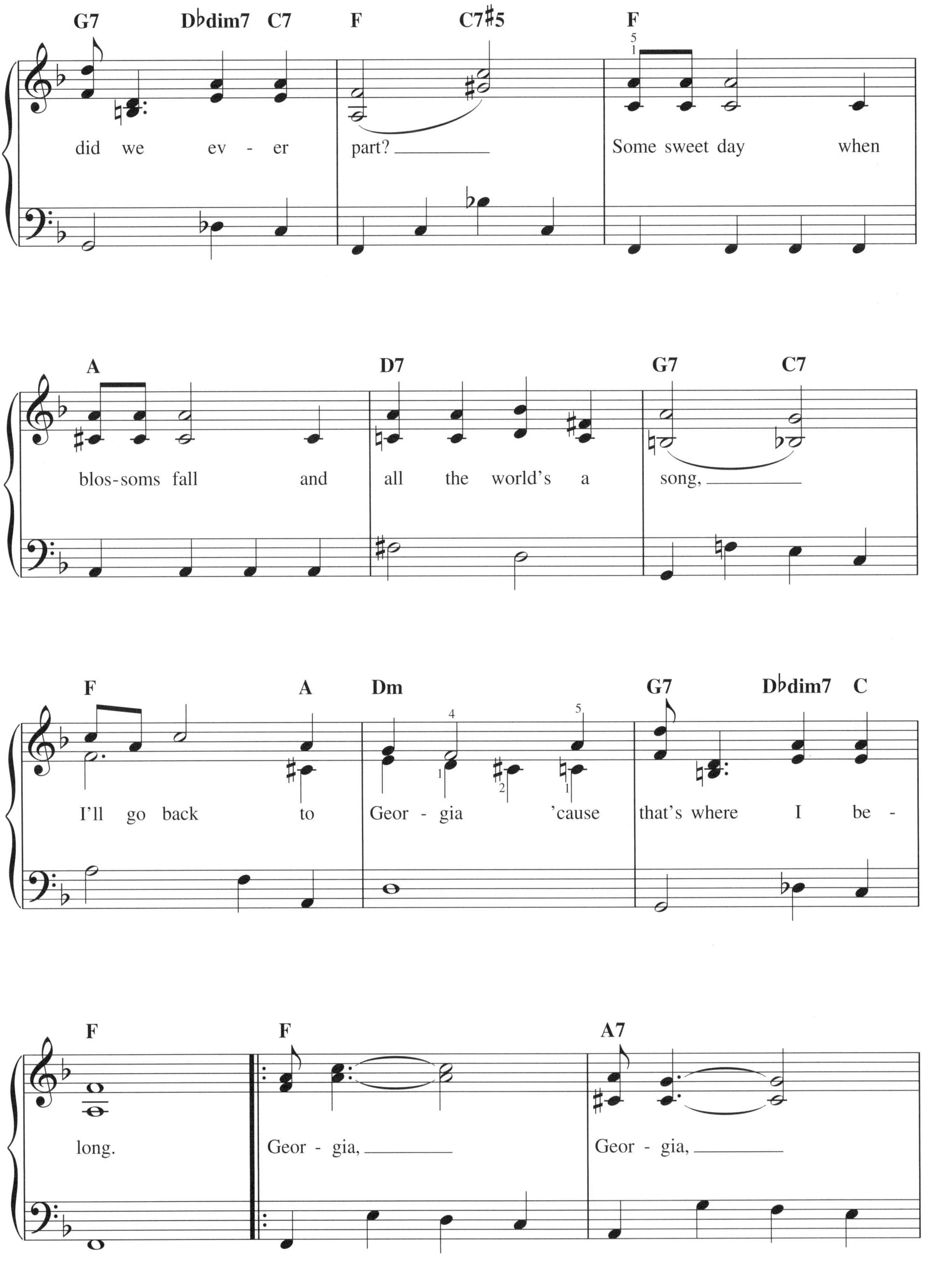
G7 D♭dim7 C7 F C7♯5 F
did we ev - er part? Some sweet day when
A D7 G7 C7
blos-soms fall and all the world's a song,
F A Dm G7 D♭dim7 C
I'll go back to Geor - gia 'cause that's where I be -
F F A7
long. Geor - gia, Geor - gia,

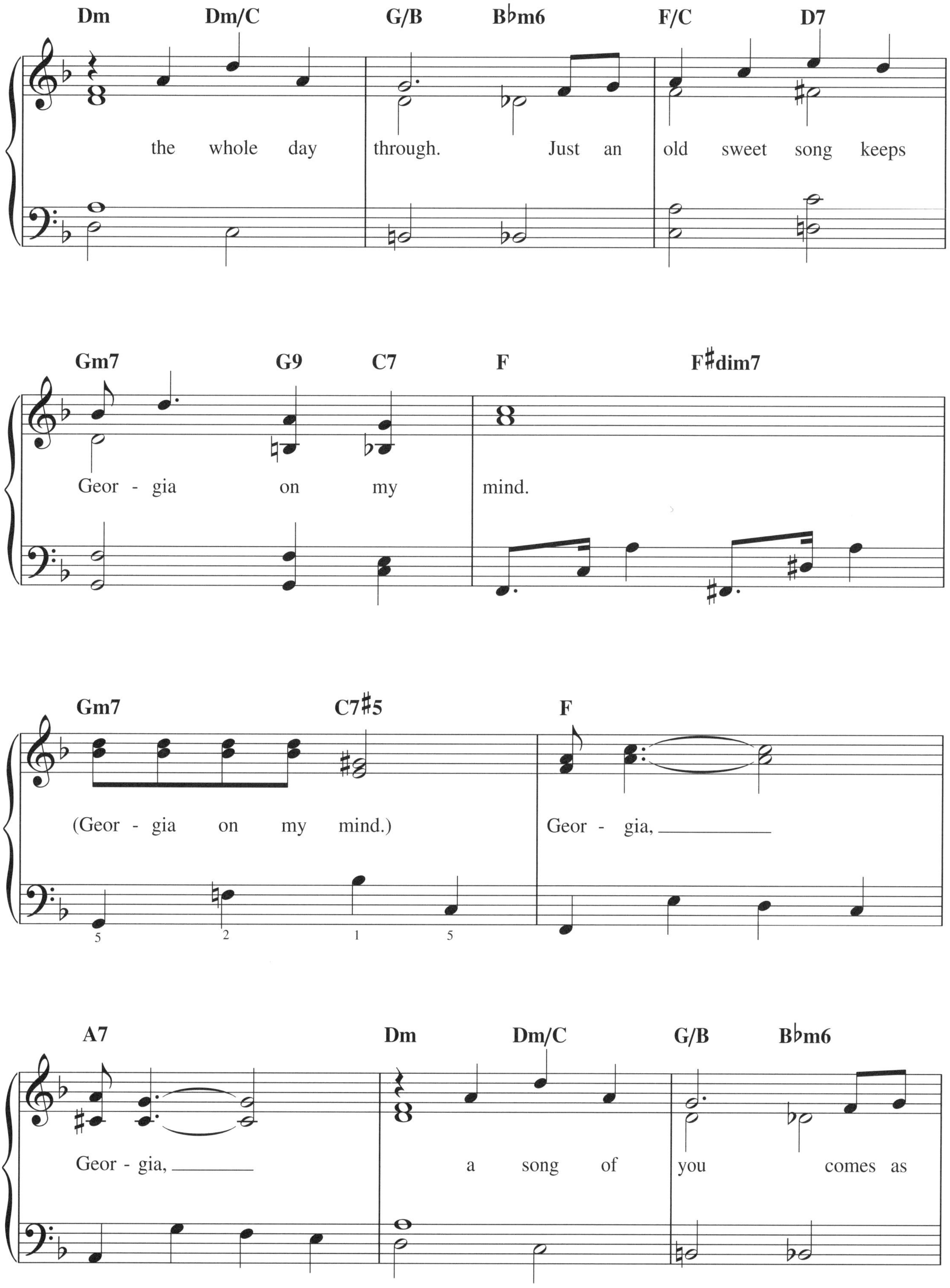
Dm Dm/C G/B B♭m6 F/C D7
the whole day through. Just an old sweet song keeps
Gm7 G9 C7 F F♯dim7
Geor - gia on my mind.
Gm7 C7♯5 F
(Geor - gia on my mind.) Geor - gia,
5 2 1 5
A7 Dm Dm/C G/B B♭m6
Geor - gia, a song of you comes as

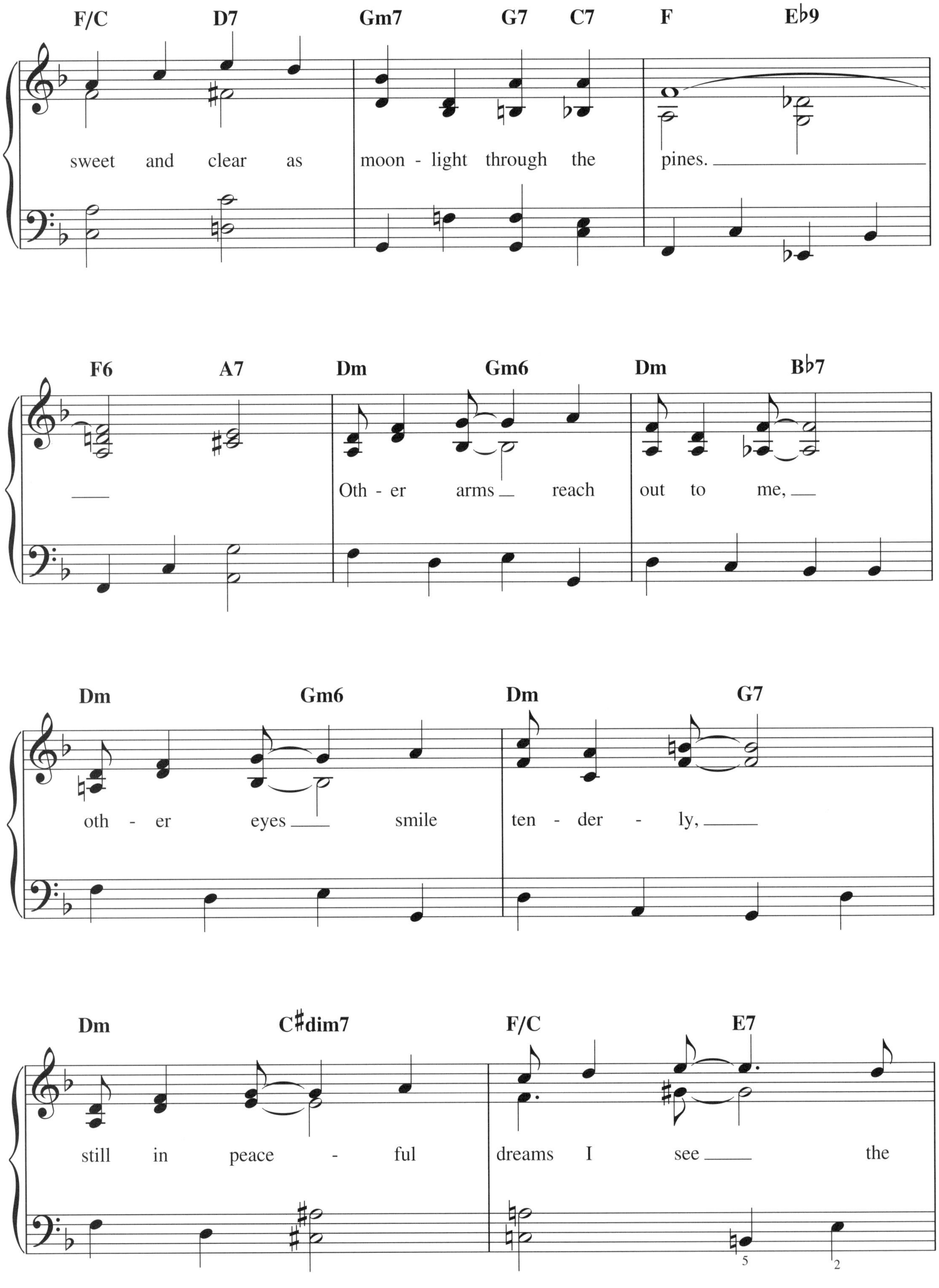
F/C D7 Gm7 G7 C7 F E♭9
sweet and clear as moon - light through the pines.
F6 A7 Dm Gm6 Dm B♭7
Oth - er arms reach out to me,
Dm Gm6 Dm G7
oth - er eyes smile ten - der - ly,
Dm C♯dim7 F/C E7
still in peace - ful dreams I see the

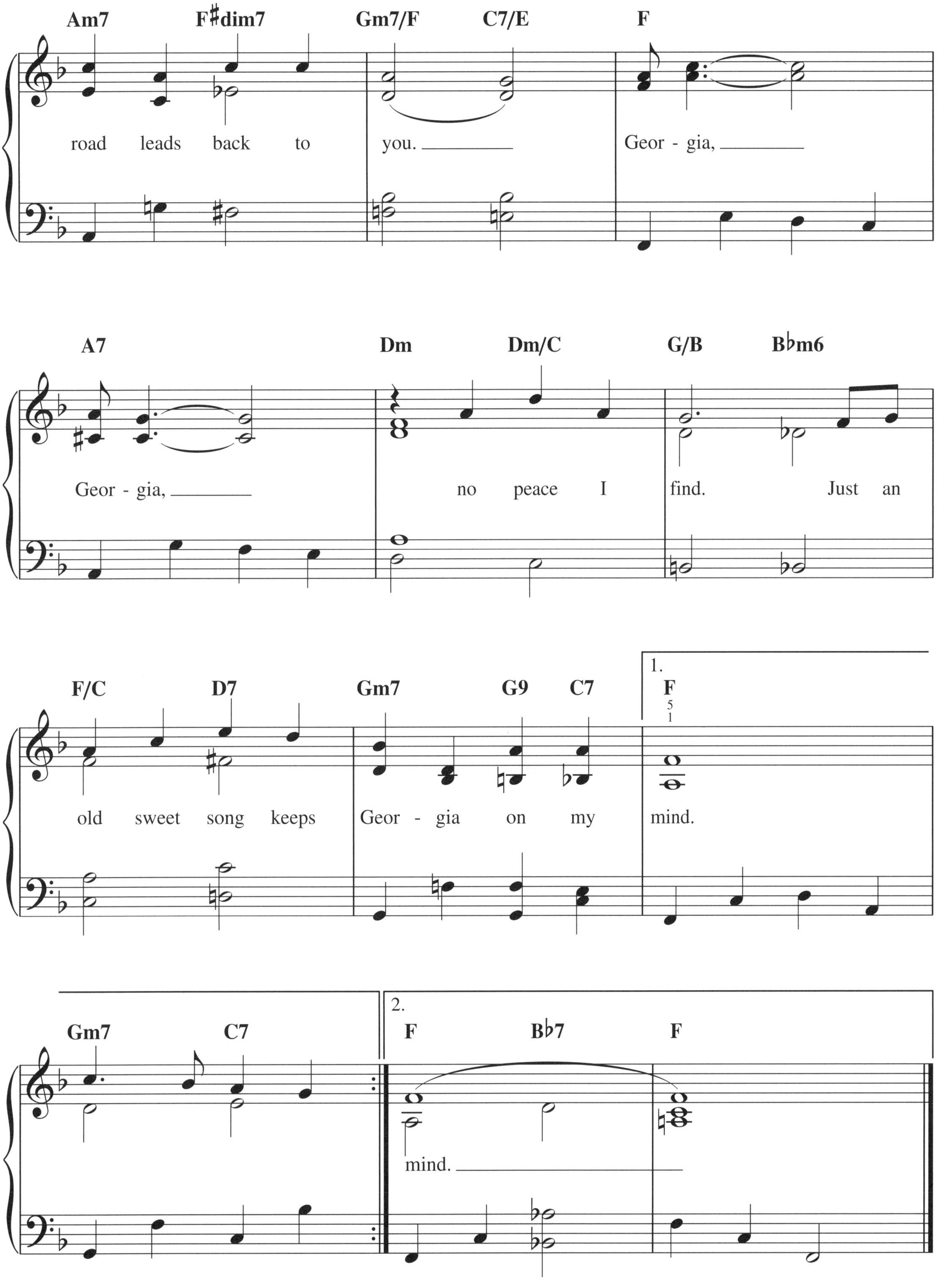
Am7 F♯dim7 Gm7/F C7/E F
road leads back to you. Geor - gia,
A7 Dm Dm/C G/B B♭m6
Geor - gia, no peace I find. Just an
F/C D7 Gm7 G9 C7
1. F
old sweet song keeps Geor - gia on my mind.
Gm7 C7
2. F B♭7 F
mind.

God Only Knows

Words and Music by BRIAN WILSON
and TONY ASHER

Moderately

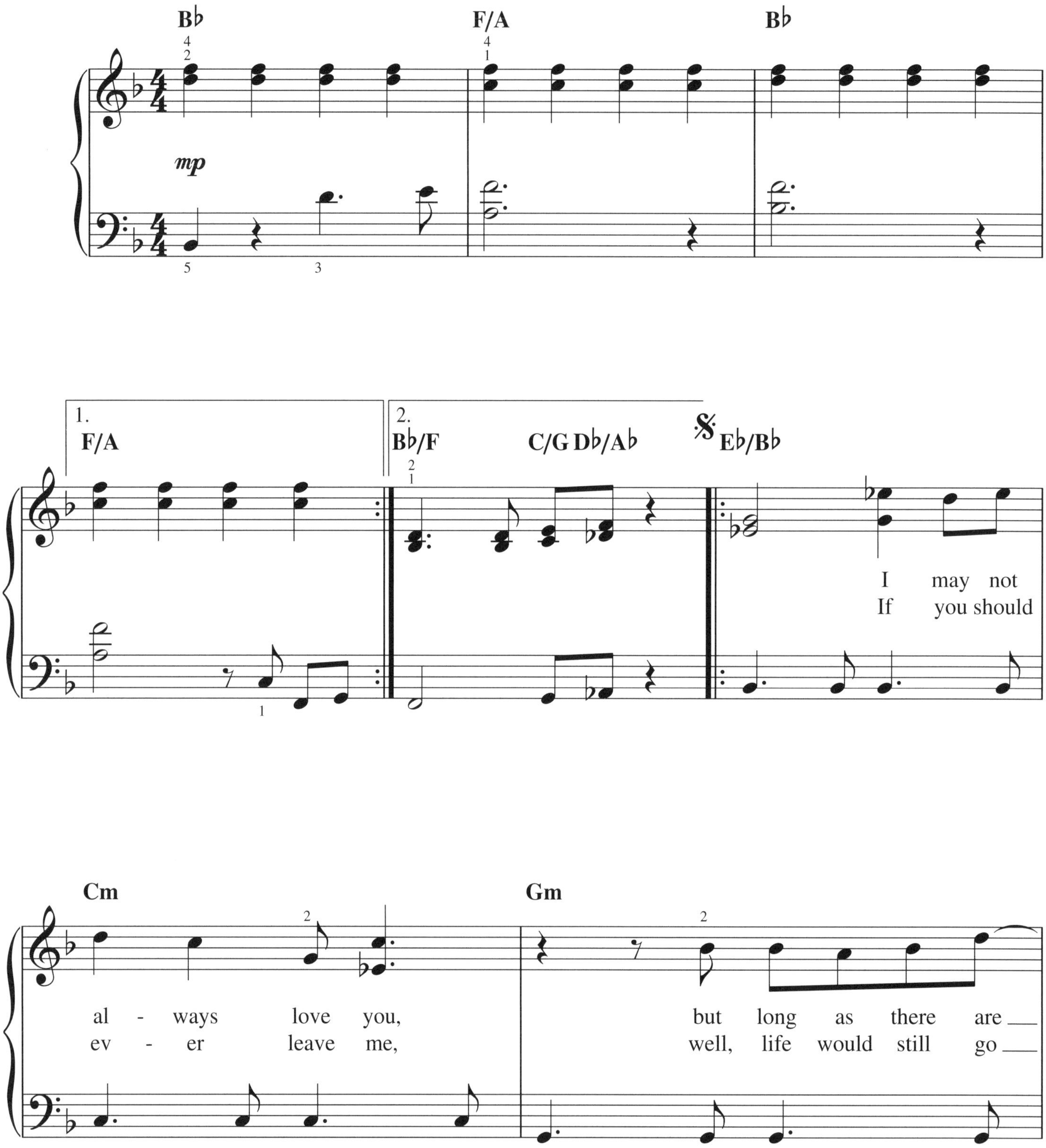

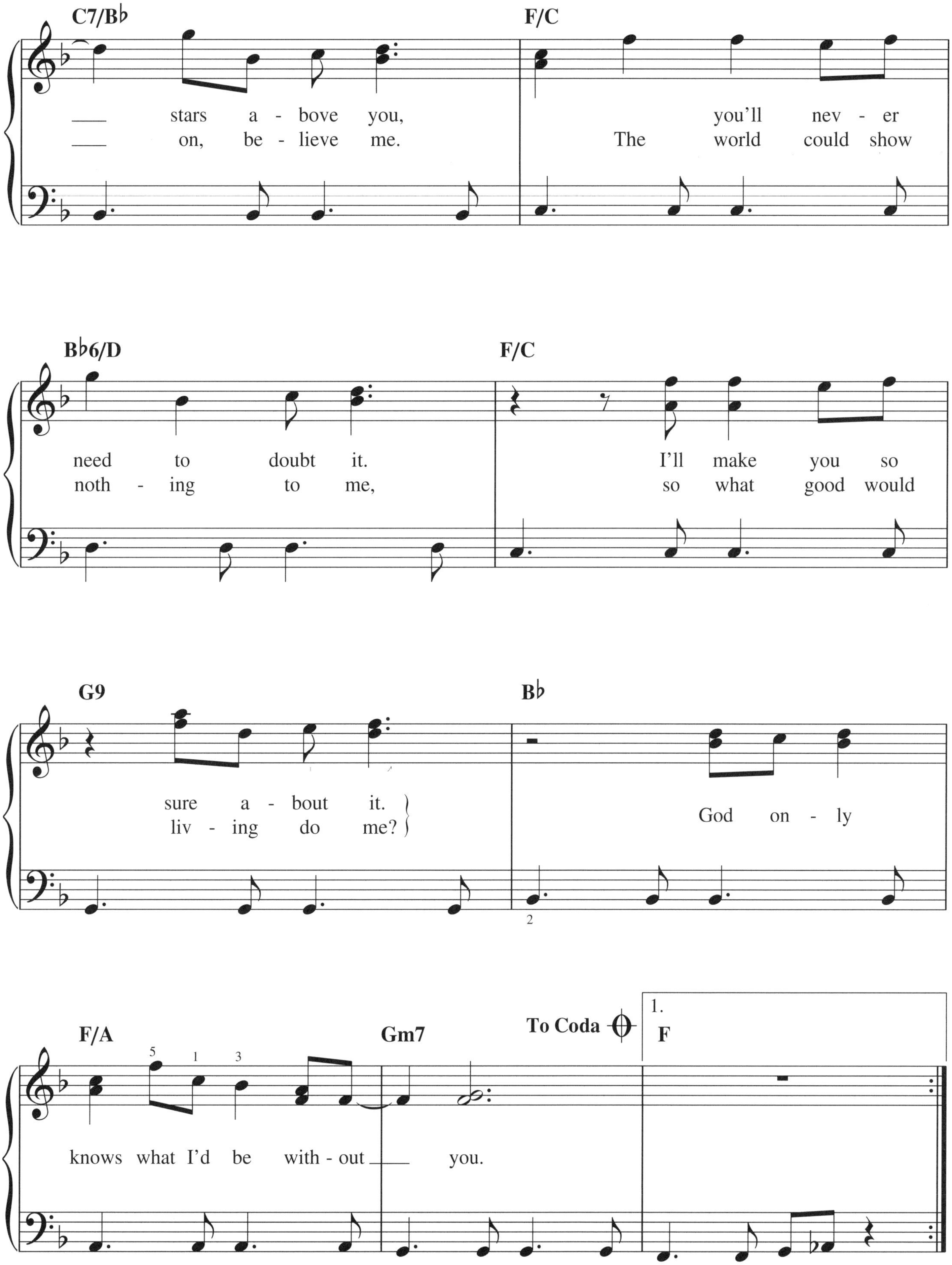
C7/B♭
F/C
___ stars a - bove you, you'll nev - er
___ on, be - lieve me. The world could show
B♭6/D
F/C
need to doubt it. I'll make you so
noth - ing to me, so what good would
G9
B♭
sure a - bout it.
liv - ing do me?
God on - ly
2
F/A
Gm7
To Coda
1.
F
5 1 3
knows what I'd be with - out ___ you.

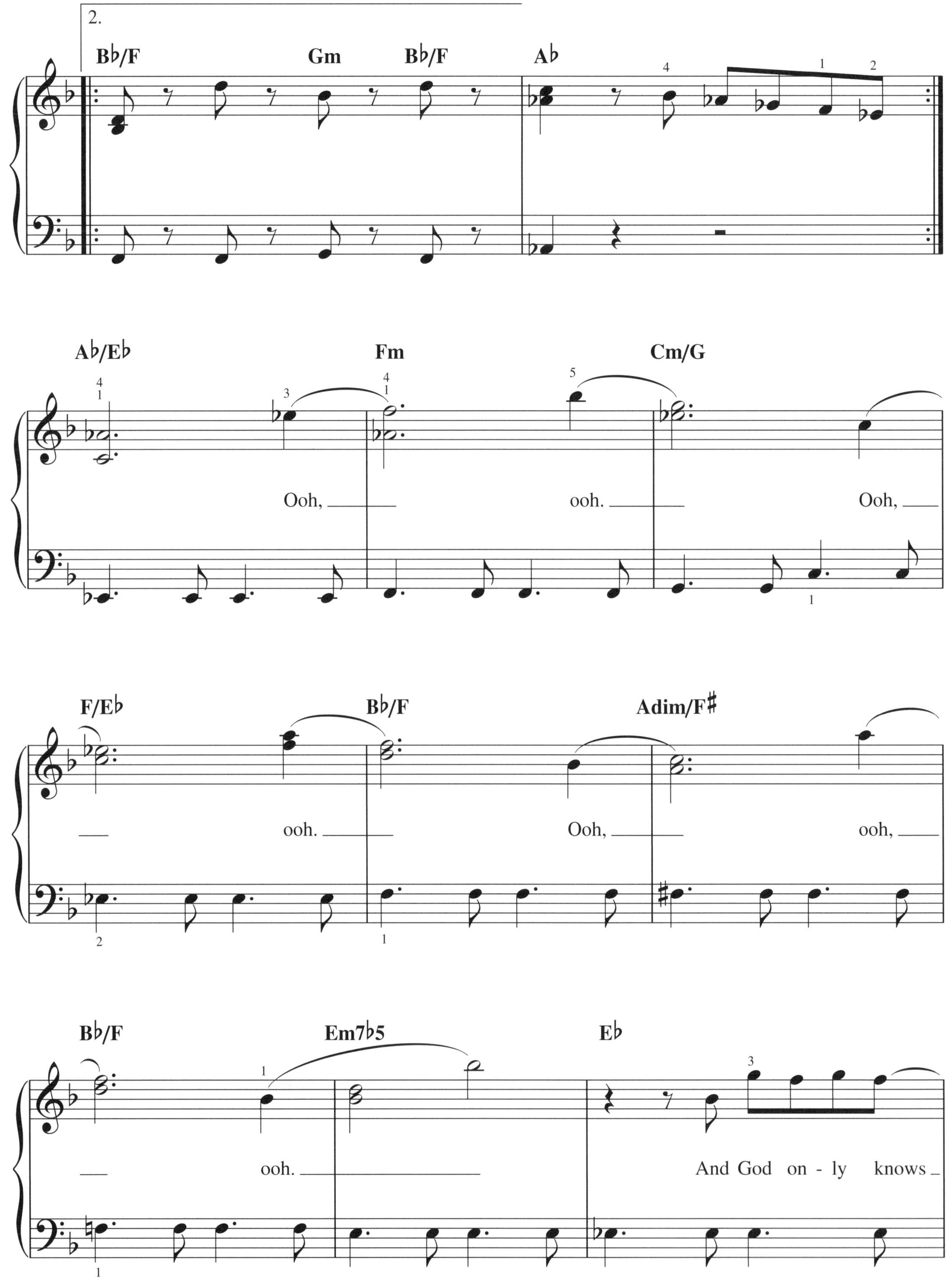
2.
Bb/F Gm Bb/F Ab
Ab/Eb Fm Cm/G
Ooh, ooh. Ooh,
F/Eb Bb/F Adim/F#
ooh. Ooh, ooh,
Bb/F Em7b5 Eb
ooh.
And God on - ly knows

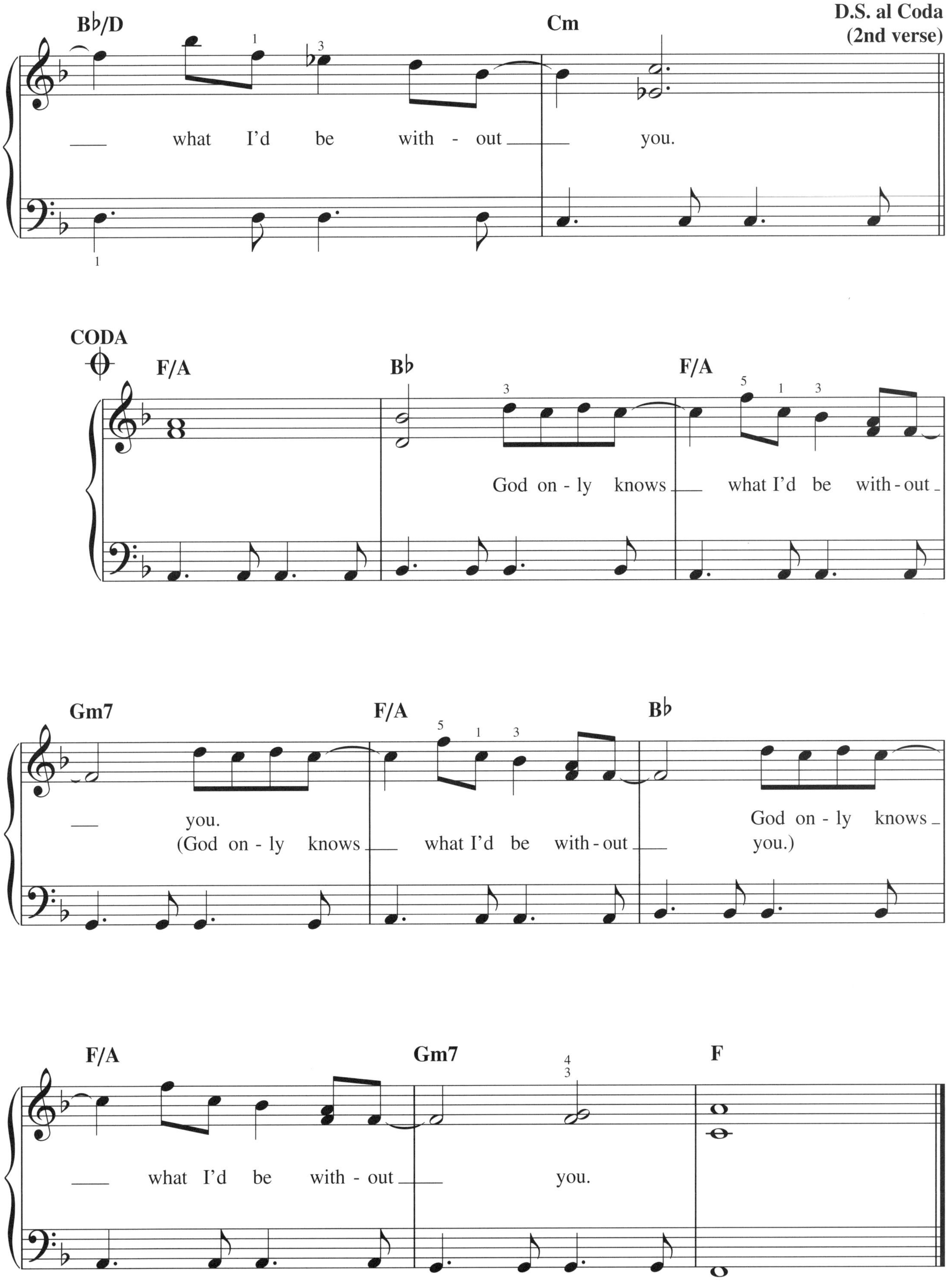
B♭/D
Cm
D.S. al Coda
(2nd verse)
what I'd be with - out
you.
CODA
F/A
B♭
F/A
God on - ly knows
what I'd be with - out
Gm7
F/A
B♭
you.
(God on - ly knows
what I'd be with - out
God on - ly knows
you.)
F/A
Gm7
F
what I'd be with - out
you.

Heart and Soul

Words by FRANK LOESSER
Music by HOAGY CARMICHAEL

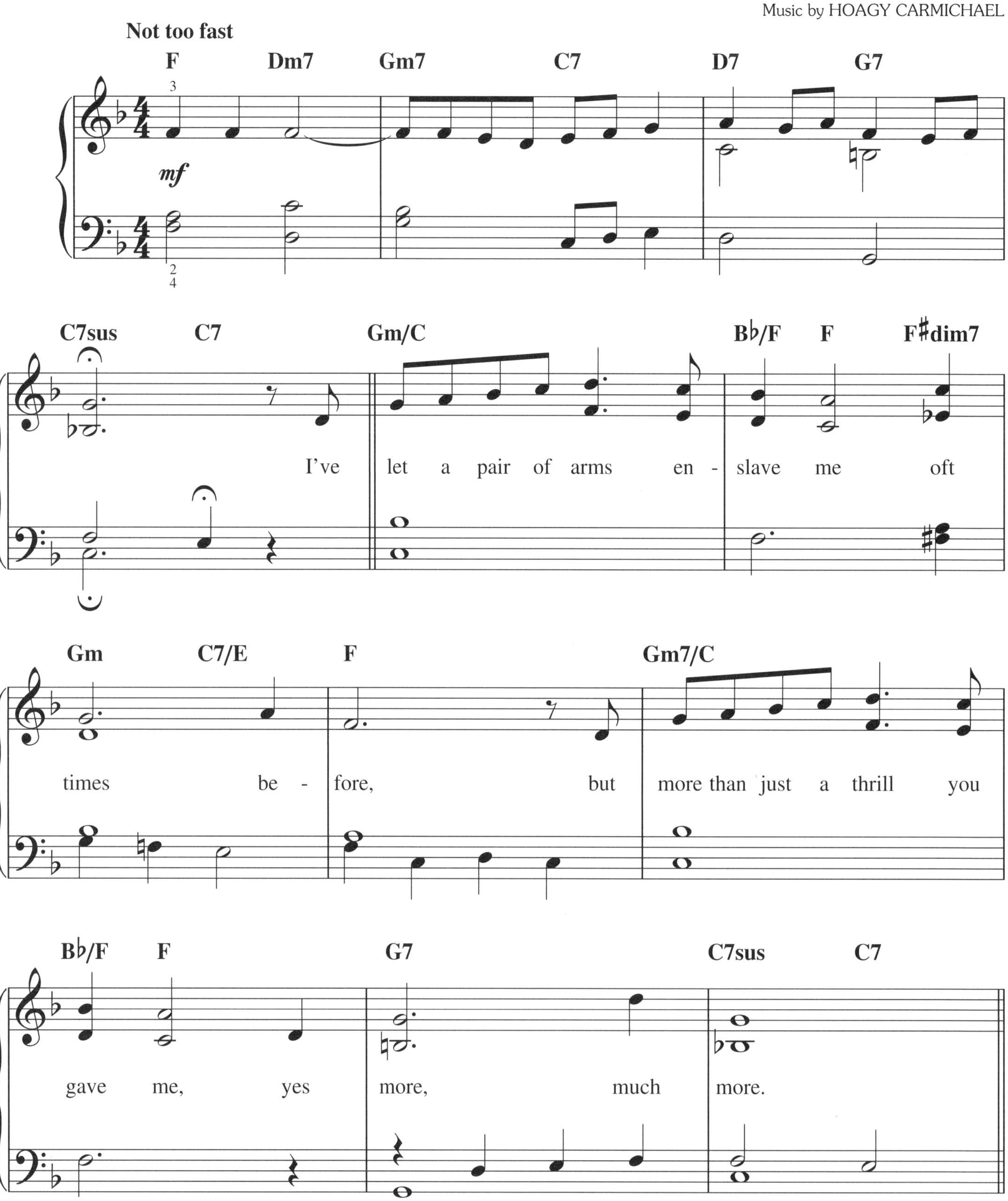

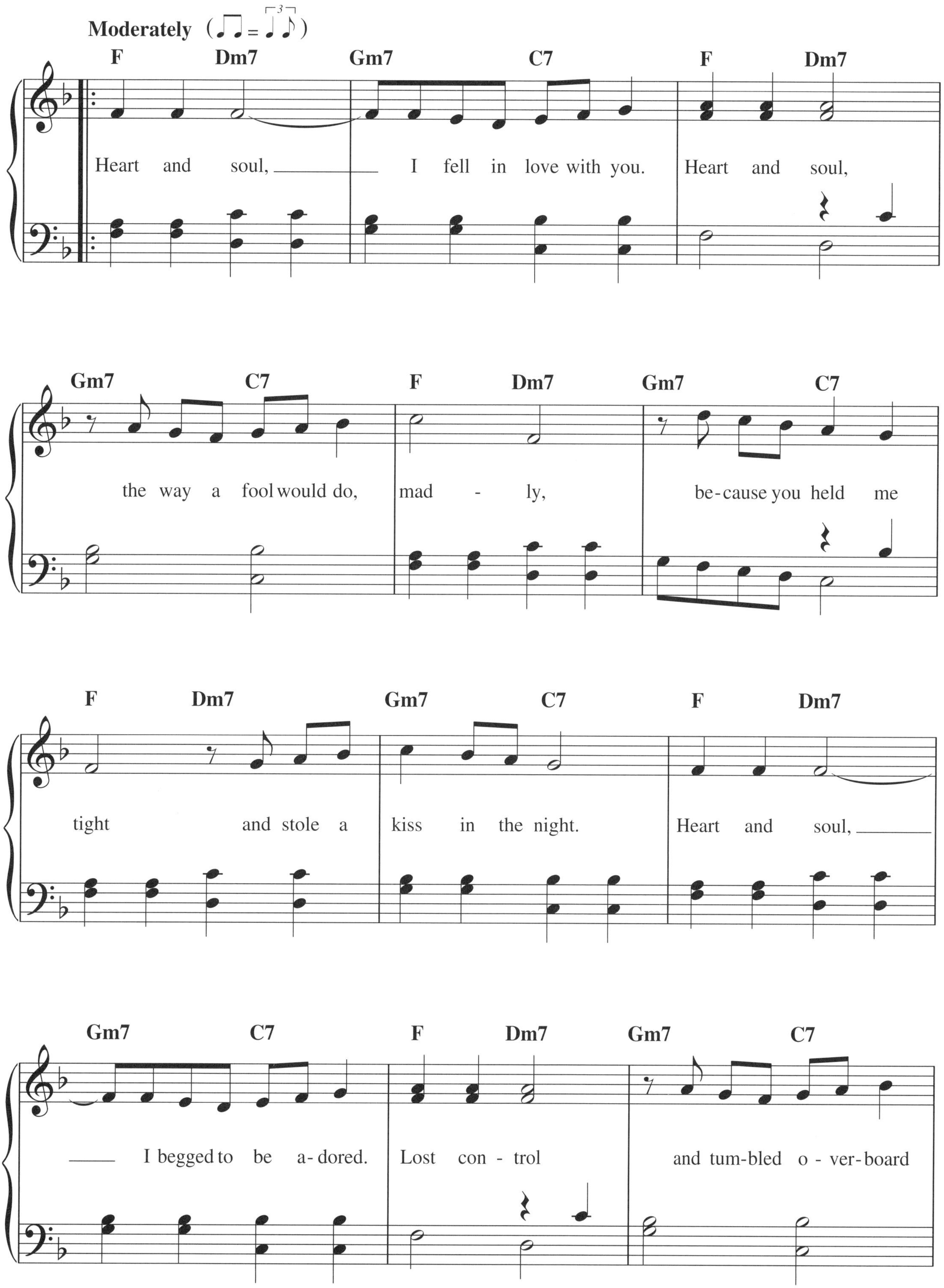
Moderately
F Dm7 Gm7 C7 F Dm7
Heart and soul, I fell in love with you. Heart and soul,
Gm7 C7 F Dm7 Gm7 C7
the way a fool would do, mad - ly, be-cause you held me
F Dm7 Gm7 C7 F Dm7
tight and stole a kiss in the night. Heart and soul,
Gm7 C7 F Dm7 Gm7 C7
I begged to be a-dored. Lost con - trol and tum-bled o - ver-board

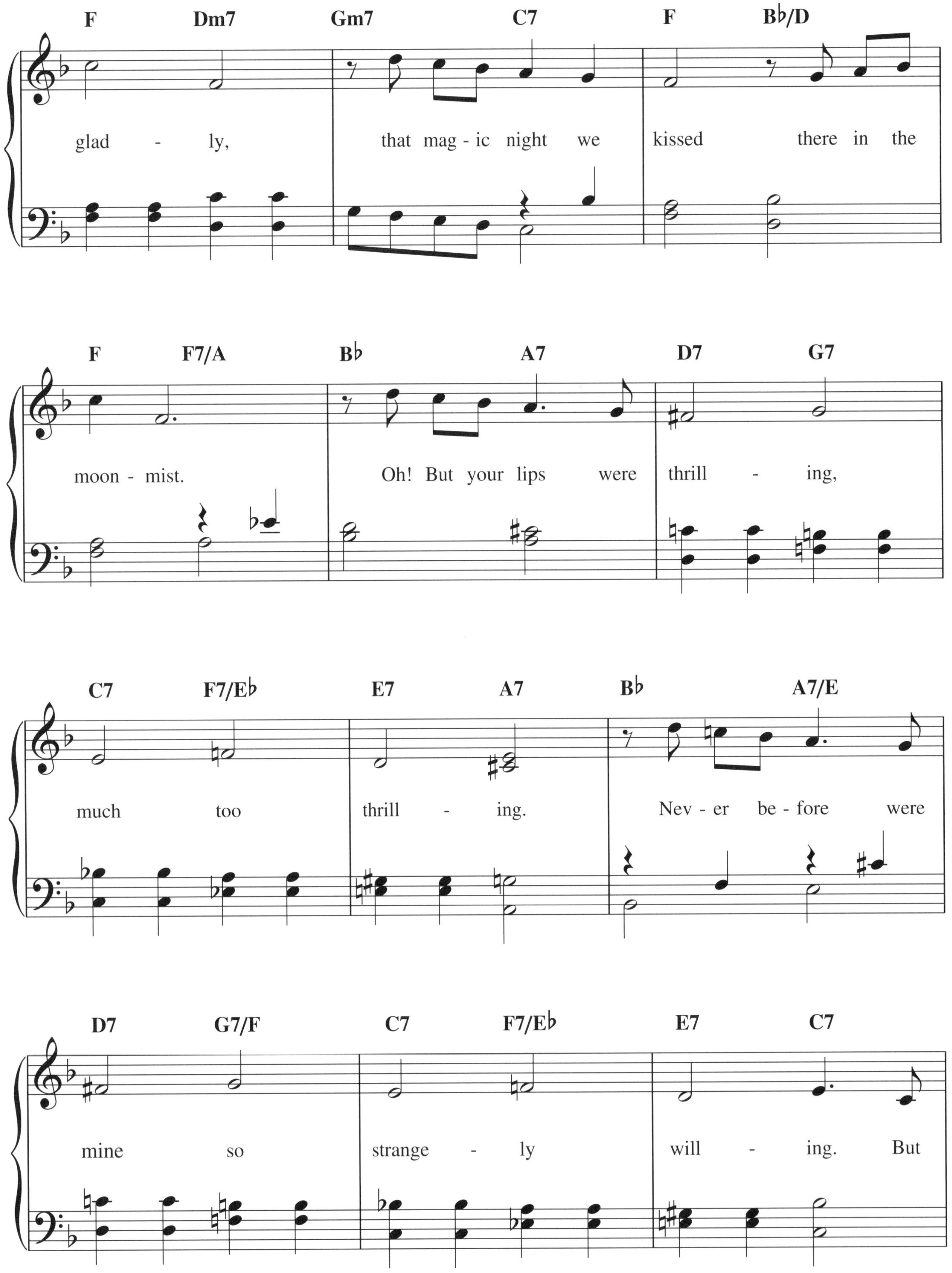
F Dm7 Gm7 C7 F B♭/D
glad - ly, that mag - ic night we kissed there in the
F F7/A B♭ A7 D7 G7
moon - mist. Oh! But your lips were thrill - ing,
C7 F7/E♭ E7 A7 B♭ A7/E
much too thrill - ing. Nev - er be - fore were
D7 G7/F C7 F7/E♭ E7 C7
mine so strange - ly will - ing. But

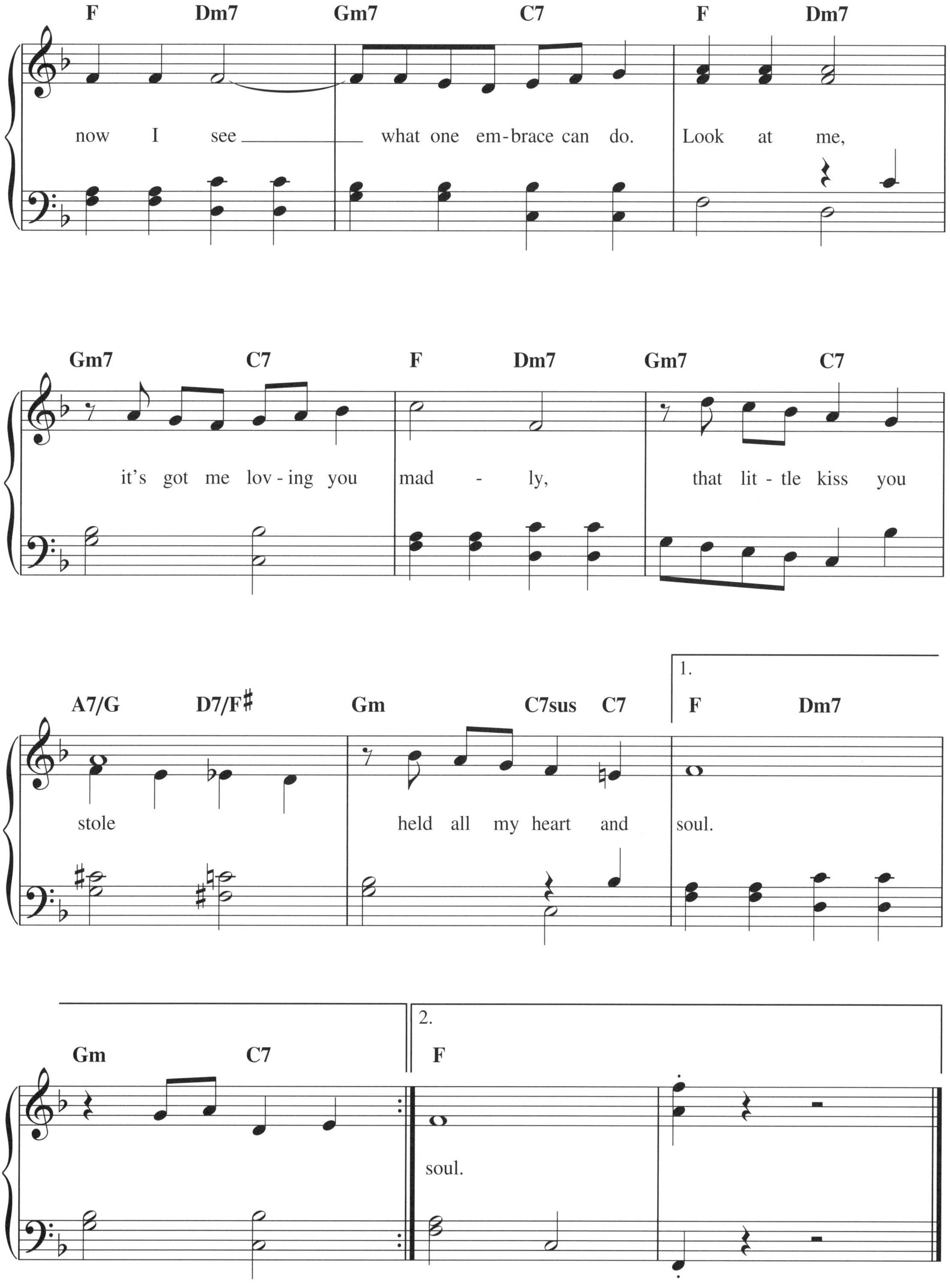
F Dm7 Gm7 C7 F Dm7
now I see what one em-brace can do. Look at me,
Gm7 C7 F Dm7 Gm7 C7
it's got me lov-ing you mad - ly, that lit - tle kiss you
A7/G D7/F♯ Gm C7sus C7
1.
F Dm7
stole held all my heart and soul.
Gm C7
2.
F
soul.

Hey, Soul Sister

Words and Music by PAT MONAHAN,
ESPEN LIND and AMUND BJORKLAND

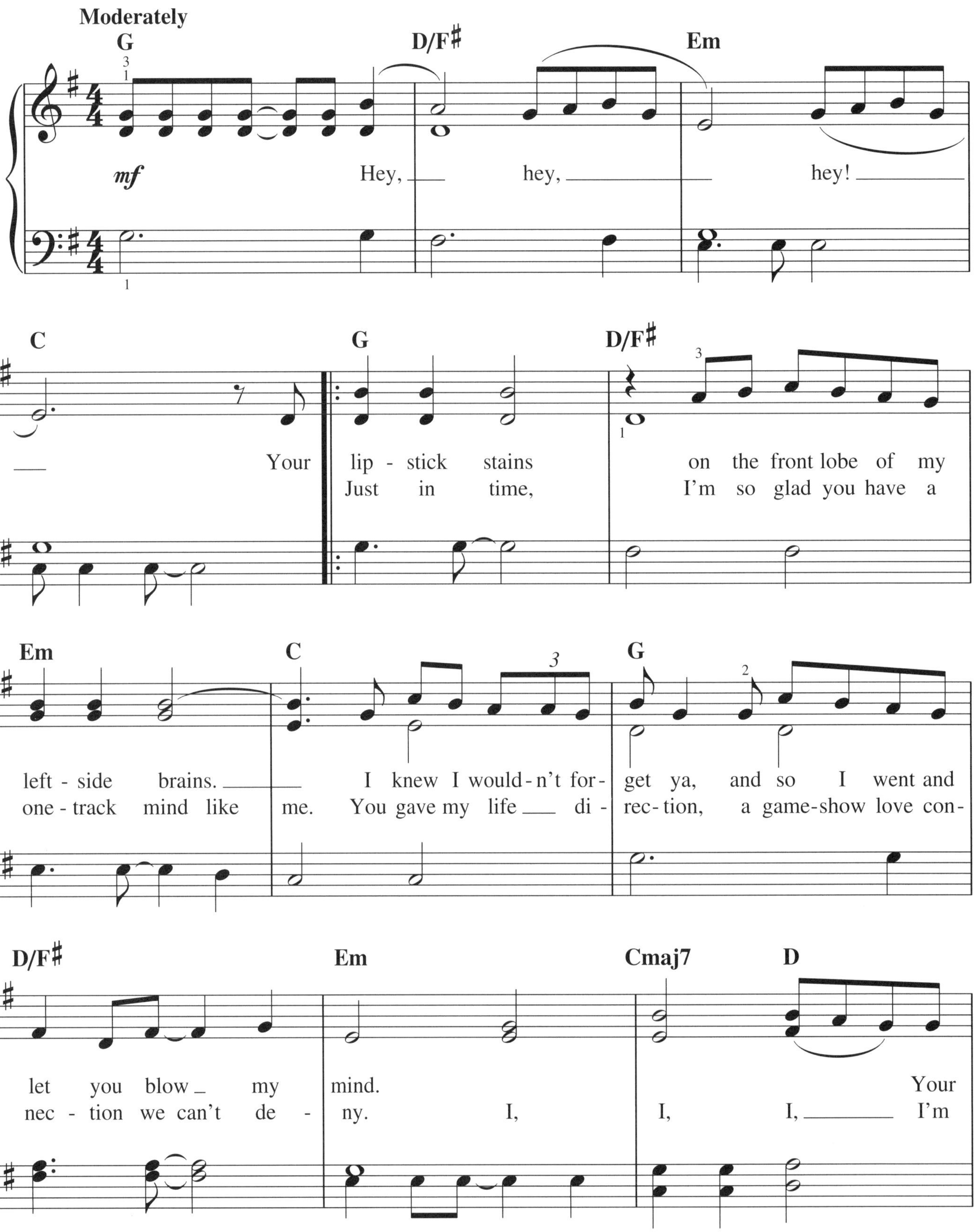

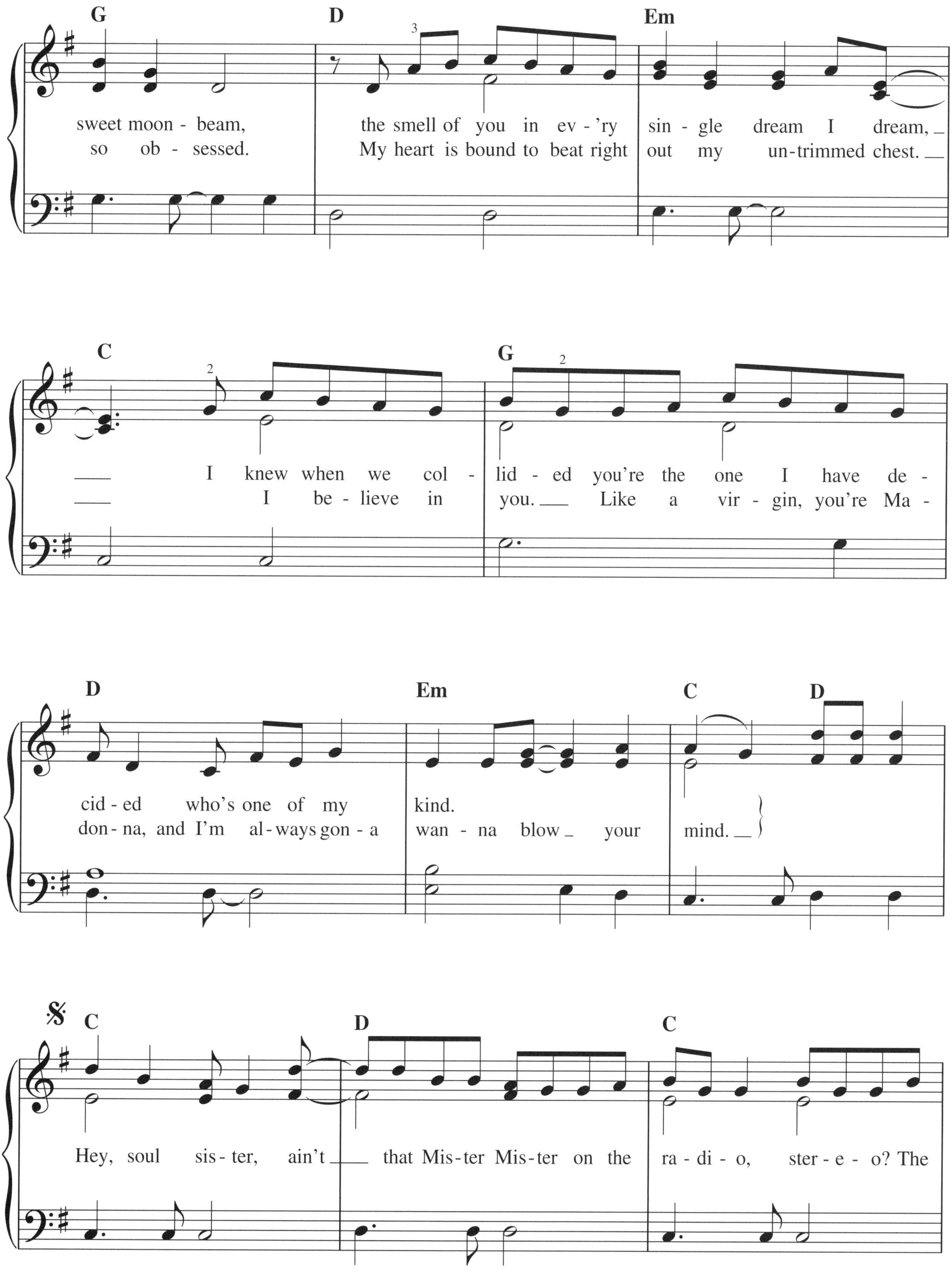
G
D
Em
sweet moon - beam, the smell of you in ev - 'ry sin - gle dream I dream,
so ob - sessed. My heart is bound to beat right out my un-trimmed chest.
C
G
I knew when we col - lid - ed you're the one I have de -
I be - lieve in you. Like a vir - gin, you're Ma -
D
Em
C
D
cid - ed who's one of my kind.
don - na, and I'm al - ways gon - a wan - na blow your mind.
C
D
C
Hey, soul sis - ter, ain't that Mis - ter Mis - ter on the ra - di - o, ster - e - o? The

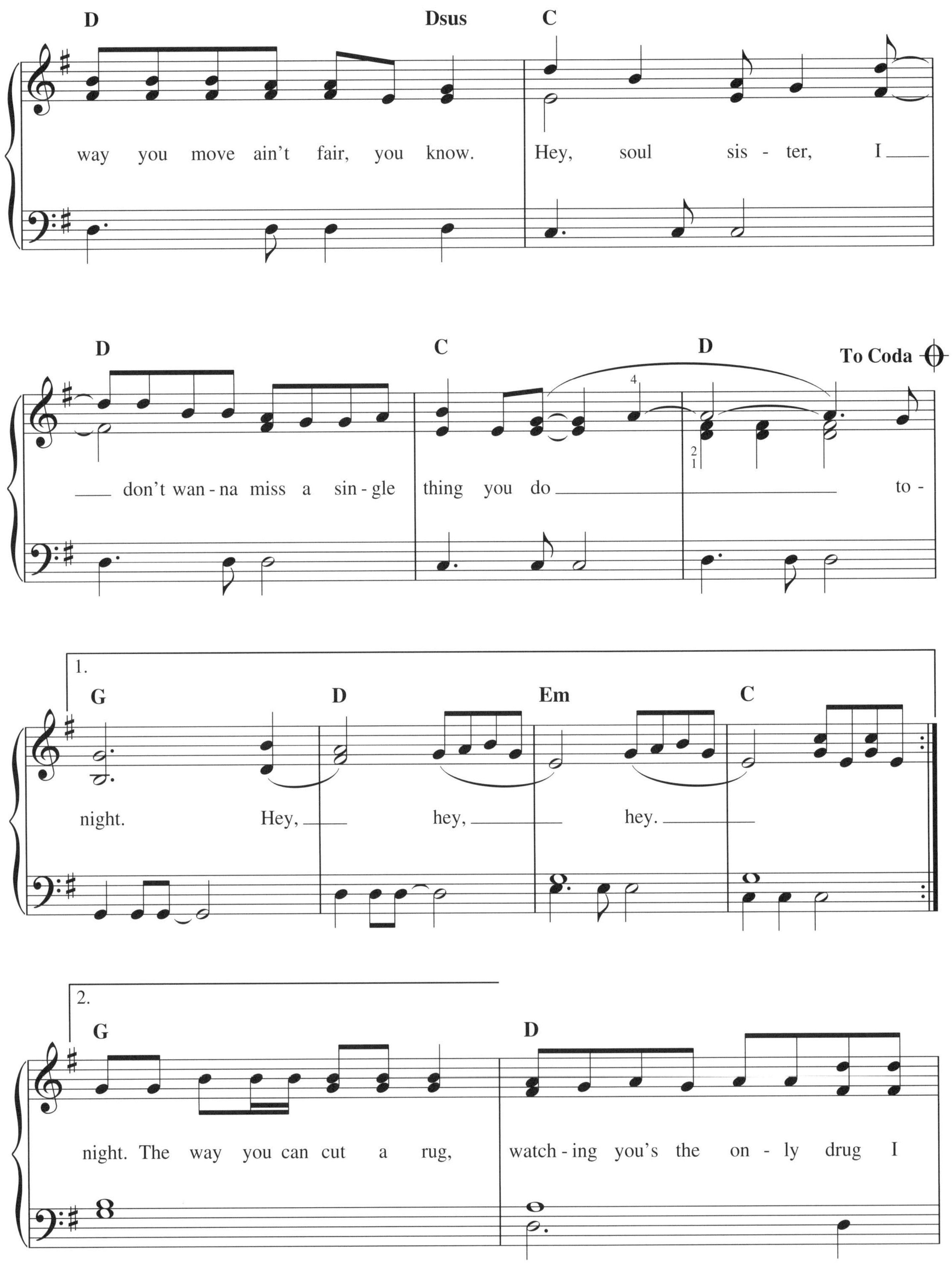
D
Dsus
C
way you move ain't fair, you know.
Hey, soul sis - ter, I
D
C
D
To Coda
don't wan - na miss a sin - gle
thing you do
to -
1.
G
D
Em
C
night.
Hey,
hey,
hey.
2.
G
D
night. The way you can cut a rug,
watch - ing you's the on - ly drug I

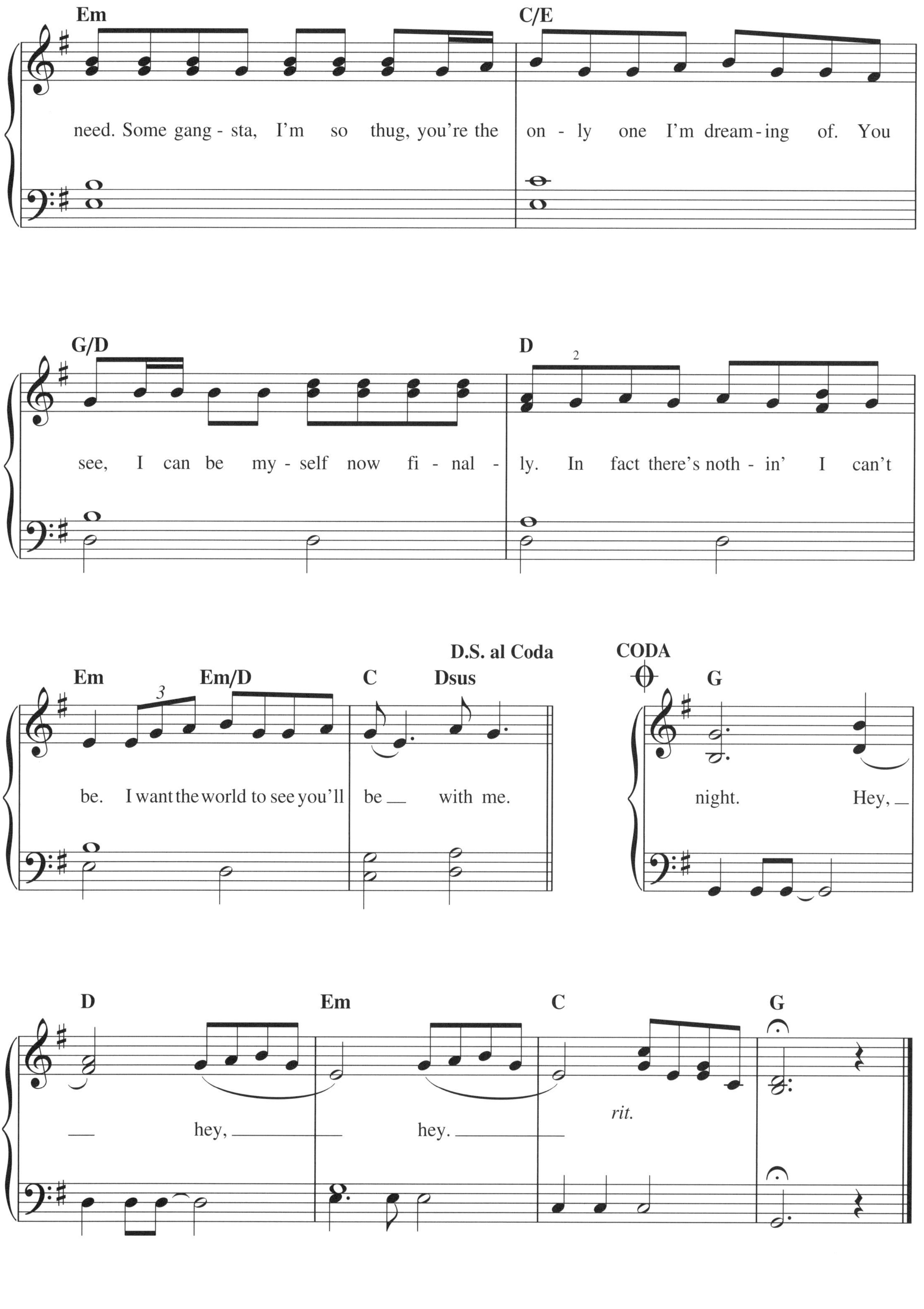
Em
C/E
need. Some gang - sta, I'm so thug, you're the
on - ly one I'm dream - ing of. You
G/D
D
2
see, I can be my - self now fi - nal -
ly. In fact there's noth - in' I can't
D.S. al Coda
CODA
Em
Em/D
C
Dsus
G
3
be. I want the world to see you'll
be with me.
night. Hey,
D
Em
C
G
hey,
hey.
rit.

I Have a Dream

Words and Music by BENNY ANDERSSON
and BJÖRN ULVAEUS

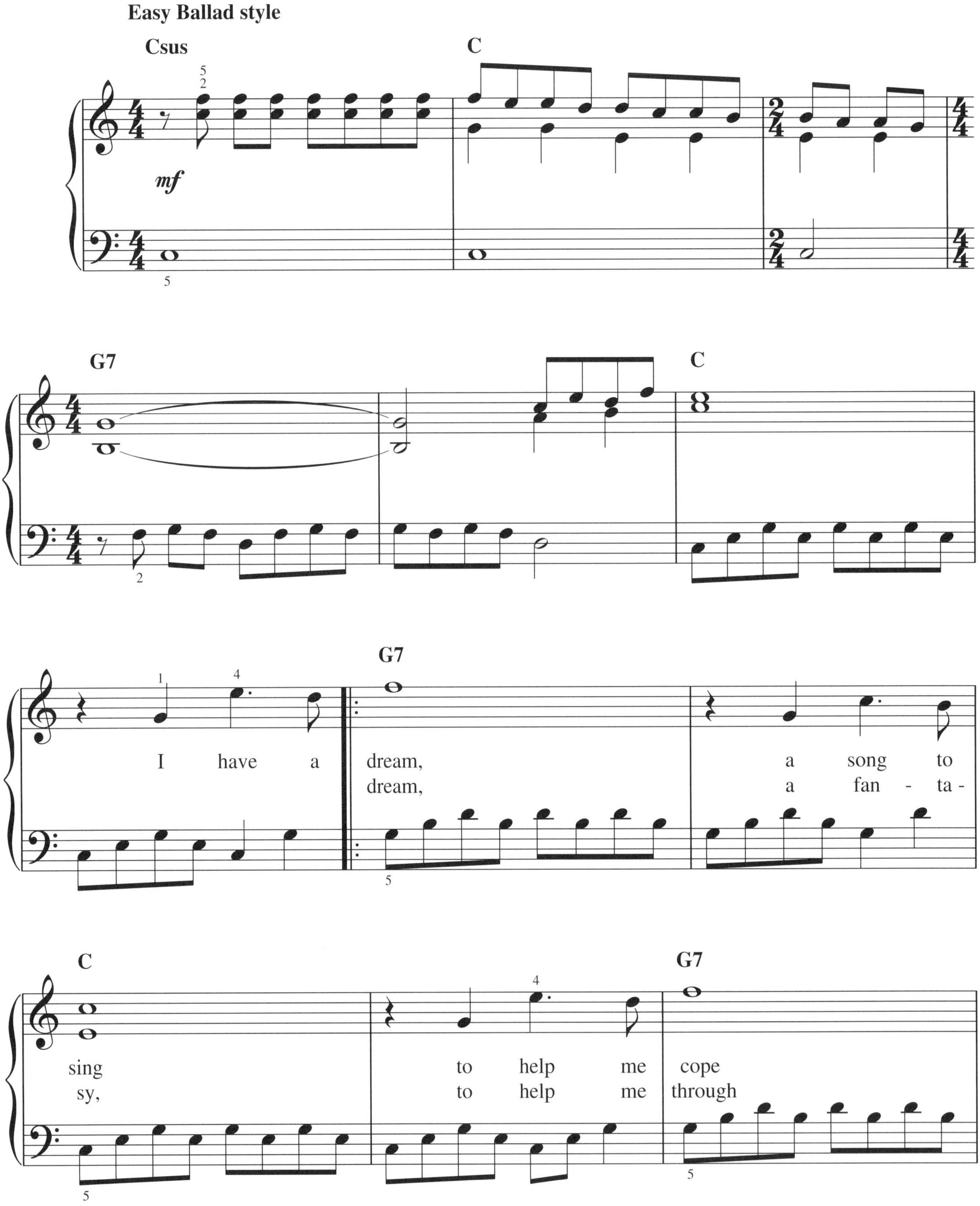

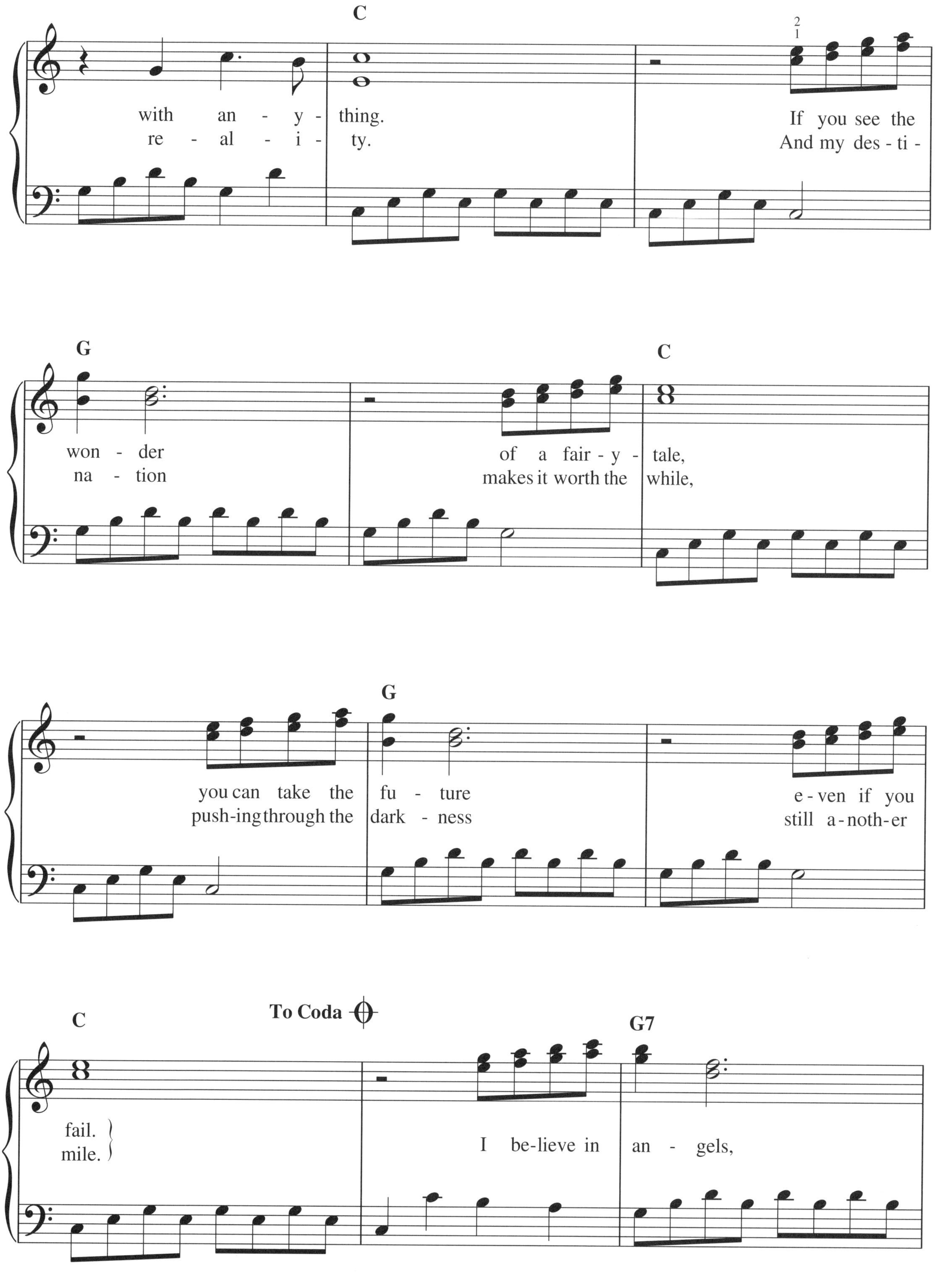
C
with an - y - thing.
re - al - i - ty.
If you see the
And my des - ti -
G
won - der
na - tion
of a fair - y - tale,
makes it worth the while,
C
you can take the
push-ing through the
G
fu - ture
dark - ness
e - ven if you
still a - noth - er
C
fail.
mile.
To Coda
I be-lieve in
G7
an - gels,

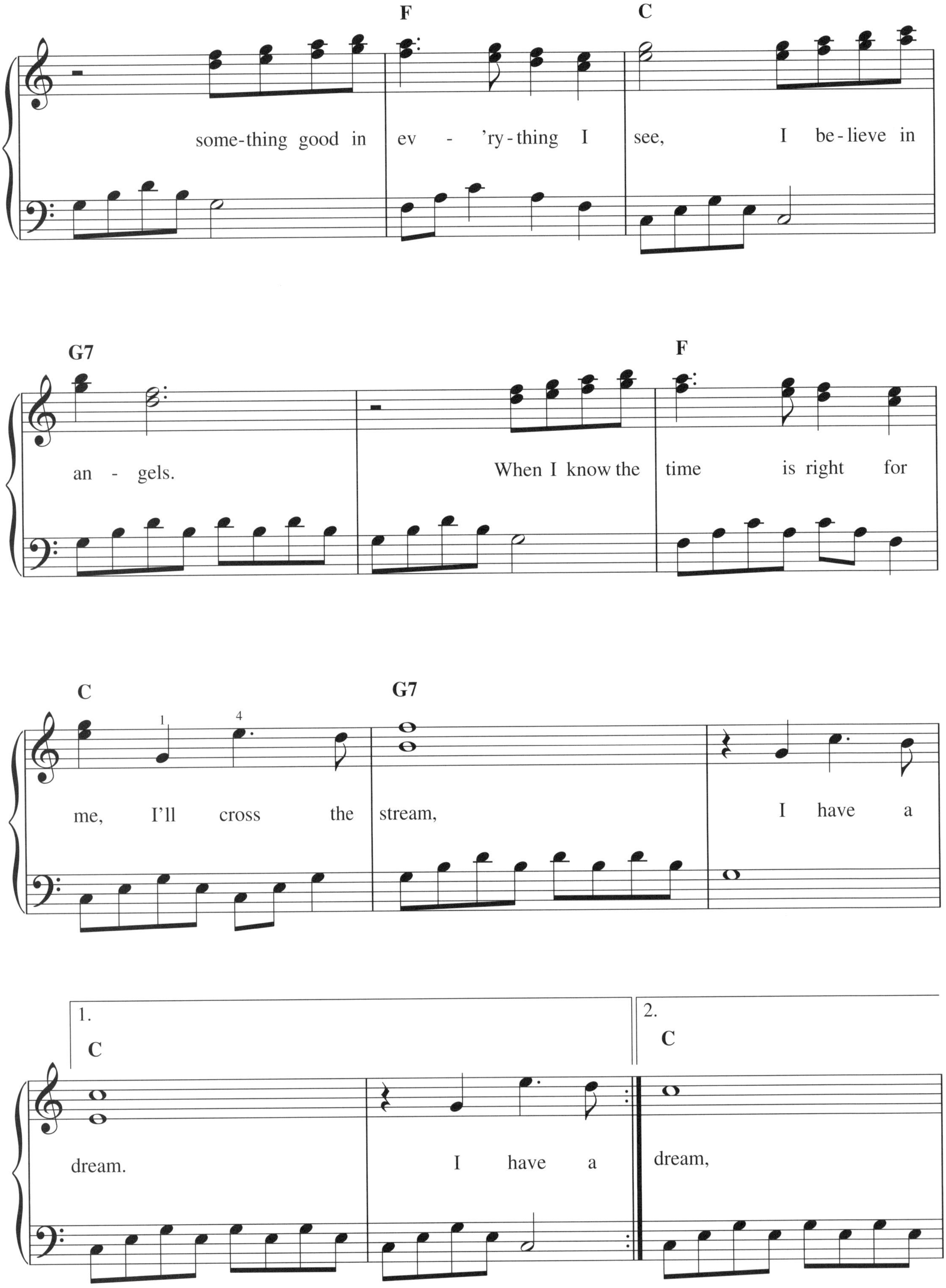
F
C
some-thing good in ev - 'ry-thing I see, I be-lieve in
G7
F
an - gels. When I know the time is right for
C
1
4
G7
me, I'll cross the stream, I have a
1.
C
2.
C
dream. I have a dream,

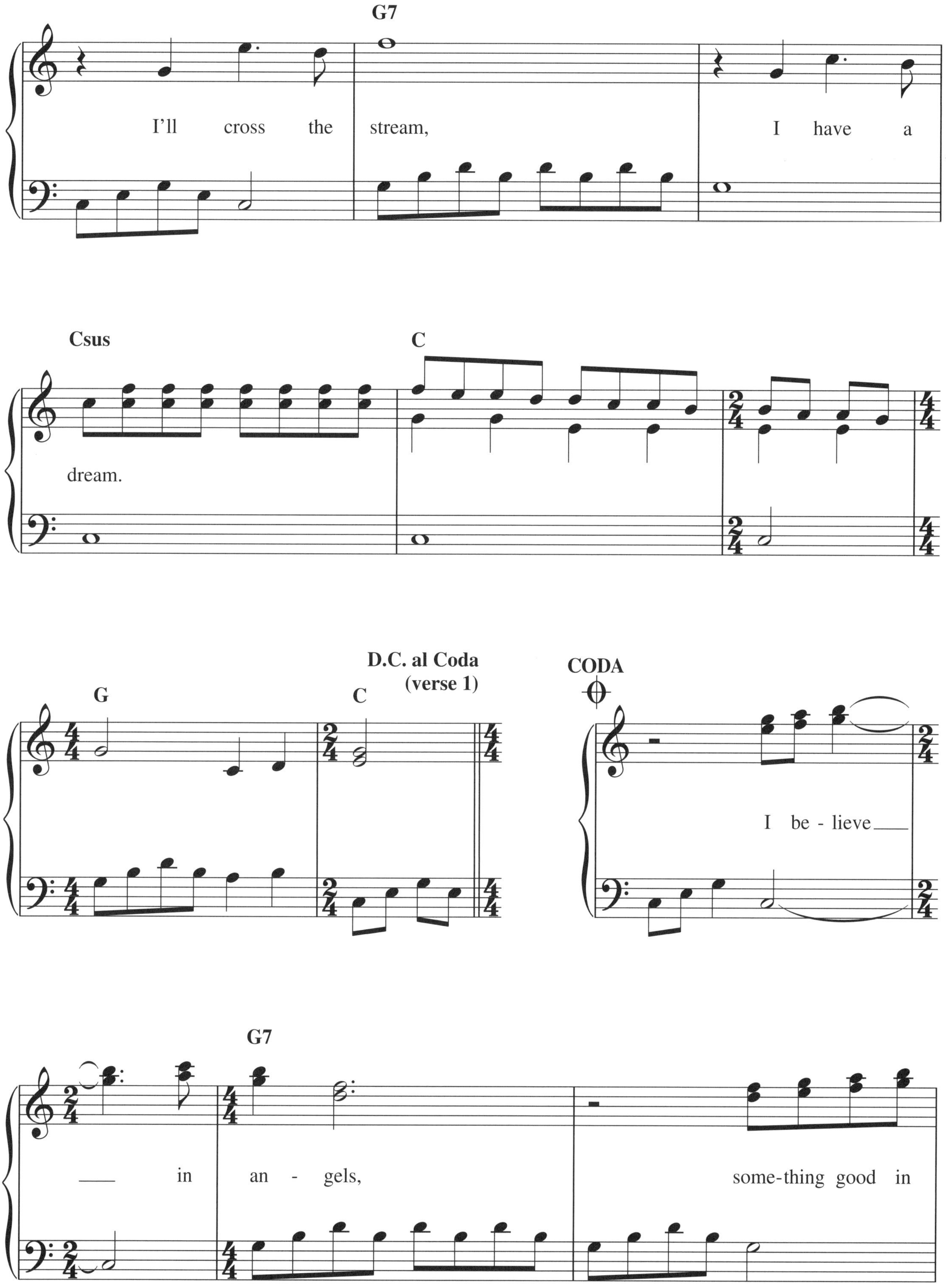
G7
I'll cross the stream, I have a
Csus
C
dream.
G
D.C. al Coda
(verse 1)
C
CODA
I be - lieve
in an - gels,
G7
some-thing good in

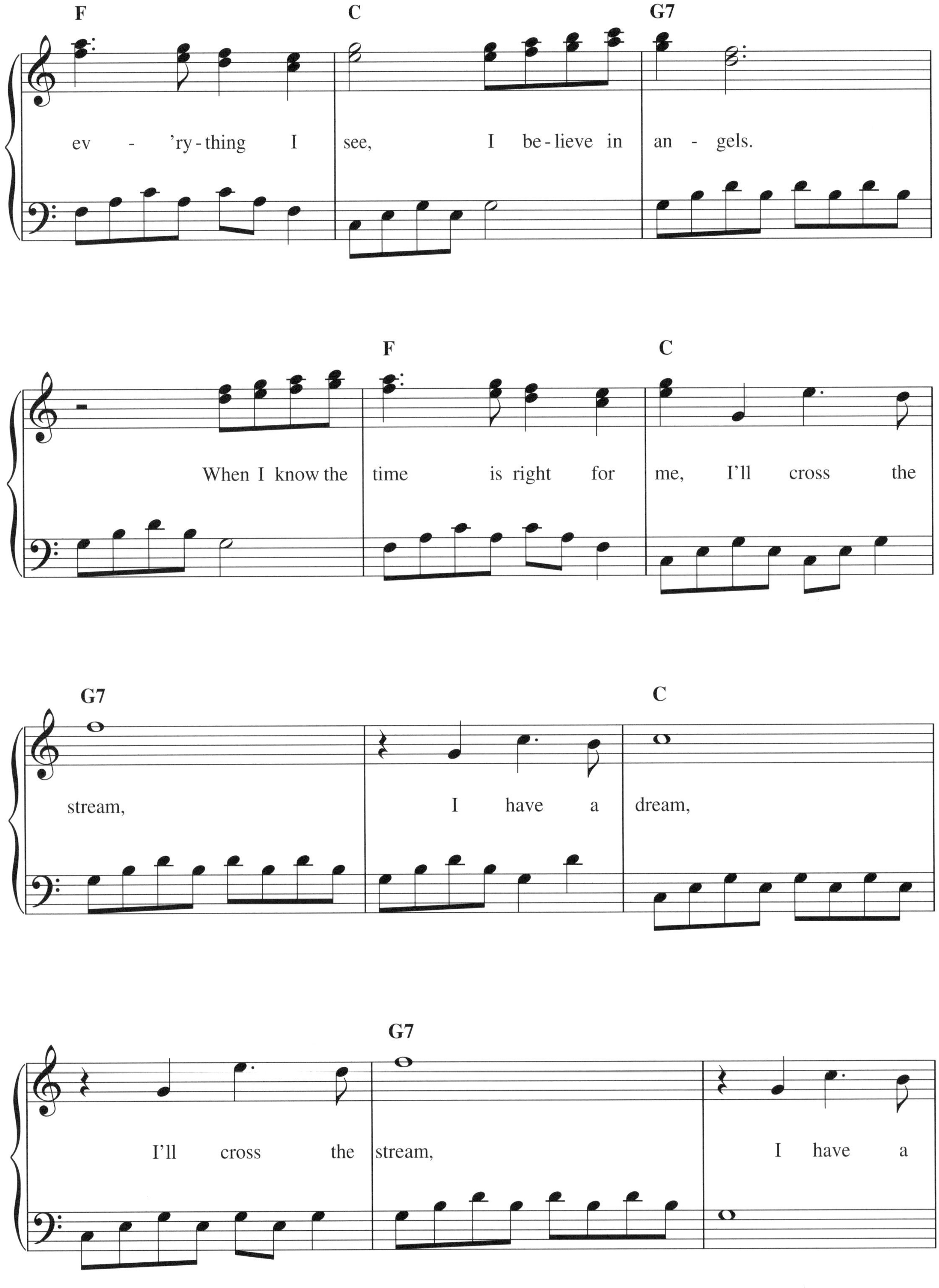
F
C
G7
ev - 'ry - thing I see, I be - lieve in an - gels.
F
C
When I know the time is right for me, I'll cross the
G7
C
stream, I have a dream,
G7
I'll cross the stream, I have a

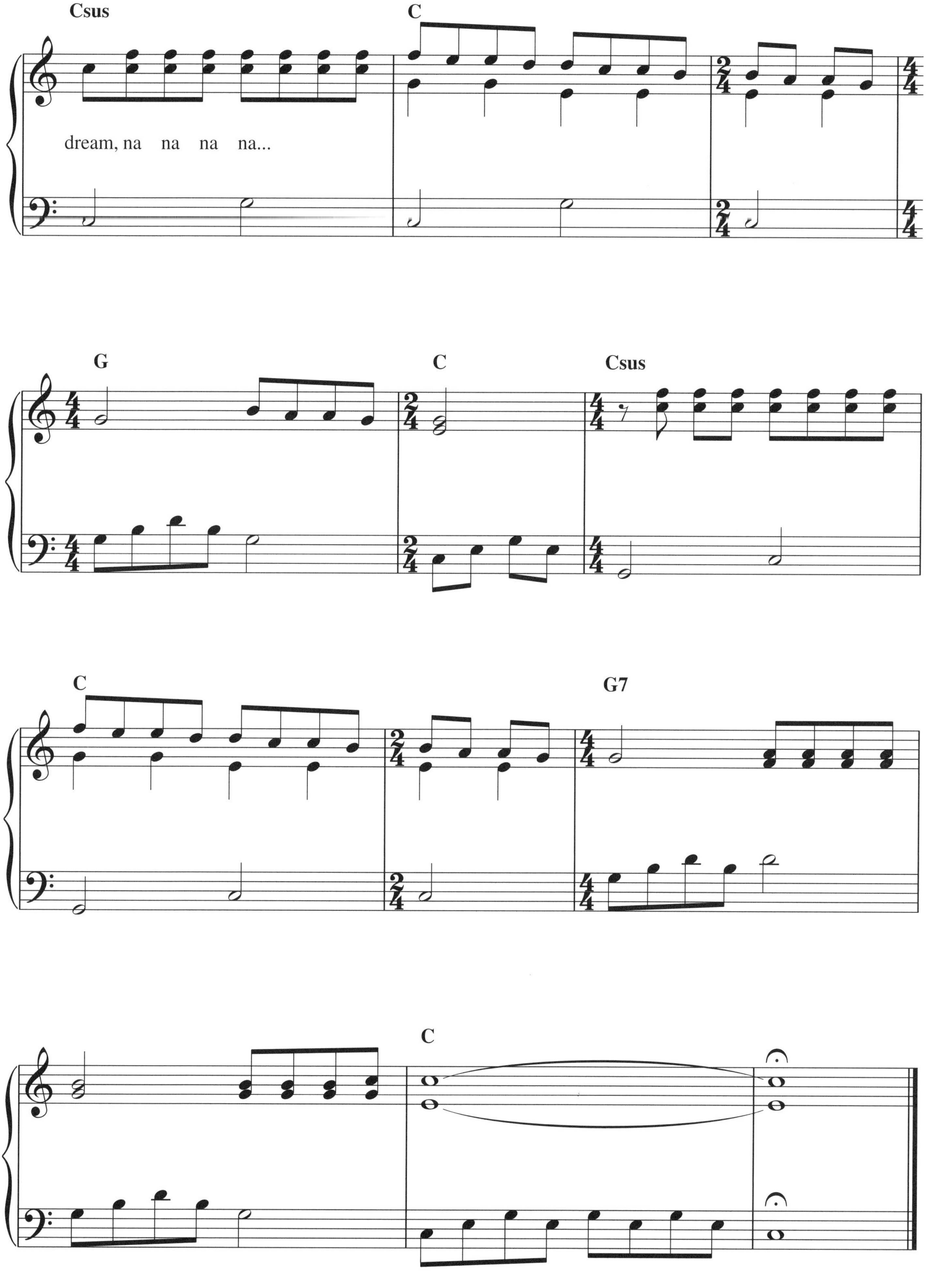
Csus
C
dream, na na na na...
G
C
Csus
C
G7
C

Performance Notes

Back to December *(Page 6)*

Taylor Swift became one of country's biggest stars in 2006, when she released her self-titled album at the tender age of 16. But by the time her third studio album, *Speak Now*, came out in 2010, Swift was one of the most acclaimed artists of any genre. From that album, "Back to December" follows Swift's typical narrative approach to songwriting; the song is an apology to a former beau for the ways in which she apparently did him wrong. As you'll see, the tune, which peaked at #3 on the Country Songs chart, translates quite nicely to our easy arrangement.

TECHNICAL STUFF

As indicated at the beginning of the song by the "C" with a vertical line through it, [¢] "Back to December" is in what's known as *cut time,* a meter found often in faster selections, marches, and country tunes. Feel this meter by counting in half notes, two per bar, rather than in quarter notes, four per bar. This will help ensure that you achieve the proper groove for the song. As you begin to learn the song, study the left- and right-hand fingerings in advance. These fingering suggestions — and all the others in this book — will help you navigate the keys easily and smoothly.

Blowin' in the Wind *(Page 14)*

Few songs have defined an era as powerfully as "Blowin' in the Wind" — the song, written in 1962, that transformed Bob Dylan from a folk singer-songwriter into a cultural sensation. The tune answers a series of rhetorical questions with the ambiguous refrain, "The answer, my friend, is blowin' in the wind," universally addressing injustice in the world. It wasn't actually Dylan, but the folk trio Peter, Paul and Mary, who released the first commercially successful version of this beloved song. It's been covered by notables like Sam Cooke, Dolly Parton, and Stevie Wonder, among so many other artists in a range of styles — a testament to the song's great durability.

TIP

While this piano arrangement of "Blowin' in the Wind" sounds lovely and is not difficult to play, the song is most closely associated with the guitar, so you might want to take out that old six-string for this one. As shown in the chord symbols atop the treble staff, the song has only three basic chords, F, G, and C, and so even if you've got the most casual relationship with the guitar this will be an easy song for you to learn. (When playing the guitar, novices may choose to ignore any of the sus, or suspended chords throughout; for example, play a C chord instead of Csus.) When you first play through the song, strum the chords in a straight fashion. Then, try matching the basic rhythm of the original Bob Dylan recording: Play a chord's lowest note on each beat 1, the full chord on beat 2, the bass note and then the chord on beat 3 (in a pair of eighth notes), and the full chord again on beat 4.

Blue Skies (Page 17)

Written by Irving Berlin in 1926 as a last-minute addition to the Rodgers and Hart musical *Betsy*, "Blue Skies" is now part of the Great American Songbook — a canon of the most influential popular tunes of the 20th century, most composed 1920–1960. This cheerful song has been interpreted many times over the years, by everyone from the clarinetist and bandleader Benny Goodman to the country-western legend Willie Nelson. Despite its musical sophistication, "Blue Skies" works out quite nicely as an easy piano arrangement.

CAUTION!

A jazzy number, "Blue Skies" is chockfull of accidentals — notes that depart from the prevailing key, like the A♯ in the left hand of bar 2 and the D♯ in the right hand of bar 4. Accidentals can trip up an instrumentalist of any skill level. So when playing this or any song for that matter, you can minimize mistakes by taking things very slowly at first and constantly scanning ahead as you read through the music, so that those pesky sharps and flats do not come as last-minute surprises. If need be, you could even use a highlighter to make the accidentals in the notation more prominent.

Bridge Over Troubled Water (Page 23)

"Bridge Over Troubled Water" was the pop singer-songwriter duo Simon and Garfunkel's fifth and final album together, and one of the biggest-selling albums of the 1970s. The recording's lovely gospel-influenced title track is sung largely as a solo by Garfunkel and driven by a piano part that is pretty complex and dense with lots of chordal movement. To simplify things for you, we've distilled the music to its essence in an arrangement that's easy on the fingers.

TIP

At the beginning of the song, below the first bar of "Bridge Over Troubled Water" you'll see the indication *With pedal,* calling for you to depress the *sostenuto* (sustaining) pedal. But don't keep the pedal held down throughout the piece; this will cause it to sound very muddy. Use your judgment to engage and release the pedal where it feels natural, allowing the notes to ring smoothly together without overwhelming the music. Avoid the temptation to overuse the pedal — you might benefit from recording yourself and having a critical listen to make sure you're not doing so.

California Girls (Page 20)

The fairer sex of The Golden State is celebrated in "California Girls," one of the Beach Boys' most popular numbers, not to mention one of the perfect pop songs of all time, covered by everyone from Jan and Dean to David Lee Roth. Part of what makes the original recording so great is its intricately crafted arrangement with churning organs, swelling horns, thunderous drums, and walls of vocal harmonies. But stripped of all these effects, "California Girls" makes a pretty great piano arrangement that you should be able to play in no time at all.

CHAMPION STRATEGY #1

The bass line of "California Girls" is positively infectious, and if you glance through the notation you'll see that the same riff appears throughout most of the song. So, in learning this arrangement, it would be a good idea to isolate and tackle the left-hand part before putting everything together. Starting with the bass clef of bar 1, you'll see that the somewhat jerky rhythm of a dotted eighth note followed by a 16th appears throughout the riff. Before you even touch the piano, make sure that you can feel and tap this rhythm accurately. If needed, listen to the original recording for reference. After you've absorbed the rhythms and worked out the bass notes on the piano, bring it all together.

Can't Help Falling in Love (Page 30)

You might not know the name, but George Weiss penned some of pop's most memorable songs in his work as a songwriter from the 1940s though the '70s. Weiss' songbook includes "Can't Help Falling in Love," which was, of course, made famous by The King, Elvis Presley. Based on the French chanson "Plaisir D'Amour," "Can't Help Falling in Love" was featured in his 1961 film, *Blue Hawaii,* and became Presley's signature love song. Throughout the years the song has received a diverse assortment of treatments, from interpretations by the reggae group UB40 to the Swedish pop group A-Teens and, here, just for you, an easy piano arrangement.

TECHNICAL STUFF

"Can't Help Falling in Love" is, of course, a very gentle number, so play this tune as smoothly and flowing throughout as possible, and with feeling, too. In bar 2 of the treble clef and elsewhere you'll see a rhythm that might be new to you — the quarter-note triplet, that is, three quarter notes in the space usually taken up by two. To feel this rhythm, try counting eighth-note triplets (three evenly spaced notes) on each beat: "trip-uh-let, trip-uh-let," and so on. In the span of two beats, a quarter note will then fall on the first "trip," the first "let," and the second "uh." If this rhythm is giving you trouble, count and practice it extremely slowly until you feel it naturally.

Candle in the Wind (Page 33)

One of Elton John's most popular songs, "Candle in the Wind" is a tribute to Marilyn Monroe, the actress and model who died all too soon, in 1962 at the age of 36. This elegant song, a meditation on celebrity, was originally released in 1973; a retooled version, a 1997 tribute to Diana, Princess of Wales, went to #1 around the world and is one of the best-selling singles of all time. Today, 40 years after it was released, the song has lost none of its luster, and it also translates very well to an easy piano arrangement.

CHAMPION STRATEGY

Like many of the songs in this collection, "Candle in the Wind" has a condensed form, for the sake of readability. Here's how to follow it:

1. When you get to the repeat sign (a double bar line with two dots) and the indication *D.C.* (*da capo*, or from the beginning), go back to the beginning of the arrangement and repeat the music. Play until you see the indication *D.S. al Coda* which means "from the sign to the coda mark."
2. Go to the sign at the bottom of the second page of music, play until you see the *To Coda* marking, and skip ahead to the *Coda* on the last page of music.

Knowing how the road map works before playing this (or any) song will help prevent you from getting lost in the notation.

The Climb (Page 38)

Hannah Montana: The Movie (2009), the musical film based on the Disney television series, has an outstanding soundtrack, including, most notably, the song "The Climb." This country-inflected power ballad finds singer/actress Miley Cyrus belting out about life's many challenges and rewards. It has topped the charts around the world and proved to be one of the most popular song choices of hopeful contestants on the vocal competition show *American Idol* — a distinction that will be completely understandable when you play and sing through our arrangement of this infectious tune.

The left hand of "The Climb," with its abundance of whole, half, and quarter notes, will be a breeze for you to play. But the right hand, which is more rhythmically involved, might present some little challenges, so focus on this part before combining the music on the treble and bass staves. If needed, subdivide: count "One-ee-and-uh, two-ee-and-uh, three-ee-and-uh, four-ee-and-uh," and so on. In the right hand of bar 4, for instance, you'll play nothing on beat 1, a pair of 16ths on "and" of 1, then steady eighths from beats 2 through 4, ending with two 16ths on the "and" of 4. If you take the time to break down rhythms in this fashion now, you'll be able to play them later on with ease.

Clocks (Page 44)

It's not uncommon for a promising new band to suffer a sophomore slump, but this was far from the case with Coldplay, whose second album, *A Rush of Blood to the Head* (2002), yielded what has proven one of their biggest hits to date — the single "Clocks." On the album, this song, with its urgent lyrics, might sound powerful due to an accompaniment of a wall of piano and drums supported by shimmering strings and guitars. But the tune's driving *arpeggios* (broken chords) sound just as good when negotiated in a piano solo, as you'll soon find out.

The main progression in "Clocks" is built around just three chords: D (D-F♯-A), Am (A-C-E), and Em (E-G-B) played as a piano solo on the first page of our arrangement. What makes this part sound so good is its economical movement between chords. The D and Am chords, for instance, share the note A. So that note, positioned in the middle of each chord, remains constant, while the upper note moves down just a step between the chords, from D to C, and the lower note does the same, from F♯ to E. Accordingly, you can keep your second finger stationed on the note A, to play the arpeggios in the smoothest way.

Dancing Queen (Page 55)

The Swedish pop group ABBA enjoyed a major hit, its only #1 song in the U.S., with the 1976 single "Dancing Queen." In this spirited song about a visit to the disco, ABBA blends European influences, a sophisticated melody, stately strings, and syncopated synth lines with the American dance beat so wildly popular at the time to create a carefully crafted arrangement. While the disco craze has long since passed, the song remains a favorite on the radio and at dance clubs — one that you can have fun with in our streamlined arrangement.

This arrangement of "Dancing Queen" achieves a disco feel through the rhythms of its bass line, so that's the most important part to focus on in learning the song. Begin by trying to play the left-hand part only. If this presents any difficulties, try playing all the rhythms using just a single pitch, playing along with a metronome on a slow setting. Gradually increase the tempo until you can run through the bass part, again on just one note, at a comfortable dance beat, then play the part as written. Next, learn the right-hand part before combining both hands, remembering that this is a song intended for dancing.

Daniel (Page 50)

The Elton John song "Daniel" is commonly thought to have been a tribute to cowriter Bernie Taupin's brother. But, the tune, in fact, refers to a fictional character, a veteran who was blinded in the Vietnam War. Recorded in 1972, "Daniel" was a hit the following year, ascending to #2 on the Pop chart and #1 on Adult Contemporary for two weeks, earning John a GRAMMY® nomination for Best Male Pop Vocal Performance. The song has seen some unusual covers, including an interpretation by the great eccentric Bonnie 'Prince' Billy & Tortoise; our version, though, is more faithful to the original.

TIP

At the beginning of "Daniel," between the staves you'll see the indication *p*; in bar 9, an *mp*, and on the third page of music, *mf*. These are known as *dynamic* markings; *p* calls for you to play the music *piano*, or soft, while *mp* means *mezzo-piano*, moderately soft, and *mf* means *mezzo-forte*, moderately loud. Play the song in a gently flowing way, and be sure to observe the dynamic markings throughout. This will help lend expressiveness to your playing and dramatic heft to the song, especially when you amp things up, playing *mf* for the song's chorus section.

Defying Gravity (Page 64)

Not to be confused with the Keith Urban album of the same name, "Defying Gravity" is the signature song from *Wicked*, the musical that debuted on Broadway in 2003. Based on the 1995 Gregory Maguire novel *Wicked: The Life and Times of the Wicked Witch of the West*, the musical is a story told from the perspective of the witches from *The Wonderful Wizard of Oz*. "Defying Gravity" is sung mostly as a solo by Elphaba, the Wicked Witch of the West. Outside of Broadway, the song has been placed in a number of interesting contexts, from an episode of television's *Glee* to, appropriately enough, the wake-up music on a 2010 space shuttle mission.

TECHNICAL STUFF

In some ways, "Defying Gravity" is one of the more challenging selections in this collection. The song begins in the key of D major but goes through some *modulations* (changes of key). In the last bar of the fifth page of music, the music is suddenly in the key of B♭ major; at the end of the following page it moves to A minor; then, on the last system of the next page it returns to D major. So, in learning the song you'll want to take things very slowly, scanning ahead so that the modulations do not come as a surprise. Heads-up on the quick time signature change on the sixth page, from 4/4 to 3/4. Count carefully, trying not to lose the beat as you toggle between these meters.

Fever (Page 74)

"Fever" is a song originally recorded by the R&B singer Little Willie John in 1956 but later made famous in a version that the jazz-pop singer Peggy Lee recorded two years later, with its cool finger-snapping on beats 2 and 4. Lee's interpretation peaked at #8 on the *Billboard* Hot 100 and earned the singer a GRAMMY nomination for Record of the Year in 1959. The song has seen a number of covers throughout the years, by artists as disparate as Elvis Presley, Madonna, and Michael Bublé.

TECHNICAL STUFF

Peggy Lee's version of "Fever" modulates through many keys between sections, but our arrangement sticks to the easy key of A minor. At the beginning of the song you'll see some note values in parentheses indicating that the song is to be played with a swing feel, a rhythmic style that features prominently in jazz. In Swing, a pair of consecutive eighth notes is played not evenly but long-short, at a ratio of roughly two-to-one. Play the rhythms with a little bounce — think of the sound of a jazzy hi-hat and a walking bass as you're playing through the music.

Georgia on My Mind (Page 79)

Though "Georgia on My Mind" was written by Hoagy Carmichael and Stuart Gorrell in 1930, the song didn't achieve widespread popularity until it was released by Ray Charles, the great R&B singer and Georgia native, in 1960. The song has since been covered to excellent effect by artists ranging from the country legend Willie Nelson to the jazz saxophonist Gerald Albright, and in 1979 it became the official state song of Georgia. Though it's packed with jazzy chords, our arrangement will put this peach of a song well within your grasp.

TECHNICAL STUFF

"Georgia on My Mind" achieves a jazzy flavor through the extensive use of *dominant seventh* chords. Symbolized by a 7 after a note name (the root, or lowest note of the chord), a dominant seventh chord is a major triad with a lowered seventh. An A7 chord, for instance, is spelled A-C♯-E-G and D7, D-F♯-A-C. To get a sense of what a big difference the seventh makes, play these two chords without the 7th notes, and you'll hear that the basic triads sound relatively plain.

God Only Knows (Page 84)

"God Only Knows" might be one of the Beach Boys' greatest hits, but when it was released in 1966, the song barely registered on the Top 40 charts. This lovely tune is one of the most complex numbers in their catalog, both musically, with its sophisticated harmony, and lyrically, with an emphasis not on the beach, girls, and cars, but on spiritual matters. It's been said that "God Only Knows" took a mere 15 minutes to compose, and with our relaxed arrangement you can be playing the song in about the same amount of time.

TECHNICAL STUFF

Part of what makes the chord progression in "God Only Knows" so interesting is the preponderance of *slash* chords. Normally, the name of a chord symbol is also its root, or lowest note. But in a slash chord, the note to the left of the slash represents the overall chord and the note to the right stands for a pitch other than the root to be played as the lowest note. Slash chords add harmonic color while making for a smooth bass line. For example, you'll see that the second chord in the notation, F/A, comes between two B♭ chords. This means that instead of jumping around the keyboard, the bass notes travel only a short distance, a half step, between the chords.

Heart and Soul (Page 88)

Composed in 1938 by Frank Loesser and Hoagy Carmichael, "Heart and Soul" was one of the biggest hits of 1939, with three different versions charting at once, by the singers Larry Clinton (#1), Eddy Duchin (#12), and Al Donahue (#16). The song has since received many different treatments, from an R&B reading by the Cleftones to a rock-inflected version by Jan and Dean, and it has been used in many advertisements as well, including a recent spot for the iPad Mini. The original 1938 version is the source for our arrangement of this great American standard.

CHAMPION STRATEGY

Like so many songs in the Great American Songbook, "Heart and Soul" is based on the 32-bar AABA form, in which each section (A and B) is eight bars long. This means that once you've learned the A section, you've essentially learned three-quarters of the song! Starting on the second page of music, see if you can identify the A and B sections, then isolate the first A section before learning the B section. After that, it should be easy to put the whole song together. You can apply this strategy to any piece of music you learn: being aware of the structure can help you tackle new songs with greater efficiency.

Hey, Soul Sister *(Page 92)*

"Hey, Soul Sister" (2009) is a catchy mid-tempo song, powered by an irresistible ukulele part, by the American rock band Train. The lead single from Train's fifth album, *Save Me, San Francisco*, the song is their biggest hit to date, having been the top-selling song on iTunes in 2010, and achieving six-time platinum status (selling six million copies) in 2012. It has also enjoyed great exposure on television, having been heard in shows like *CSI: NY* and *Glee*.

At times, the notation to "Hey, Soul Sister" has multiple layers of rhythmic activity in the same hand. For instance, in bar 2, a whole-note D is held beneath a more active melody on top; in bar 3, a G sits above the E-based bass line. If you experience any difficulties in learning the song, feel free to strip away some of the layers, focusing on a skeletal version of our arrangement before adding the missing parts. In doing so, remember to take things slowly enough to ensure you can play with rhythmic accuracy.

I Have a Dream *(Page 96)*

Another great song by ABBA, "I Have a Dream" (1979) is a song of hope in which the Swedish group's already impressive wall of vocal harmony is bolstered by a large children's choir in the final chorus. While this moving song reached #1 in Austria, Belgium, Switzerland, and the Netherlands, it didn't chart in the U.S. Curiously, it was not released in this country. However, a 1981 version by the country-gospel singer Cristy Lane took the song to #17 on the U.S. Country Singles chart, proving that the song is powerful in any type of setting.

"I Have a Dream" is played in the easy key of C, without any accidentals, and with pretty straightforward rhythms in a relaxed tempo, so it should be a breeze for you to learn this song. Though only one dynamic marking, *mf* (mezzo-forte, or moderately loud) is indicated in the notation, "I Have a Dream" is an expressive number that is a good platform for adding your own dynamics. Try playing loudly and softly as you see fit, and strive for a smoothly flowing performance throughout, especially with the left-hand arpeggios, which could become mechanical-sounding without careful attention.

I Heard It Through the Grapevine *(Page 116)*

Originally recorded by Smokey Robinson & the Miracles in 1966, the Motown song "I Heard It Through the Grapevine" was initially rejected for release. Instead, a version by Gladys Knight & the Pips was released in 1967, climbing to #2 on the *Billboard* chart. But it was Marvin Gaye's version, released in 1968, that made "I Heard it Through the Grapevine" a certifiable R&B classic. It might be the song's propulsive bass line, smooth strings, and sweet background vocals that help make Gaye's rendition sound so good, but our version captures the essence while being highly playable on the piano.

As you're likely aware, Motown is all about the groove. And the groove on this song came through the lines laid down by the house bassist James Jamerson. So, in preparation for learning "I Heard It Through the Grapevine," it would be a good idea to listen to the original recording, really honing in on the feel of the bass as you work on the left-hand part. Even though our version is simplified, this will help you lock in with the groove, enabling you to play more soulfully when you put together both hands as a piano solo.

If I Were a Carpenter (Page 119)

In the mid-1960s, in the middle of the British Invasion, the focus was on sounds from the UK. At the time, the American pop singer Bobby Darin was experiencing a dry spell, without a hit record in several years. His luck changed when he recorded "If I Were a Carpenter," the 1966 song by the folk musician Tim Hardin. The song went to #8 on the U.S. charts, and Darin returned the favor by writing "Simple Song of Freedom," which became a Top 10 hit for Hardin. "If I Were a Carpenter" has been covered by heavyweight musicians like Johnny Cash and Led Zeppelin's leader, Robert Plant, and now you, too, can play this lovely song with our piano arrangement.

TIP

"If I Were a Carpenter" is arranged here in the key of E♭ major, which uses three flats: B♭, E♭, and A♭. This is one of the more challenging keys in this book, and to help get it under your fingers you might first begin by playing the E♭ major scale: E♭-F-G-A♭-B♭-C-D-E♭ in each hand. When learning the song, always look ahead for the accidentals D♭ and C♭. C♭ is *enharmonic* (equivalent in pitch) to the note B-natural. Isolate any problematic areas of the song, repeating them until you can play them easily before proceeding.

Just the Way You Are (Page 122)

Not to be confused with the Billy Joel song of the same name, "Just the Way You Are" is the debut single by the singer Bruno Mars. Though the tune is only a few years old, it is one of the best-selling singles of all time, already having sold more than 12.5 million copies worldwide. "Just the Way You Are," with its simple structure and direct message, owes a clear debt to songs like Joe Cocker's "You Are So Beautiful" and Eric Clapton's "Wonderful Tonight." As such, it translates nicely to the solo piano format, as you'll see in our arrangement.

CHAMPION STRATEGY #1

"Just the Way You Are" has a particularly easy bass line, consisting of the most basic note values, mostly whole, half, and quarter notes. The right hand contains a fair amount of *syncopation,* or offbeat rhythms, and is not quite as straightforward. So, in learning the song you might want to first isolate the right-hand part before playing hands together. Take things slowly, paying close attention to the rhythmic placement of each note and keeping a hip-hop beat in mind as you play, with strong accents on beats 2 and 4. Then, work the song up to its full moderate tempo.

Layla (Page 130)

Written by Eric Clapton and Jim Gordon, and originally released by their blues-rock band, Derek and the Dominoes in 1971, "Layla" is one of rock's greatest love songs. While the title of the song is inspired by *Layla and Majnun*, a work by the 12th-century Persian poet Nizami Ganjavi, the muse behind the tune is Patti Boyd, who first married The Beatles' George Harrison and then Eric Clapton. Unlike the typical rock song, "Layla" includes two discrete movements, each with a great riff, the signature opening guitar part and the piano-based outro. You'll be playing both parts in no time with our easy arrangement.

CAUTION!

Before you play through the music, be aware that "Layla" has a number of key changes. It starts in G minor, moves down a half step to F♯ minor for the verses, then back to G minor for the chorus and finally to F major for the outro. Look through the song to spot each of these changes; you might even use a highlighter to make them more noticeable. While "Layla" is in 4/4 time, the very first measure has only one and a half beats. This is not a typo; rather, the song begins with a *pick-up*, or incomplete measure, coming in on the "and" of beat 3. Heads up, too, on the quick time signature changes, and take care to maintain a steady beat during these transitions.

Leaving on a Jet Plane (Page 127)

"Leaving on a Jet Plane," a bittersweet song about having to leave a loved one behind, was a huge hit for the folk trio Peter, Paul & Mary in 1967. Originally titled "Babe, I Hate to Go," the song was written a year earlier by a young John Denver, then in the Chad Mitchell Trio and yet to embark on his solo career. While the vocal harmonies are really what make Peter, Paul & Mary's version shine, the bones of the piece, a wistful melody propped up by a plain but sturdy chord progression, are rather satisfying to play as a simplified piano arrangement.

TIP

"Leaving on a Jet Plane," is in the key of G major. With no accidentals and simple rhythms, it shouldn't pose any great difficulties on the piano, but the music can sound lifeless if attention is not paid to phrasing. Sing the lyrics as you play through the piece, and try to channel the story with your fingers. Make sure that individual vocal phrases are played with a bit of separation, and for the *melismatic* bits (the same vocal syllable assigned to more than one pitch), as indicated by the *slurs* (curved lines connecting a series of notes), see to it that the indicated notes blend seamlessly together.

Let It Be (Page 134)

It's commonly assumed that The Beatles' "Let It Be," which makes reference to a "Mother Mary," is a religious song. However, the Mary in question happens to be Paul McCartney's own mother, who died when Paul was 14. In a dream McCartney had as an adult he was reunited with his mother, who told him, "It will be all right, just let it be." This idea received a piano treatment, and one of the most memorable songs in The Beatles' catalog, in fact in all of popular music history, was born.

TECHNICAL STUFF

The notation used in "Let It Be" might contain a few symbols that are unfamiliar to you. Here are some quick explanations: On the last page of music, in the seventh bar, the squiggly vertical line calls for the notes to be rolled in rapid succession; play the G just slightly ahead of the E. In the last three bars, the diagonal lines indicate that the right hand should travel between the treble and bass clefs; be sure to observe the suggested fingering for the smoothest performance here. Then, on the last chord of the piece, the semicircles with dots [𝄐] are *fermata* markings, which indicate to hold the notes longer than notated, at your discretion.

Love Story (Page 141)

"Love Story" is another great country-pop confection by the singer-songwriter Taylor Swift. Like many of Swift's pieces, the song has a strong narrative; channeling *Romeo and Juliet*, it tells the tale of a love interest who was not viewed kindly by friends and family. "Love Story," which has sold over eight million copies worldwide, has proven to be a resounding commercial success, in fact one of the best-selling singles of all time. With its gently rolling arpeggios, the song is perfectly suited for our piano arrangement.

TECHNICAL STUFF

While the chord progression is fairly basic, "Love Story" contains some colorful harmonies that help add wistfulness to the proceedings. For instance, at the end of the first page, instead of a plain old B♭ chord (B♭-D-F), there's a B♭sus2 (suspended second), essentially a B♭ chord in which the third (D) has been replaced by the second (C). To best appreciate the sound of the sus chord, spend a moment playing and comparing it to the B♭ chord. Similarly, at the first ending, check out the F(add9) chord, which adds the ninth (G) to an F chord (F-A-C), making the music a little more poignant.

Maybe I'm Amazed (Page 138)

Paul McCartney wrote "Maybe I'm Amazed" in 1969, shortly before The Beatles broke up, later dedicating the song to his wife, Linda McCartney, who really helped get him through the disbandment. The song, featuring Paul on lead vocals, guitar, bass, piano, organ, and drums, and Linda on background vocals, was first released on the 1970 album *McCartney*, and in 1976 it was heard as a live single by the McCartney's husband-and-wife band, Wings. "Maybe I'm Amazed," which ranks not just as one of McCartney's greatest love songs but as one of the best rock songs of all time, remains a centerpiece of his concerts to this day.

The melody of "Maybe I'm Amazed" sounds conversational due to its syncopated 16th-note rhythms — note values that might prove a little challenging to some and which cannot be fudged. If you fall into this category, then it would serve you well to isolate the right-hand part and focus on the rhythms, at first simply tapping them or playing them on a single note. Subdivide if needed. (For more on this, see the notes for "The Climb.") Don't take any shortcuts on this critical step; make sure that you have absolutely nailed those right-hand rhythms before moving forward with the song.

Moon River (Page 148)

Written by Johnny Mercer and Henry Mancini, "Moon River" just might be the only song in pop history that has had a river named after it. The song, which was inspired by Mercer's formative experiences in the American South, made its debut in the 1961 film *Breakfast at Tiffany's* sung by the lead actress, Audrey Hepburn. Television's Andy Williams was so fond of the song that he sang the first eight bars as an intro to his variety show, and many artists ranging from the jazz legend Louis Armstrong to the indie rock group R.E.M. have also made it their own. You can do the same with our arrangement.

Here's something to notice right off the bat. Be aware that in the first four bars of the song and also in the last two measures of the first ending, both hands play notes written in the treble clef. Written in 3/4, the song is a classic *waltz,* a dance rhythm with three quarter notes per bar. Play with a slight emphasis on the first beat of each measure, and count, "one, two, three" throughout. Imagine that you're playing the song for a group of dancers. A final small detail: In the third bar from the end, you'll see the indication *dim. e rit.* (*diminuendo* and *ritardando*), calling for you to play the music more quietly and slowly as you bring the piece to a close.

The Pink Panther (Page 151)

Few cartoon themes have proven as successful with children and adults alike as "The Pink Panther," from the movie of the same name. Henry Mancini wrote this instrumental piece for the 1963 film, and when it was released the following year as a single, it hit the Top 10 on *Billboard*'s Adult Contemporary chart and received an Academy Award nomination as well as three GRAMMY awards. As you'll soon find out, the jazzy theme, which evokes a panther slinking around, feels great under the fingers on the piano.

"The Pink Panther" kicks off with both hands in the bass clef. This, in conjunction with a bunch of *chromatic* notes, those outside of the composition's key, E minor, gives the music a fittingly mysterious air. Throughout, the piece makes excellent use of rests. For example, the dotted eighth-note rests in the treble clef of the ninth full bar and the quarter-note rests in the bass. Be sure to give all rests their full value and avoid the temptation to rush them, inadvertently throwing off the groove. Remember: When you don't play is often as important as when you do play.

Raindrops Keep Fallin' on My Head (Page 154)

Featured in the 1969 movie *Butch Cassidy and the Sundance Kid*, "Raindrops Keep Fallin' on My Head" is one of the greatest hits from the songwriting team of Hal David and Burt Bacharach. The song was a #1 hit internationally for the singer who recorded it, B. J. Thomas, and it has made a number of notable other movie and television appearances, in *Forrest Gump*, *Spider-Man 2*, and *The Simpsons*, among other settings. The song's signature jaunty ukulele strumming is captured nicely here in our piano arrangement.

"Raindrops Keep Fallin' on My Head" has a sophisticated sound thanks to its use of jazzy harmonies, in particular, *seventh* chords. For example, in the fourth bar you'll find an Fmaj7 (major seventh) chord, which is an F triad (F-A-C) with the addition of the major seventh (E), which lends a winsome sound. Three bars later marks the appearance of an Am7 (minor seventh) chord, an A minor triad (A-C-E) with the minor seventh (G), imparting a soulful flavor. To best appreciate these seventh chords, take a moment to compare them to the basic triads, and let their sounds resonate in your ears.

Rolling in the Deep (Page 164)

In 2010, the British singer-songwriter Adele achieved a commercial and artistic breakthrough with the single "Rolling in the Deep," from her second studio album, *21*. The song, which neatly merges blues, gospel, and disco in a style all its own, reached #1 in eleven countries and sold more than ten million copies around the world; it's the second best-selling digital song ever in the U.S. Try your hand at the highly emotive "Rolling in the Deep" with our adaptation for piano.

It won't be overly difficult for you to put together "Rolling in the Deep;" just look out for those sneaky 16th notes in the right hand, subdividing if required to render them accurately. The left hand, played in steady eighth notes or quarters, is so simple that you may be able to sight read it. Something neat about the bass part is that it borrows from rock-guitar vocabulary (and in fact is an adaptation of the original guitar part). The first pages of the music are packed with what are known as *power chords;* chords containing only roots and fifths, indicated as chord symbols by a root name followed by a 5. As you play through this part, imagine that you are strumming, somewhat aggressively, on a guitar.

Silly Love Songs (Page 157)

The Beatles' Paul McCartney was sometimes taunted for writing songs with fluffy subject matter, and in response, he, with the help of his wife, Linda McCartney, penned the great tune "Silly Love Songs." Released by the group Wings in 1976, the disco-inflected song spent five weeks at #1 on *Billboard*'s Hot 100. It has since been covered by artists ranging from the rock group Red House Painters to the singer Stevie B and was even heard on a Valentine's Day episode of television's *Glee.*

In the fourth measure of "Silly Love Songs" and elsewhere in the notation you'll find *accent* marks, [>] adjacent to the notehead. An accent mark simply calls for you to play the indicated note(s) with a little extra emphasis, but not so much that you're banging on the piano. This will help add expressiveness and rhythmic excitement to your performance of "Silly Love Songs."

Sing *(Page 172)*

The PBS children's television show *Sesame Street* has long been known for its hip music. One of the show's best-loved songs is "Sing," a jazzy song that the Carpenters covered in 1973, making it a big hit among general listening audiences. The song, which was written by *Sesame Street*'s staff songwriter, the late Joe Raposo, has since seen a surprisingly wide range of interpretations, from a hardcore version by the Dutch group Nakatomi to a country-tinged take by the Dixie Chicks. Our version, though, is patterned after the original.

Like much of the fare heard on *Sesame Street,* "Sing" has a lively kid-friendly melody supported by a jazz-inspired progression containing a handful of seventh and ninth chords. So, as you play through it, take the time to appreciate the song's harmonic sophistication. Also, as indicated at the beginning of the song, it is to be played with a Swing feel. Remember, a pair of consecutive eighth notes, like those on beat 2 of the first bar, will be played not evenly as written, but long-short, with a bit of a bounce.

Stardust *(page 180)*

One of the oldest songs in this collection, "Stardust" was composed in 1927 by Hoagy Carmichael, with lyrics added in 1929 by Mitchell Parish. Kind of a song within a song about love, this great American standard is one of the most recorded numbers of the 20th century, with more than 1,500 unique recordings by artists ranging from great vocalists like Frank Sinatra to jazz cats like the pianist Dave Brubeck to country musicians like the legendary Willie Nelson. Our arrangement will give you an easy way to sound like a jazz pianist in a version that sticks closely to the original song.

When playing "Stardust," be sure to observe the little details that can make the difference between a good performance and an inspired one. For example, in bar 16, when you see the *caesura* mark, or two slanted lines, [//] give the music a dramatic pause before playing each of the next three notes, with their *fermata* markings, with a generous duration. Three bars later you'll see that the whole-note chord in the treble clef is to be *rolled* (played quickly from lowest note to highest). Feel free to add this ornament elsewhere as you see fit, even if not indicated in the notation. Then, in the third bar from the end, where you see the indication *rall.*(*rallentando*), begin gradually slowing down until you come to rest on the final chord.

Sway (Quien Será) *(Page 175)*

The classic Latin-inflected song "Sway" is an English adaptation of the 1953 Mambo hit "¿Quién será?" by the Mexican bandleader Pablo Beltrán Ruiz. "Sway" was a big hit for the American singer Dean Martin in 1954, and it has been recorded by an impressive range of other popular artists, from the soul singer Ben E. King to the Canadian vocalist Michael Bublé. In 2010, fans of the TV show *Glee* were treated to a version of "Sway" as performed by the main character, William Schuester.

In our arrangement of "Sway," a good portion of the vocal line is harmonized in thirds, with the main melody falling in the higher notes and the supportive melody in the lower notes. Harmonizing in thirds is a great way to sweeten any melody, as you can hear when isolating the higher notes of the melody before playing the higher and lower notes together. Another thing to consider is that the song is driven by a strong Latin beat, and if this feel is unfamiliar to you, listen to the original version by Dean Martin and perhaps to some assorted selections by bandleaders like Machito and Mario Bauzá, keeping their fiery rhythms in your mind's ear as you play "Sway" on the piano.

Twist and Shout (Page 184)

Originally titled "Shake It Up, Baby," the R&B tune "Twist and Shout" received a number of different recorded interpretations shortly after it was written in 1961, with versions from the Top Notes, the Isley Brothers, and The Beatles. This rock 'n' roll standard has also been a staple of the live shows of some of the biggest names, like the Who and Bruce Springsteen with his E Street Band. And now you can incorporate this great song into your own repertoire with a minimum of fuss, thanks to our streamlined arrangement.

At only two pages long, there isn't a whole lot of music to learn for "Twist and Shout," especially considering that the song is based on a repeating two-bar chord progression of C-F-G. To most efficiently learn the song, begin by learning the left-hand part of the first two bars — a riff, played in thirds, appearing continually until the very last chord of the song. Be sure to follow the suggested fingering, and play with a rock groove, with high energy and a little extra emphasis on beats 2 and 4, while not forgetting to nail that accent on the "and" of beat 4. Make sure that you can play this part impeccably before adding the right hand, which, consisting almost entirely of single notes, will be pretty easy for you to play.

The Way You Look Tonight (Page 186)

"The Way You Look Tonight" was originally heard in the 1936 musical comedy *Swing Time*, as sung by Fred Astaire. One of the great pop and jazz standards, "The Way You Look Tonight" has been recorded by vocal legends like Ella Fitzgerald, Billie Holiday, Frank Sinatra and instrumental heavyweights like the pianists Art Tatum and Oscar Peterson. More recently, the pop band Maroon 5 gave the song an old-school treatment, and so can you with our traditional but easy arrangement.

In the first four bars of the music you'll see a *decrescendo* sign. [>] As indicated, the song begins *f* (*forte*, or loudly), and gradually gets quieter until you reach the closed end of the sign at the end of bar 4. Though no other dynamics are indicated in the notation, you might try experimenting with some of your own. For example, follow the rise and fall of the phrase shape as you sing and play. This will help add an emotional dimension to the song.

We Are the Champions (Page 190)

"We Are the Champions," the power ballad by the British rock band Queen, is celebrated for its anthemic quality — not something that happened after the fact. The composer, Queen's Freddie Mercury, had football chants in mind when he penned the piece. One of Queen's most popular songs, "We Are the Champions" was a smash hit around the world, reaching #4 on the *Billboard* Hot 100 and #2 on the UK Singles chart. It also owns the distinction of having been discovered by a team of researchers to be the catchiest song in the history of pop, and in playing through our arrangement we think you'll not be surprised by this honor.

"We Are the Champions" is played in waltz time. (For more on this meter see the notes to "Moon River.") It starts with the verse, which is a bit subdued and based in the somewhat mournful key of D minor. When the chorus kicks in the song modulates to the brighter key of G major, lending a triumphant effect that helps maintain the listener's interest. To get the most out of this change in tonality, you might try playing the verse in a more pensive way, then getting more exuberant for the chorus, adding subtle dynamic changes within each section as you see fit.

Yellow Submarine (Page 206)

One of the quirkiest numbers in The Beatles' catalog, "Yellow Submarine" is commonly interpreted as containing political and social messages. It was initially conceived as a nonsensical children's story, which is why the lyrics contain short words. The song went to #1 on all the British charts shortly after its 1966 release and #2 on the *Billboard* Hot 100. Part of what makes the original recording so interesting is the use of many special effects, but the song sounds just as fun when played as an easy arrangement for piano.

TIP

While "Yellow Submarine" was originally written in the key of G♭ major, we've arranged it here for you in the much easier key of F major. The song is taken at a moderate March tempo, requiring it be rendered with rhythmic precision. This will not be a difficult task, since most of the note values are very basic. But before you begin, be sure that you can accurately feel the rhythm of a dotted eighth note followed by a 16th note, because this rhythm appears in almost every bar of the treble clef. If need be, take things slowly enough that you can count the piece in 16th notes: "One-ee-and-uh, two-ee-and-uh, etc." A dotted eighth note will always fall squarely on a beat, while the 16th note will fall on the syllable "uh."

You Belong with Me (Page 196)

Taylor Swift received the inspiration for "You Belong with Me," from her second studio album, *Fearless*, after hearing a male friend argue defensively with his girlfriend on the telephone and feeling sympathetic to his position. Peaking at #1 on both the U.S. Adult Contemporary and Country Songs charts, and #2 on the U.S. Hot 100, Pop Songs, and Adult Pop Songs charts, the song has achieved quadruple Platinum status while receiving GRAMMY nominations for Song of the Year, Record of the Year, and Best Female Pop Vocal Performance. Swift's original version is reduced to its essence in our highly playable arrangement.

CHAMPION STRATEGY

While the tempo indication instructs you to play "You Belong with Me" moderately fast, it might be best to take things slowly when learning this song, for while it might seem simple, some of the eighth-note syncopations could potentially throw you off. Try setting a metronome to the very slowest tempo at which you can confidently play the music, gradually increasing your tempo until you can comfortably play the piece at the original tempo. But don't focus just on playing the notes — remember, this is a song of yearning, so regardless of the tempo, play the song with expression.

You Don't Know Me (Page 202)

Written by Cindy Walker and Eddy Arnold, "You Don't Know Me" was first recorded by Arnold and released as a single in 1956. While a version by Jerry Vale peaked at #14 on *Billboard*'s Pop chart that same year, it wasn't until 1962 that the song's best-selling version was released; Ray Charles took it to #2 on the Hot 100 chart that year, having released the song on his #1 album *Modern Sounds in Country and Western Music.* "You Don't Know Me" would subsequently be covered by hundreds of artists, most notably Bob Dylan, Willie Nelson, and Elvis Presley, certifying its status as a golden pop standard.

CHAMPION STRATEGY

"You Don't Know Me" is a slow ballad with the eighth notes played not exactly as written but with a *swing* feel. If this rhythmic style is still elusive for you, try this: set a metronome so that it plays eighth-note triplets (three per beat) at a slow tempo. Count along with the metronome: "One-uh-let, two-uh-let, three-uh-let, four-uh-let," etc., with a syllable coinciding with each click. Now try playing along on the piano. In the treble clef of the first bar, for instance, the first and second eighth notes will fall on the "one" and the "let," respectively. Once you feel comfortable, take off the musical training wheels and see if you can play the swing feel with the metronome set to quarter notes.

I Heard It Through the Grapevine

Words and Music by NORMAN J. WHITFIELD
and BARRETT STRONG

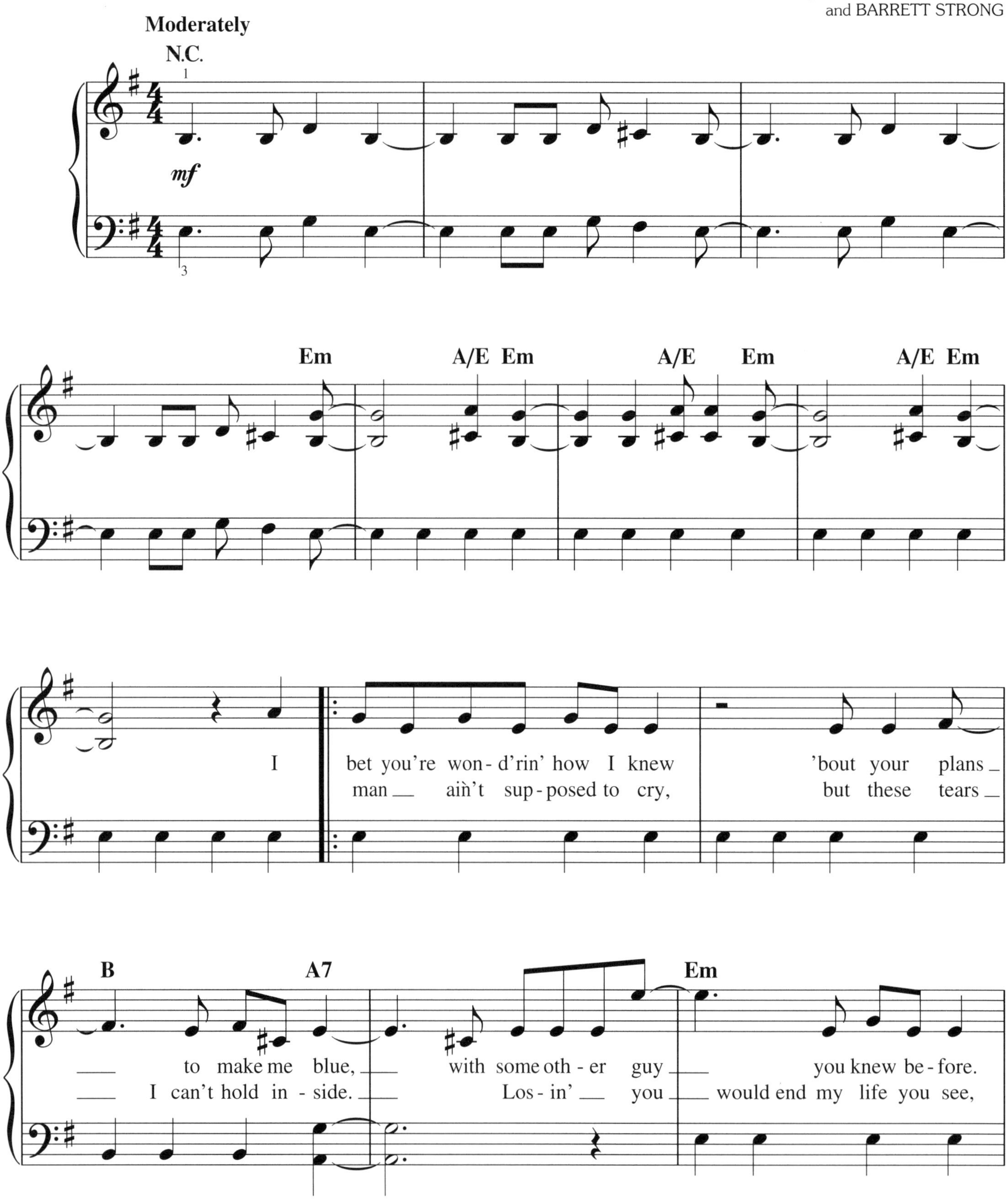

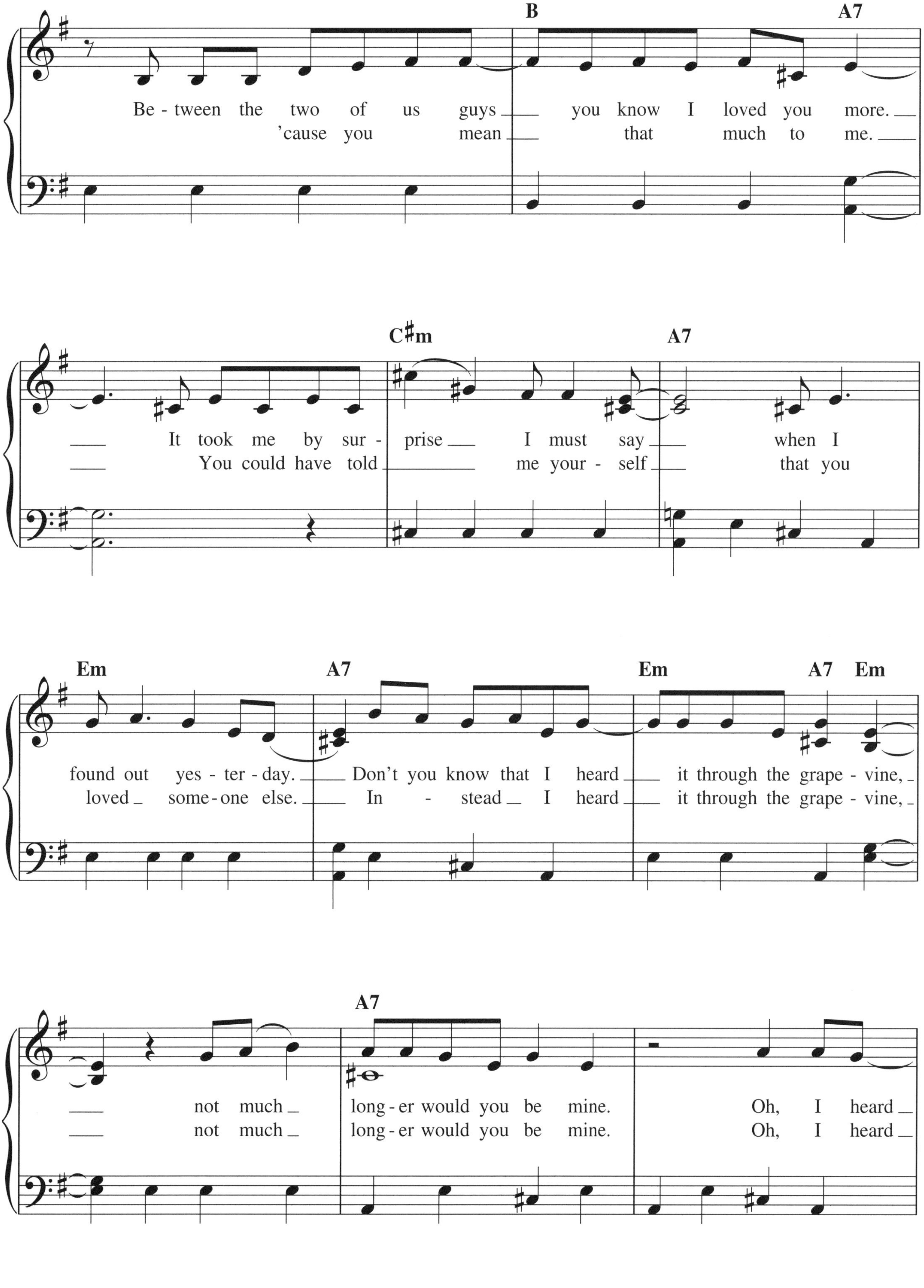
B
A7
Be - tween the two of us guys ___ you know I loved you more. ___
'cause you mean ___ that much to me. ___
C♯m
A7
___ It took me by sur - prise ___ I must say ___ when I
___ You could have told ___ me your - self ___ that you
Em
A7
Em
A7
Em
found out yes - ter - day. ___ Don't you know that I heard ___ it through the grape - vine, _
loved _ some - one else. ___ In - stead _ I heard ___ it through the grape - vine, _
A7
___ not much _ long - er would you be mine. Oh, I heard _
___ not much _ long - er would you be mine. Oh, I heard _

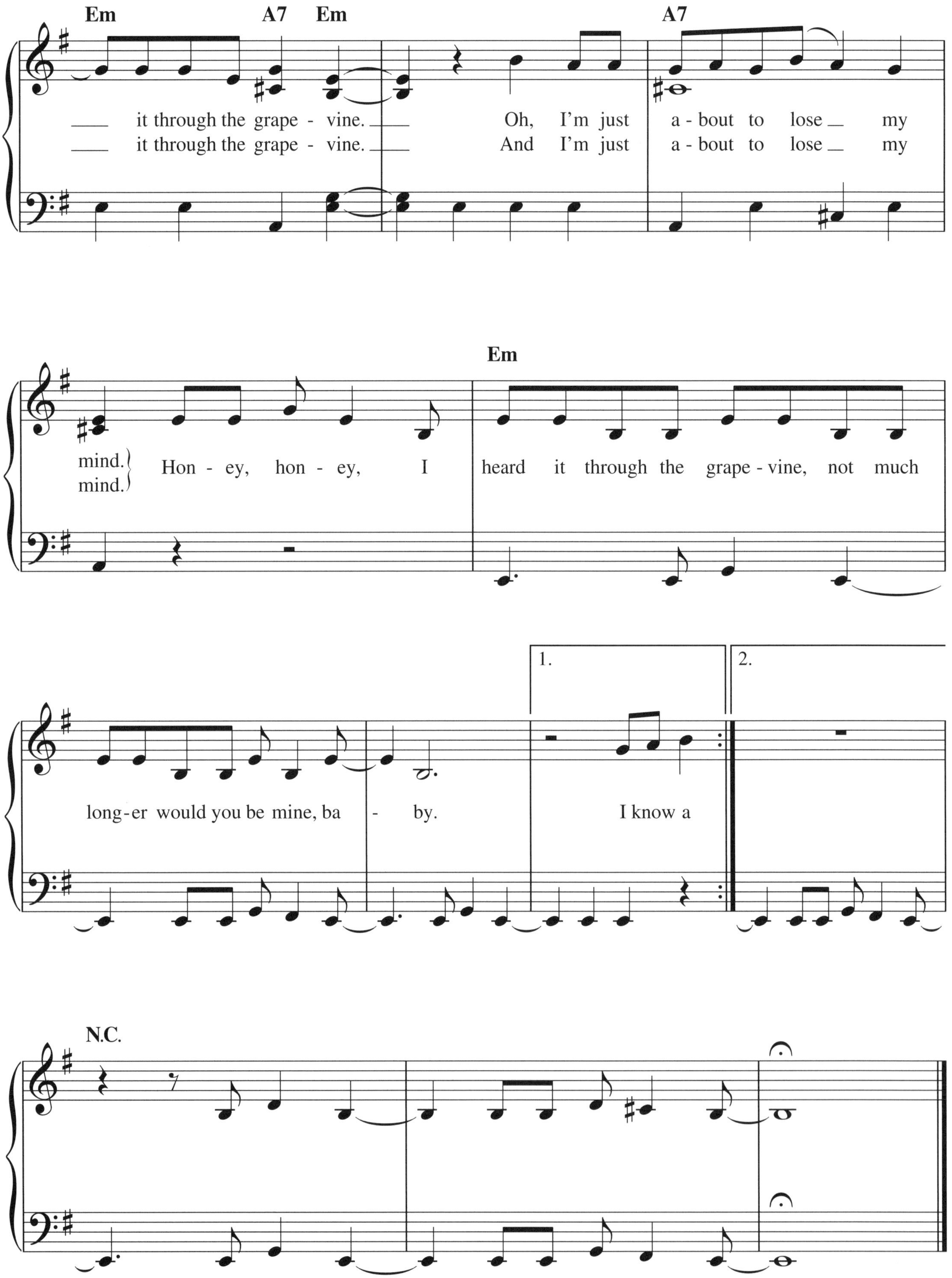
Em
A7
Em
A7
it through the grape - vine. Oh, I'm just a - bout to lose my
it through the grape - vine. And I'm just a - bout to lose my
Em
mind. mind. Hon - ey, hon - ey, I heard it through the grape - vine, not much
1.
2.
long - er would you be mine, ba - by. I know a
N.C.

If I Were a Carpenter

Words and Music by
TIM HARDIN

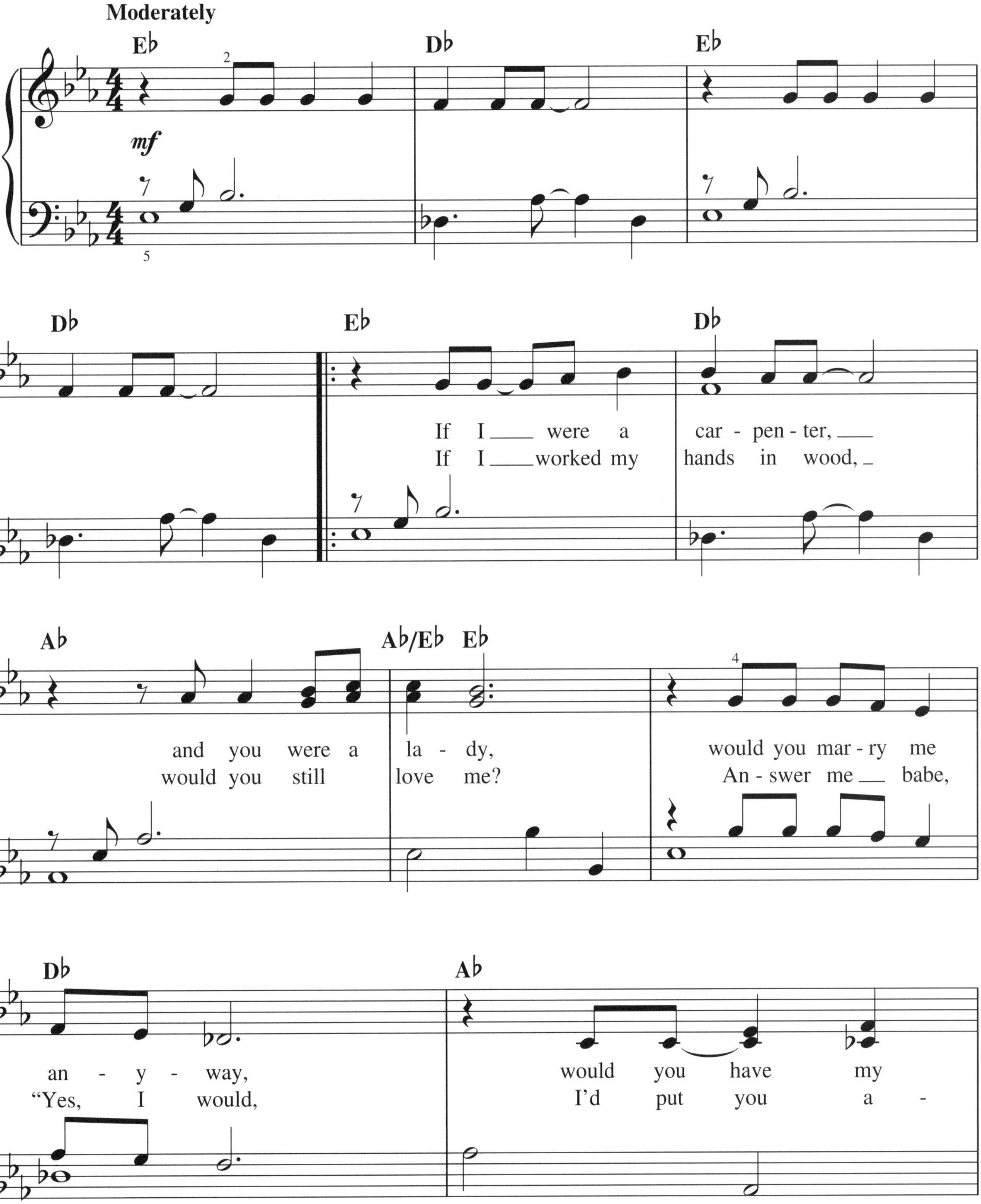
Moderately
Eb
Db
Eb
mf
Db
Eb
Db
If I were a carpenter,
If I worked my hands in wood,
Ab
Ab/Eb
Eb
and you were a lady,
would you still love me?
would you marry me
Answer me babe,
Db
Ab
anyway,
would you have my
"Yes, I would,
I'd put you a-

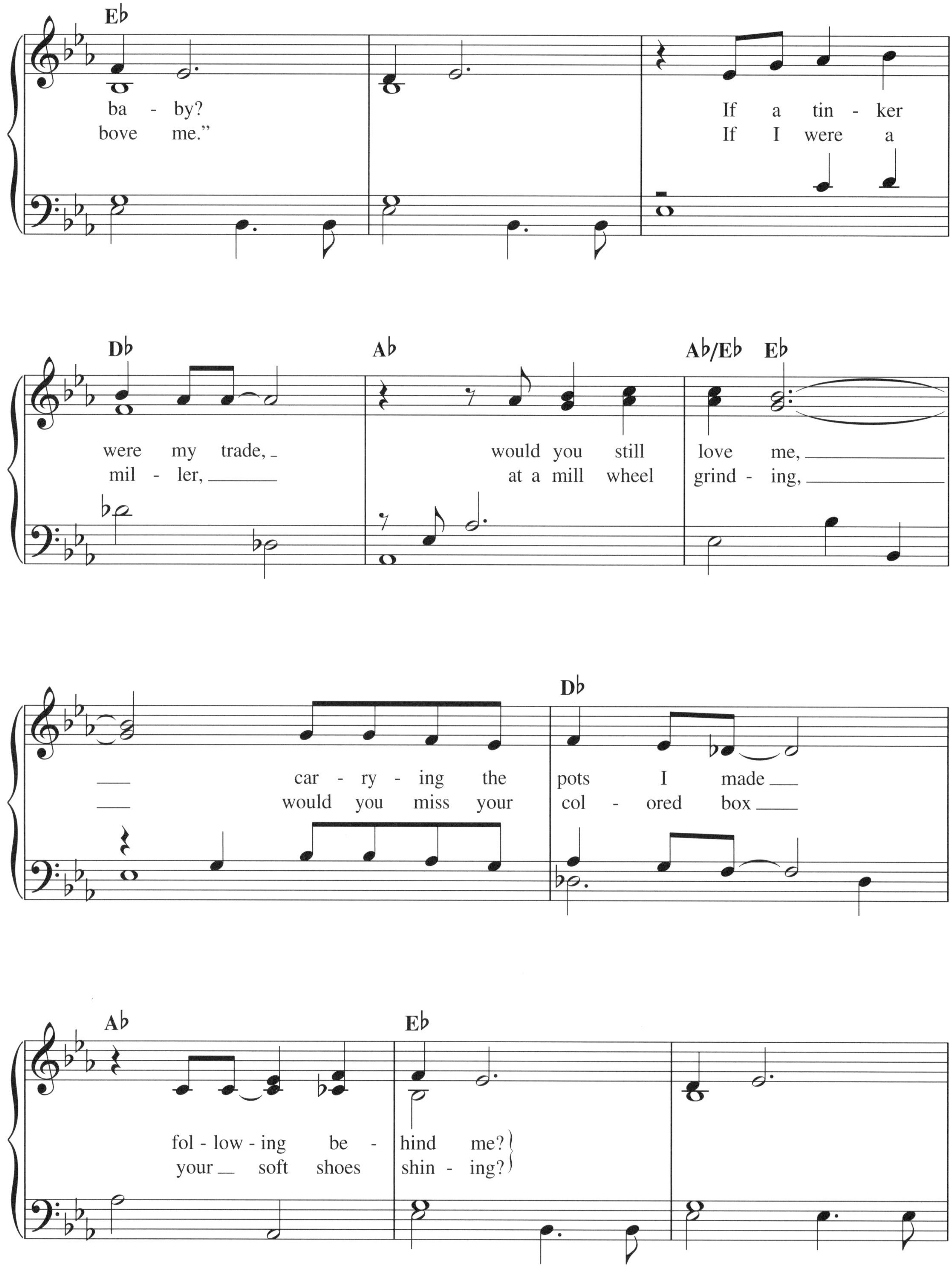
E♭
ba - by?
bove me."
If a tin - ker
If I were a
D♭
A♭
A♭/E♭
E♭
were my trade, _
mil - ler,
would you still
at a mill wheel
love me,
grind - ing,
car - ry - ing the
would you miss your
D♭
pots I made
col - ored box
A♭
E♭
fol - low - ing be - hind me?
your _ soft shoes shin - ing?

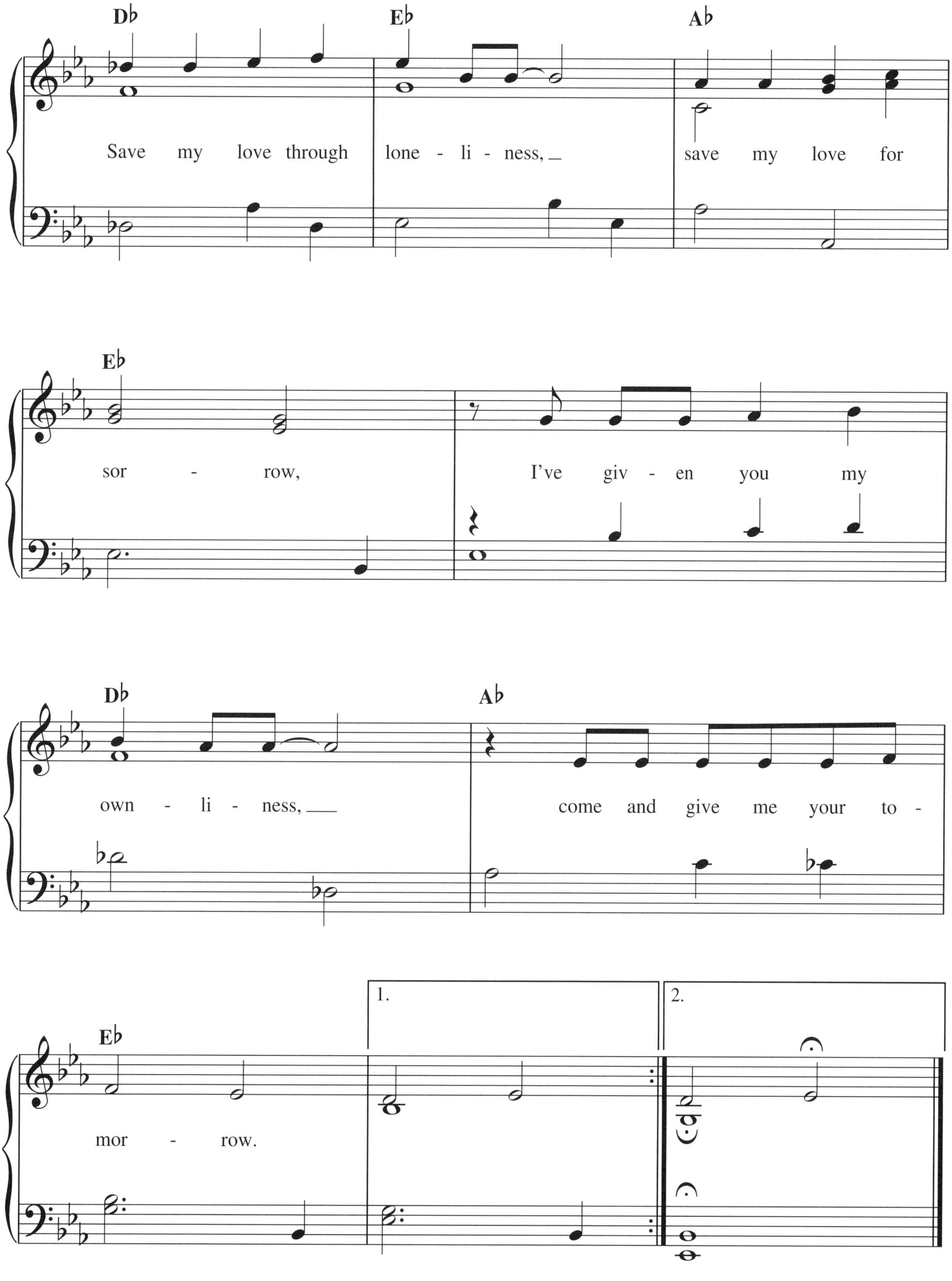
Db
Eb
Ab
Save my love through lone - li - ness, save my love for
Eb
sor - row, I've giv - en you my
Db
Ab
own - li - ness, come and give me your to -
Eb
mor - row.
1.
2.

Just the Way You Are

Words and Music by BRUNO MARS,
ARI LEVINE, PHILIP LAWRENCE,
KHARI CAIN and KHALIL WALTON

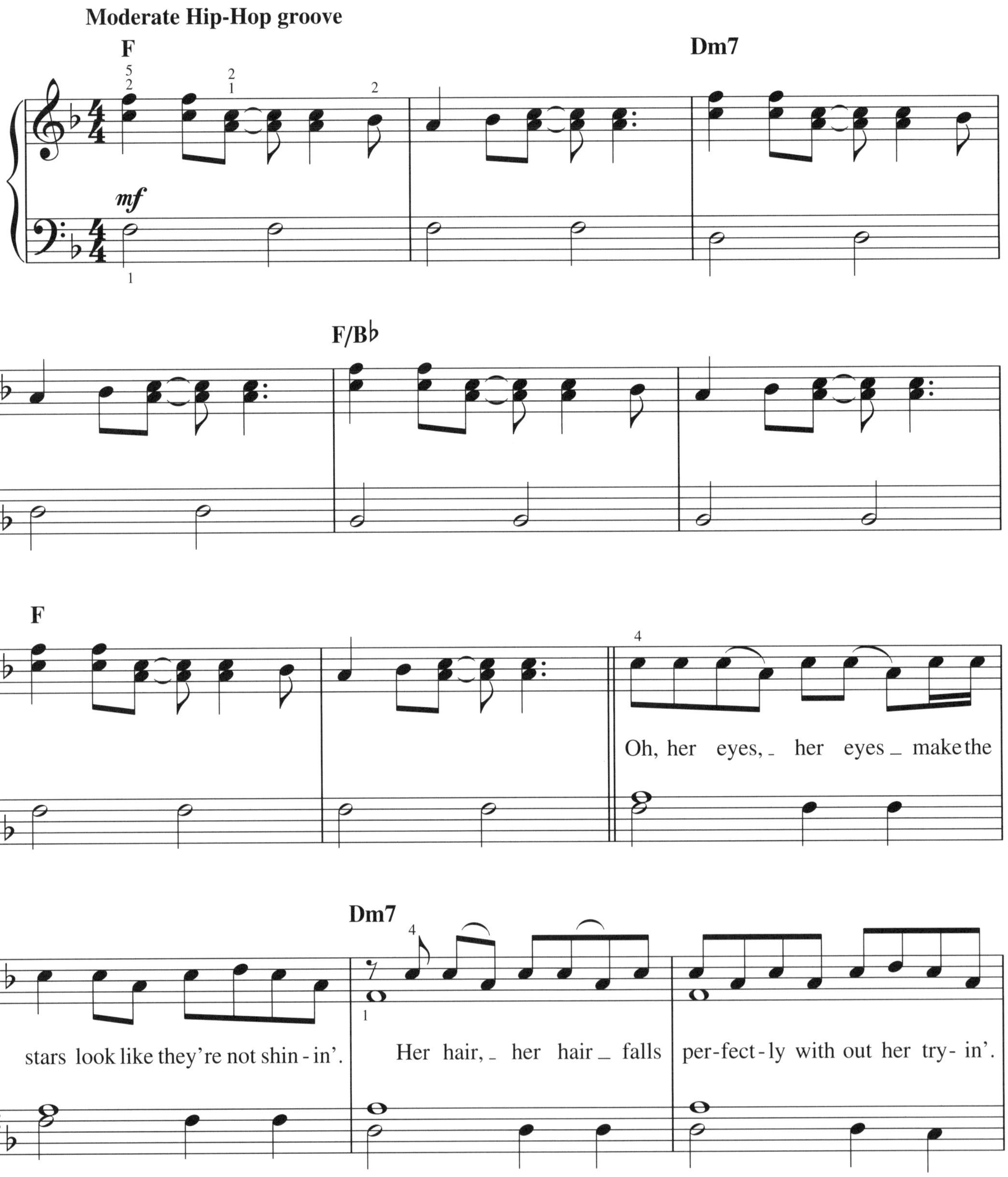

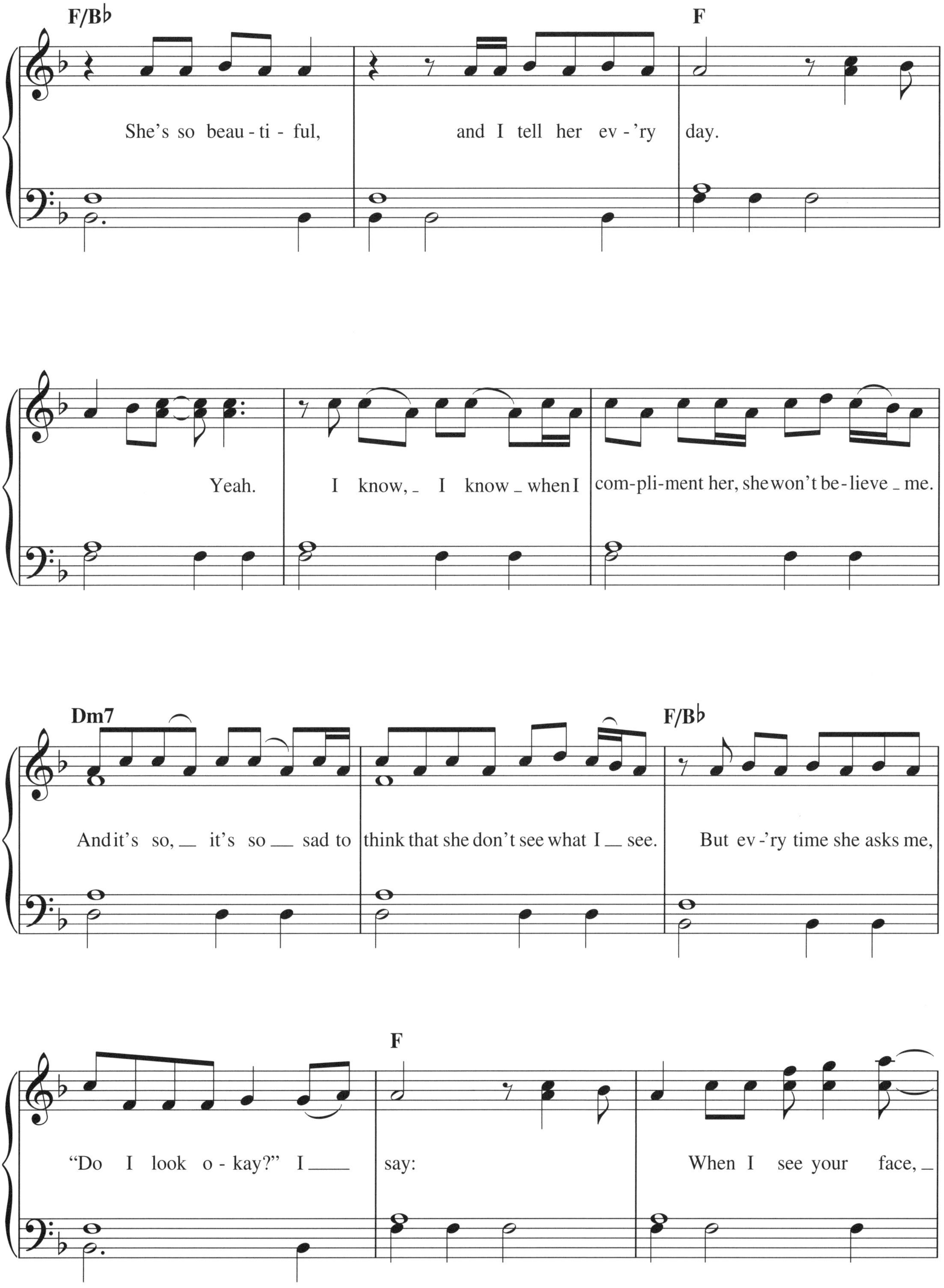
F/B♭
She's so beau - ti - ful, and I tell her ev - 'ry
F
day.
Yeah. I know, I know when I com-pli-ment her, she won't be-lieve me.
Dm7
And it's so, it's so sad to think that she don't see what I see.
F/B♭
But ev-'ry time she asks me,
"Do I look o - kay?" I
F
say:
When I see your face,

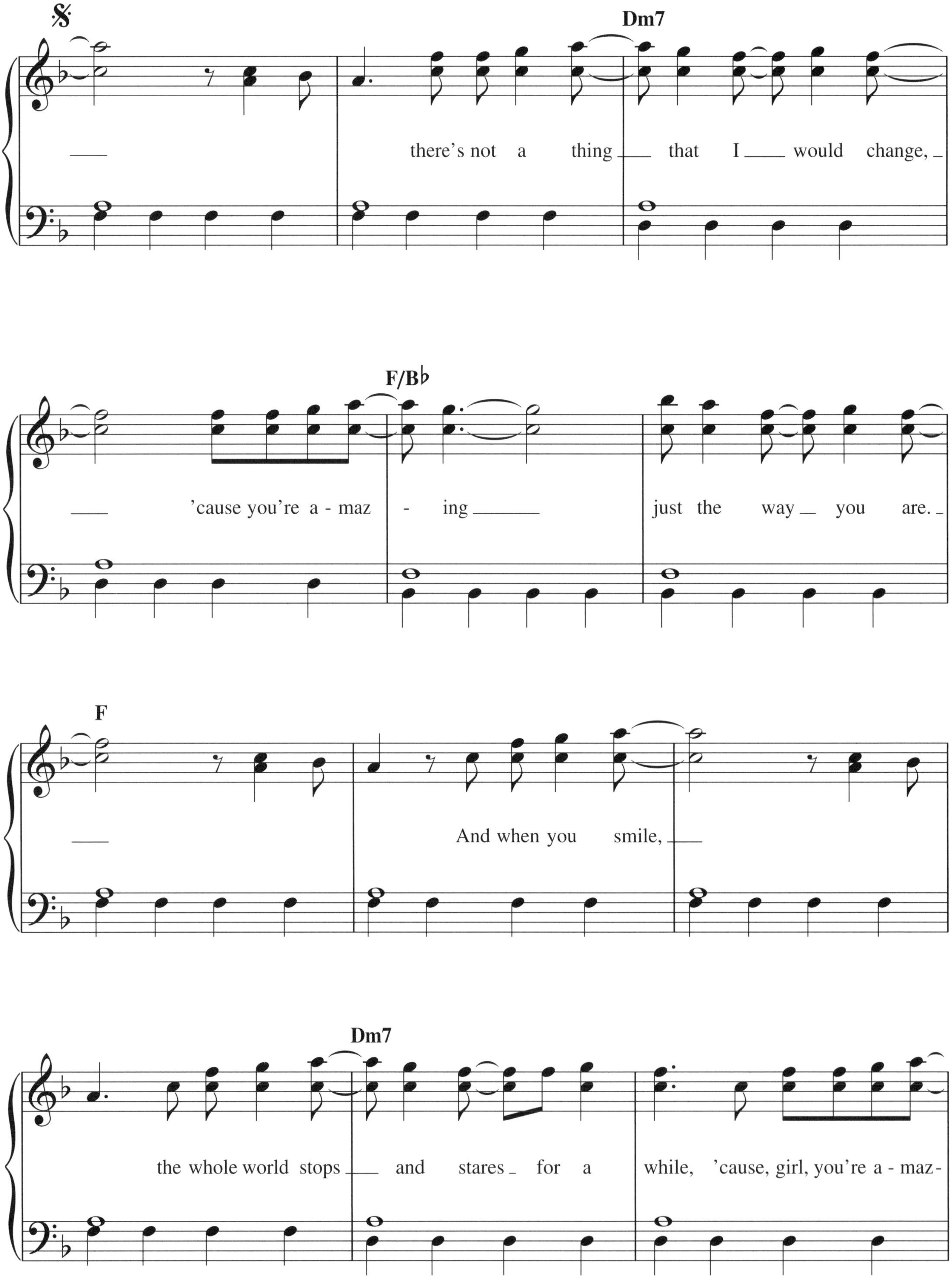
Dm7
there's not a thing that I would change,
F/B♭
'cause you're a - maz - ing
just the way you are.
F
And when you smile,
Dm7
the whole world stops and stares for a
while, 'cause, girl, you're a - maz-

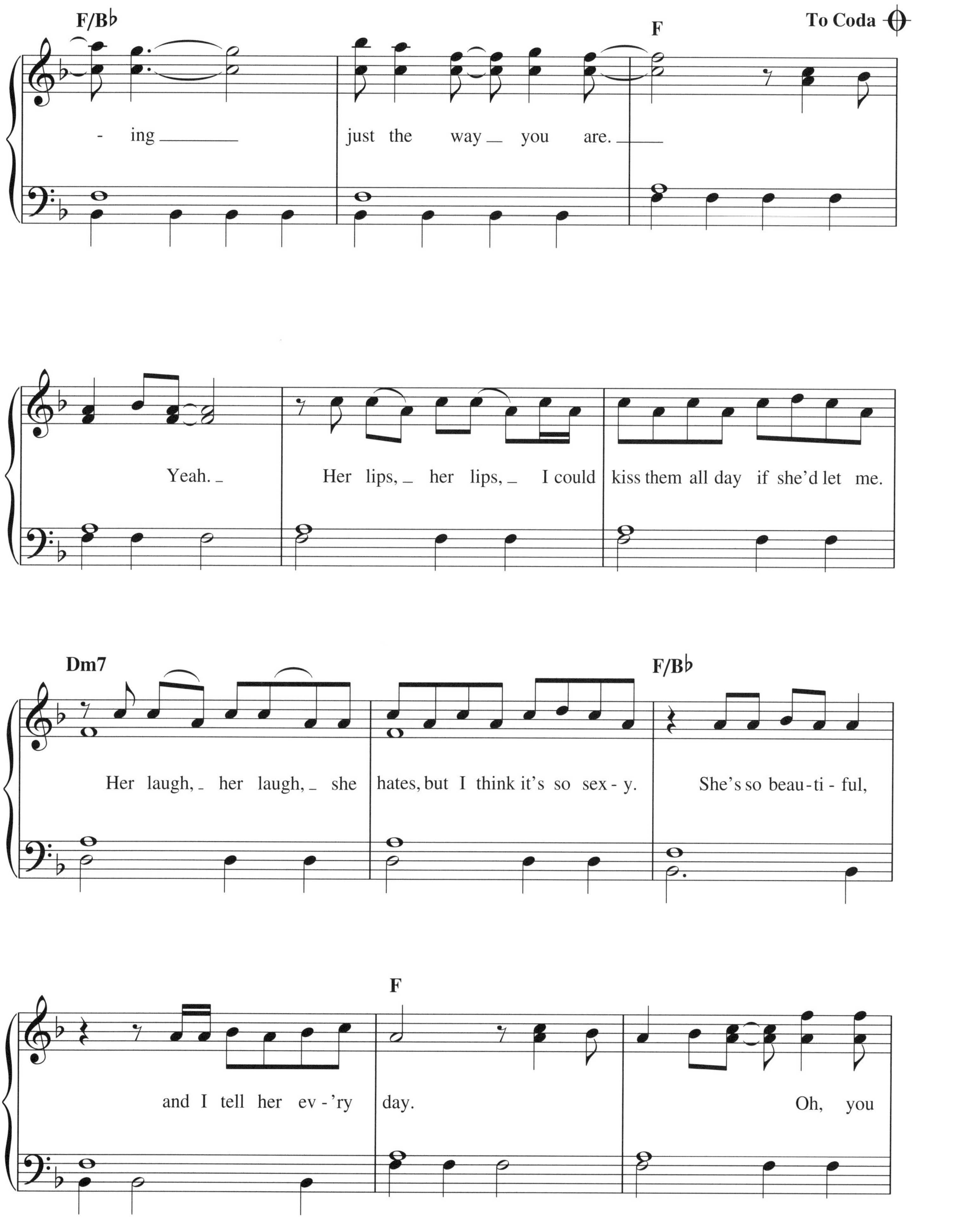
F/B♭
F
To Coda
- ing
just the way you are.
Yeah.
Her lips, her lips, I could
kiss them all day if she'd let me.
Dm7
F/B♭
Her laugh, her laugh, she
hates, but I think it's so sex - y.
She's so beau - ti - ful,
F
and I tell her ev - 'ry
day.
Oh, you

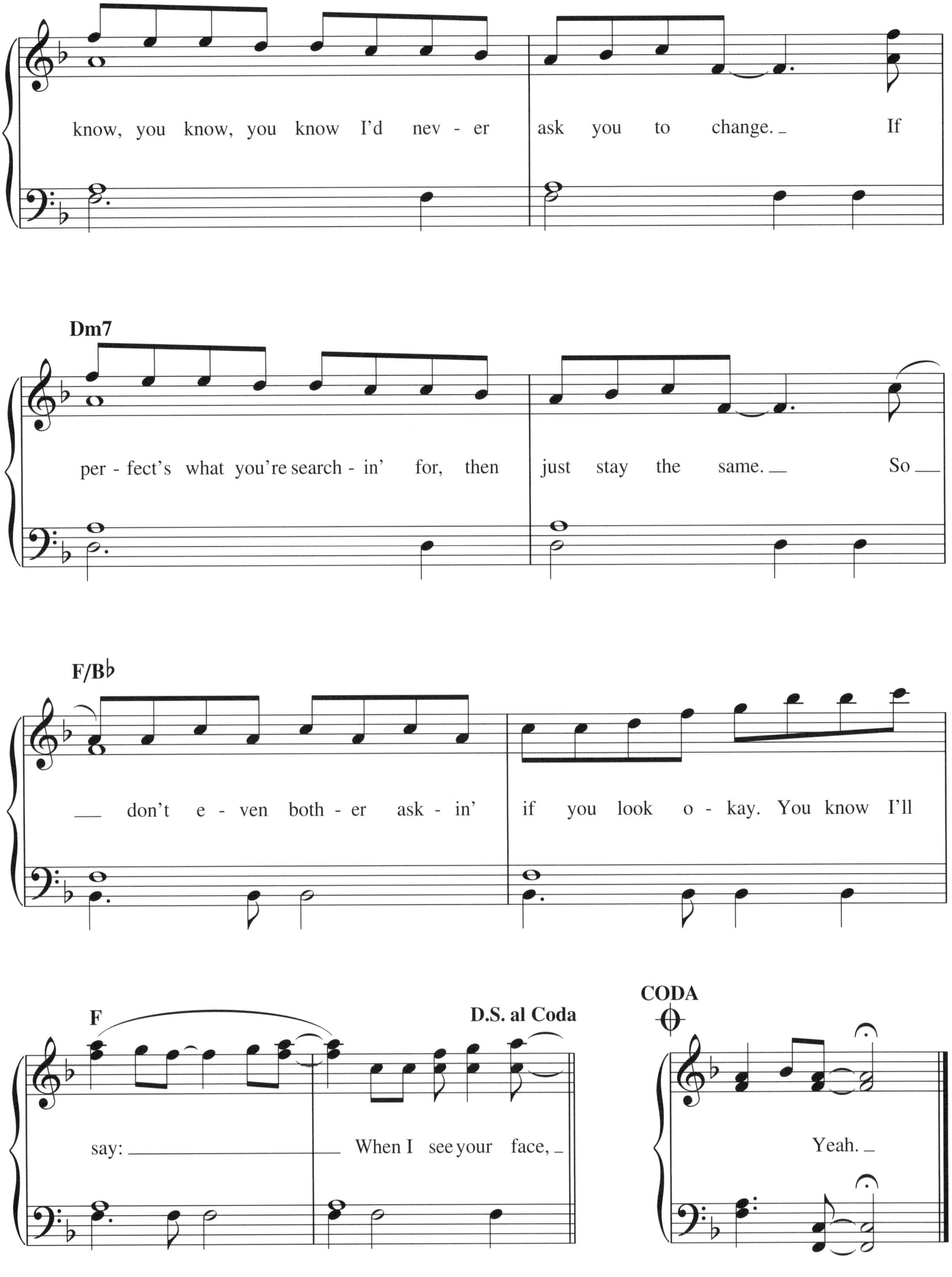
know, you know, you know I'd nev - er ask you to change. If
Dm7
per - fect's what you're search - in' for, then just stay the same. So
F/B♭
don't e - ven both - er ask - in' if you look o - kay. You know I'll
F
D.S. al Coda
say: When I see your face,
CODA
Yeah.

Leaving on a Jet Plane

Words and Music by
JOHN DENVER

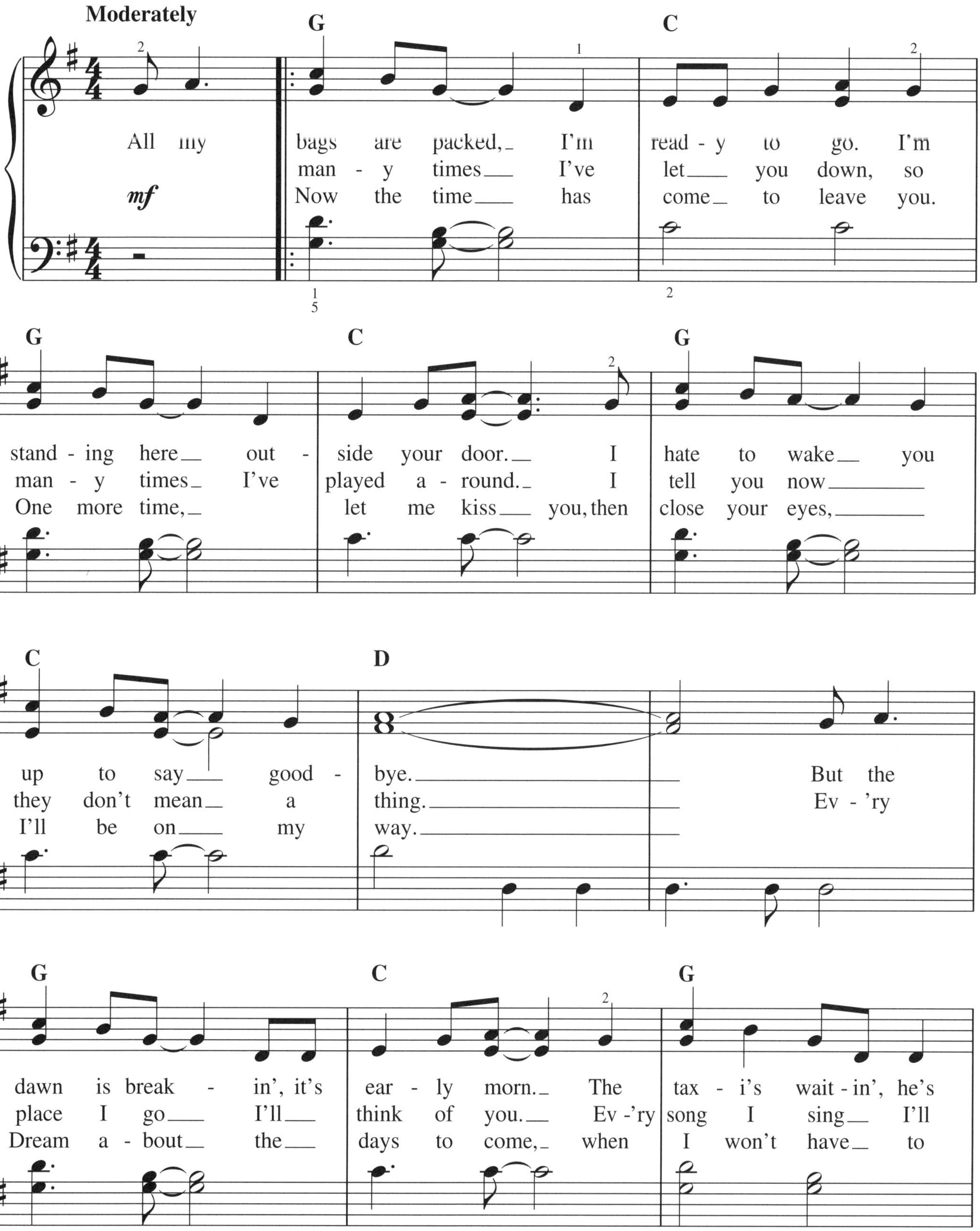

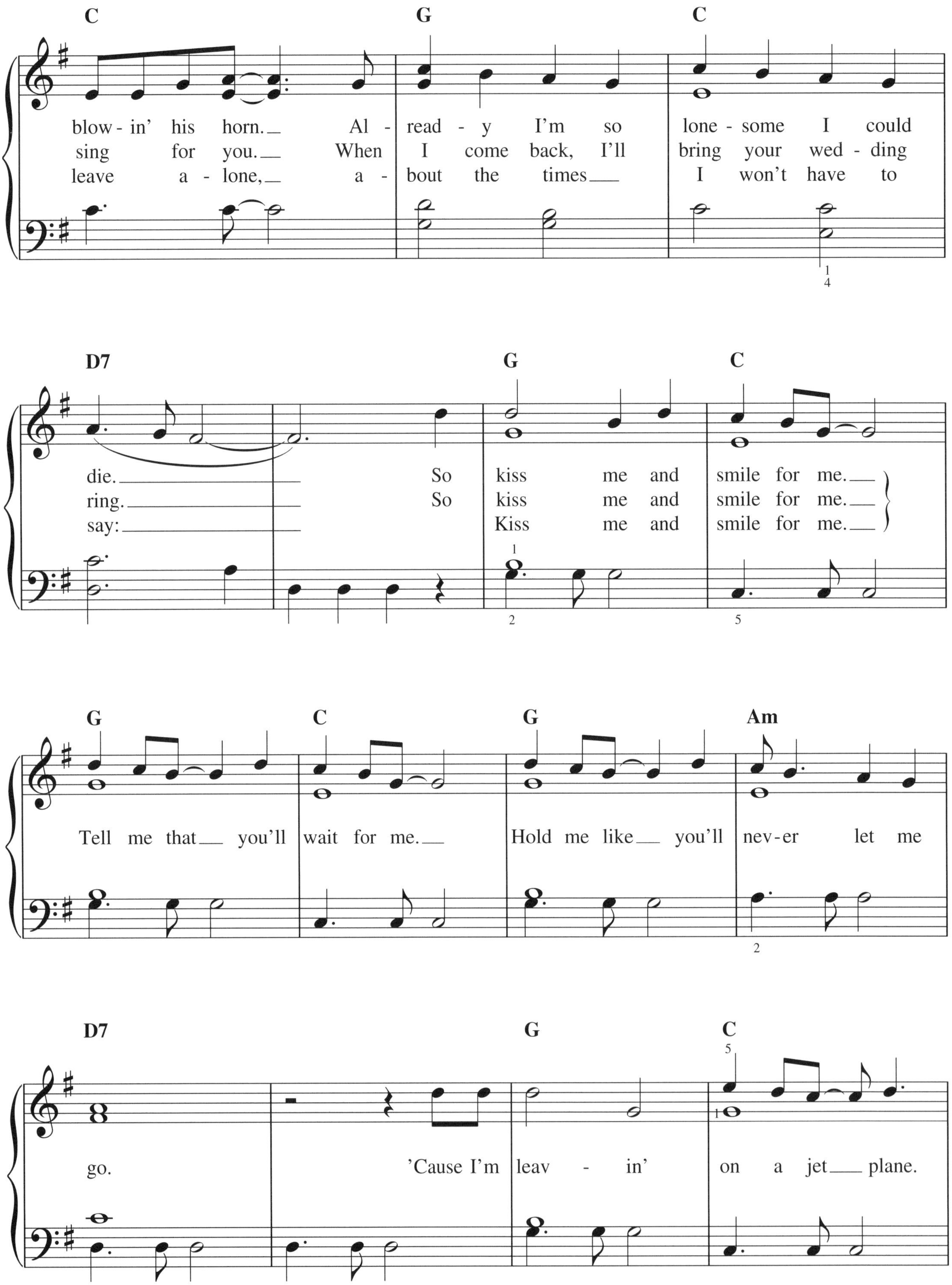
C
G
C
blow - in' his horn. Al - read - y I'm so lone - some I could
sing for you. When I come back, I'll bring your wed - ding
leave a - lone, a - bout the times I won't have to
D7
G
C
die. So kiss me and smile for me.
ring. So kiss me and smile for me.
say: Kiss me and smile for me.
G
C
G
Am
Tell me that you'll wait for me. Hold me like you'll nev-er let me
D7
G
C
go. 'Cause I'm leav - in' on a jet plane.

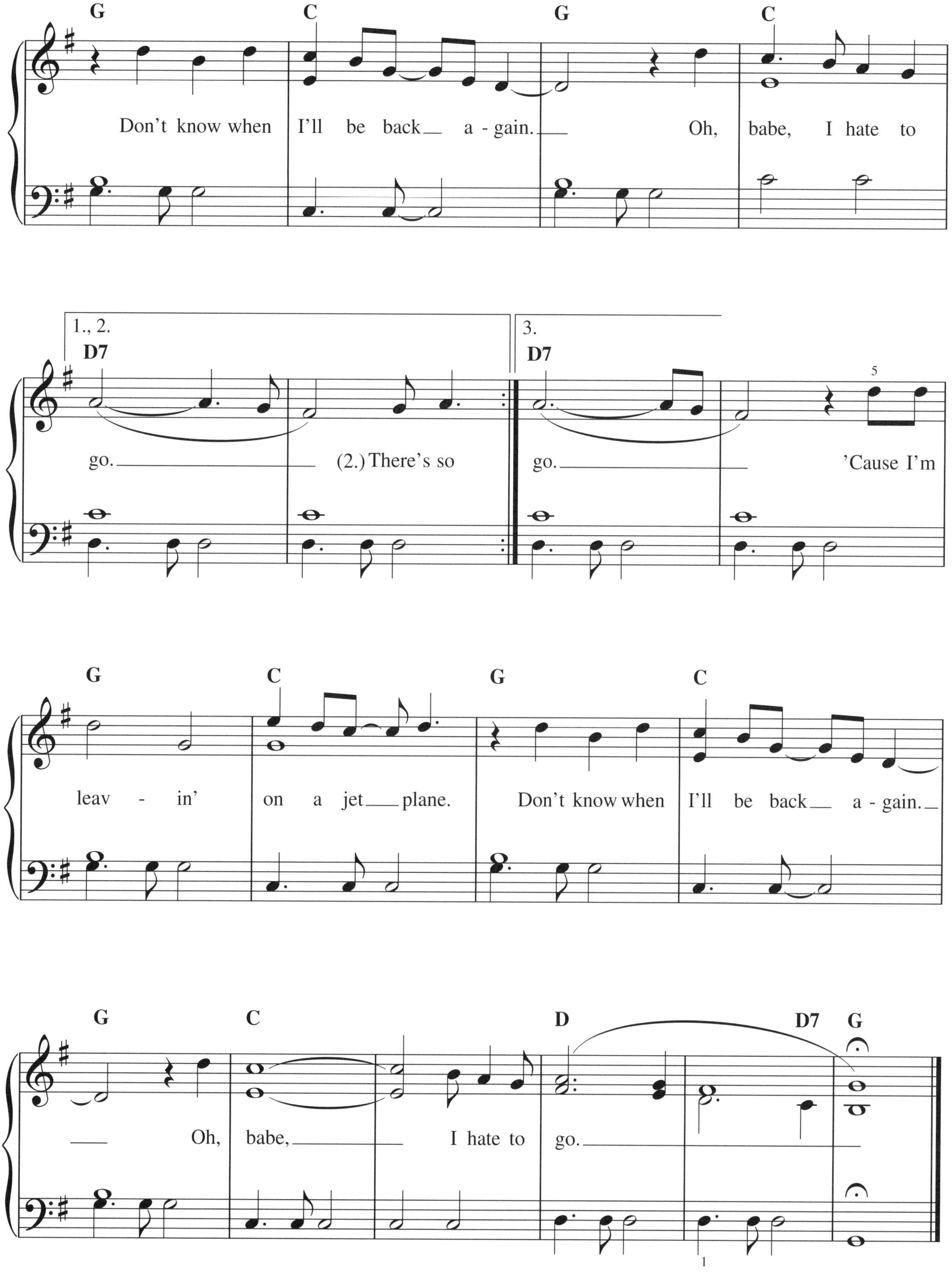
G C G C
Don't know when I'll be back a - gain. Oh, babe, I hate to
1., 2.
D7
go. (2.) There's so
3.
D7
go. 'Cause I'm
5
G C G C
leav - in' on a jet plane. Don't know when I'll be back a - gain.
G C D D7 G
Oh, babe, I hate to go.
1

Layla

Words and Music by ERIC CLAPTON
and JIM GORDON

Moderately fast Rock

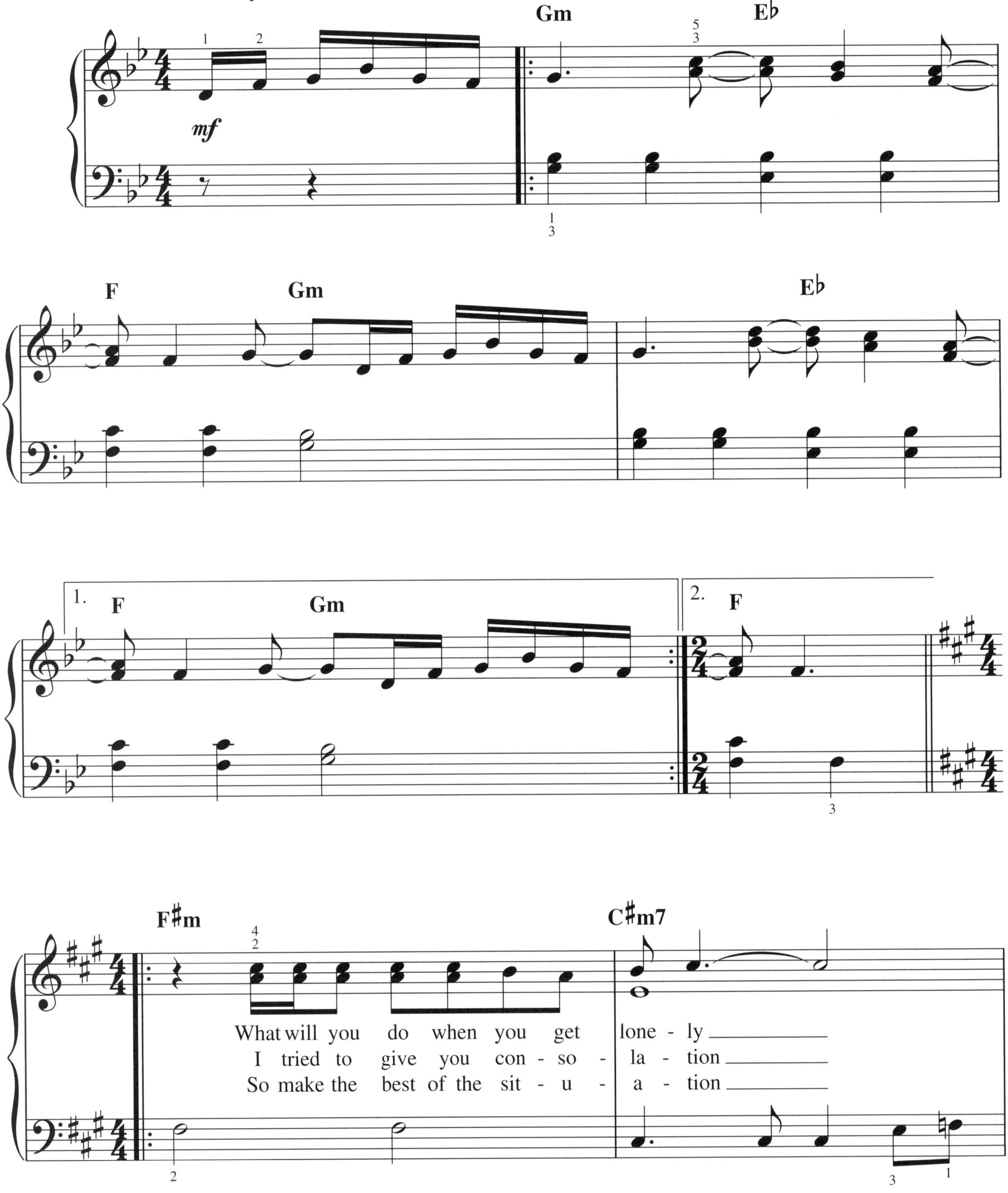
Gm
Eb
mf
F
Gm
Eb
1.
F
Gm
2.
F
F#m
C#m7
What will you do when you get lone - ly
I tried to give you con - so - la - tion
So make the best of the sit - u - a - tion

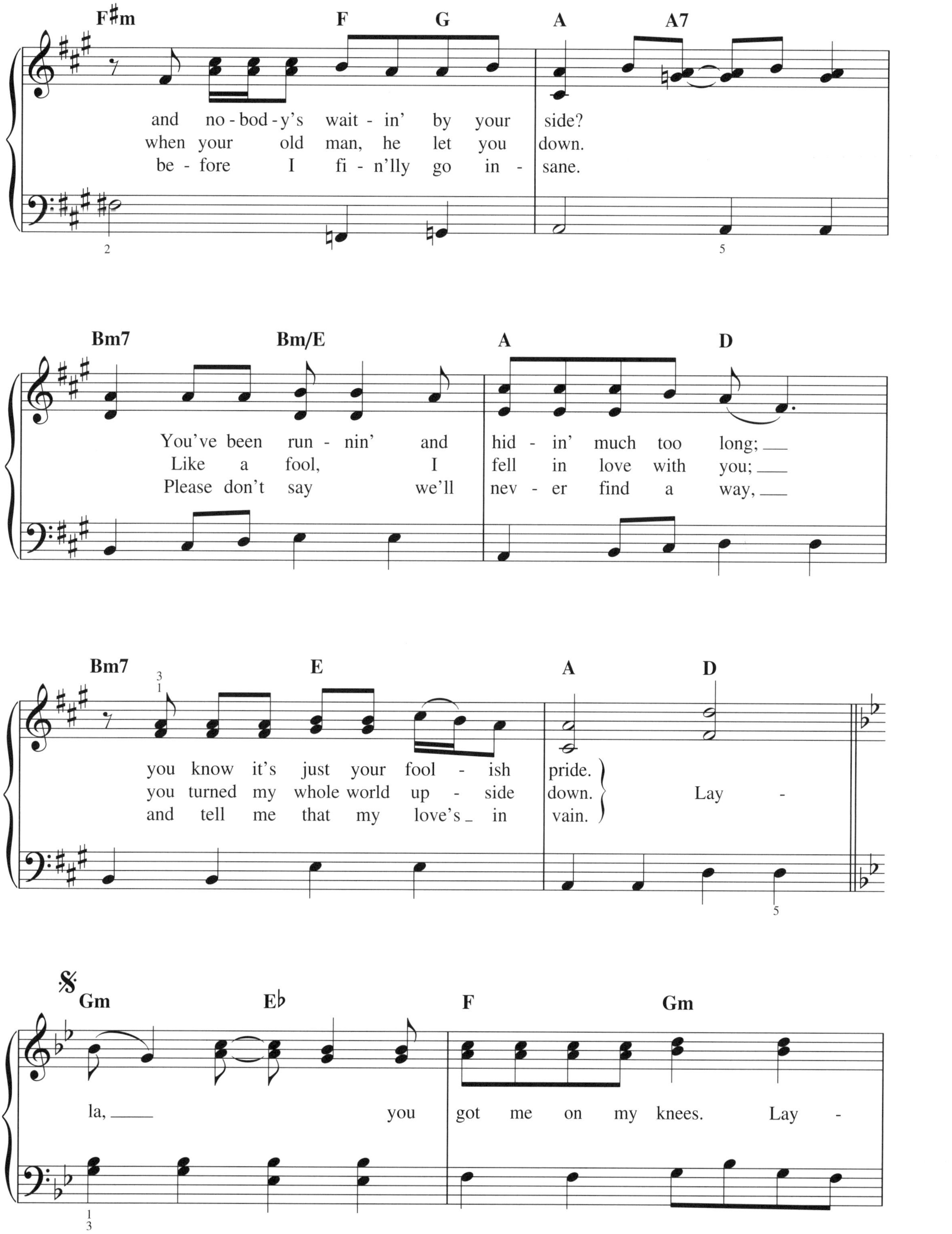
F♯m F G A A7
and no - bod - y's wait - in' by your side?
when your old man, he let you down.
be - fore I fi - n'lly go in - sane.
Bm7 Bm/E A D
You've been run - nin' and hid - in' much too long;
Like a fool, I fell in love with you;
Please don't say we'll nev - er find a way,
Bm7 E A D
you know it's just your fool - ish pride.
you turned my whole world up - side down.
and tell me that my love's in vain.
Lay -
Gm E♭ F Gm
la, you got me on my knees. Lay -

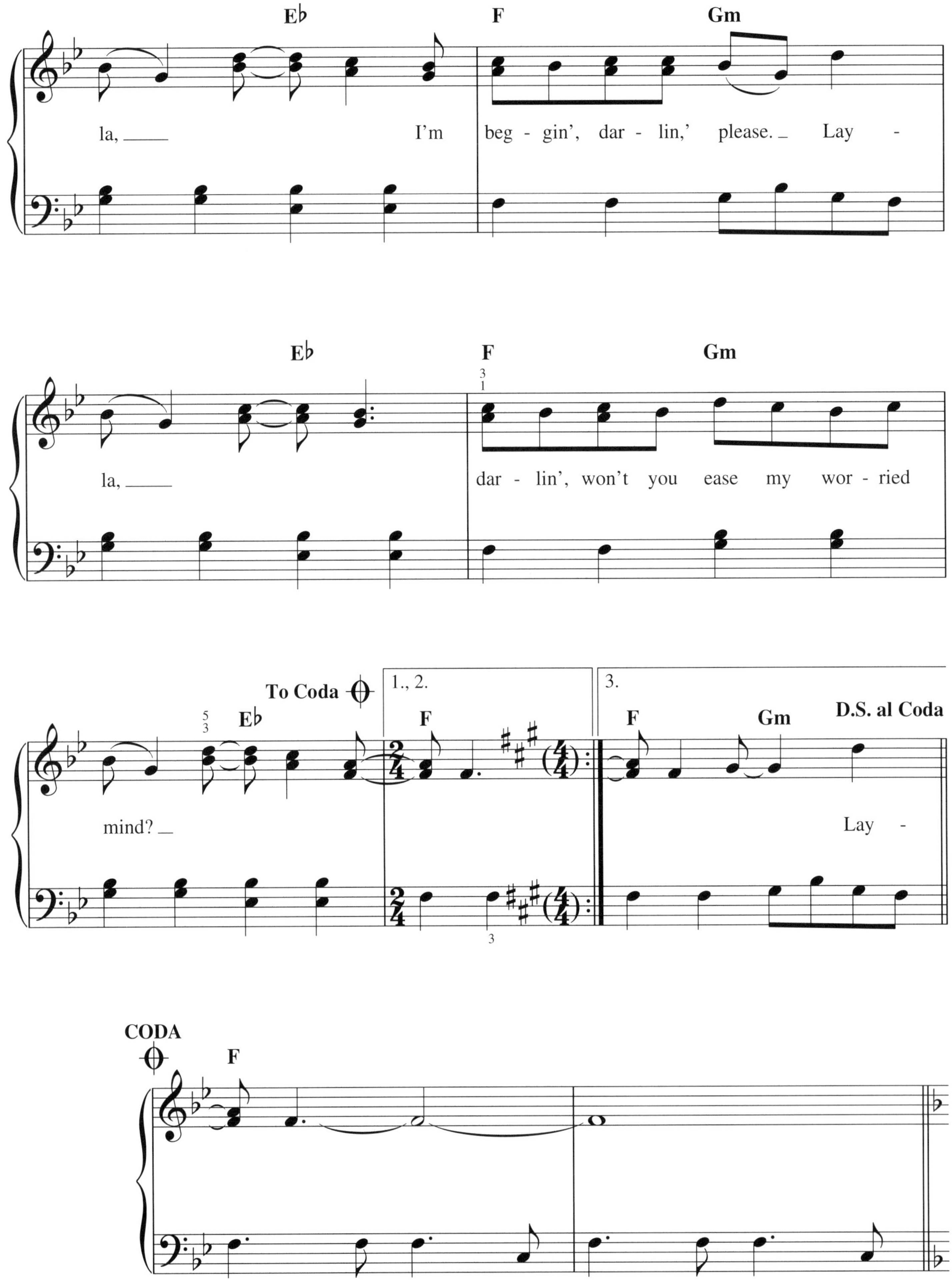
E♭
F
Gm
la, I'm beg - gin', dar - lin,' please. Lay -
E♭
F
Gm
la, dar - lin', won't you ease my wor - ried
To Coda
1., 2.
3.
E♭
F
F
Gm
D.S. al Coda
mind? Lay -
CODA
F

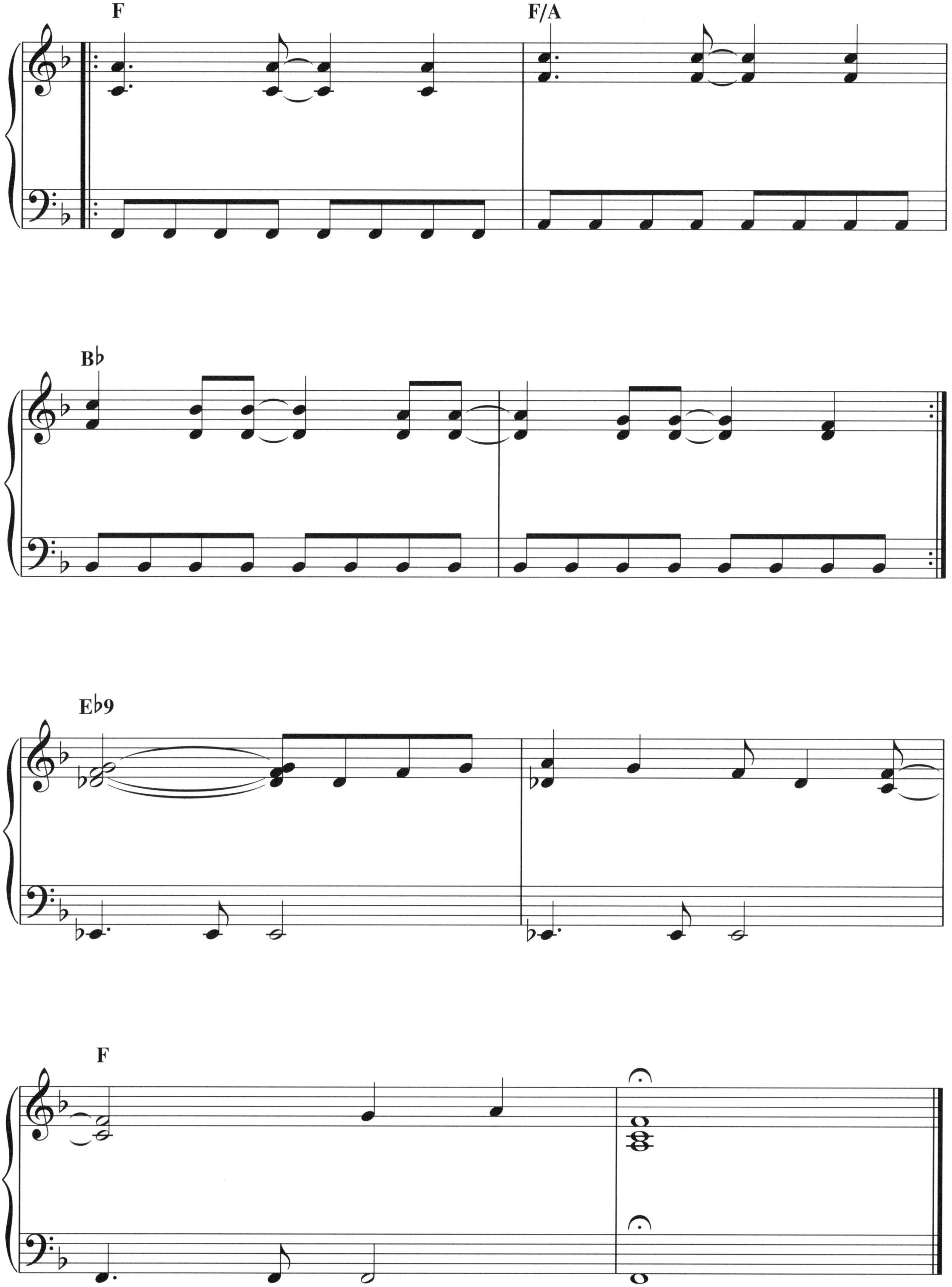
F
F/A
B♭
E♭9
F

Let It Be

Words and Music by JOHN LENNON
and PAUL McCARTNEY

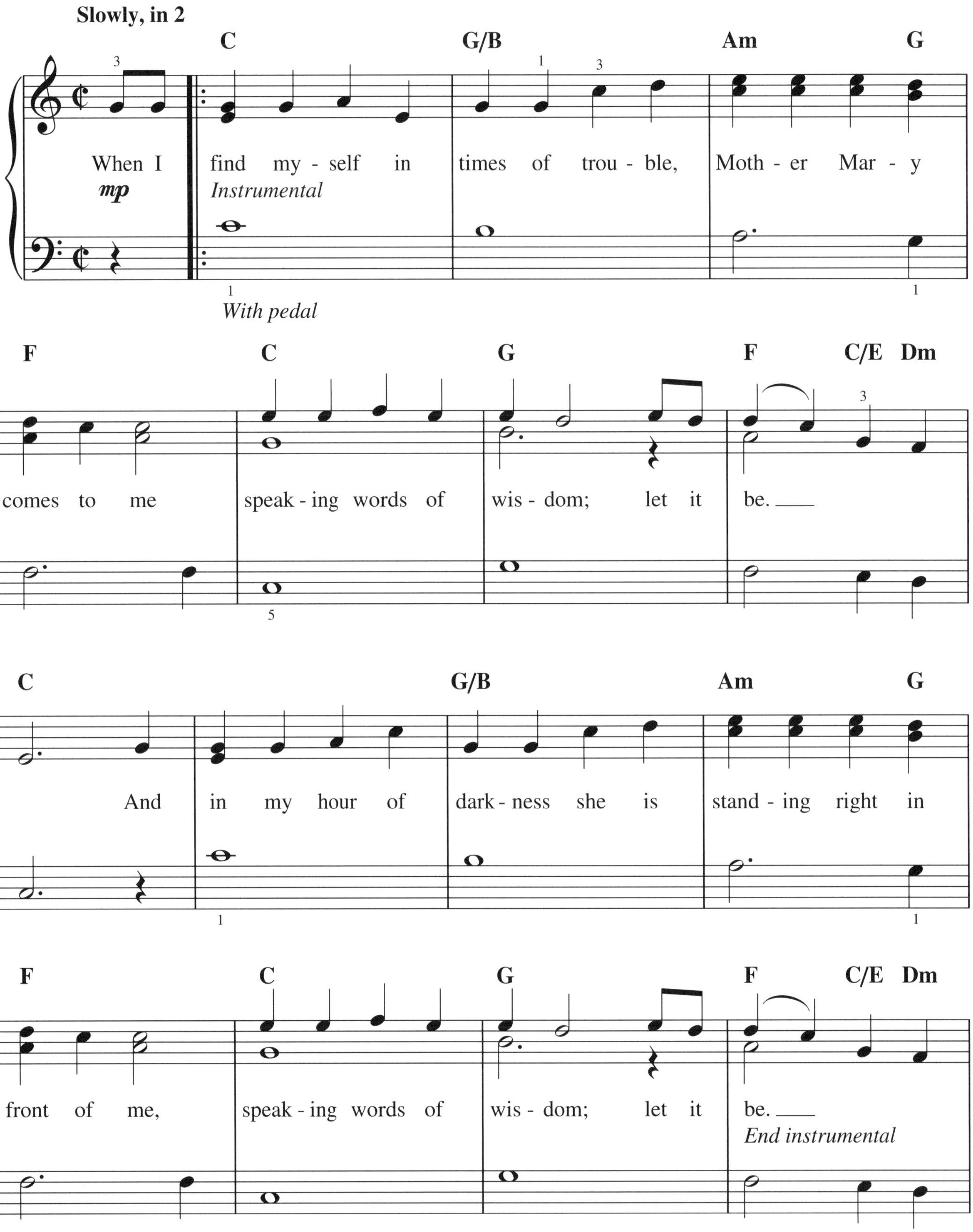

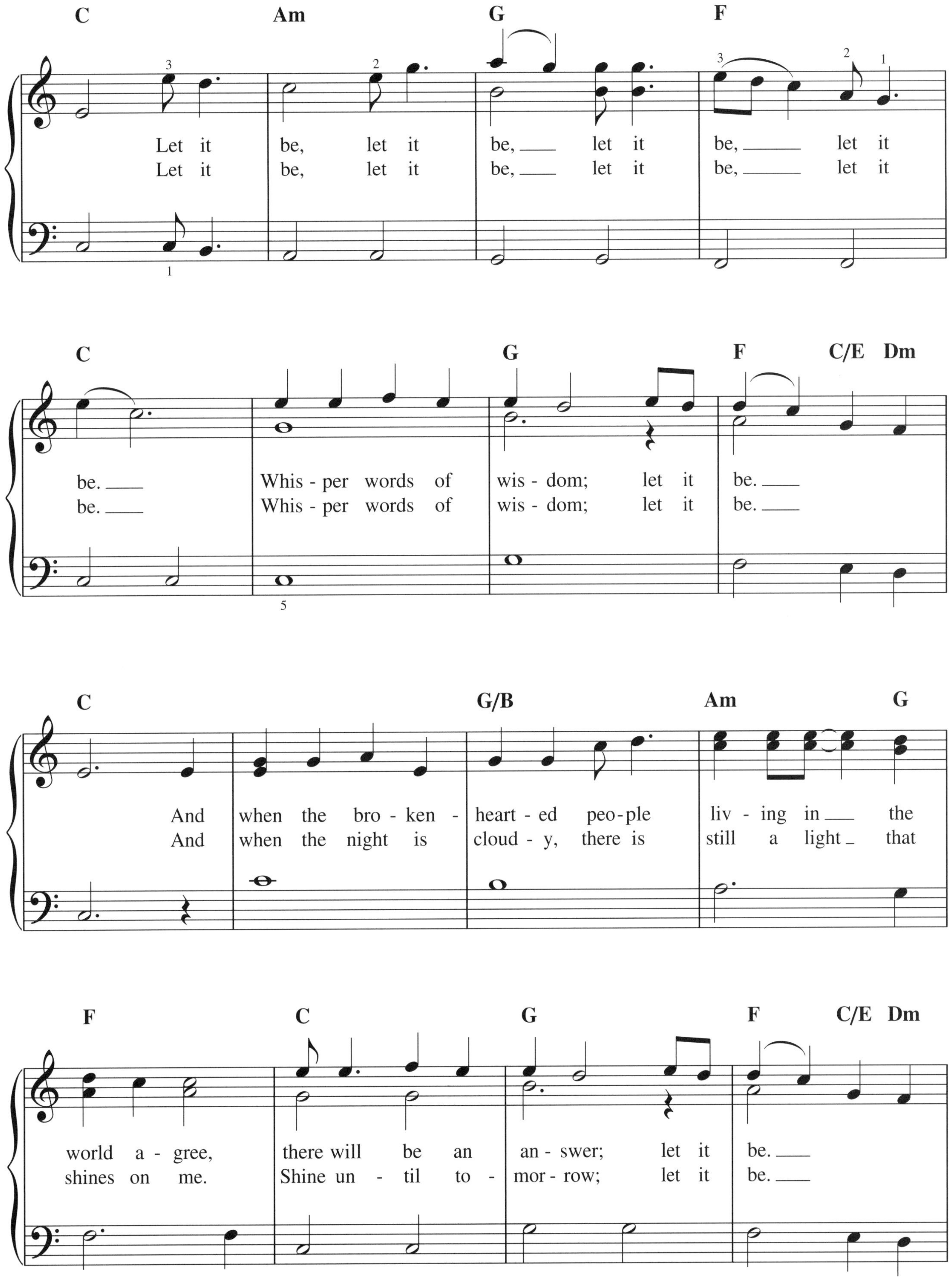
C Am G F
Let it be, let it be, let it be, let it
Let it be, let it be, let it be, let it
C G F C/E Dm
be. Whis - per words of wis - dom; let it be.
be. Whis - per words of wis - dom; let it be.
C G/B Am G
And when the bro - ken - heart - ed peo - ple liv - ing in the
And when the night is cloud - y, there is still a light that
F C G F C/E Dm
world a - gree, there will be an an - swer; let it be.
shines on me. Shine un - til to - mor - row; let it be.

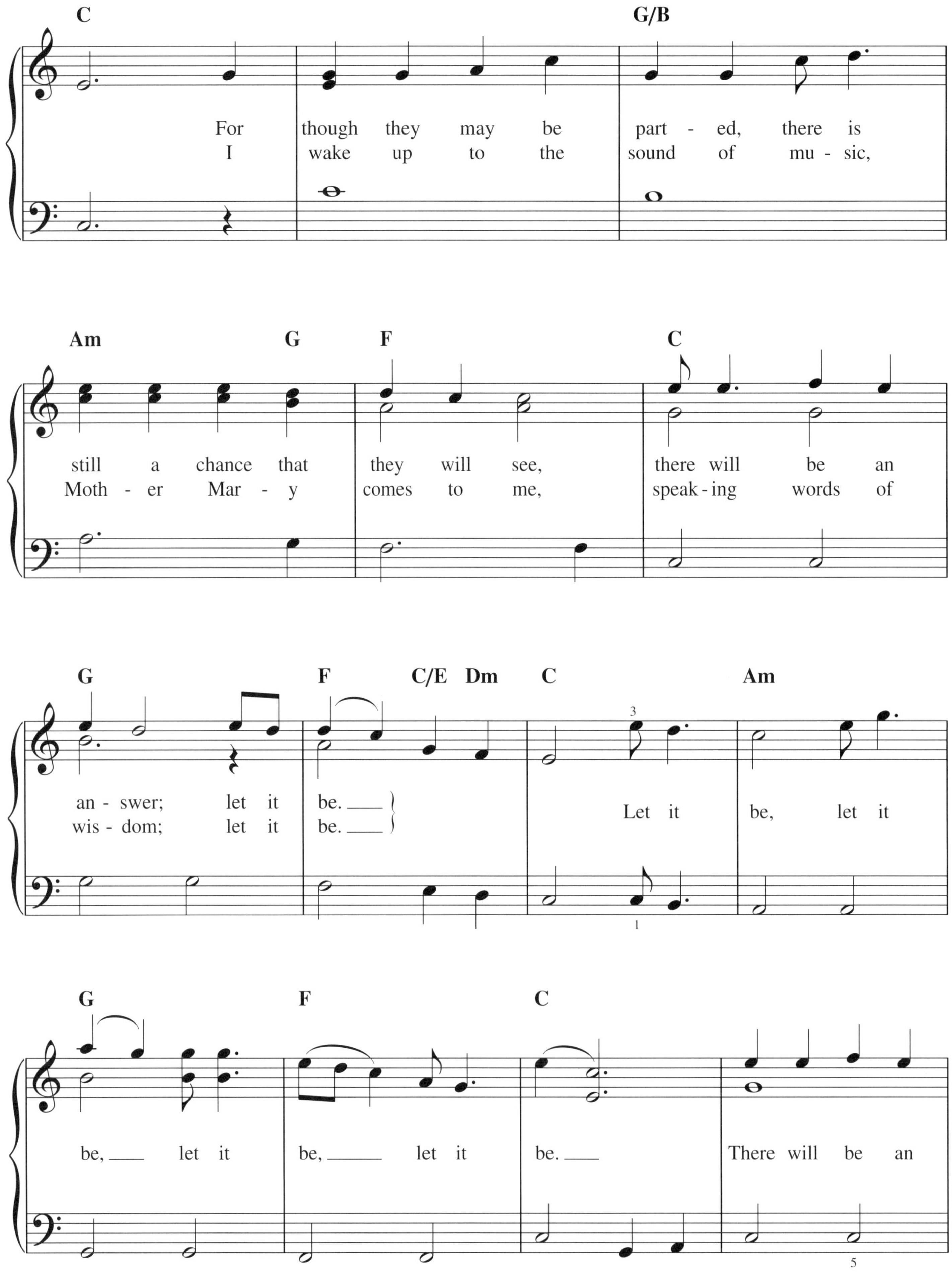
C G/B
For though they may be part - ed, there is
I wake up to the sound of mu - sic,
Am G F C
still a chance that they will see, there will be an
Moth - er Mar - y comes to me, speak - ing words of
G F C/E Dm C Am
an - swer; let it be.
wis - dom; let it be.
Let it be, let it
G F C
be, let it be, let it be.
There will be an

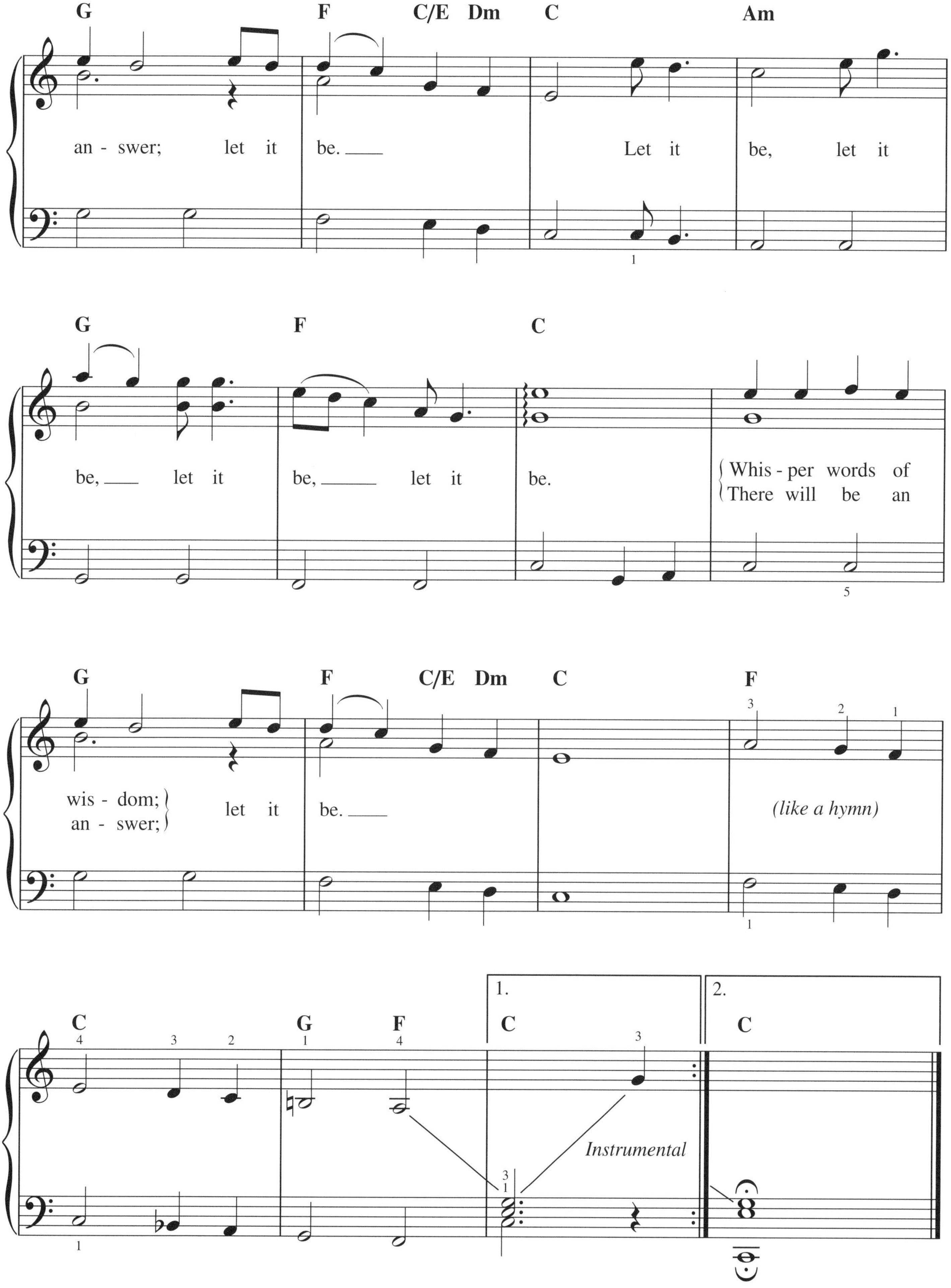
G F C/E Dm C Am
an - swer; let it be. Let it be, let it
G F C
be, let it be, let it be.
Whis - per words of
There will be an
G F C/E Dm C F
wis - dom;
an - swer;
let it be.
(like a hymn)
C G F
1. C
2. C
Instrumental

Maybe I'm Amazed

Words and Music by
PAUL McCARTNEY

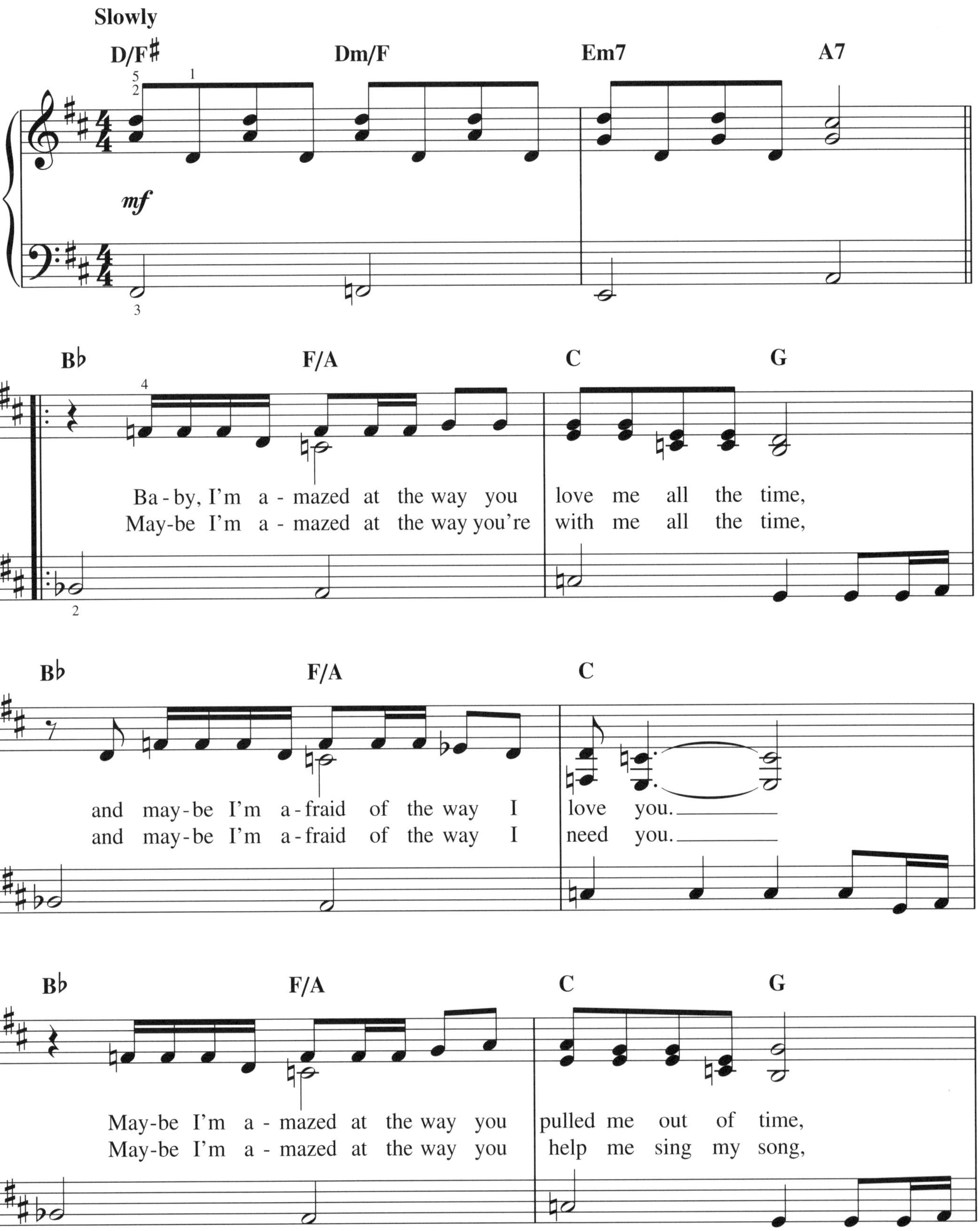

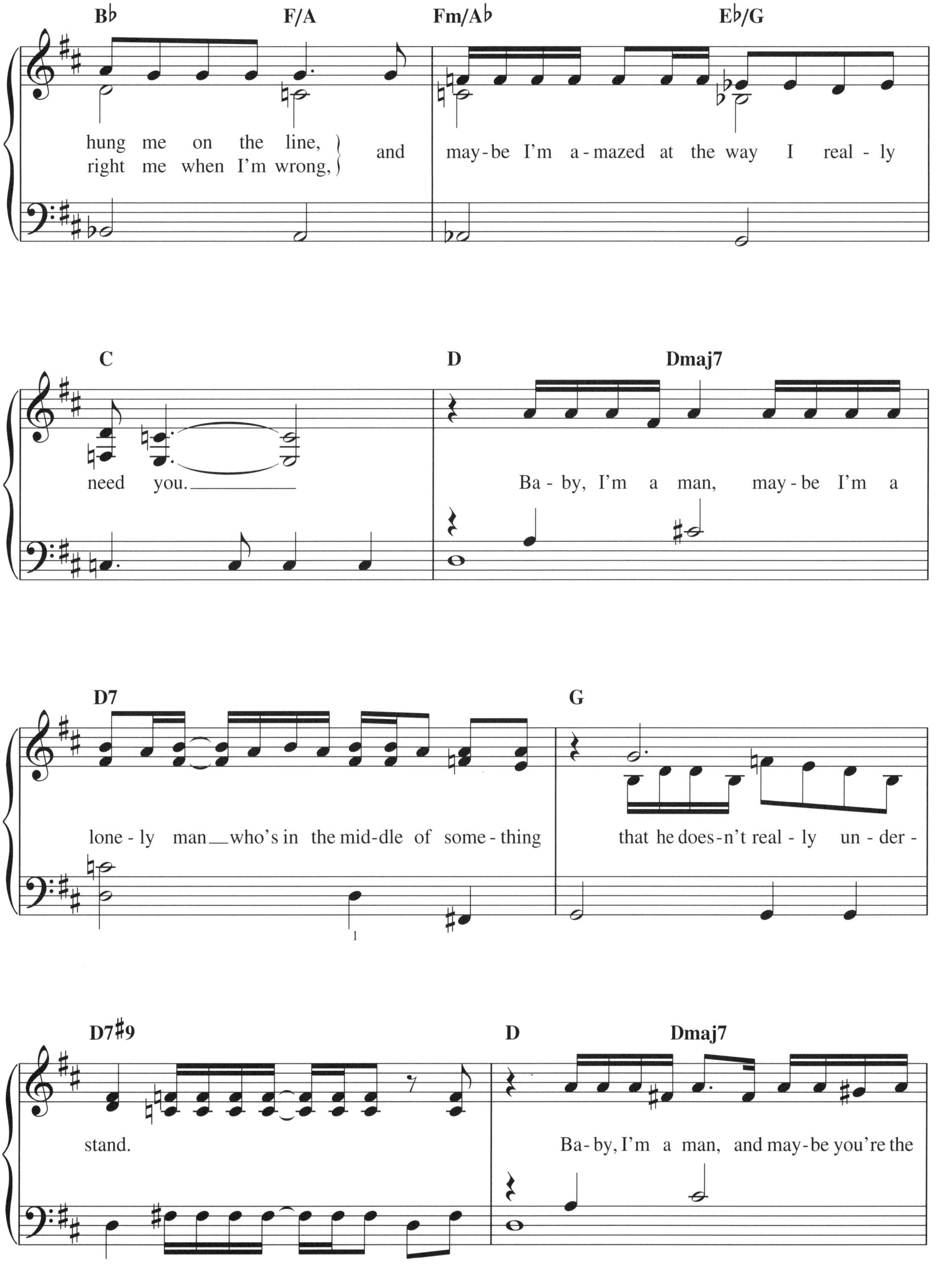
B♭
F/A
Fm/A♭
E♭/G
hung me on the line,
right me when I'm wrong,
and
may-be I'm a-mazed at the way I real-ly
C
D
Dmaj7
need you.
Ba-by, I'm a man, may-be I'm a
D7
G
lone-ly man who's in the mid-dle of some-thing
that he does-n't real-ly un-der-
D7♯9
D
Dmaj7
stand.
Ba-by, I'm a man, and may-be you're the

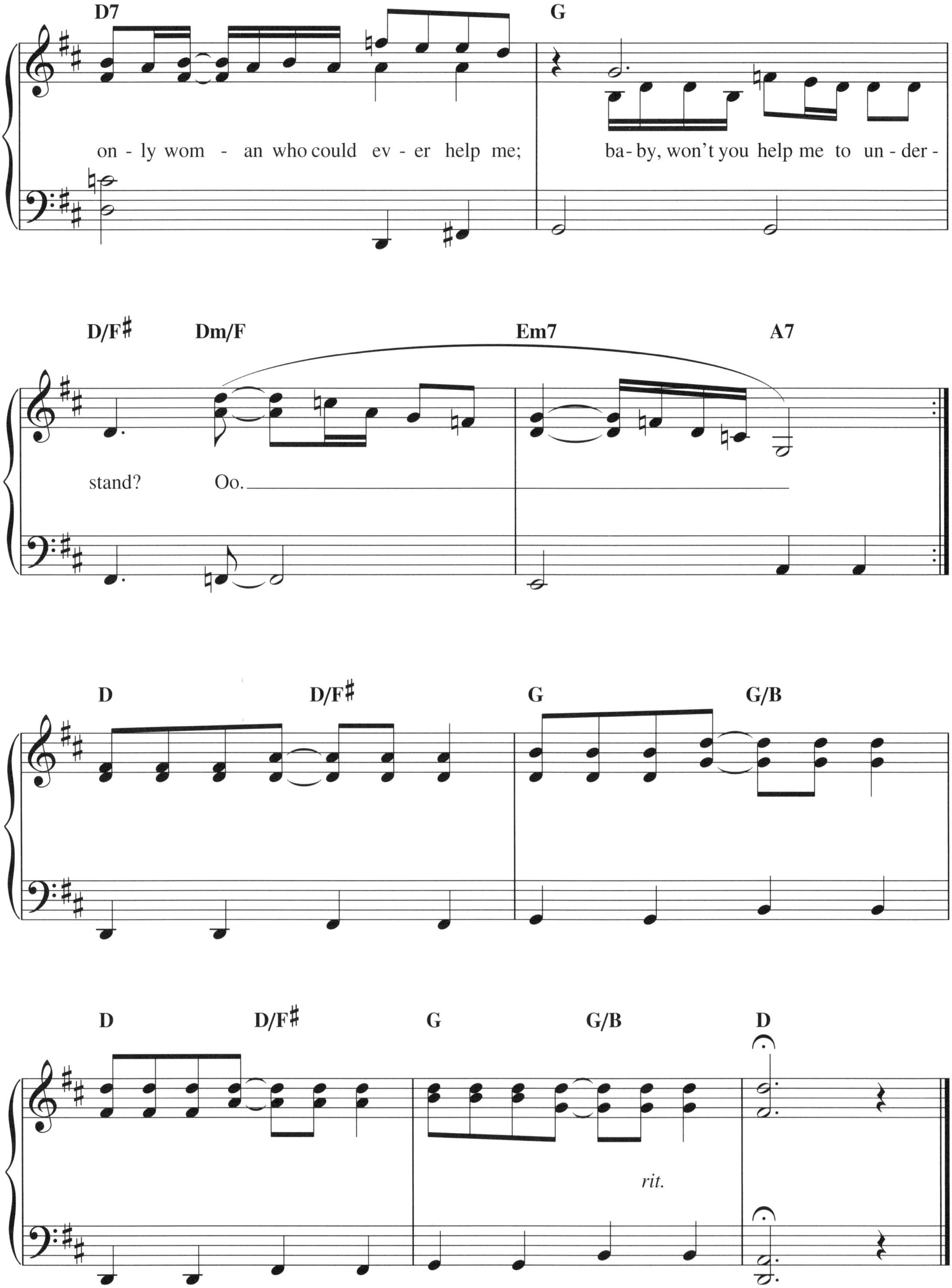
D7
G
on - ly wom - an who could ev - er help me;
ba - by, won't you help me to un - der -
D/F♯
Dm/F
Em7
A7
stand? Oo.
D
D/F♯
G
G/B
D
D/F♯
G
G/B
D
rit.

Love Story

Words and Music by
TAYLOR SWIFT

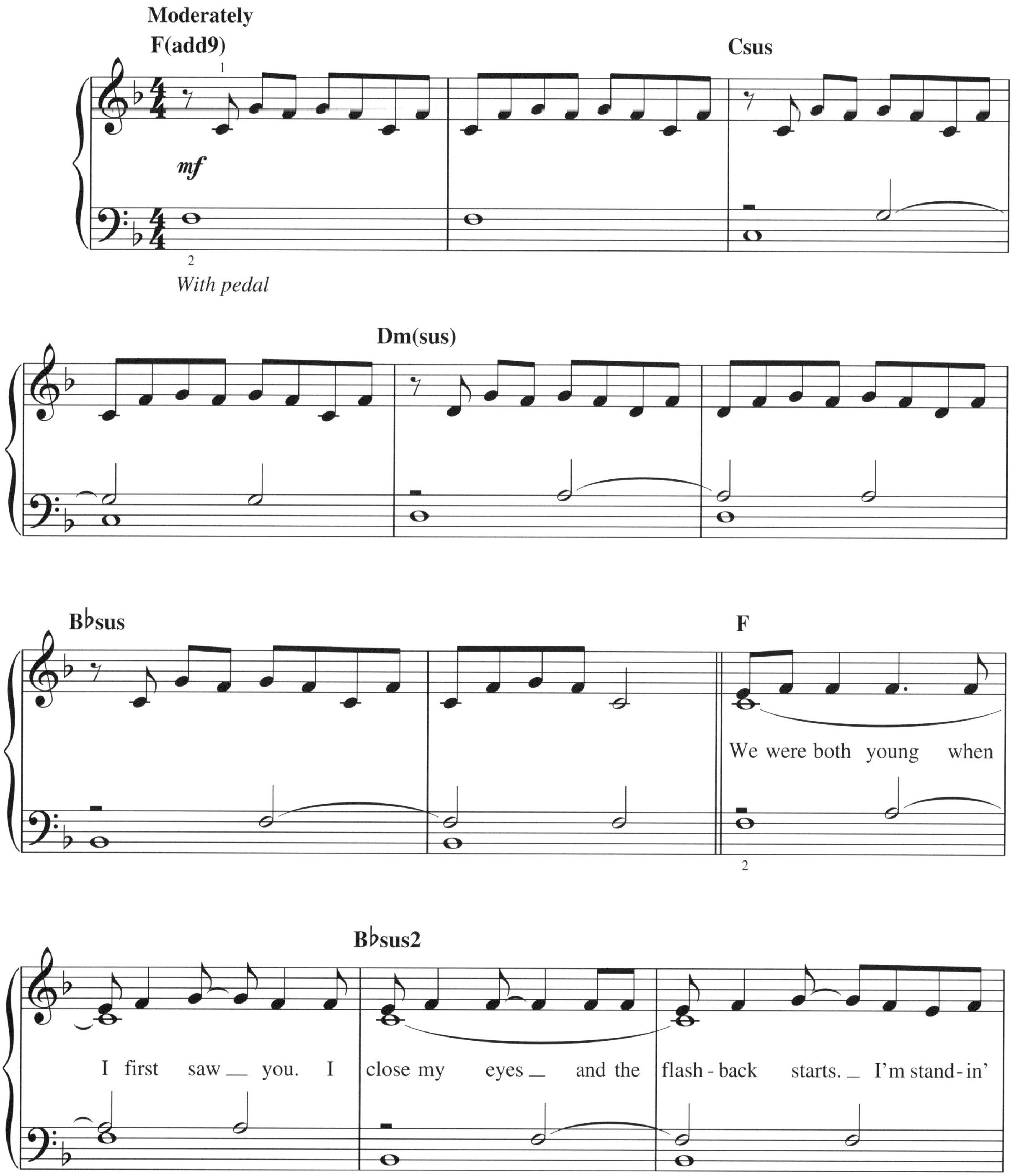

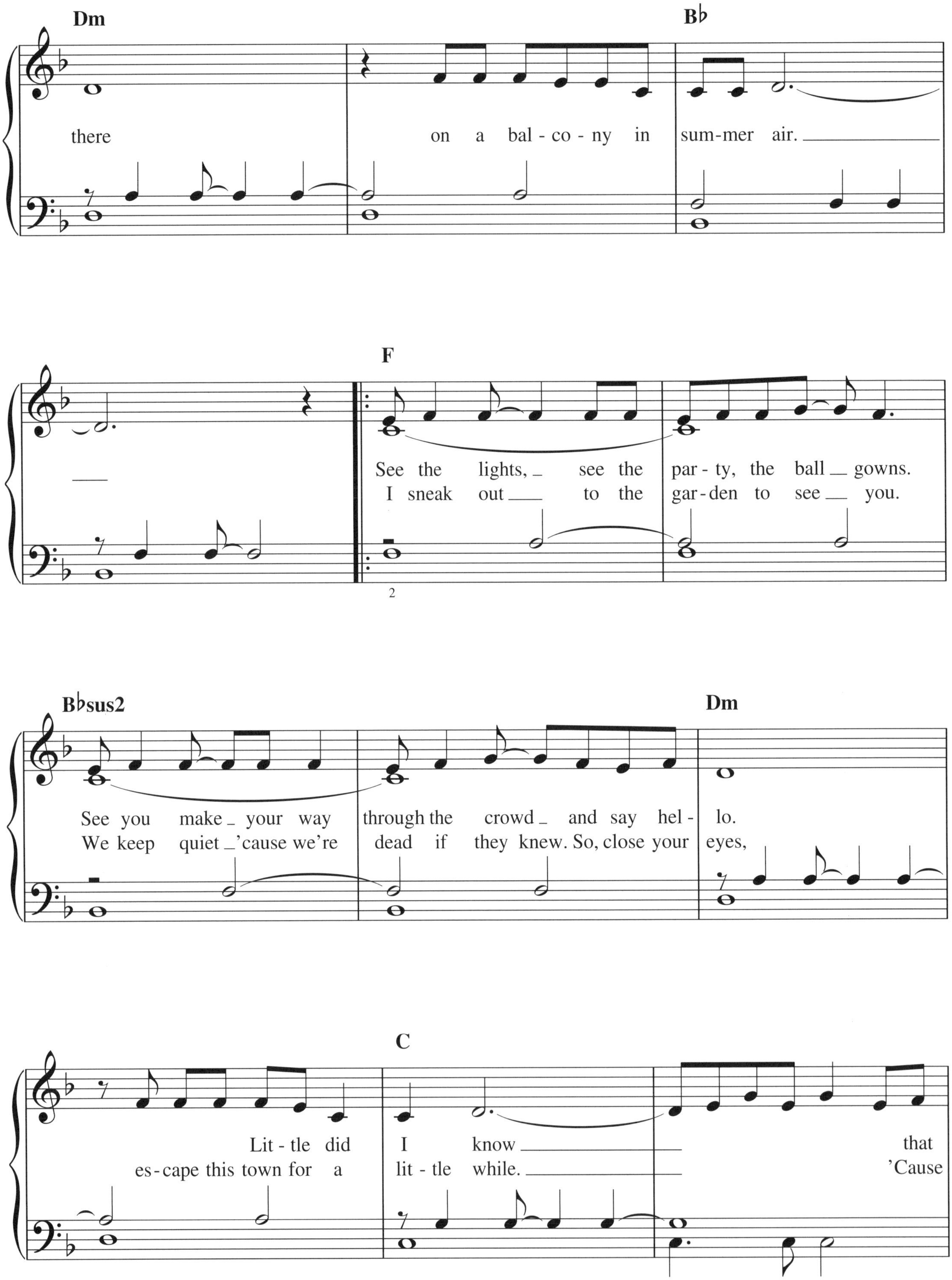
Dm
there
on a bal - co - ny in
B♭
sum-mer air.
F
See the lights, see the par - ty, the ball gowns.
I sneak out to the gar - den to see you.
2
B♭sus2
See you make your way through the crowd and say hel - lo.
We keep quiet 'cause we're dead if they knew. So, close your eyes,
Dm
Lit - tle did
es - cape this town for a
C
I know
lit - tle while.
that
'Cause

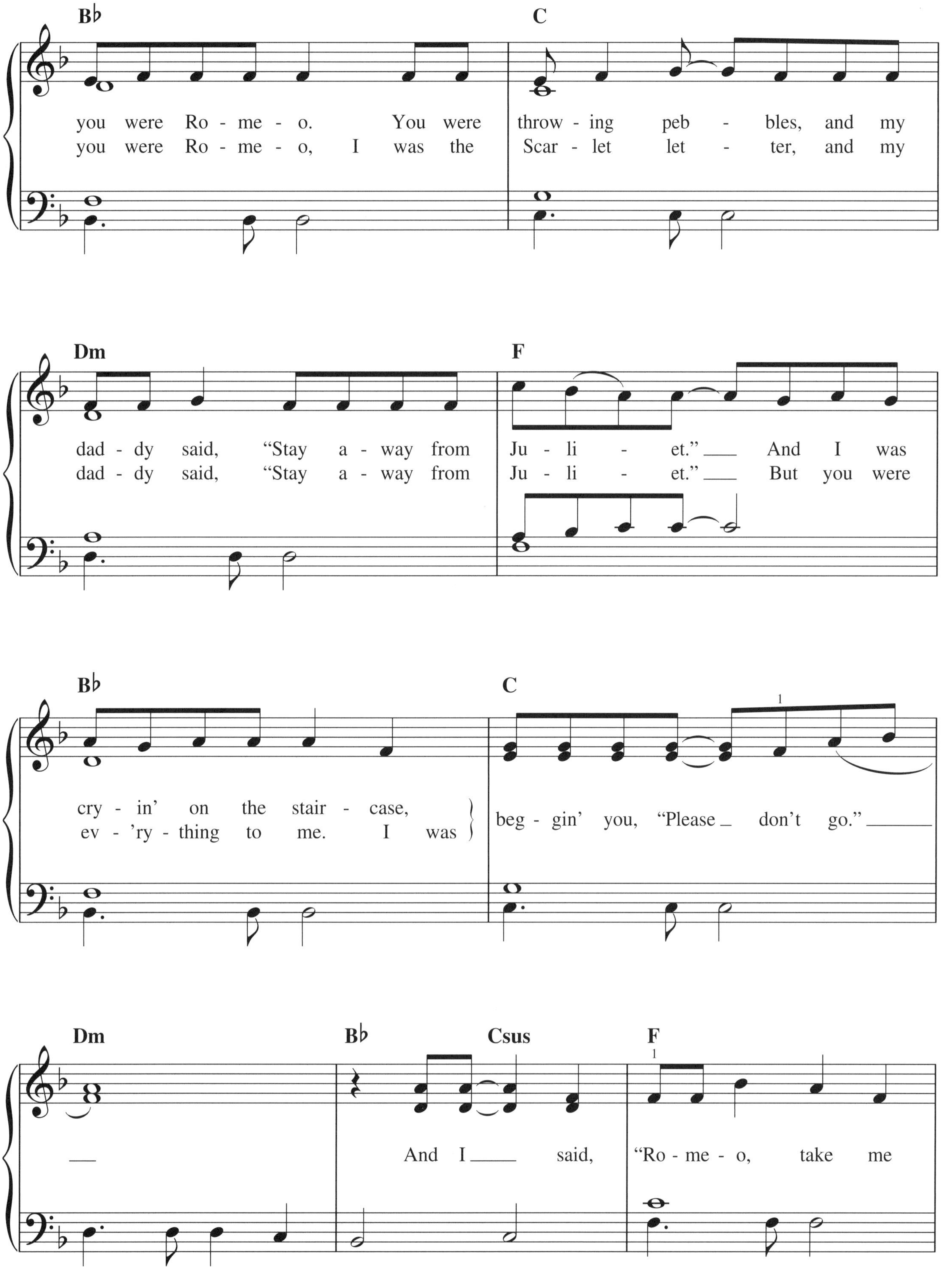
B♭
C
you were Ro - me - o. You were throw - ing peb - bles, and my
you were Ro - me - o, I was the Scar - let let - ter, and my
Dm
F
dad - dy said, "Stay a - way from Ju - li - et." And I was
dad - dy said, "Stay a - way from Ju - li - et." But you were
B♭
C
cry - in' on the stair - case,
ev - 'ry - thing to me. I was
beg - gin' you, "Please don't go."
Dm
B♭
Csus
F
And I said, "Ro - me - o, take me

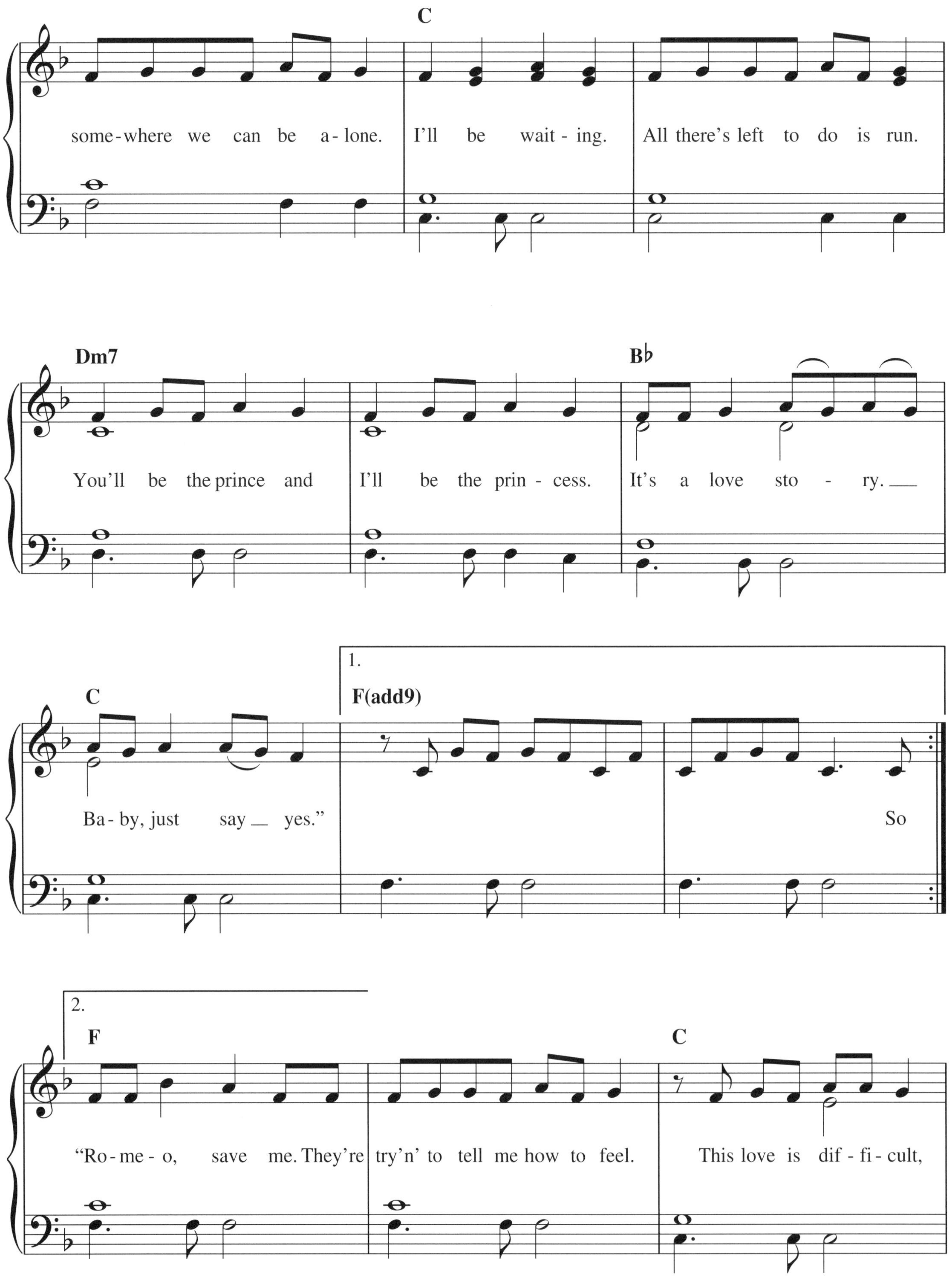
C
some-where we can be a-lone. I'll be wait-ing. All there's left to do is run.
Dm7
Bb
You'll be the prince and I'll be the prin-cess. It's a love sto-ry.
C
1.
F(add9)
Ba-by, just say yes." So
2.
F
C
"Ro-me-o, save me. They're try'n' to tell me how to feel. This love is dif-fi-cult,

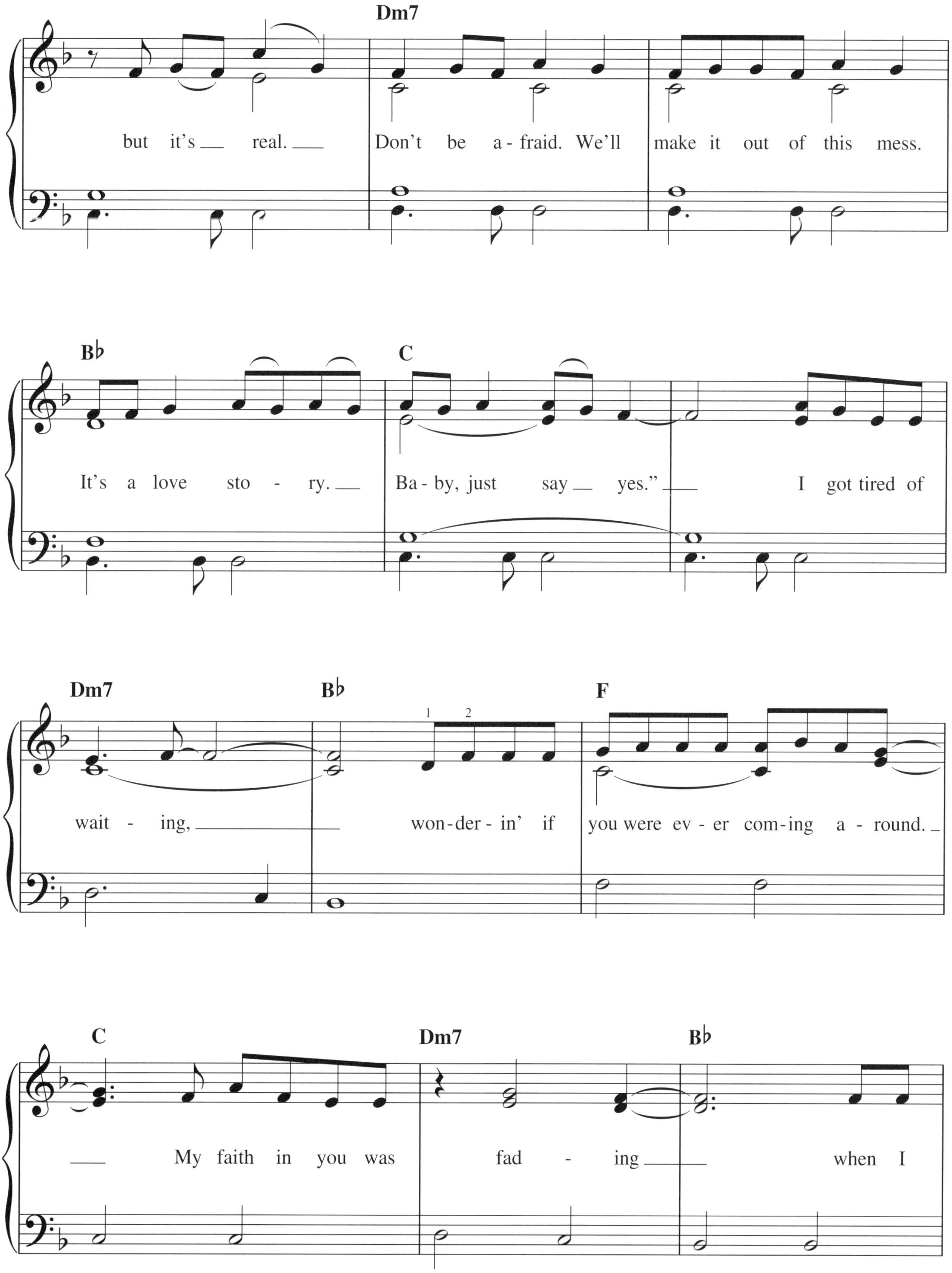
Dm7
but it's real. Don't be a-fraid. We'll make it out of this mess.
B♭
C
It's a love sto-ry. Ba-by, just say yes." I got tired of
Dm7
B♭
F
1 2
wait-ing, won-der-in' if you were ev-er com-ing a-round.
C
Dm7
B♭
My faith in you was fad-ing when I

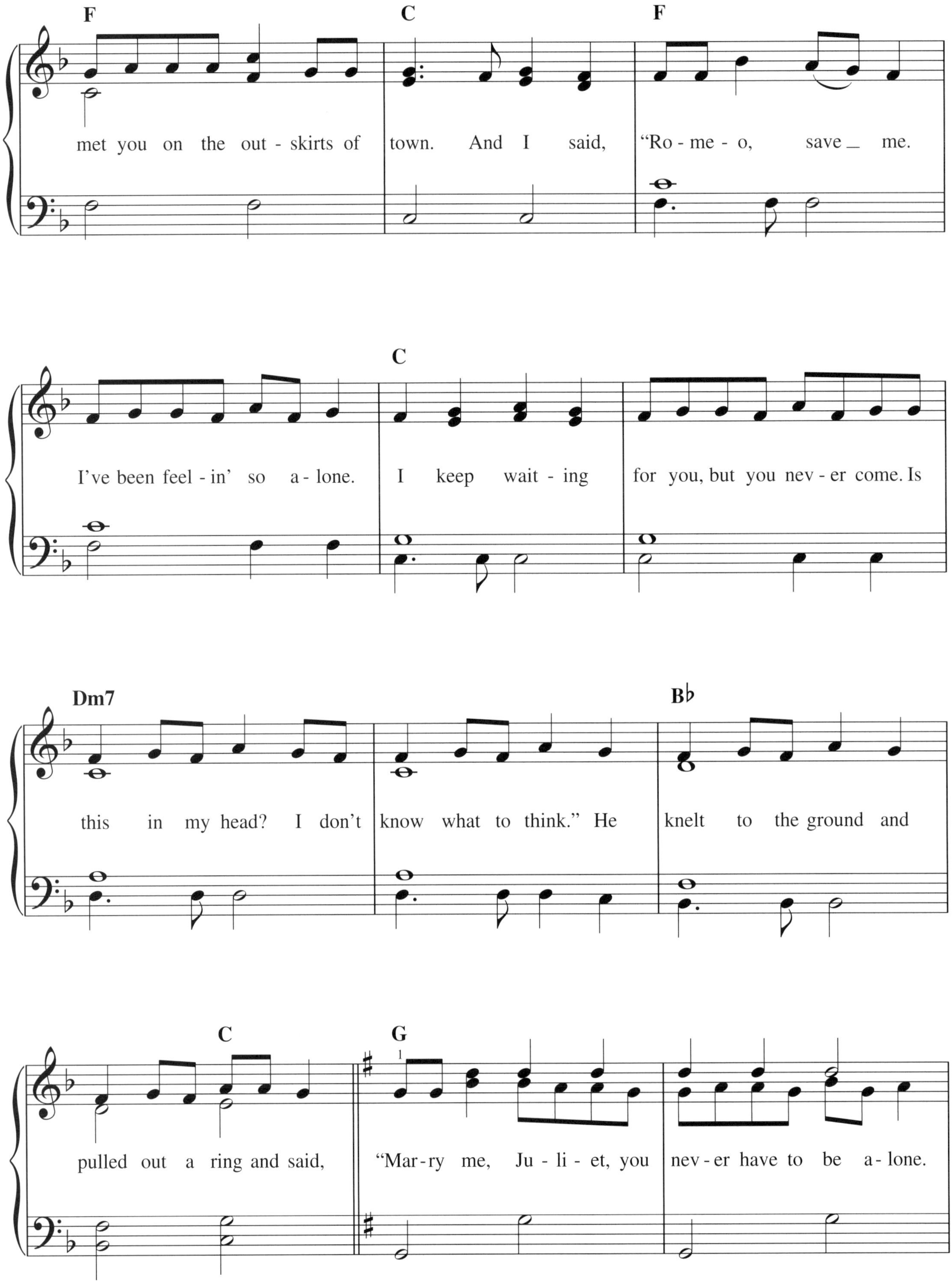
F
C
F
met you on the out - skirts of town. And I said, "Ro - me - o, save _ me.
C
I've been feel - in' so a - lone. I keep wait - ing for you, but you nev - er come. Is
Dm7
B♭
this in my head? I don't know what to think." He knelt to the ground and
C
G
1
pulled out a ring and said, "Mar - ry me, Ju - li - et, you nev - er have to be a - lone.

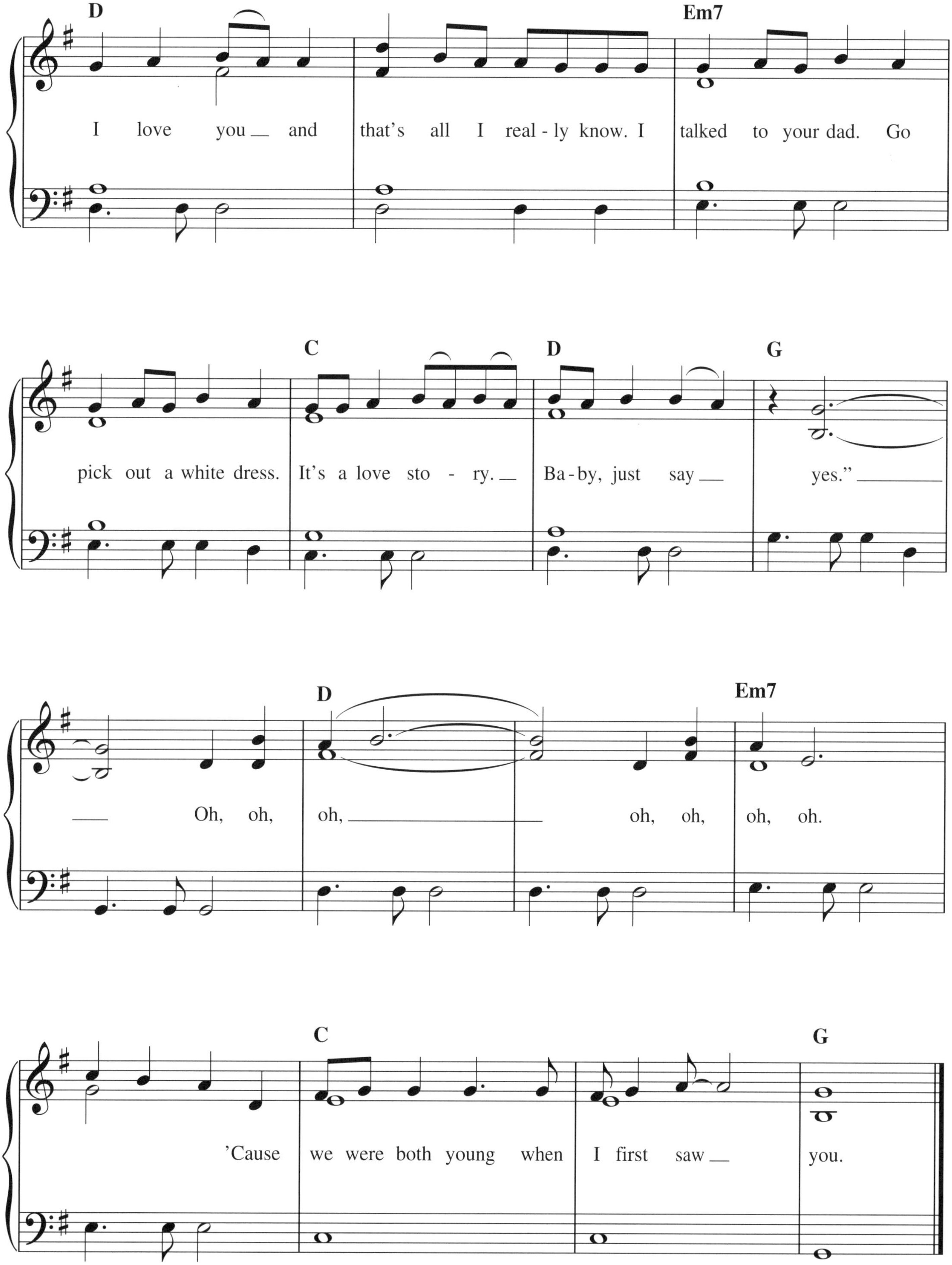
D
I love you and
that's all I real-ly know. I
Em7
talked to your dad. Go
pick out a white dress.
C
It's a love sto - ry.
D
Ba-by, just say
G
yes."
Oh, oh,
D
oh,
oh, oh,
Em7
oh, oh.
'Cause
C
we were both young when
I first saw
G
you.

Moon River

Words by JOHNNY MERCER
Music by HENRY MANCINI

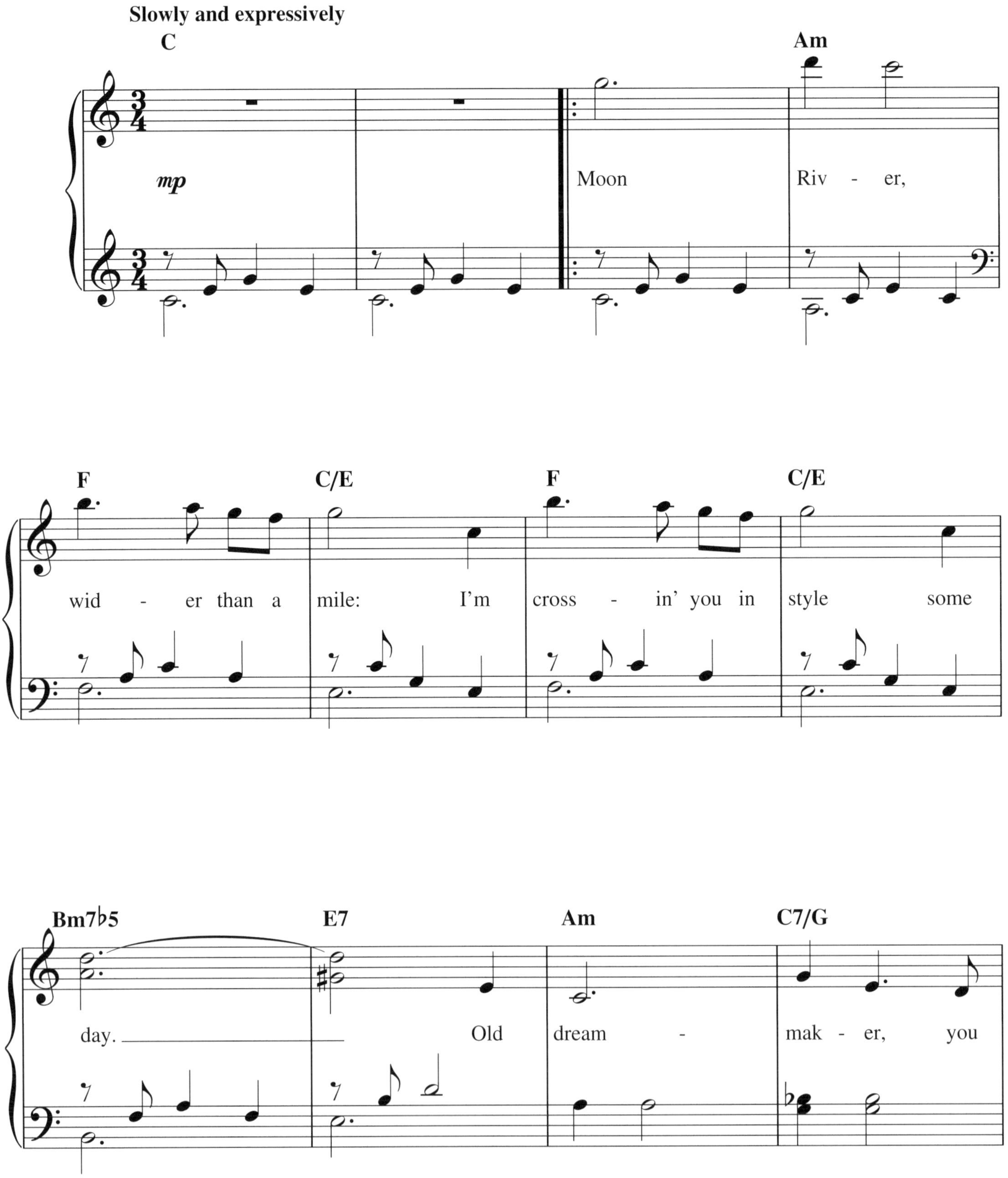

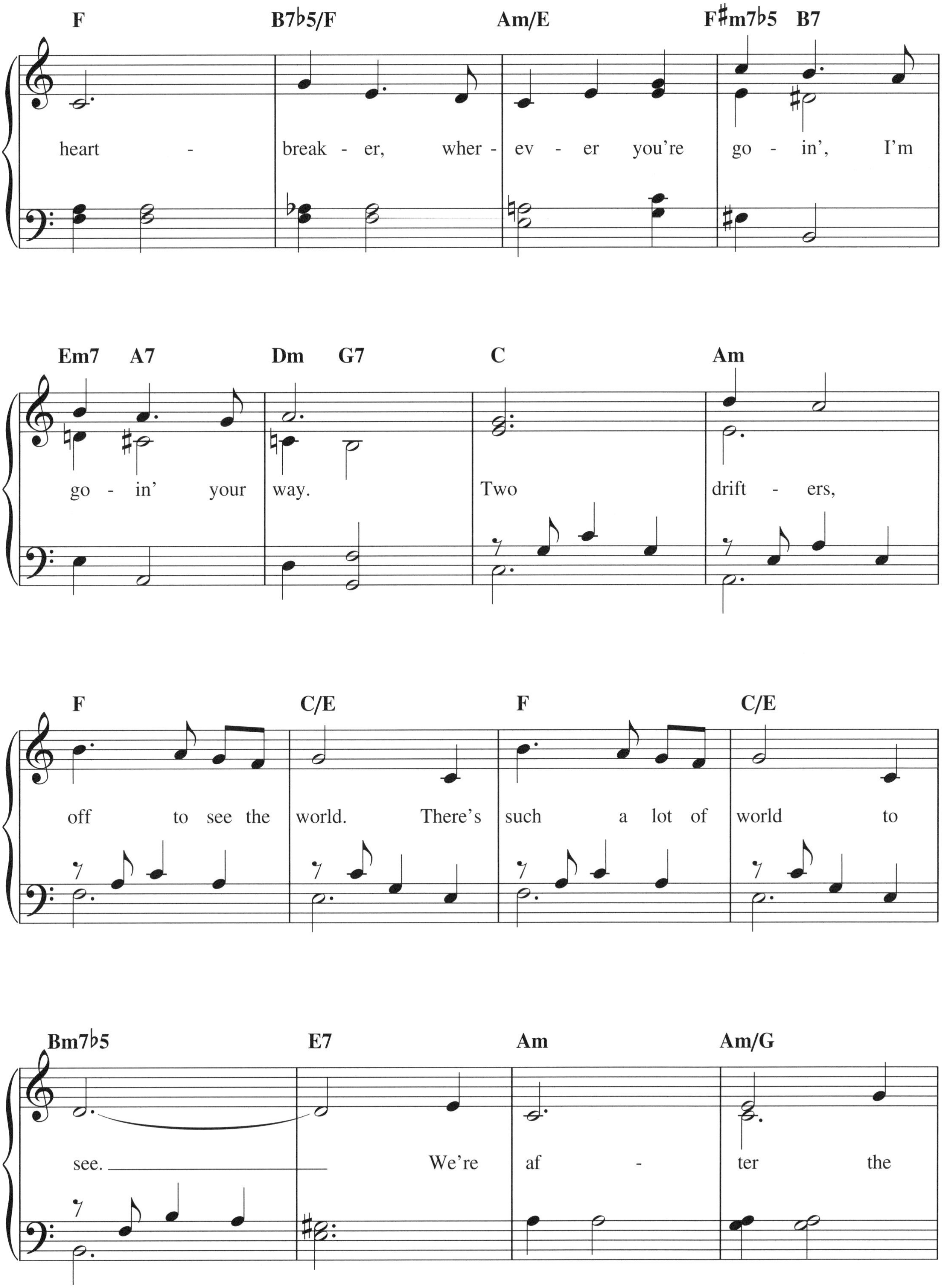
F B7♭5/F Am/E F♯m7♭5 B7
heart - break - er, wher - ev - er you're go - in', I'm
Em7 A7 Dm G7 C Am
go - in' your way. Two drift - ers,
F C/E F C/E
off to see the world. There's such a lot of world to
Bm7♭5 E7 Am Am/G
see. We're af - ter the

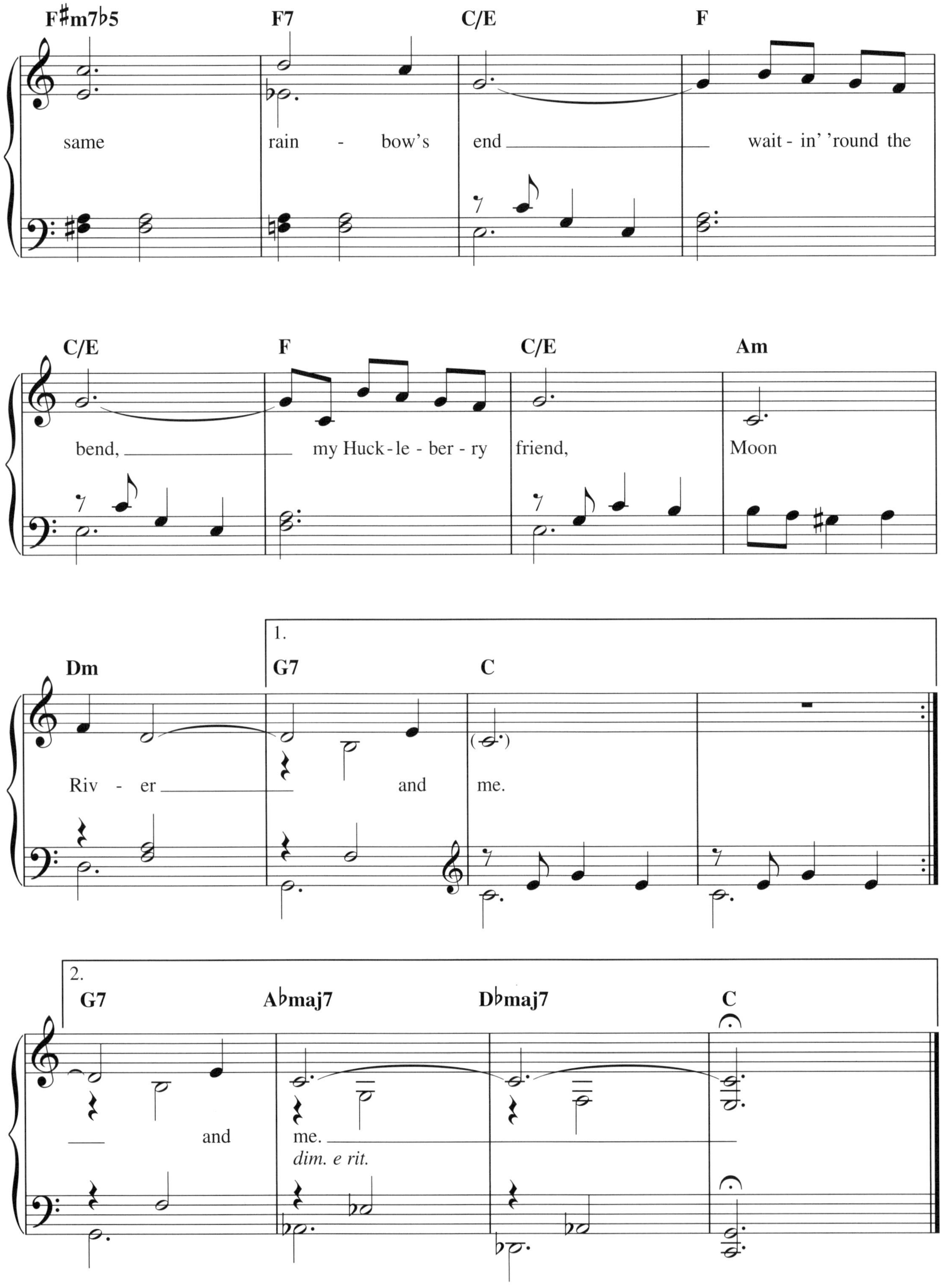
F♯m7♭5
F7
C/E
F
same rain - bow's end wait - in' 'round the
C/E
F
C/E
Am
bend, my Huck - le - ber - ry friend, Moon
Dm
1.
G7
C
Riv - er and me.
2.
G7
A♭maj7
D♭maj7
C
and me.
dim. e rit.

The Pink Panther

By HENRY MANCINI

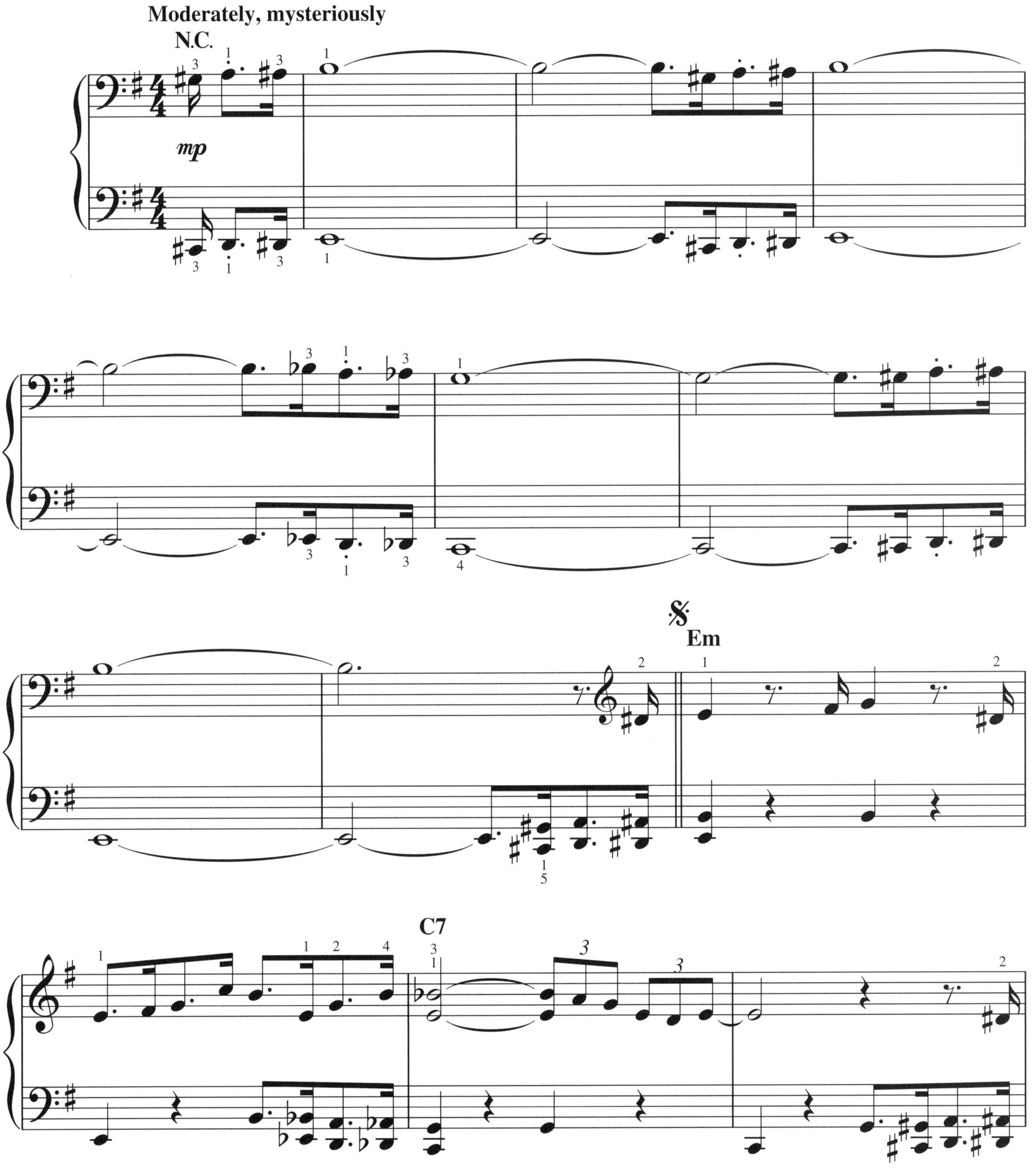

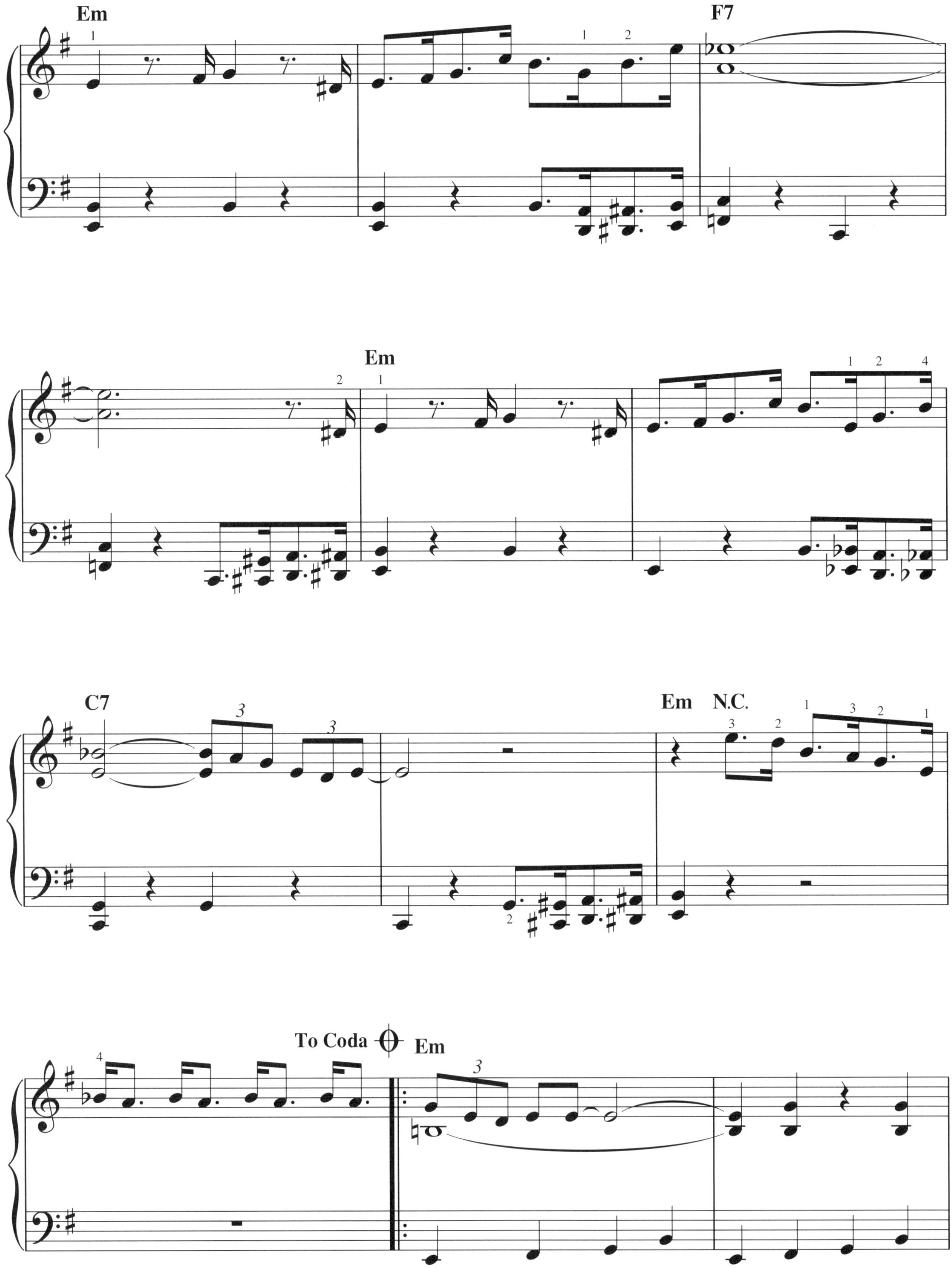
Em
F7
Em
C7
Em N.C.
To Coda
Em

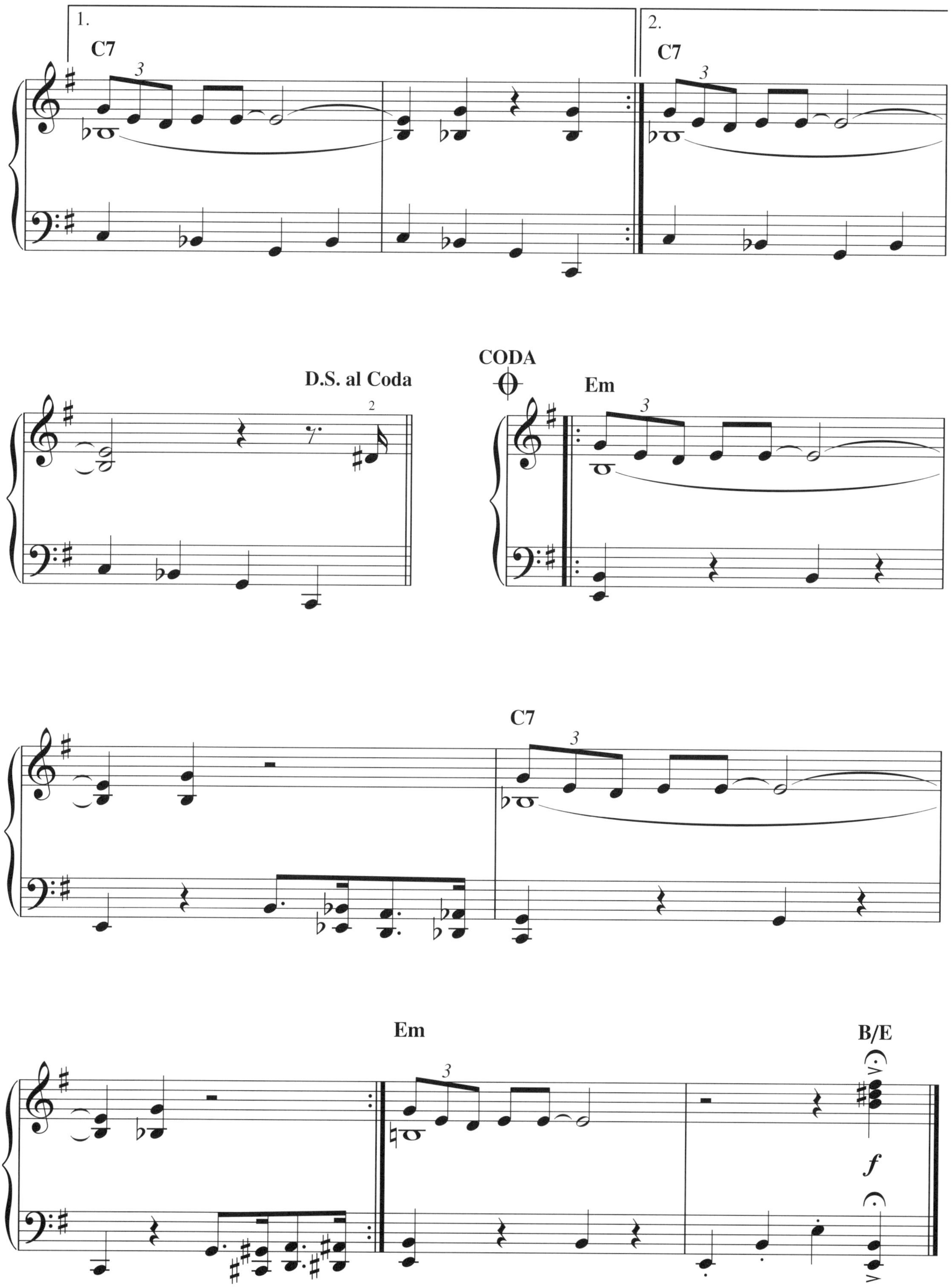
1.
C7
2.
C7
D.S. al Coda
CODA
Em
C7
Em
B/E
f

Raindrops Keep Fallin' on My Head

Lyric by HAL DAVID
Music by BURT BACHARACH

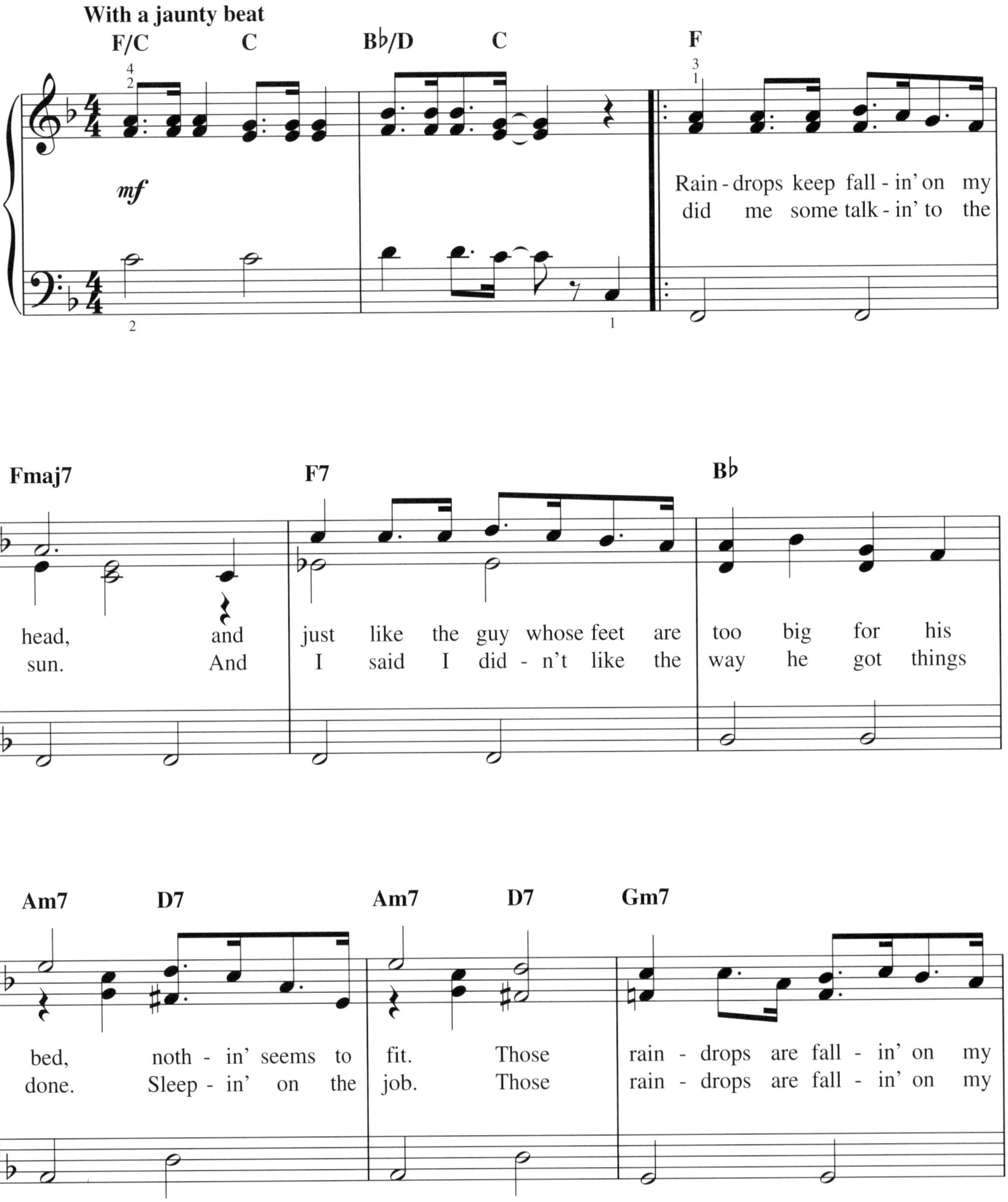

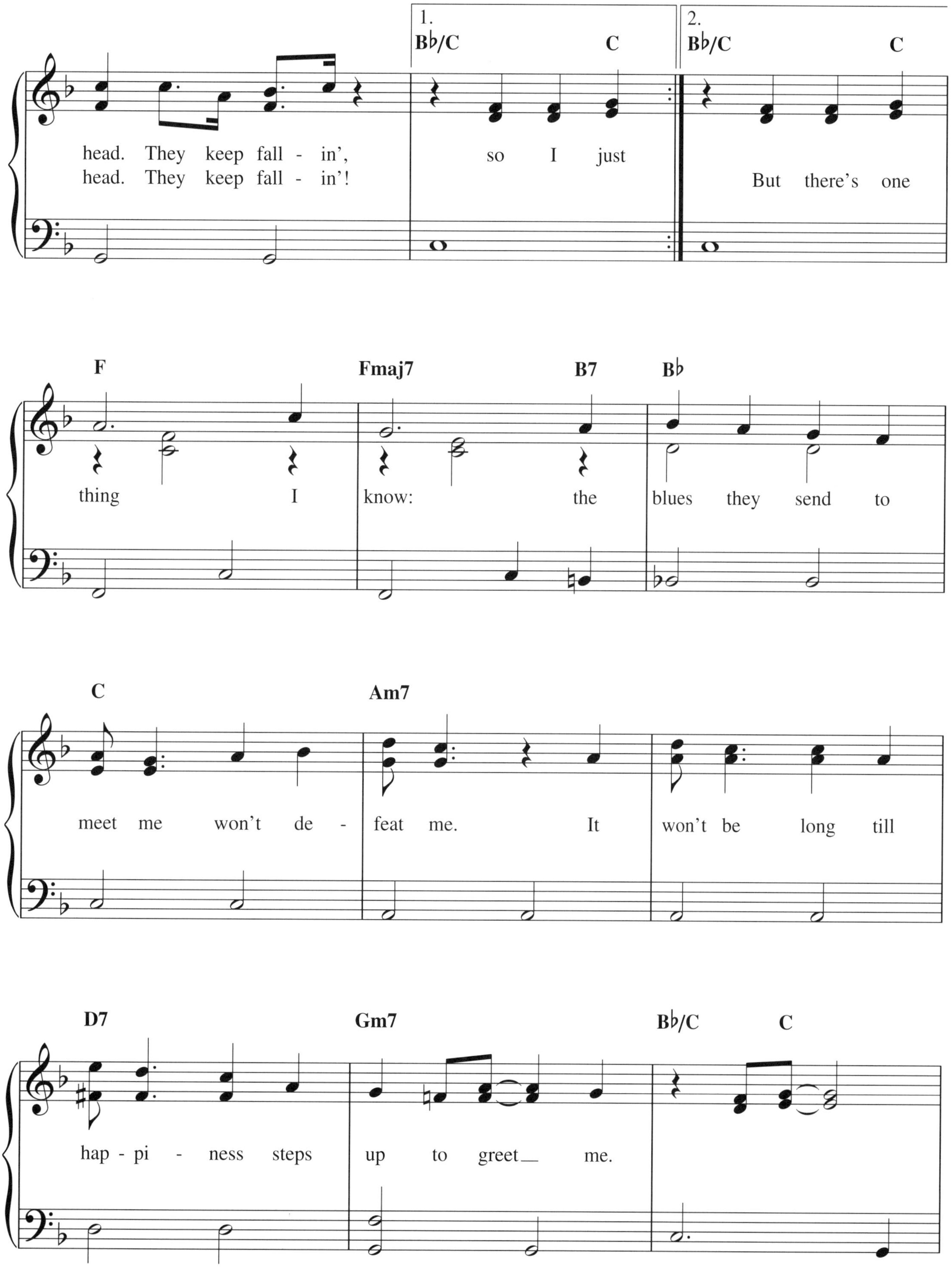
1.
Bb/C C
2.
Bb/C C
head. They keep fall - in',
head. They keep fall - in'!
so I just
But there's one
F Fmaj7 B7 Bb
thing I know: the blues they send to
C Am7
meet me won't de - feat me. It won't be long till
D7 Gm7 Bb/C C
hap - pi - ness steps up to greet me.

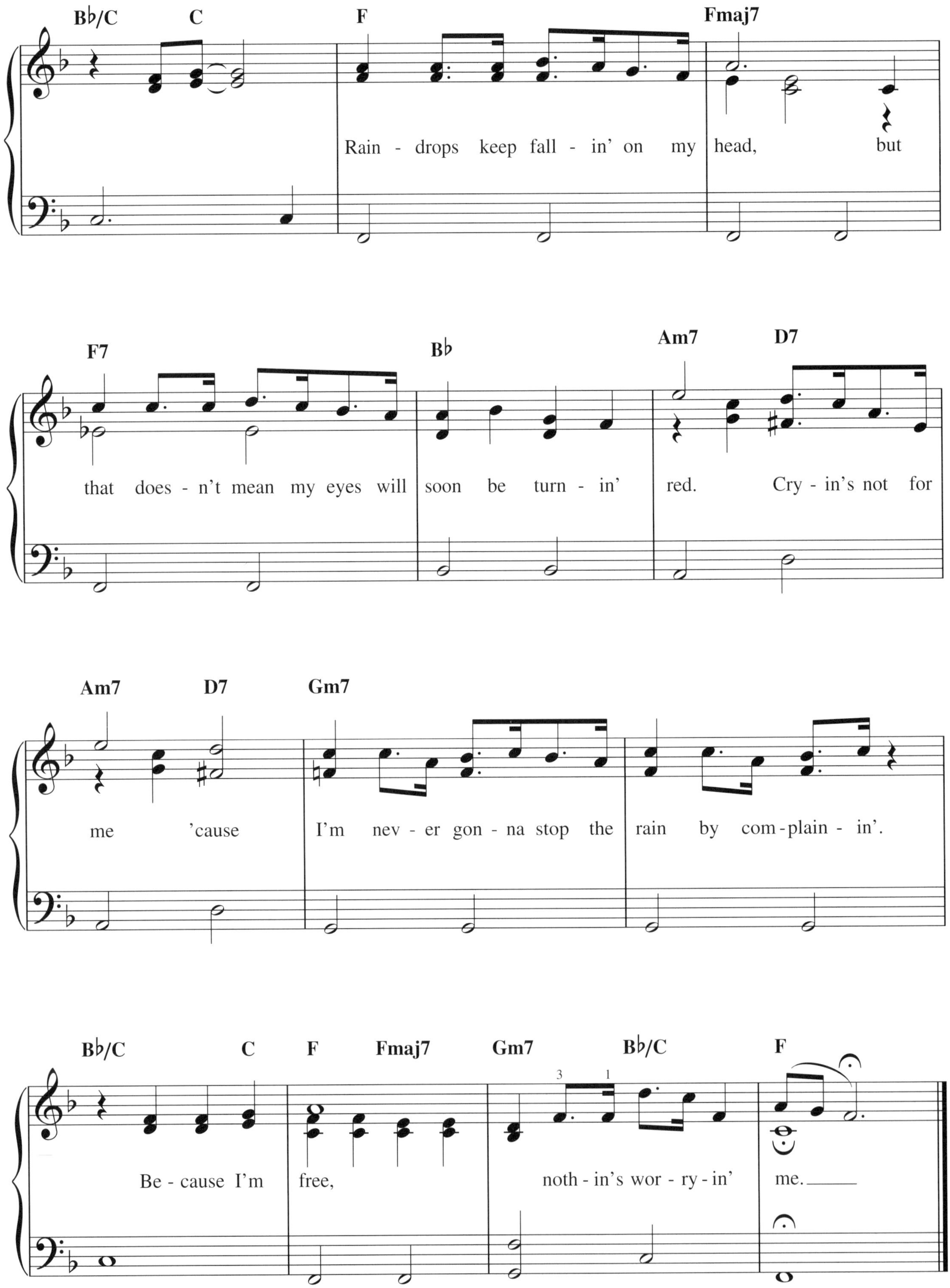
B♭/C C F Fmaj7
Rain - drops keep fall - in' on my head, but
F7 B♭ Am7 D7
that does - n't mean my eyes will soon be turn - in' red. Cry - in's not for
Am7 D7 Gm7
me 'cause I'm nev - er gon - na stop the rain by com - plain - in'.
B♭/C C F Fmaj7 Gm7 B♭/C F
Be - cause I'm free, noth - in's wor - ry - in' me.

Silly Love Songs

Words and Music by PAUL McCARTNEY
and LINDA McCARTNEY

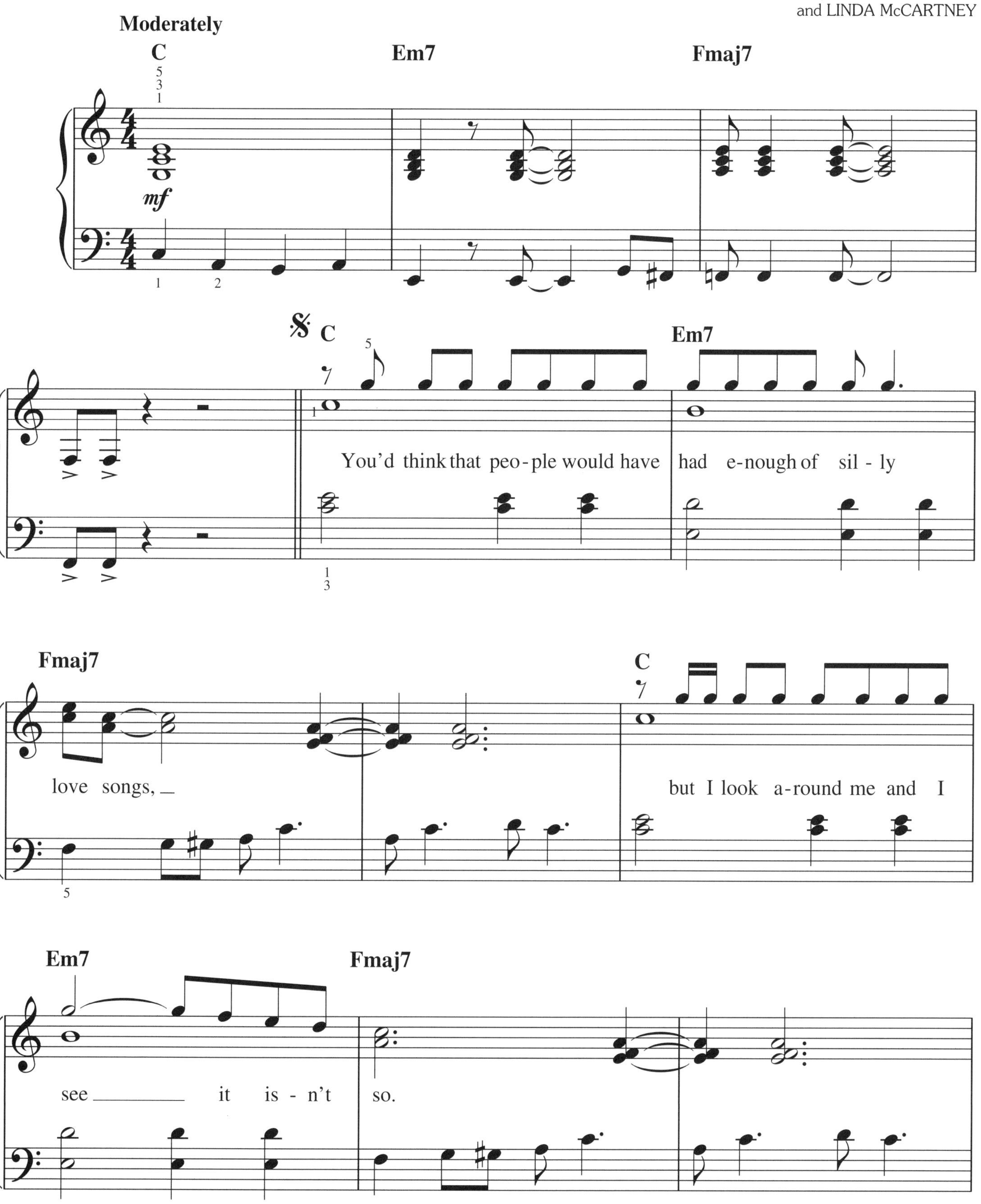

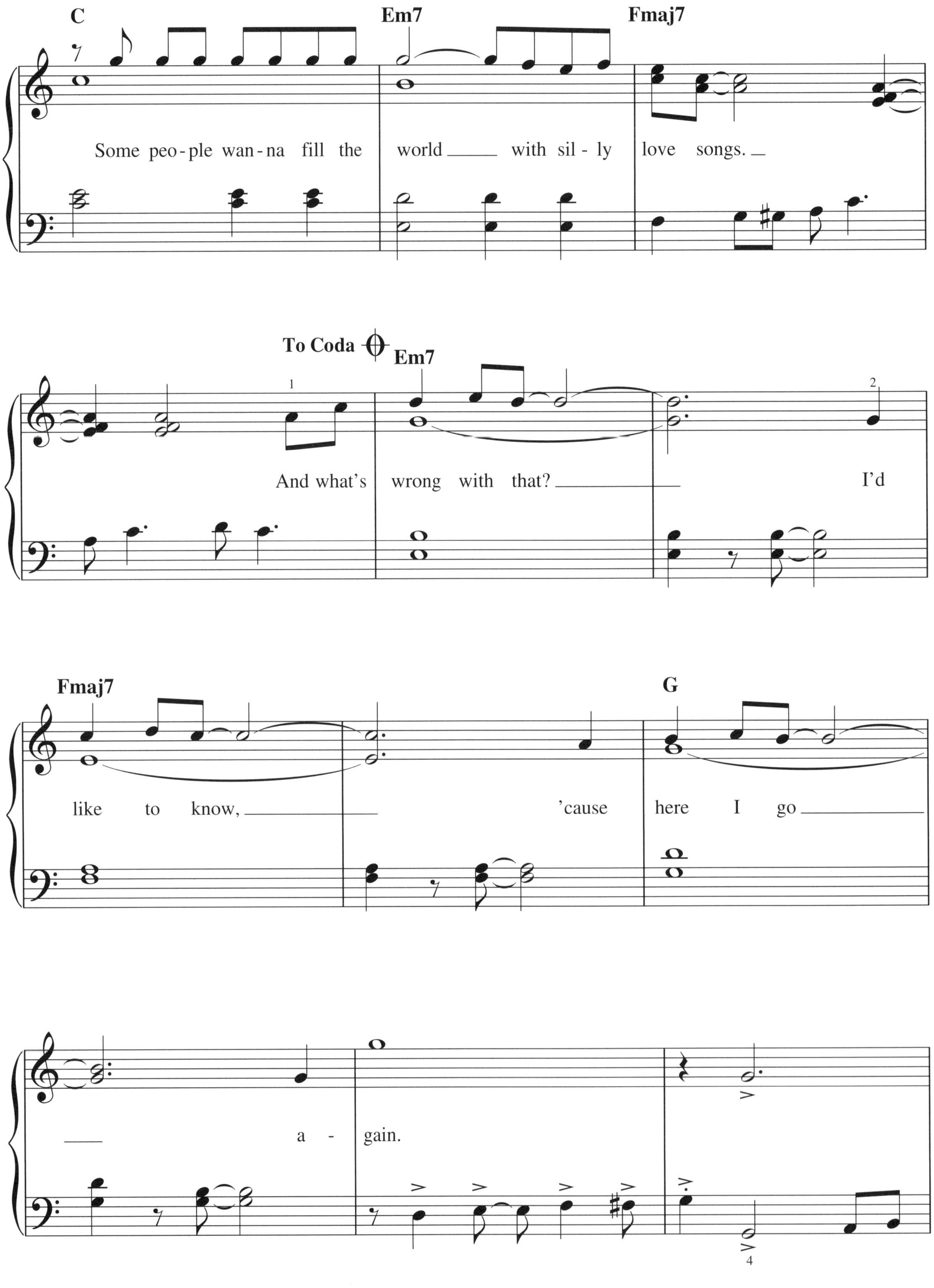
C
Em7
Fmaj7
Some peo-ple wan-na fill the world with sil-ly love songs.
To Coda
Em7
1
2
And what's wrong with that? I'd
Fmaj7
G
like to know, 'cause here I go
a - gain.
4

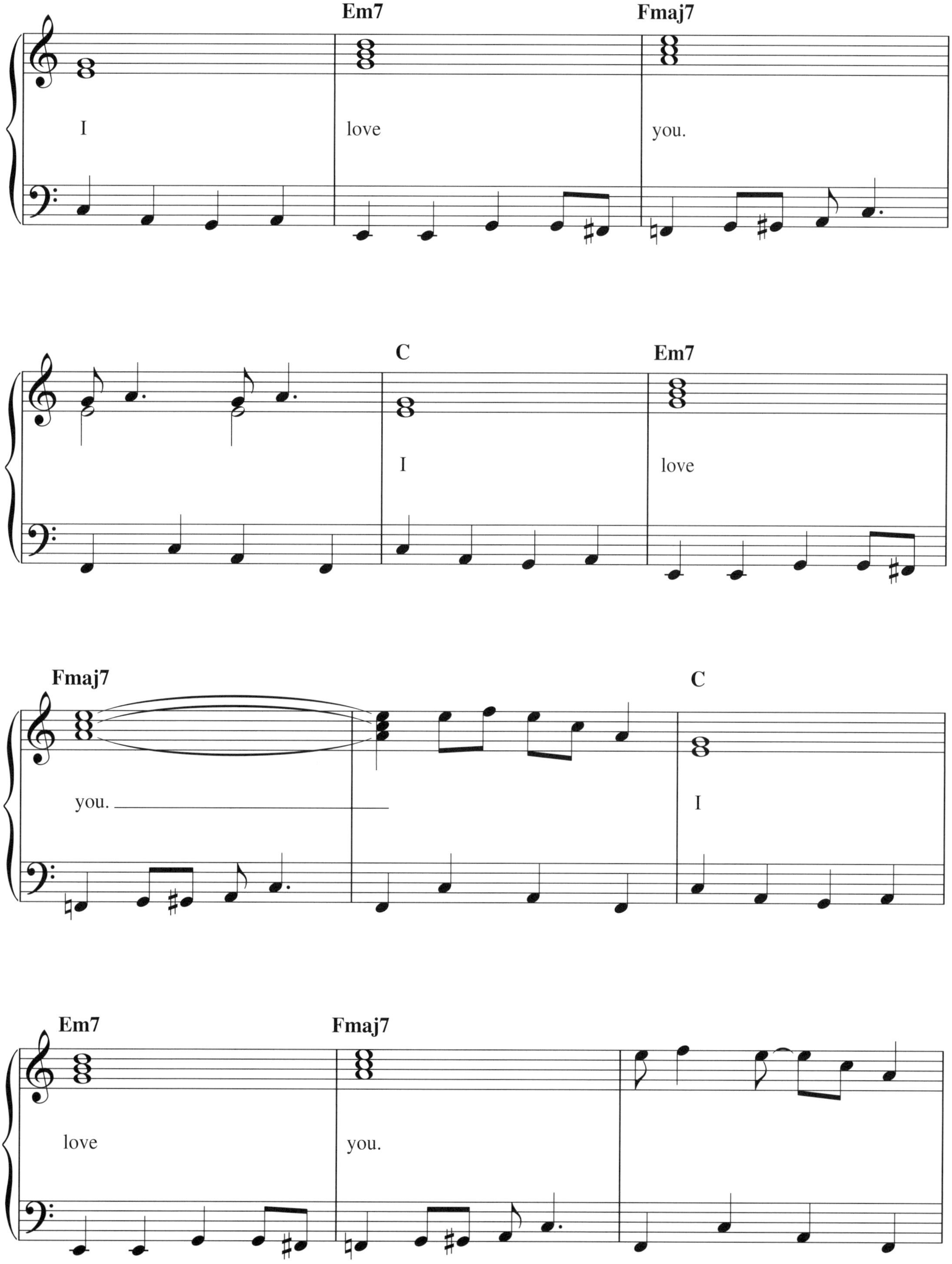
Em7
Fmaj7
I
love
you.
C
Em7
I
love
Fmaj7
C
you.
I
Em7
Fmaj7
love
you.

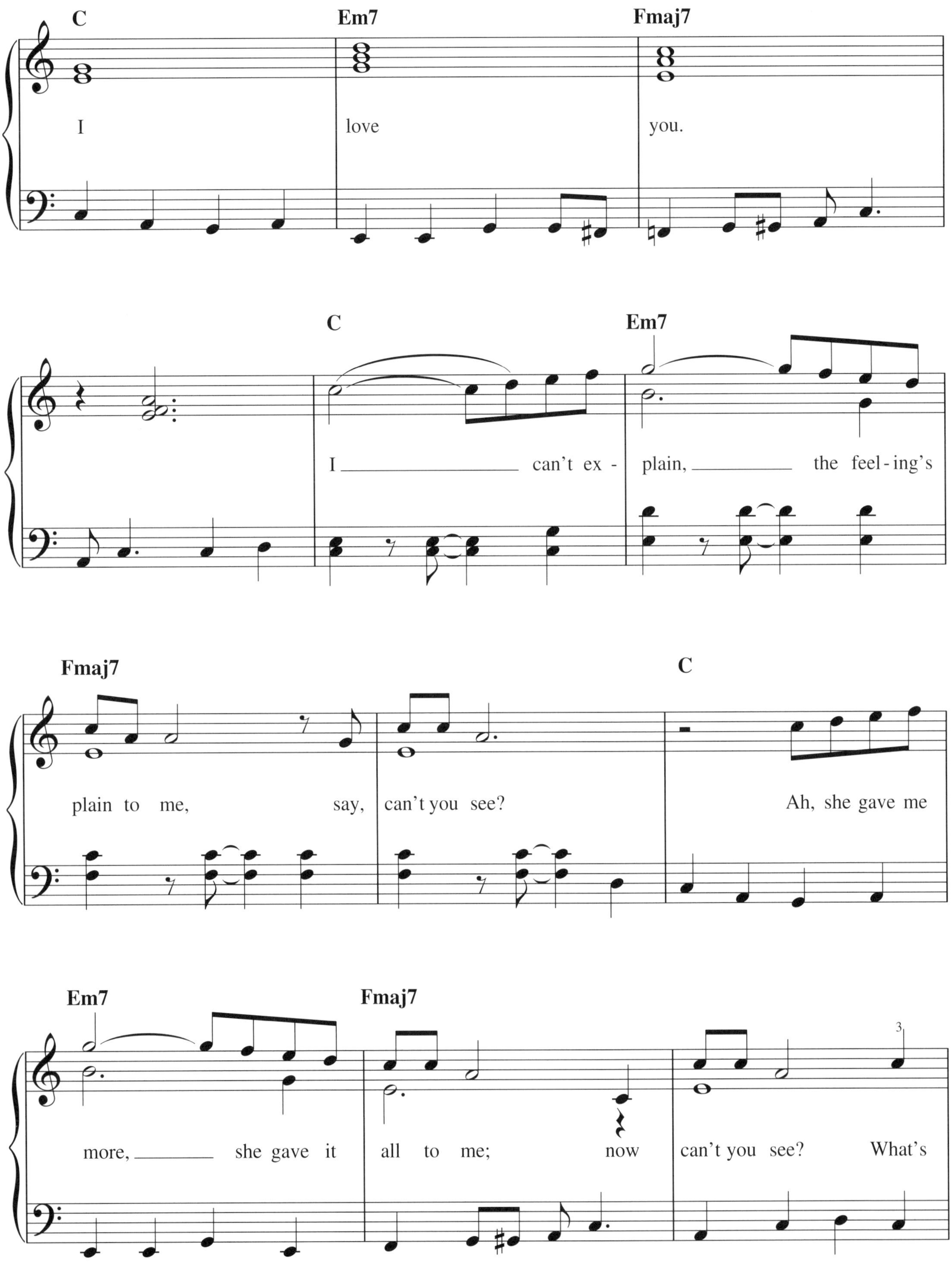
C
Em7
Fmaj7
I
love
you.
C
Em7
I can't ex - plain, the feel - ing's
Fmaj7
C
plain to me, say, can't you see? Ah, she gave me
Em7
Fmaj7
more, she gave it all to me; now can't you see? What's
3

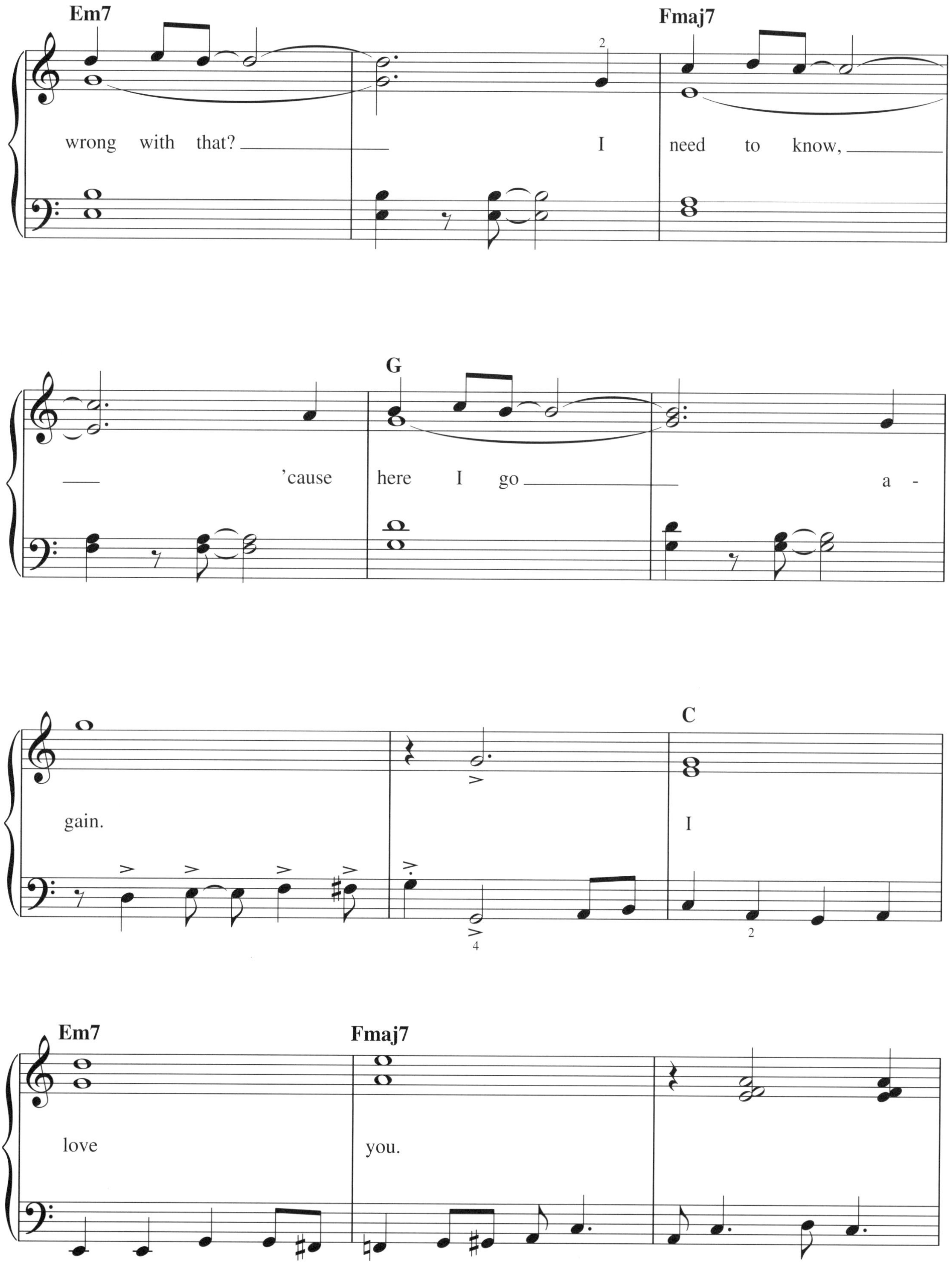
Em7
Fmaj7
wrong with that?
I need to know,
'cause
G
here I go
a-
gain.
C
I
Em7
Fmaj7
love
you.

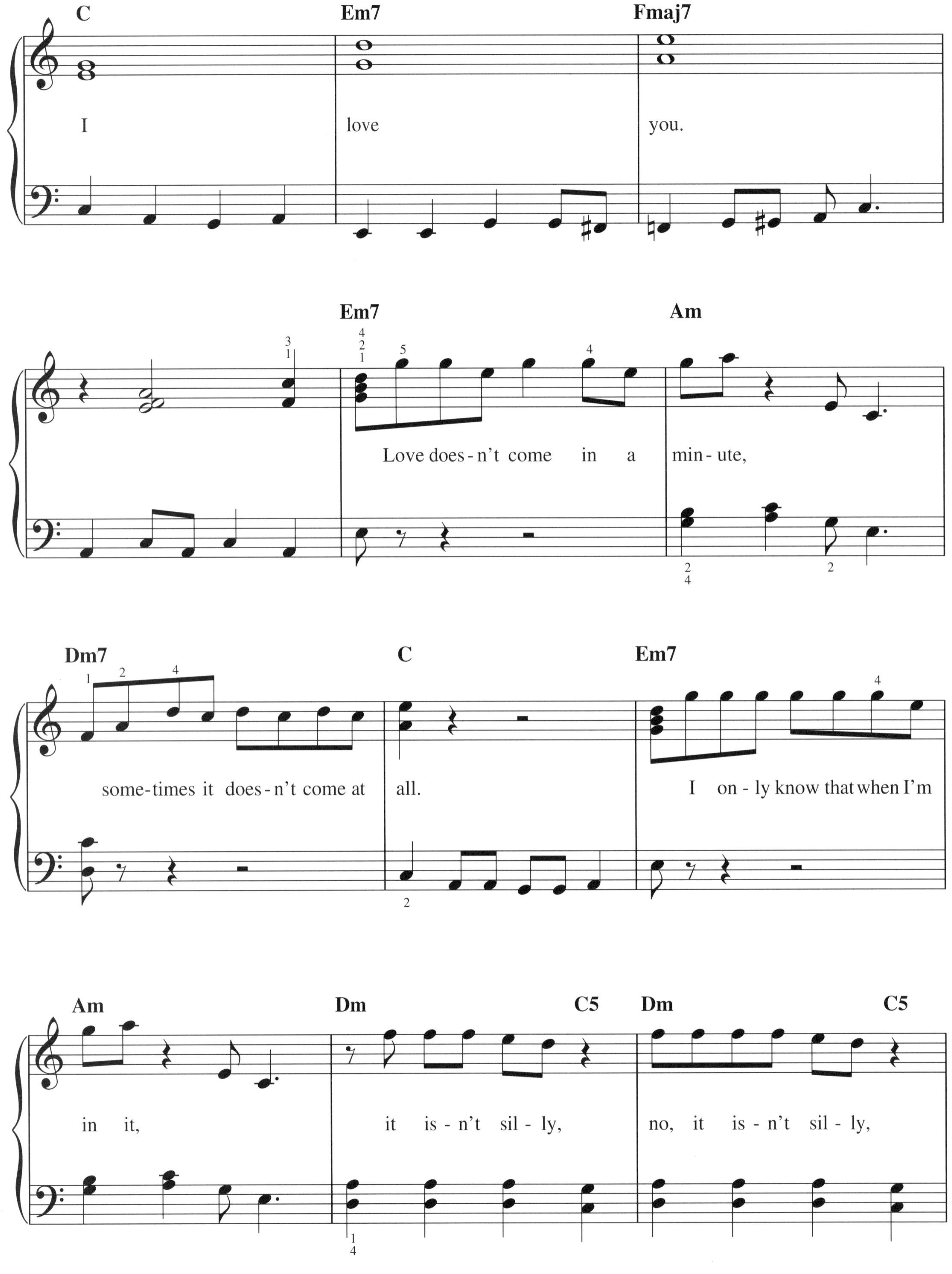
C Em7 Fmaj7
I love you.
Em7 Am
Love does-n't come in a min-ute,
Dm7 C Em7
some-times it does-n't come at all.
I on-ly know that when I'm
Am Dm C5 Dm C5
in it,
it is-n't sil-ly,
no, it is-n't sil-ly,

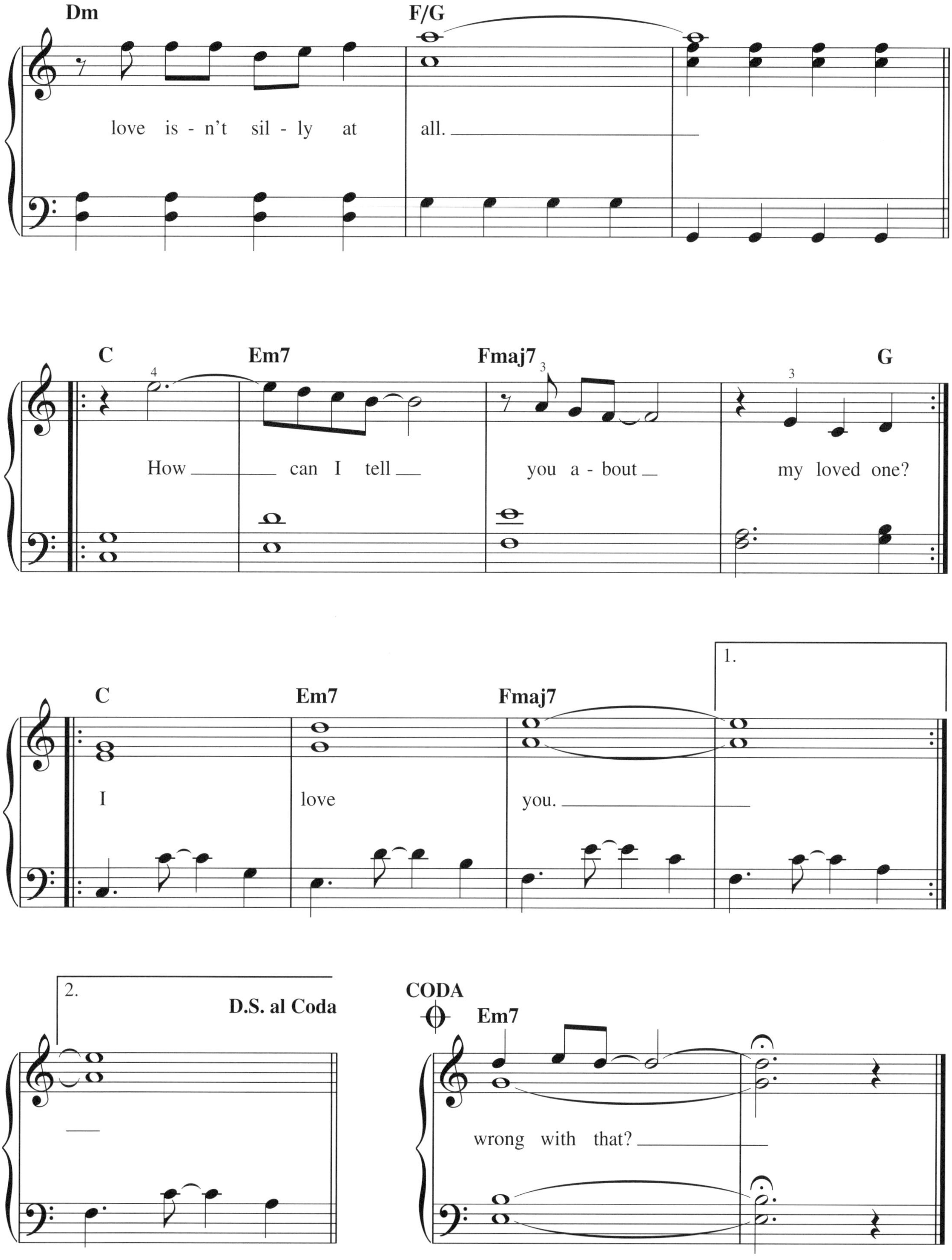
Dm
F/G
love is - n't sil - ly at all.
C
Em7
Fmaj7
G
How can I tell you a - bout my loved one?
C
Em7
Fmaj7
1.
I love you.
2.
D.S. al Coda
CODA
Em7
wrong with that?

Rolling in the Deep

Words and Music by ADELE ADKINS
and PAUL EPWORTH

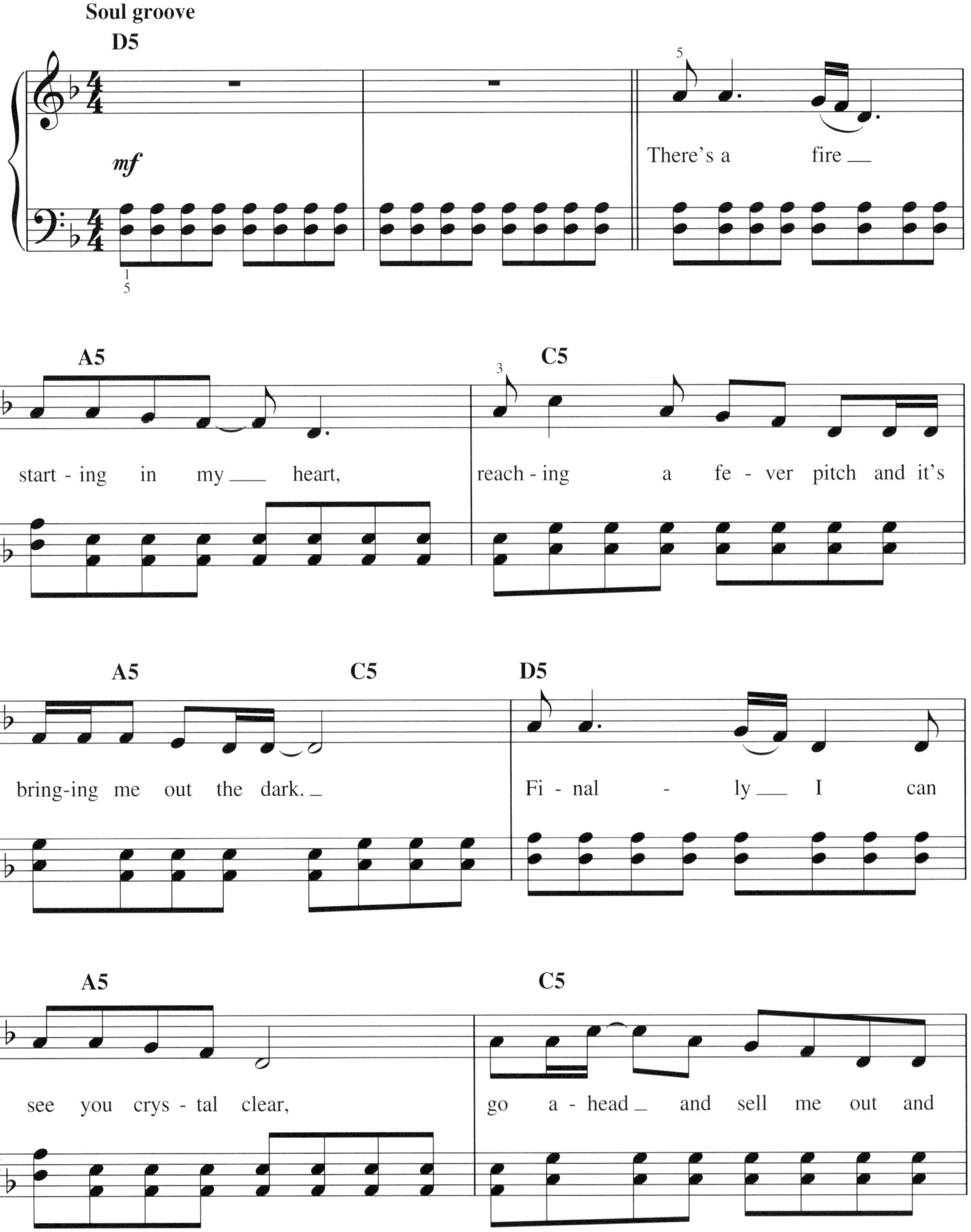

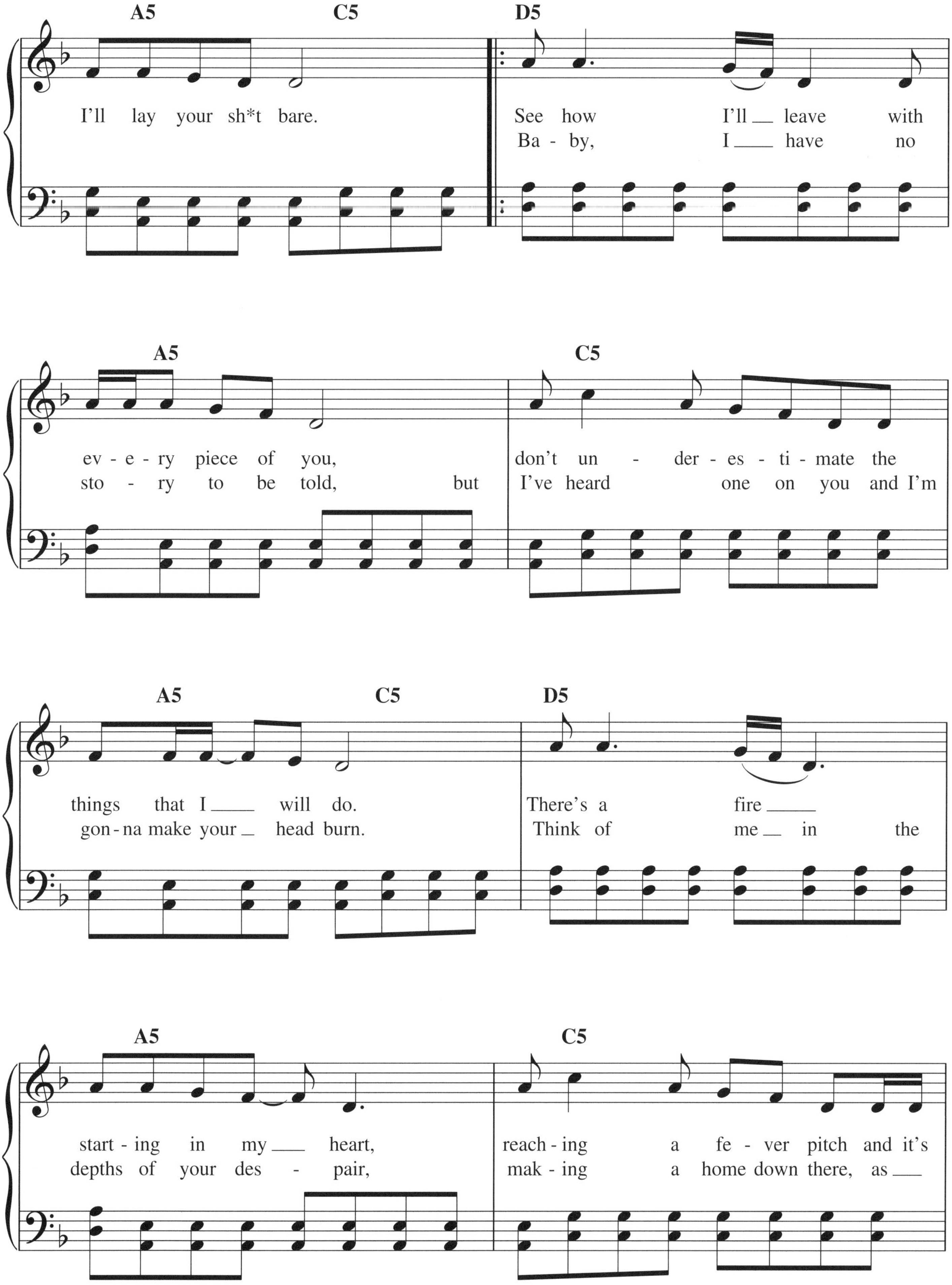
A5 C5 D5
I'll lay your sh*t bare.
See how I'll leave with
Ba - by, I have no
A5 C5
ev - e - ry piece of you, don't un - der - es - ti - mate the
sto - ry to be told, but I've heard one on you and I'm
A5 C5 D5
things that I will do. There's a fire
gon - na make your head burn. Think of me in the
A5 C5
start - ing in my heart, reach - ing a fe - ver pitch and it's
depths of your des - pair, mak - ing a home down there, as

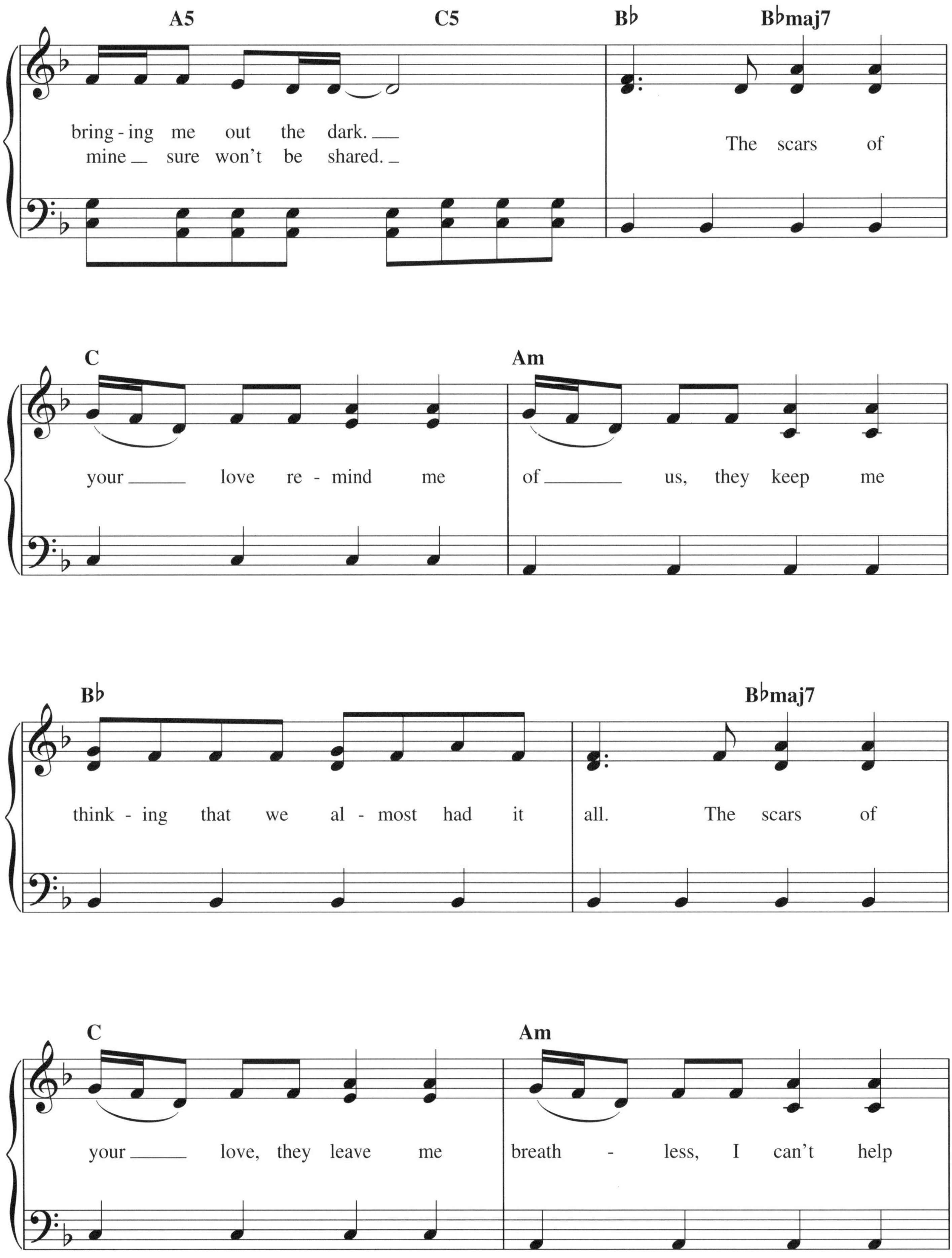
A5
C5
B♭
B♭maj7
bring - ing me out the dark.
mine sure won't be shared.
The scars of
C
Am
your love re - mind me
of us, they keep me
B♭
B♭maj7
think - ing that we al - most had it
all. The scars of
C
Am
your love, they leave me
breath - less, I can't help

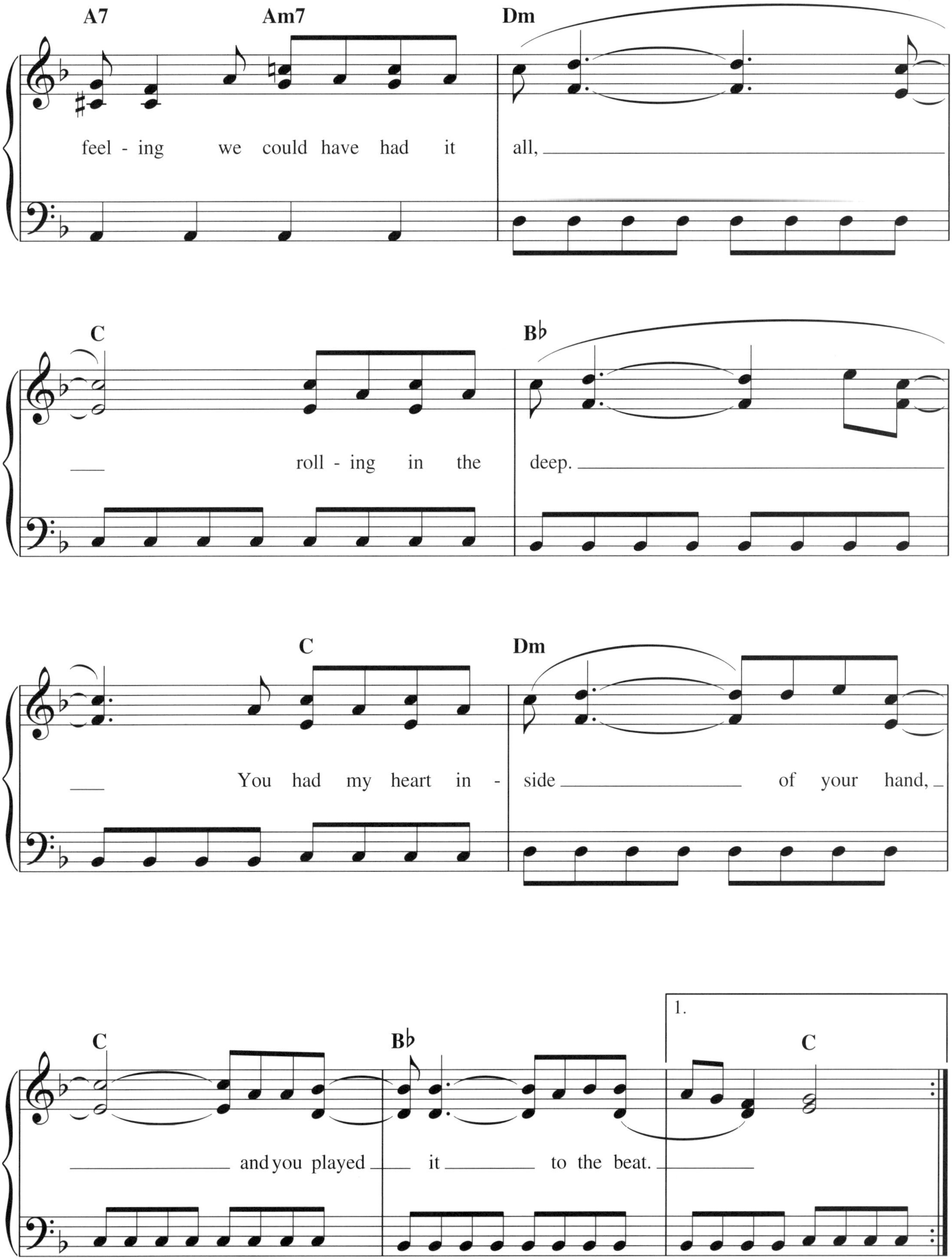
A7
Am7
Dm
feel - ing we could have had it all,
C
Bb
roll - ing in the deep.
C
Dm
You had my heart in - side of your hand,
C
Bb
1.
C
and you played it to the beat.

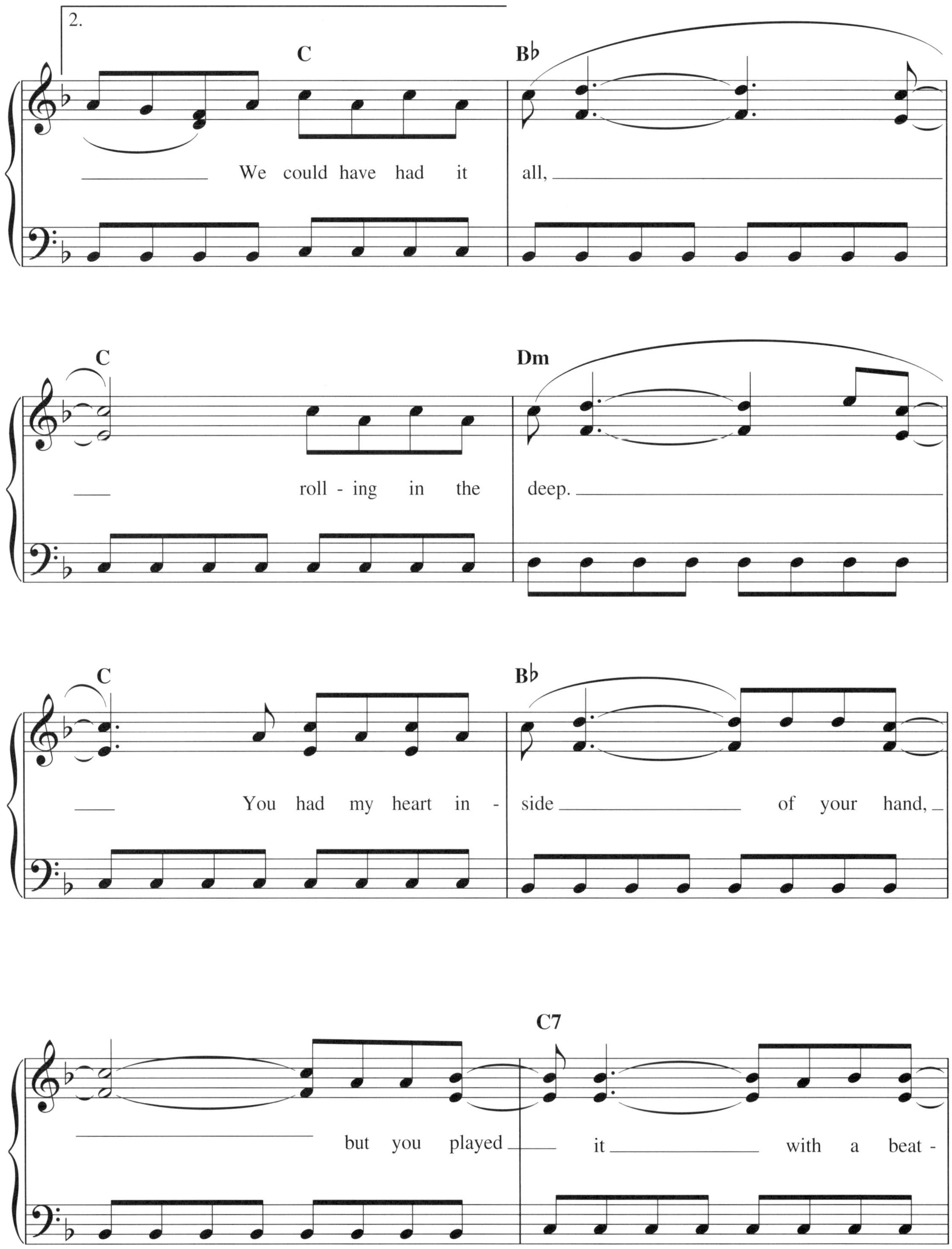
2.
C
Bb
We could have had it all,
C
Dm
rolling in the deep.
C
Bb
You had my heart inside of your hand,
C7
but you played it with a beat-

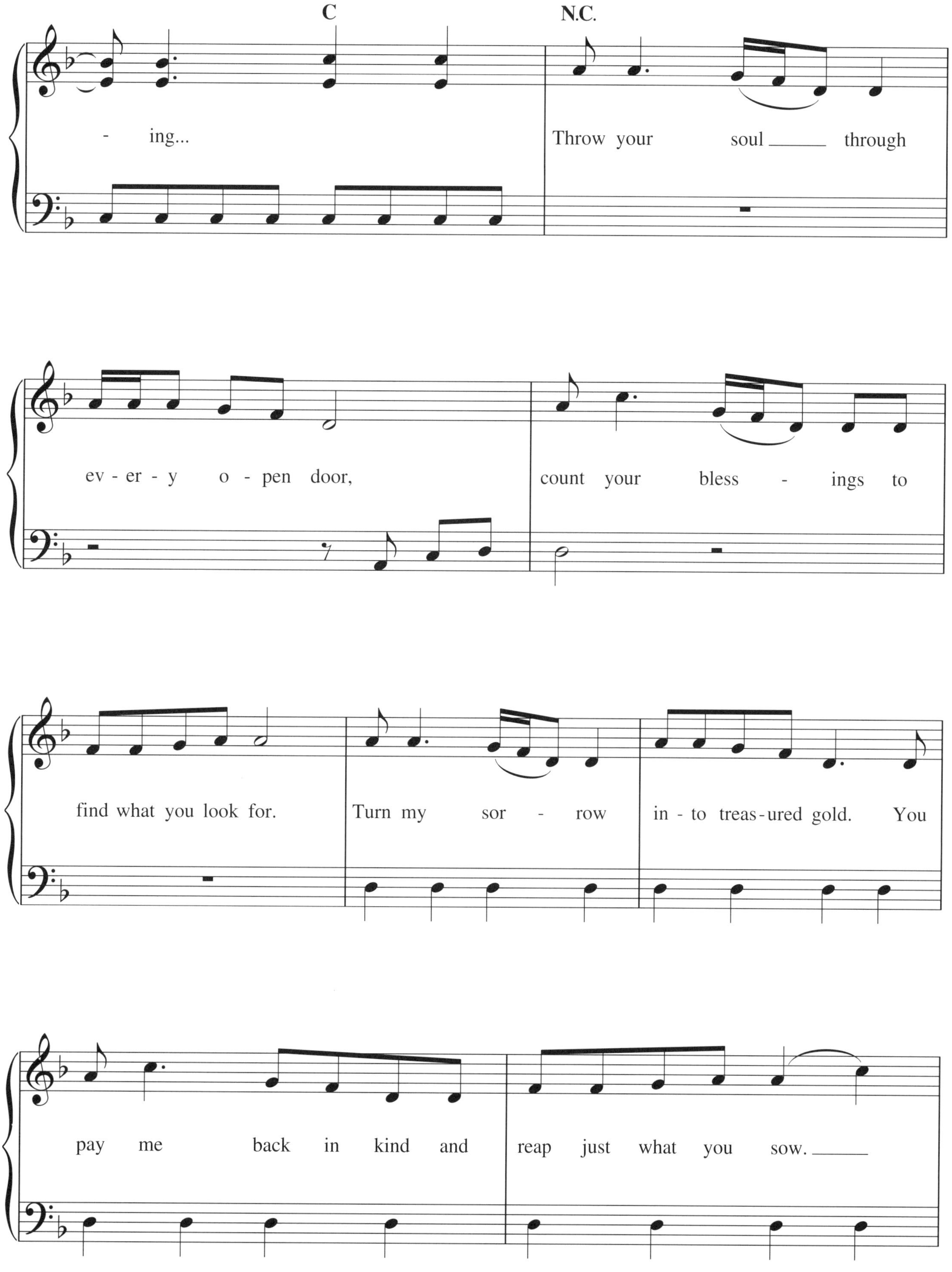
C
N.C.
- ing...
Throw your soul ___ through
ev - er - y o - pen door,
count your bless - ings to
find what you look for.
Turn my sor - row
in - to treas - ured gold. You
pay me back in kind and
reap just what you sow. ___

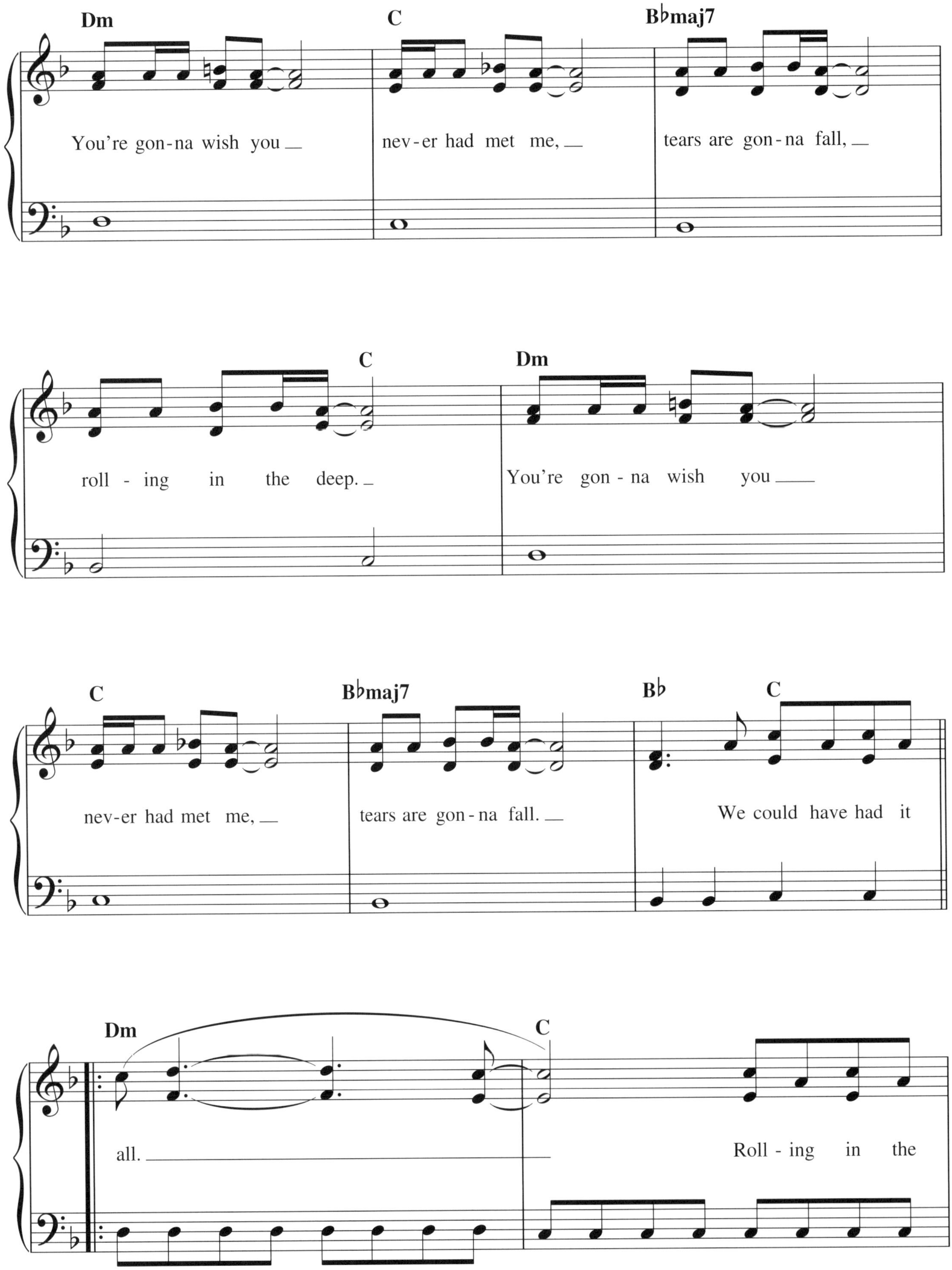
Dm
C
B♭maj7
You're gon-na wish you
nev-er had met me,
tears are gon-na fall,
C
Dm
roll - ing in the deep.
You're gon - na wish you
C
B♭maj7
B♭
C
nev-er had met me,
tears are gon-na fall.
We could have had it
Dm
C
all.
Roll - ing in the

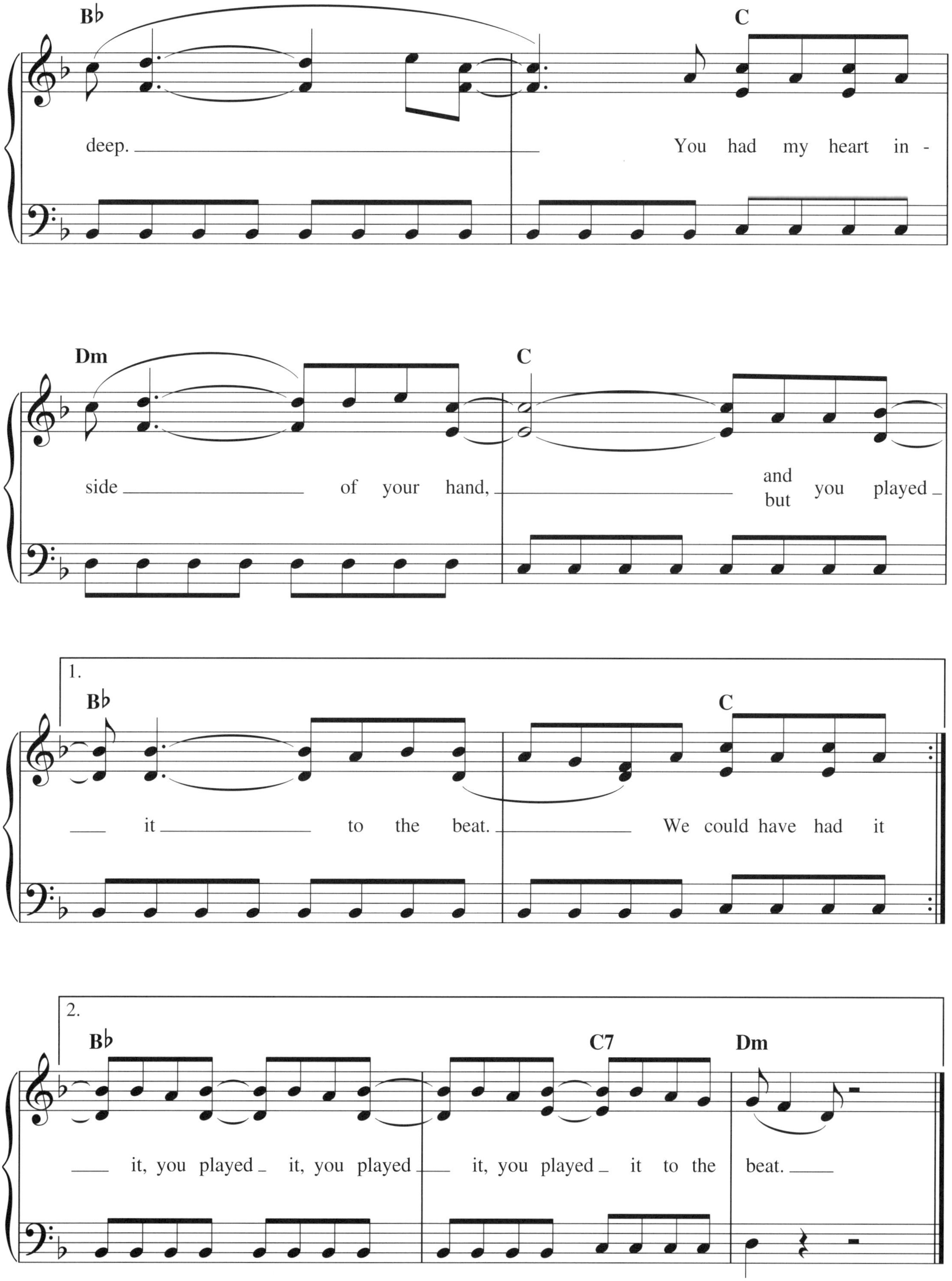
B♭
C
deep. You had my heart in -
Dm
C
side of your hand, and you played
but
1.
B♭
C
it to the beat. We could have had it
2.
B♭
C7
Dm
it, you played it, you played it, you played it to the beat.

Sing

Words and Music by
JOE RAPOSO

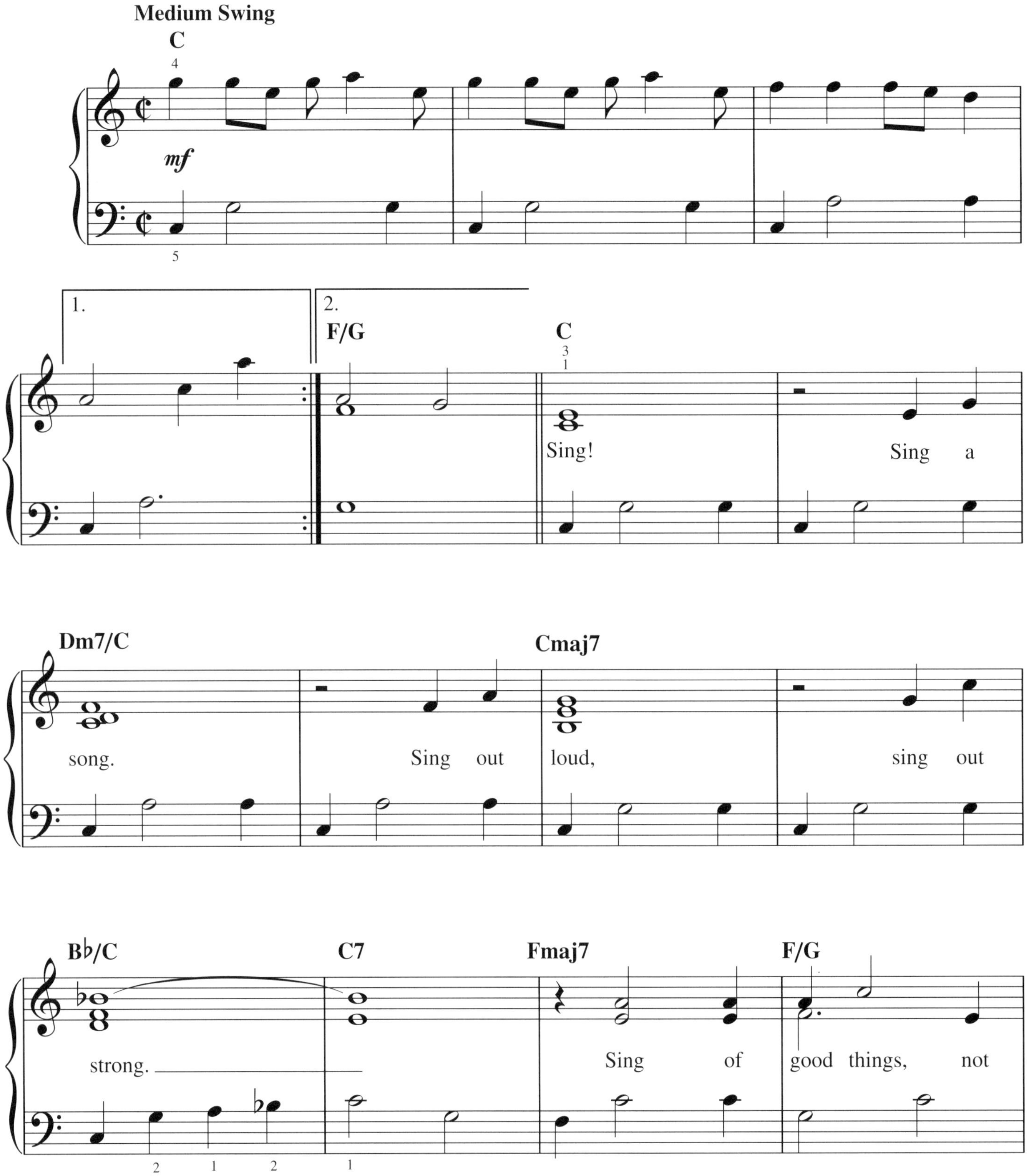

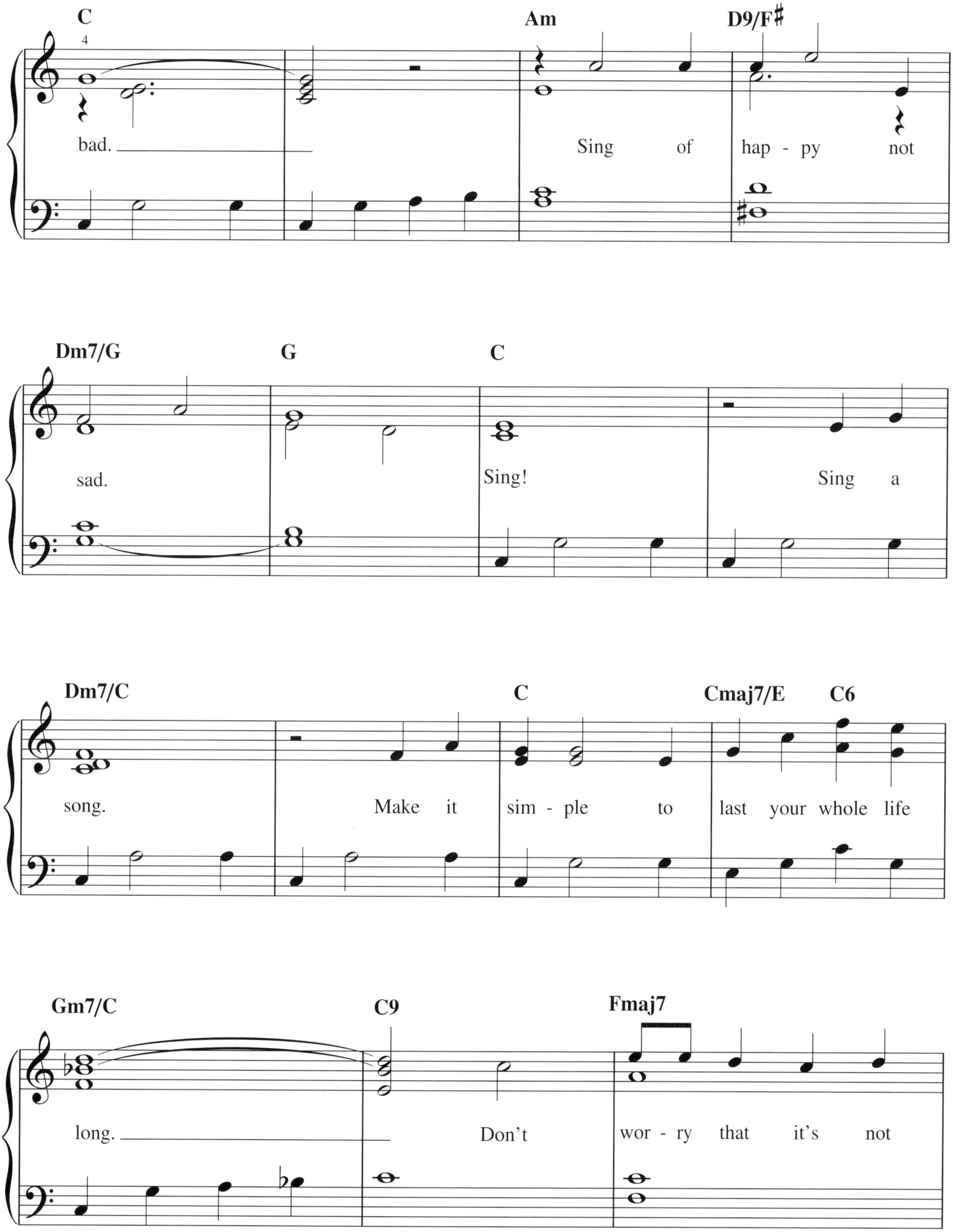
C
4
bad.
Am
Sing of
D9/F♯
hap - py not
Dm7/G
sad.
G
C
Sing!
Sing a
Dm7/C
song.
Make it
C
sim - ple to
Cmaj7/E
C6
last your whole life
Gm7/C
long.
C9
Don't
Fmaj7
wor - ry that it's not

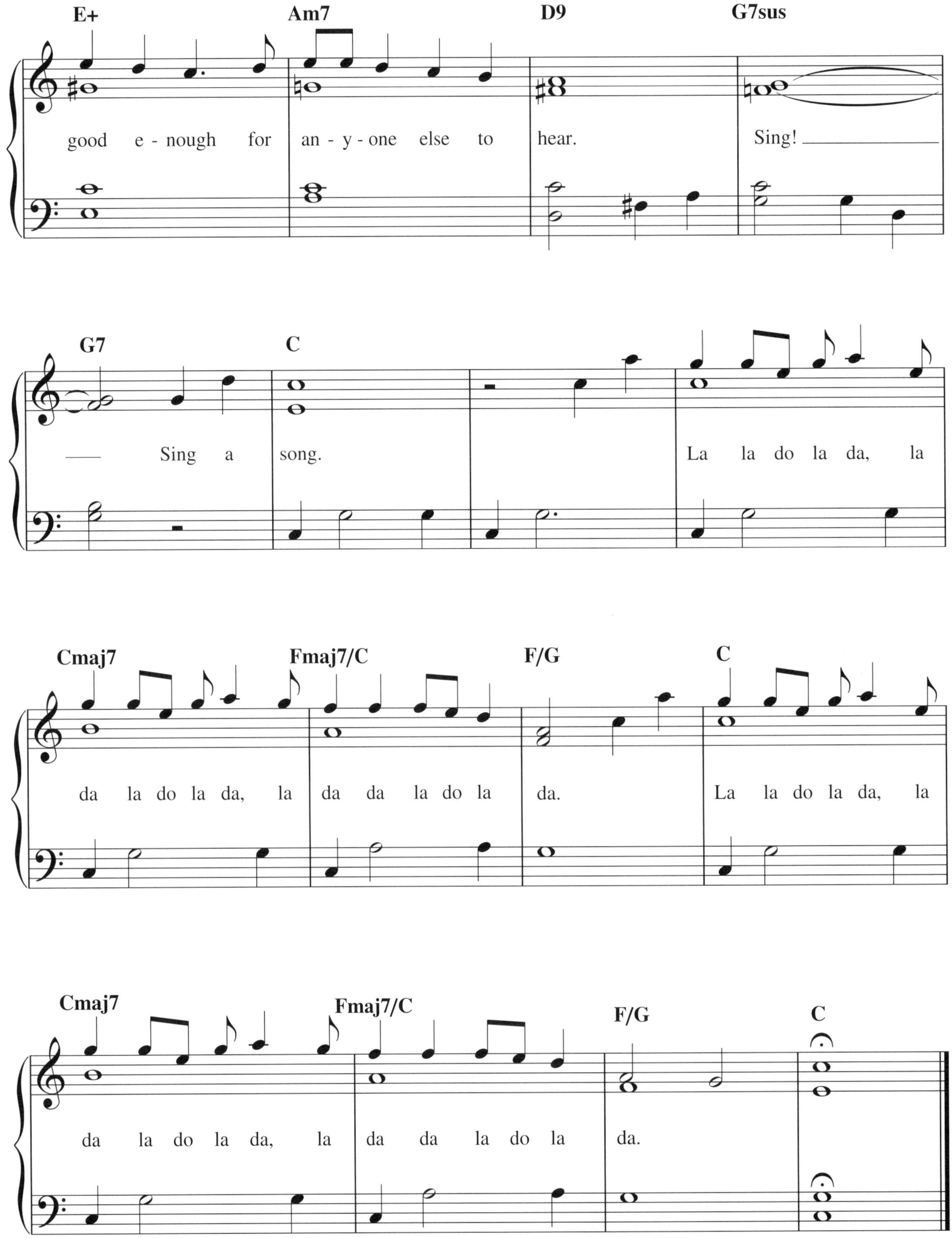
E+ Am7 D9 G7sus
good e - nough for an - y - one else to hear. Sing!
G7 C
Sing a song.
La la do la da, la
Cmaj7 Fmaj7/C F/G C
da la do la da, la da da la do la da. La la do la da, la
Cmaj7 Fmaj7/C F/G C
da la do la da, la da da la do la da.

Sway (Quien Será)

English Words by NORMAN GIMBEL
Spanish Words and Music by PABLO BELTRAN RUIZ

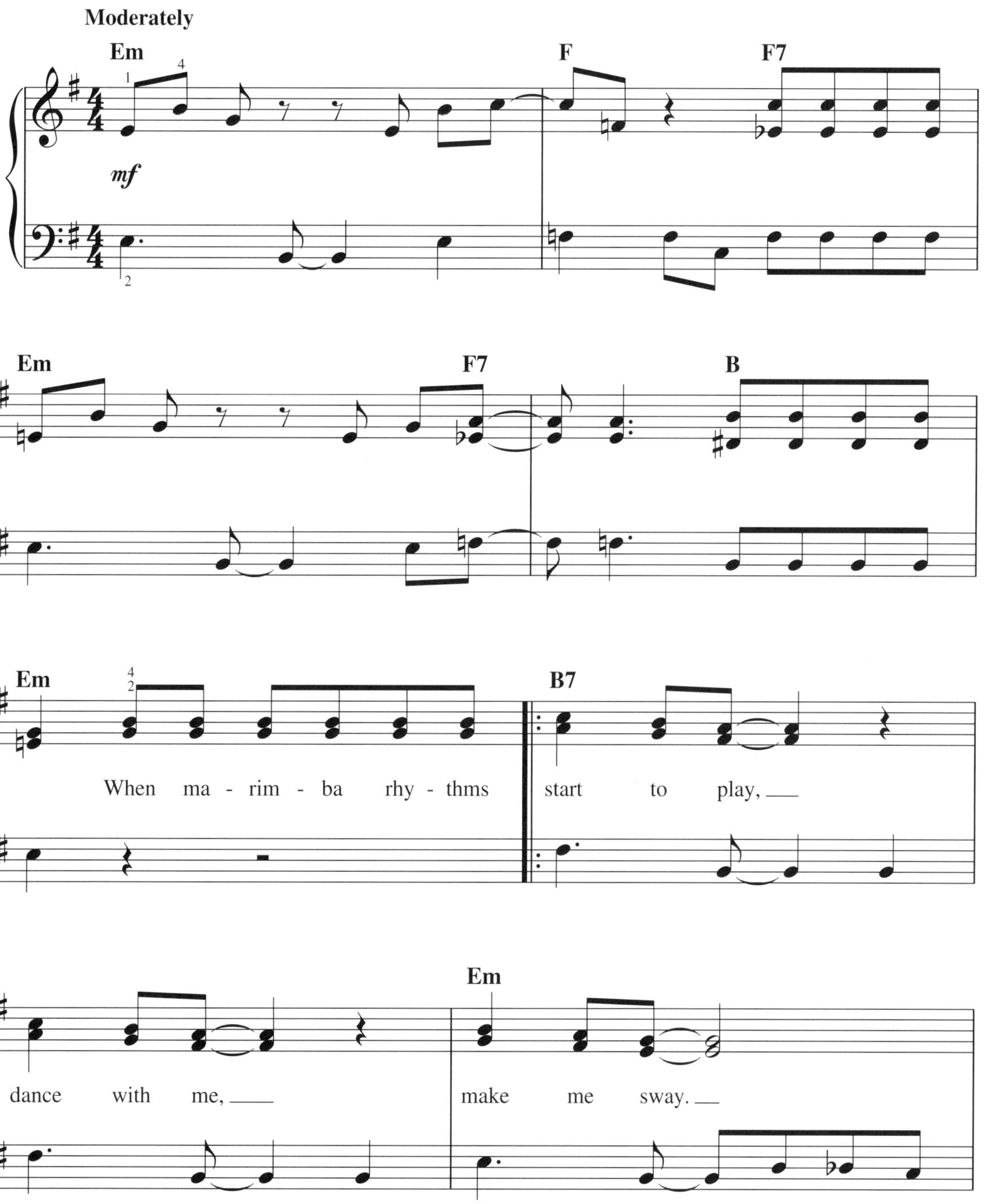

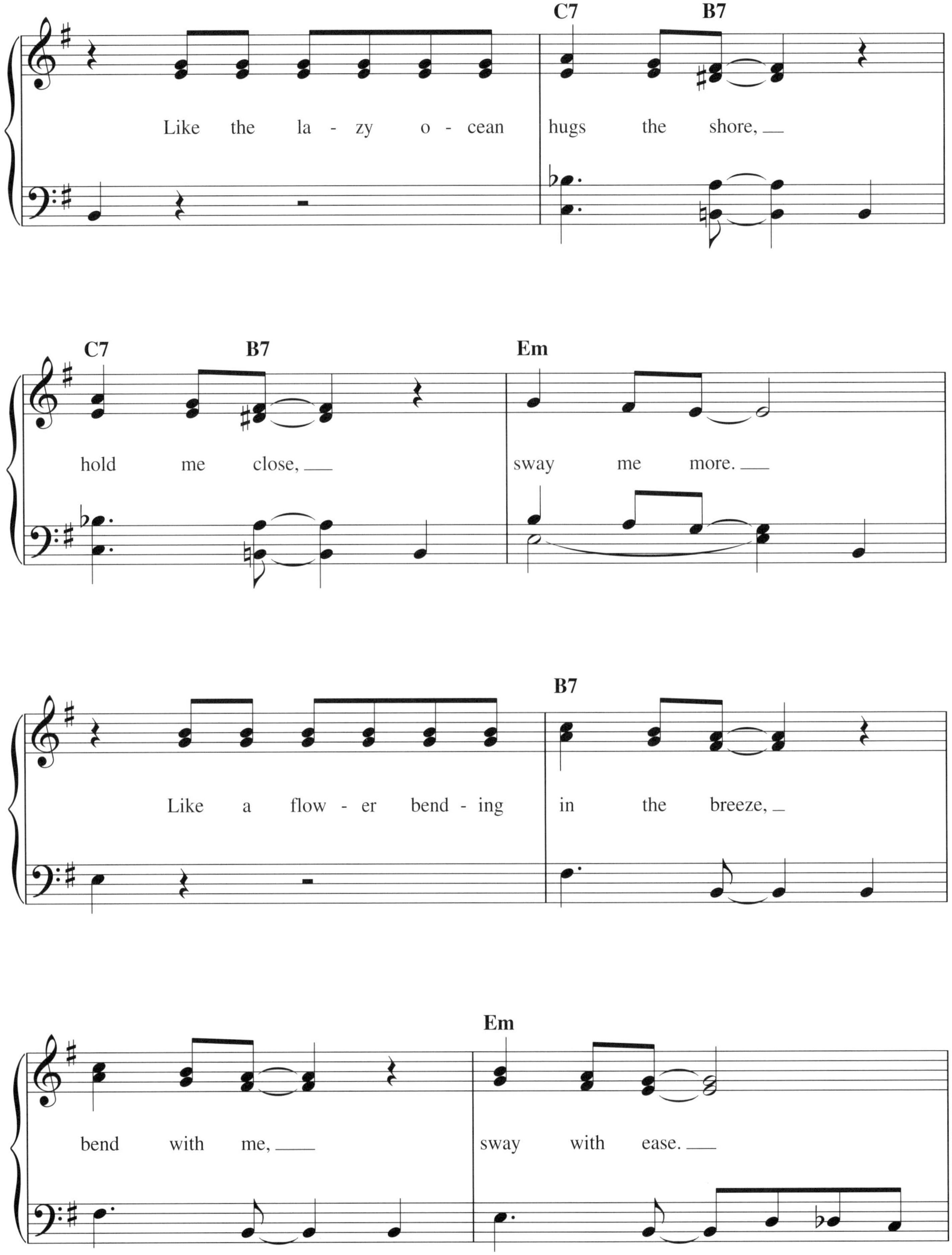
C7 B7
Like the la - zy o - cean hugs the shore,
C7 B7 Em
hold me close, sway me more.
B7
Like a flow - er bend - ing in the breeze,
Em
bend with me, sway with ease.

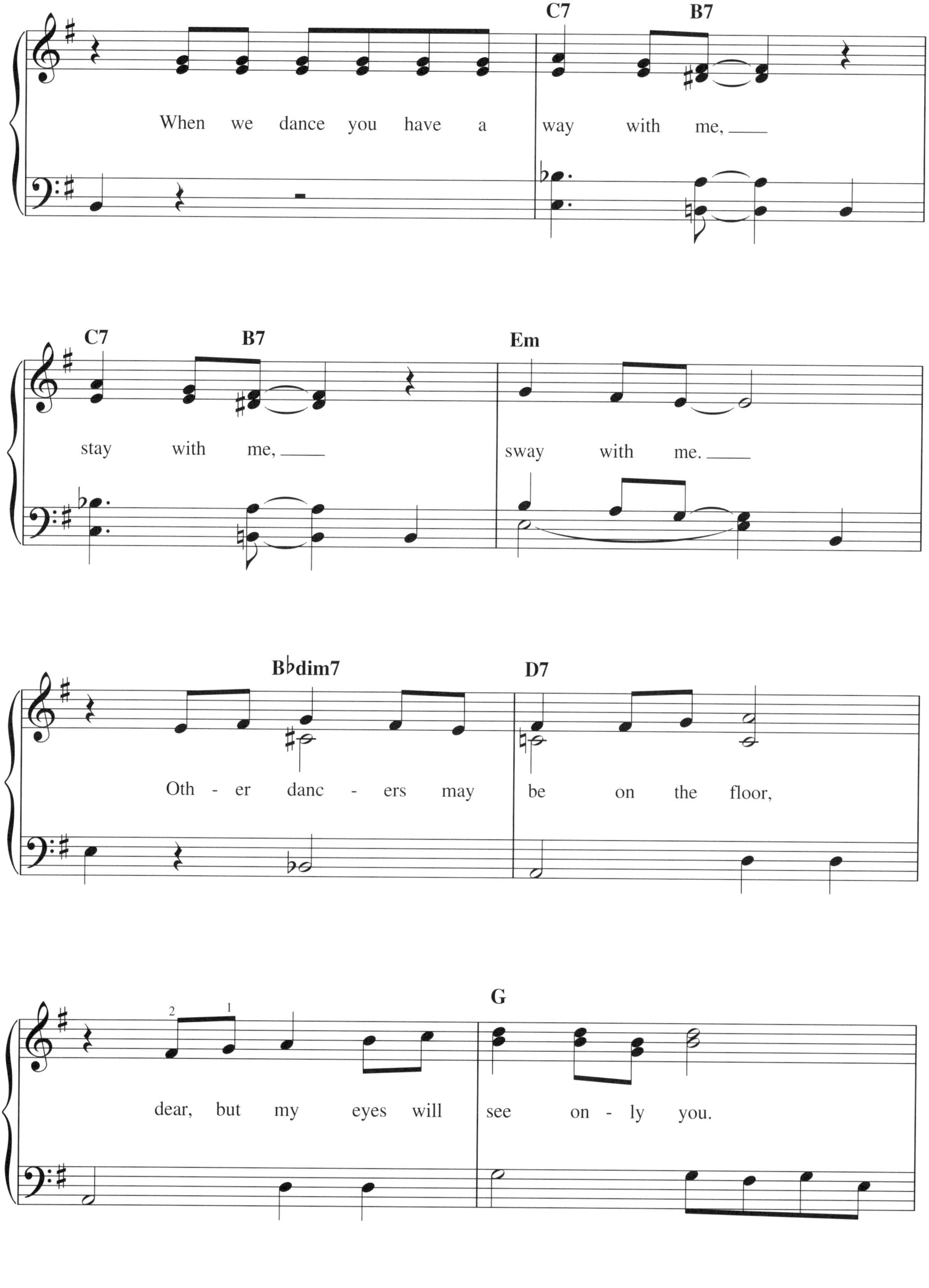
C7 B7
When we dance you have a way with me,
C7 B7 Em
stay with me, sway with me.
B♭dim7 D7
Oth - er danc - ers may be on the floor,
2 1
G
dear, but my eyes will see on - ly you.

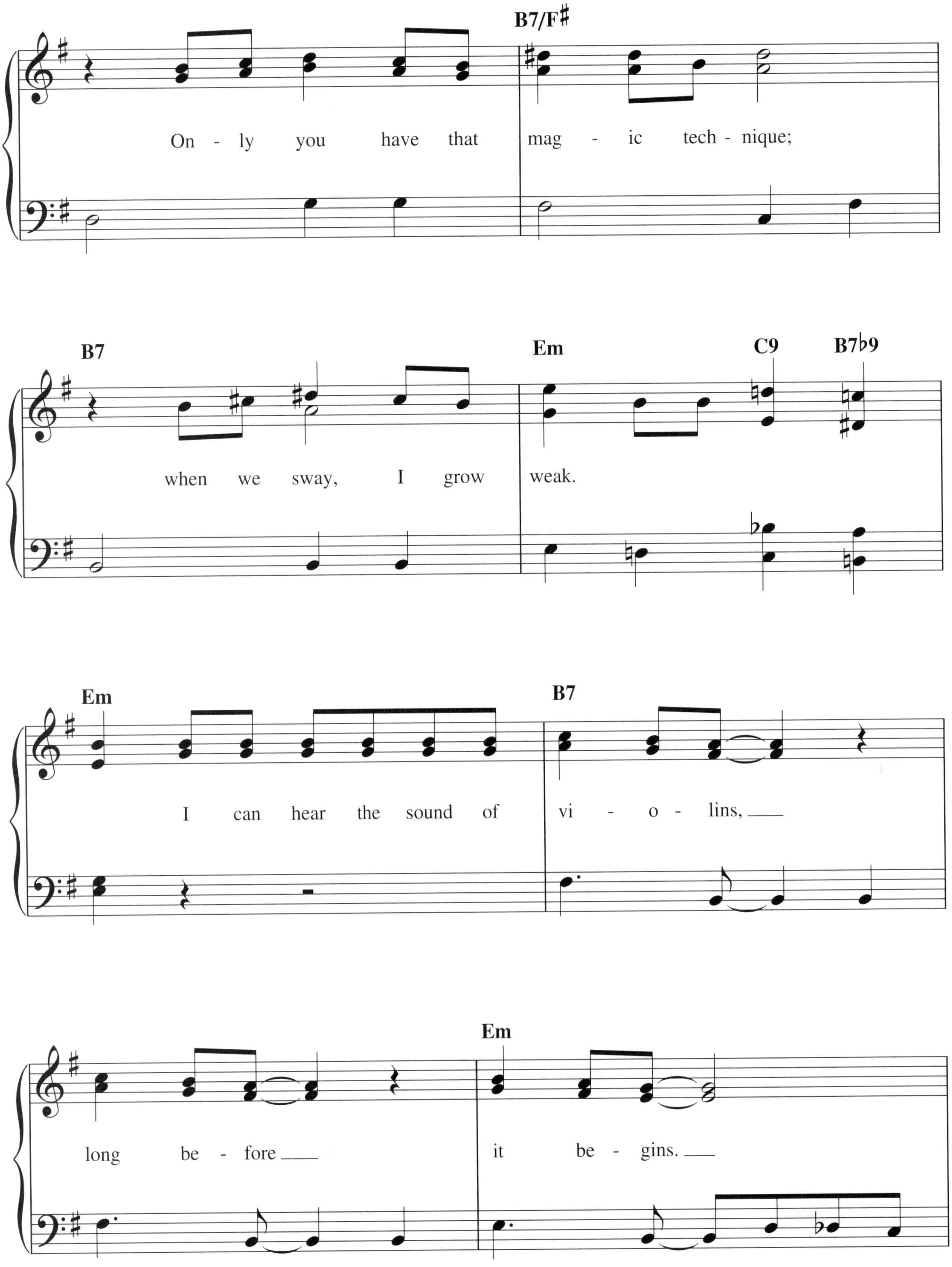
B7/F♯
On - ly you have that mag - ic tech - nique;
B7
Em
C9
B7♭9
when we sway, I grow weak.
Em
B7
I can hear the sound of vi - o - lins,
Em
long be - fore it be - gins.

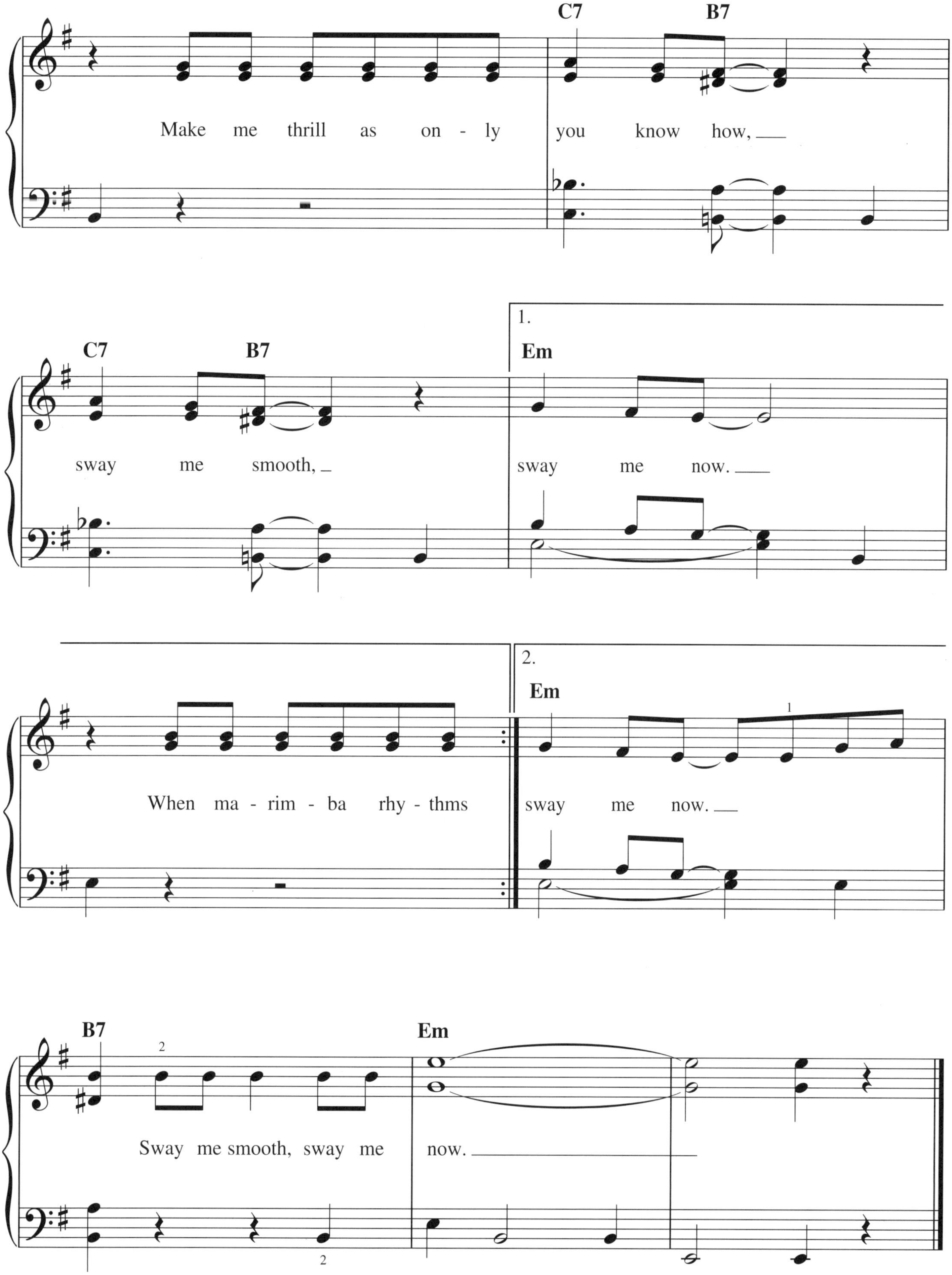
C7
B7
Make me thrill as on - ly you know how,
C7
B7
1.
Em
sway me smooth, sway me now.
2.
Em
When ma - rim - ba rhy - thms sway me now.
B7
Em
Sway me smooth, sway me now.

Stardust

Words by MITCHELL PARISH
Music by HOAGY CARMICHAEL

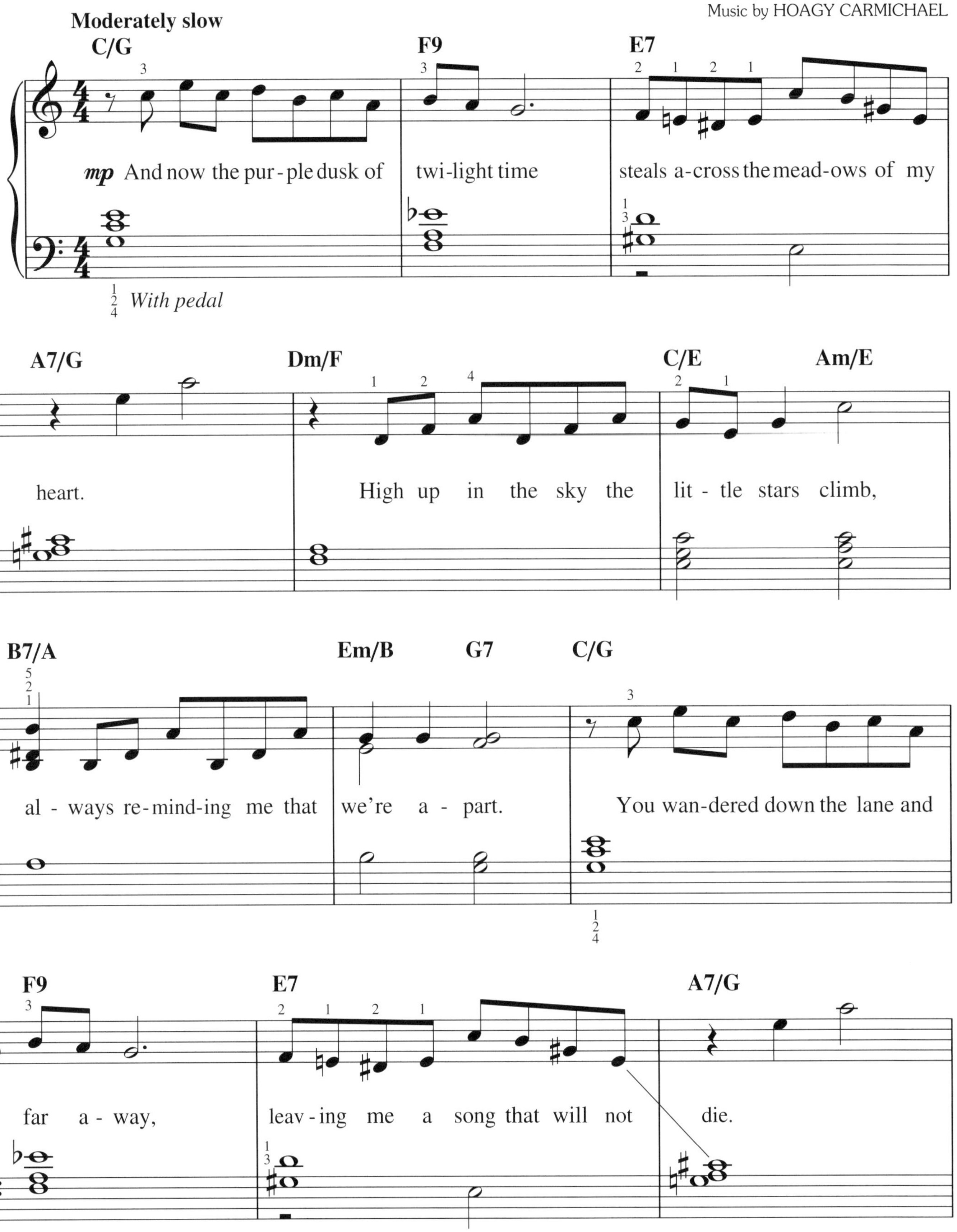

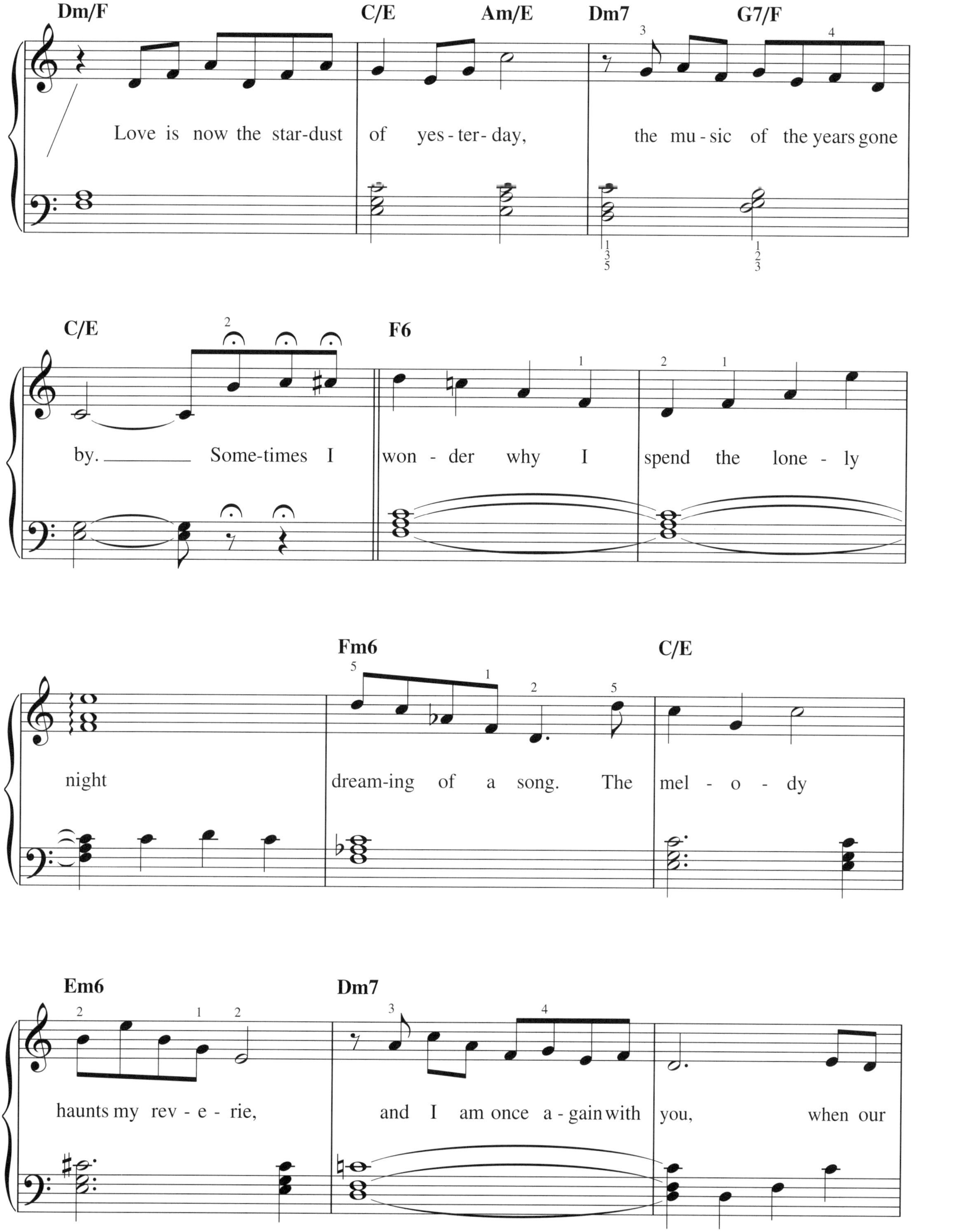
Dm/F C/E Am/E Dm7 G7/F
Love is now the star-dust of yes-ter-day, the mu-sic of the years gone
C/E F6
by. Some-times I won - der why I spend the lone - ly
Fm6 C/E
night dream-ing of a song. The mel - o - dy
Em6 Dm7
haunts my rev - e - rie, and I am once a - gain with you, when our

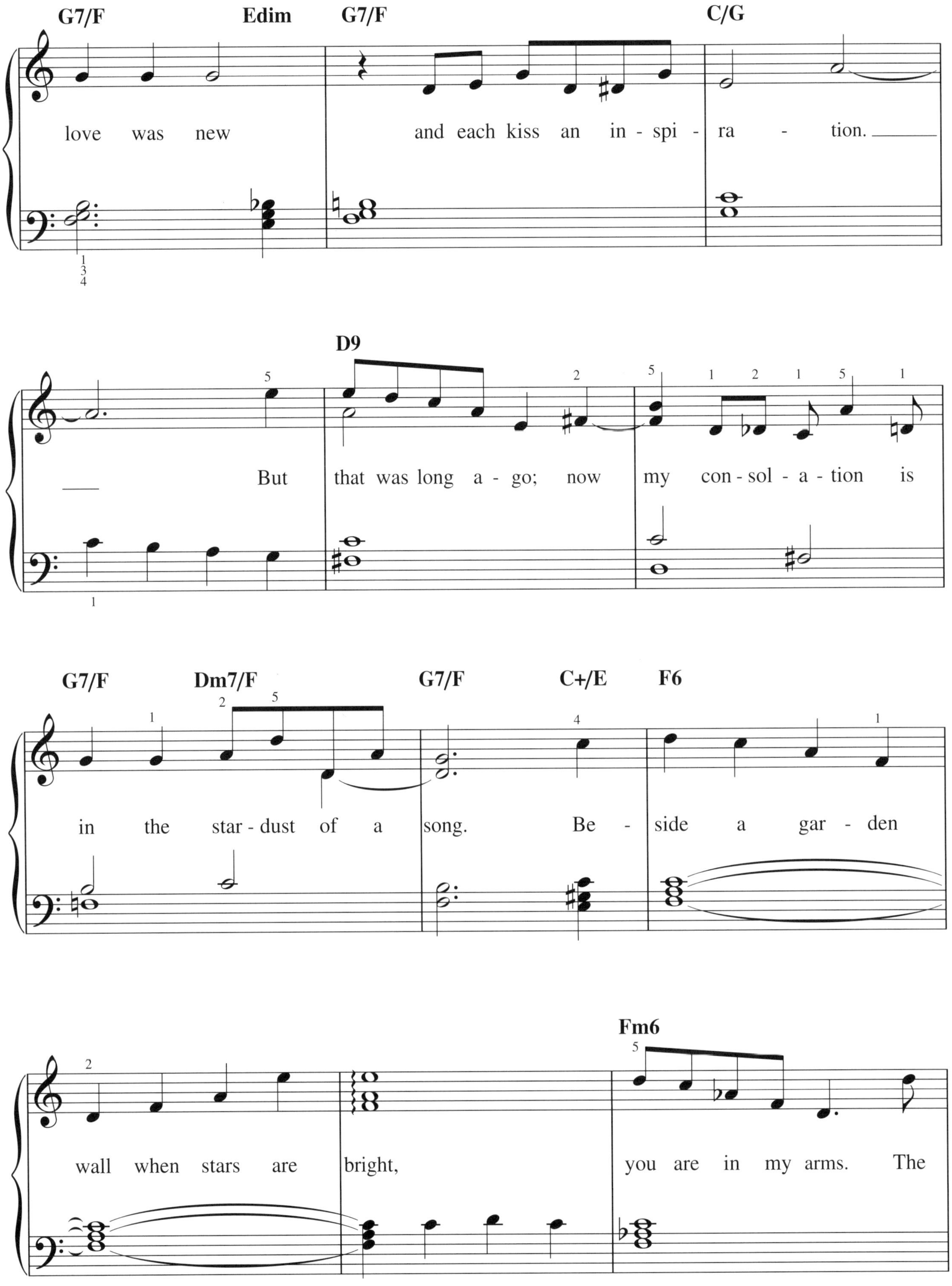
G7/F Edim G7/F C/G
love was new and each kiss an in - spi - ra - tion.
D9
But that was long a - go; now my con - sol - a - tion is
G7/F Dm7/F G7/F C+/E F6
in the star - dust of a song. Be - side a gar - den
Fm6
wall when stars are bright, you are in my arms. The

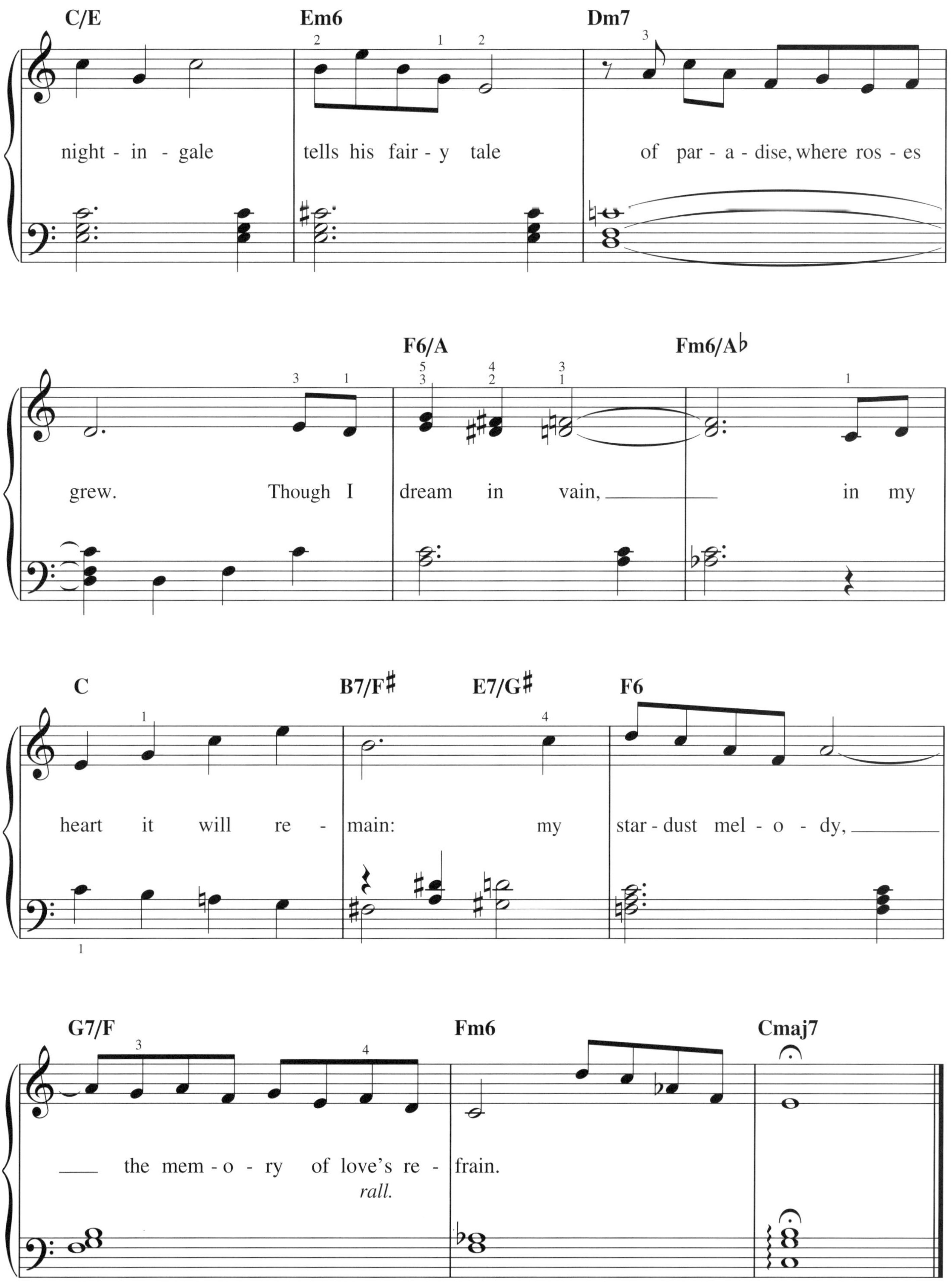
C/E Em6 Dm7
night - in - gale tells his fair - y tale of par - a - dise, where ros - es
F6/A Fm6/A♭
grew. Though I dream in vain, in my
C B7/F♯ E7/G♯ F6
heart it will re - main: my star - dust mel - o - dy,
G7/F Fm6 Cmaj7
the mem - o - ry of love's re - frain.
rall.

Twist and Shout

Words and Music by BERT RUSSELL
and PHIL MEDLEY

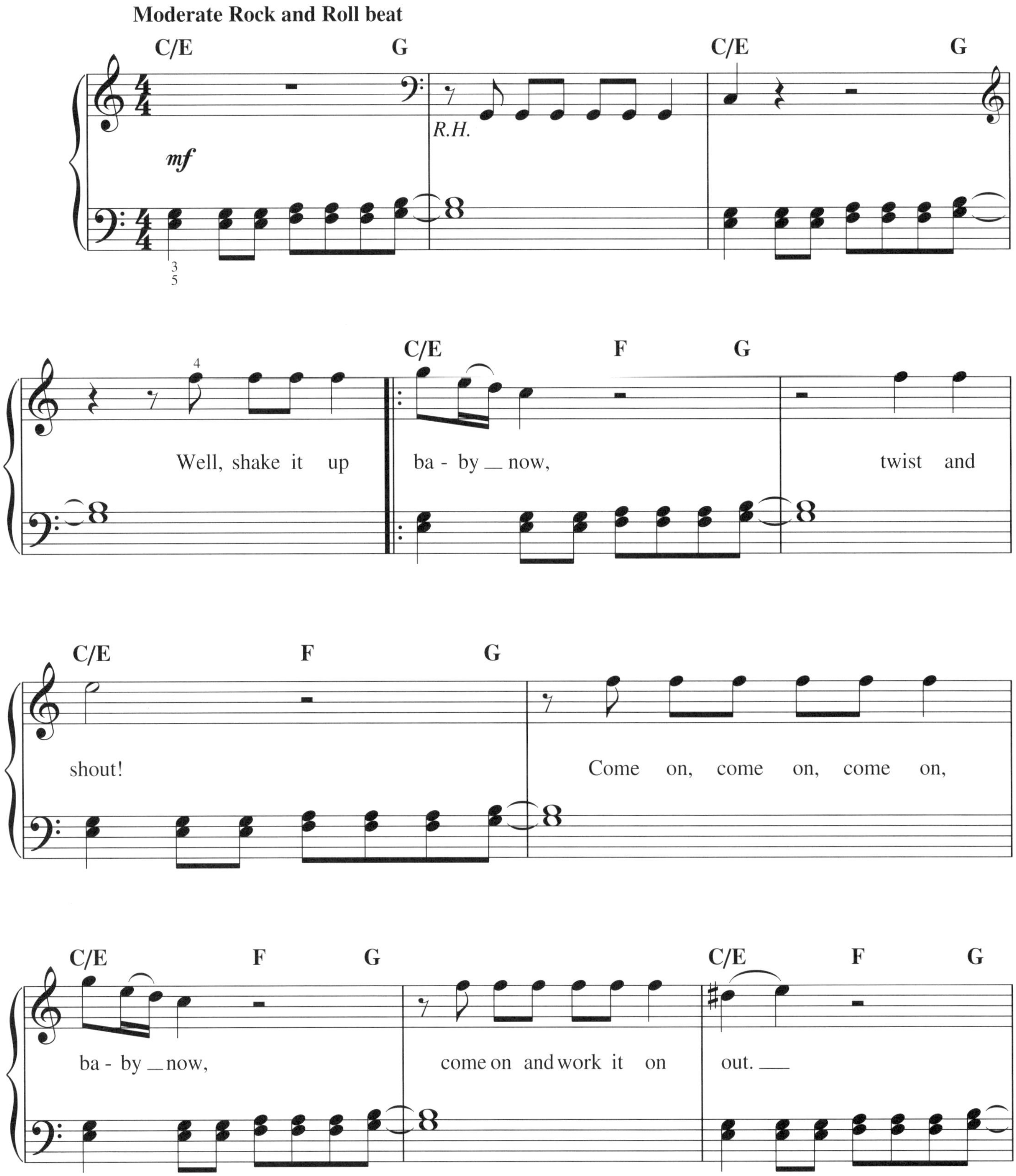
Moderate Rock and Roll beat
C/E
G
C/E
G
mf
R.H.
Well, shake it up
C/E
F
G
ba - by _ now,
twist and
C/E
F
G
shout!
Come on, come on, come on,
C/E
F
G
ba - by _ now,
come on and work it on
C/E
F
G
out. _

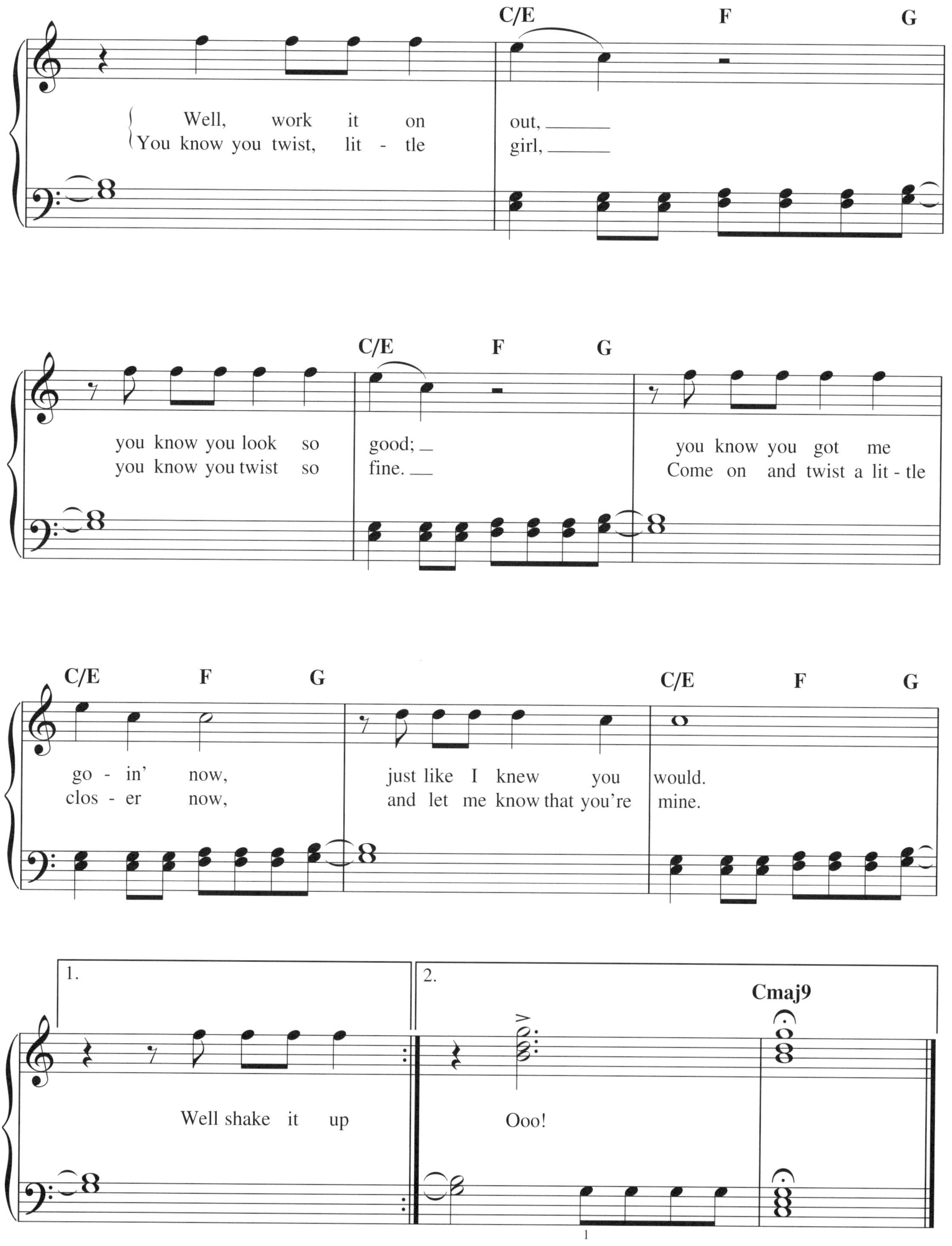
C/E F G
Well, work it on out,
You know you twist, lit - tle girl,
C/E F G
you know you look so good;
you know you twist so fine.
you know you got me
Come on and twist a lit - tle
C/E F G
go - in' now,
clos - er now,
just like I knew you would.
and let me know that you're mine.
C/E F G
1.
Well shake it up
2.
Ooo!
Cmaj9

The Way You Look Tonight

Words by DOROTHY FIELDS
Music by JEROME KERN

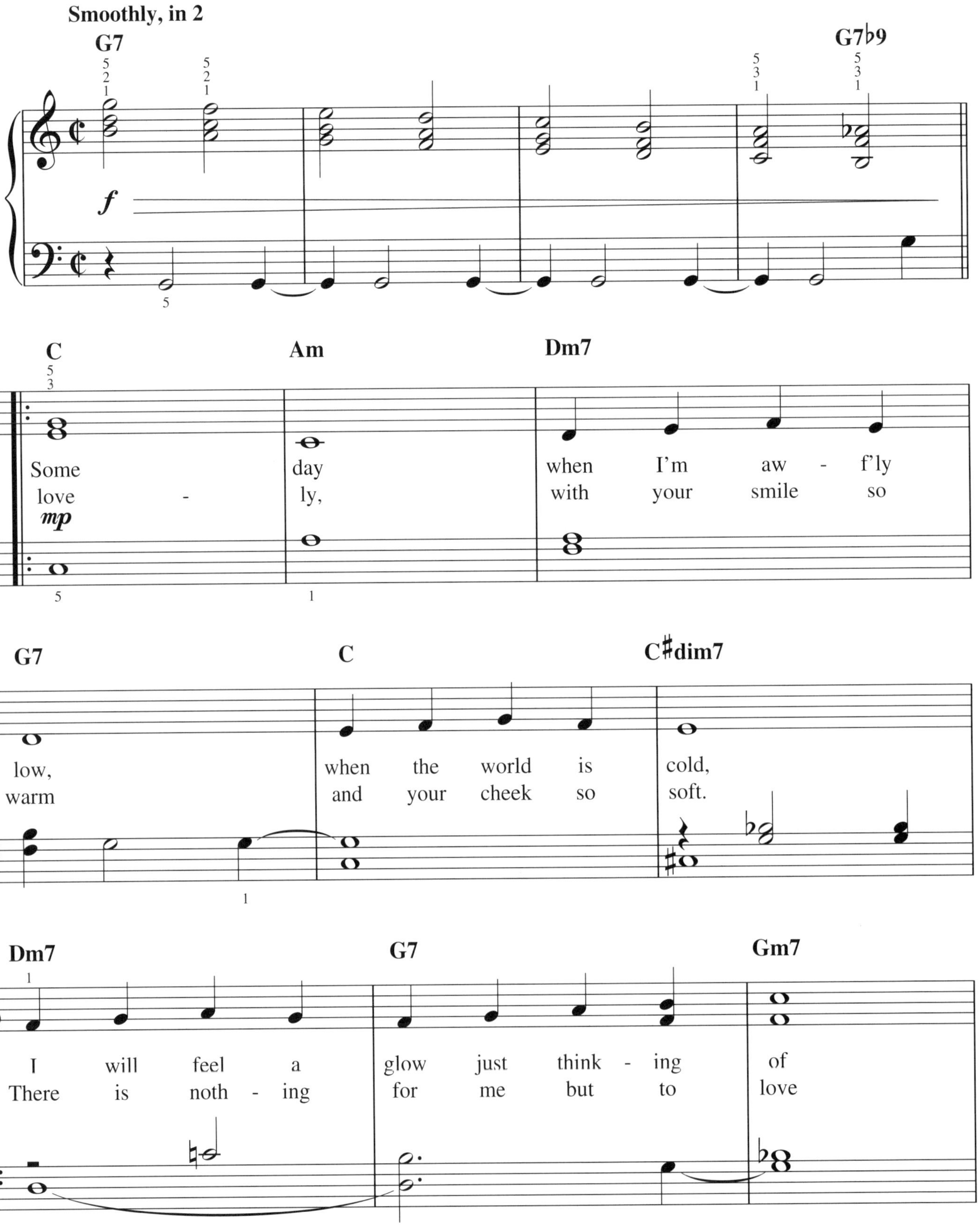

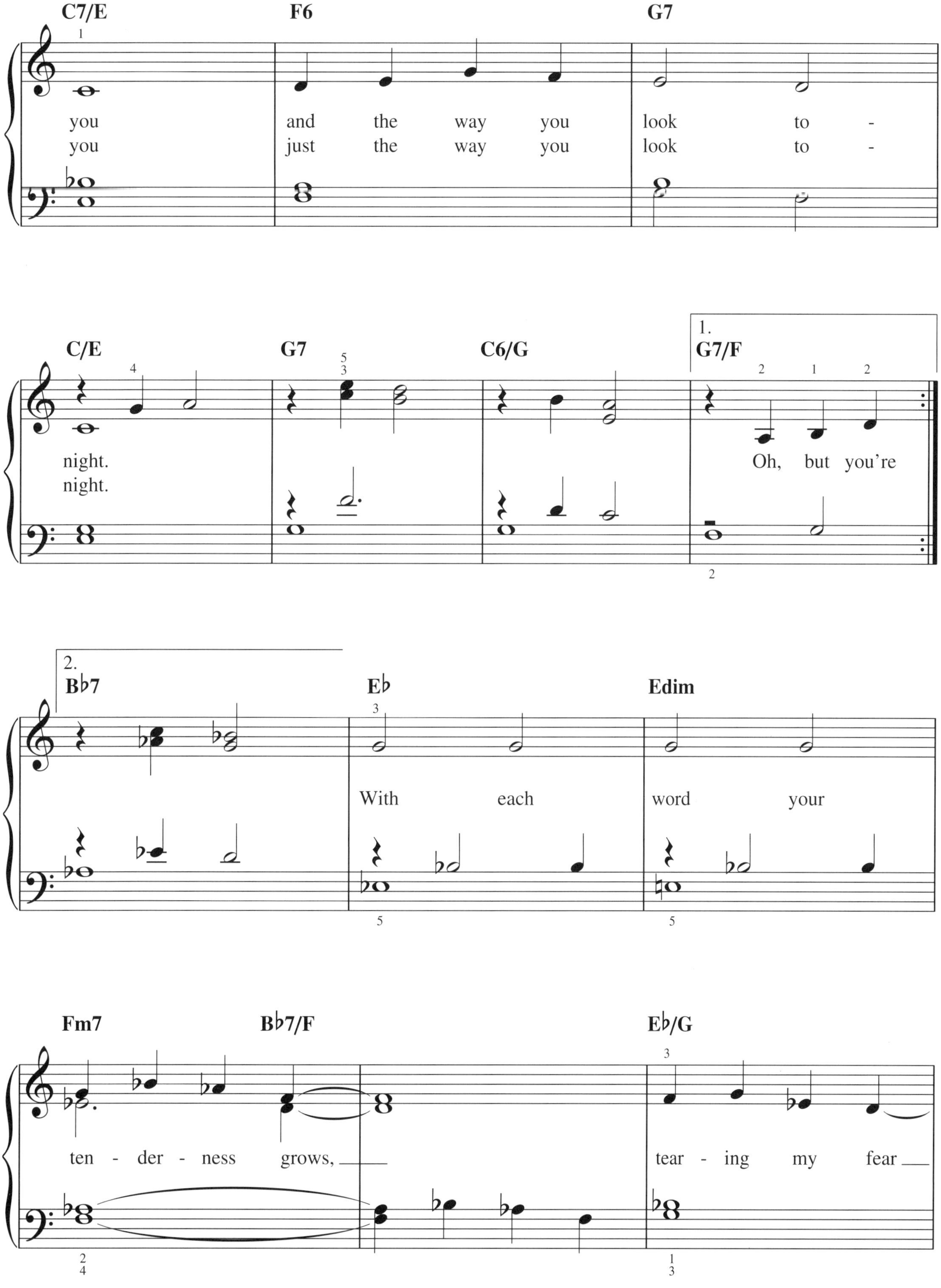
C7/E F6 G7
you and the way you look to -
you just the way you look to -
C/E G7 C6/G 1. G7/F
night. Oh, but you're
night.
2. B♭7 E♭ Edim
With each word your
Fm7 B♭7/F E♭/G
ten - der - ness grows, tear - ing my fear

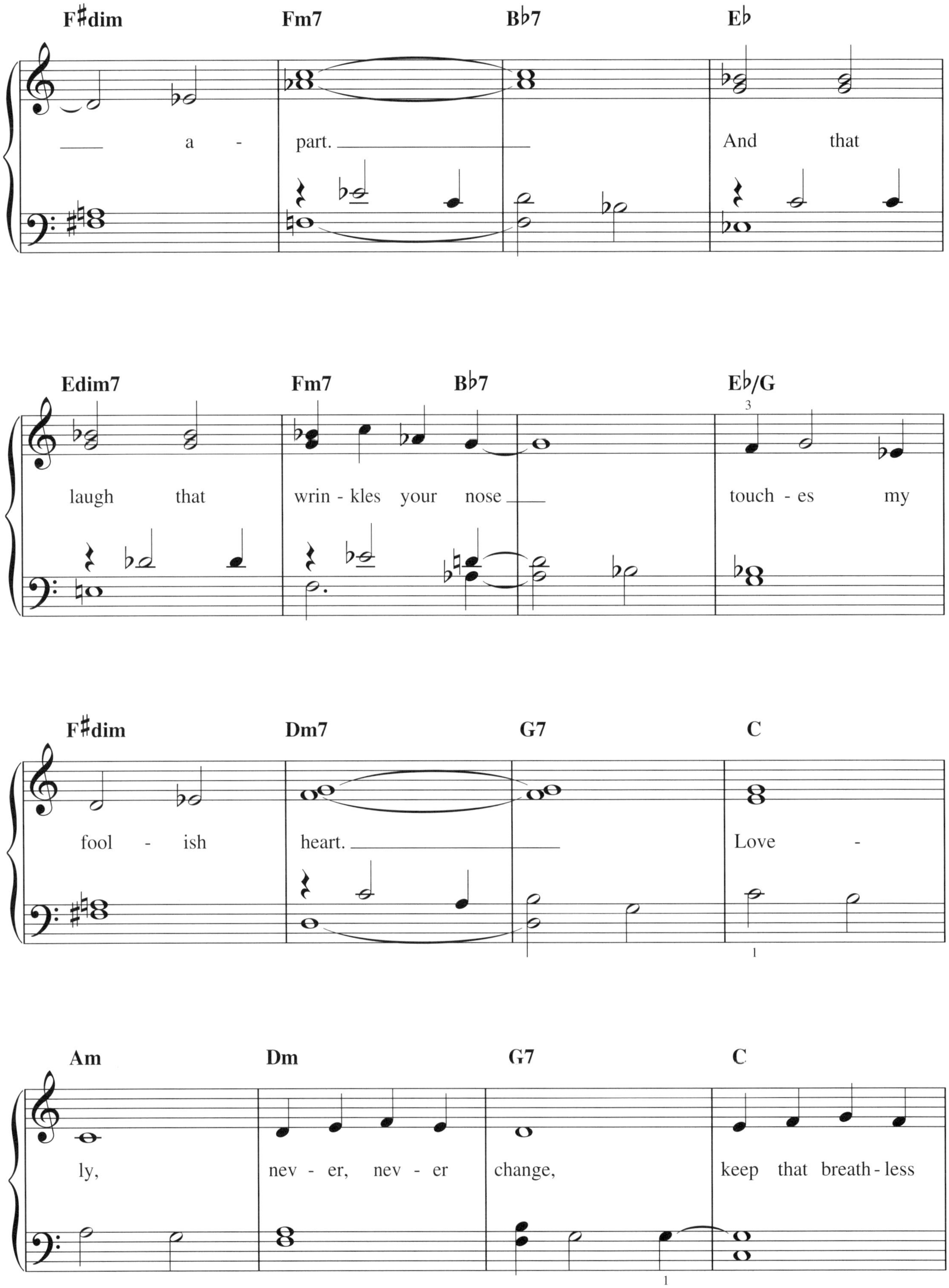
F♯dim Fm7 B♭7 E♭
a - part. And that
Edim7 Fm7 B♭7 E♭/G
laugh that wrin - kles your nose touch - es my
F♯dim Dm7 G7 C
fool - ish heart. Love -
Am Dm G7 C
ly, nev - er, nev - er change, keep that breath - less

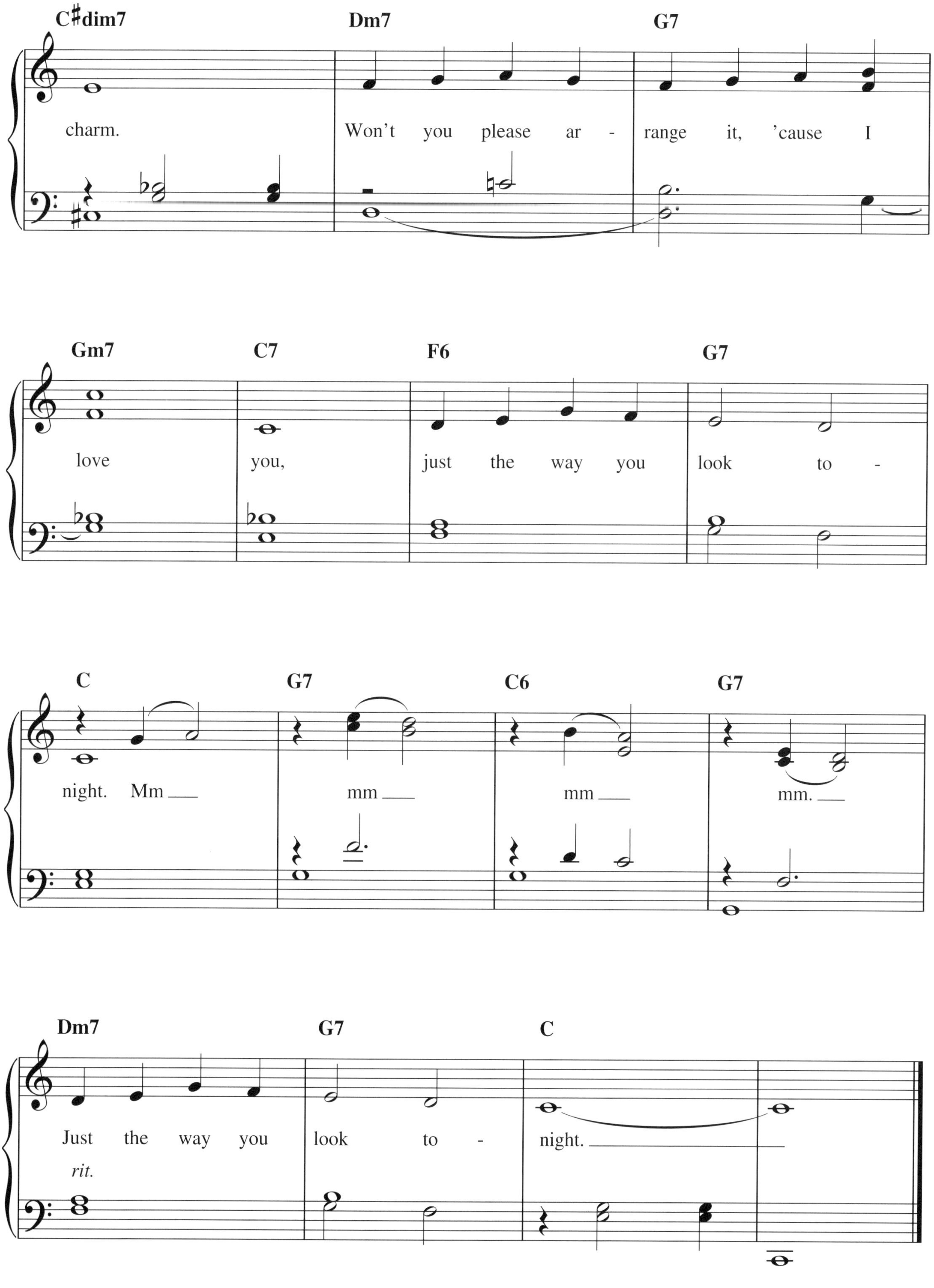
C♯dim7 Dm7 G7
charm. Won't you please ar - range it, 'cause I
Gm7 C7 F6 G7
love you, just the way you look to -
C G7 C6 G7
night. Mm mm mm mm.
Dm7 G7 C
Just the way you look to - night.
rit.

We Are the Champions

Words and Music by
FREDDIE MERCURY

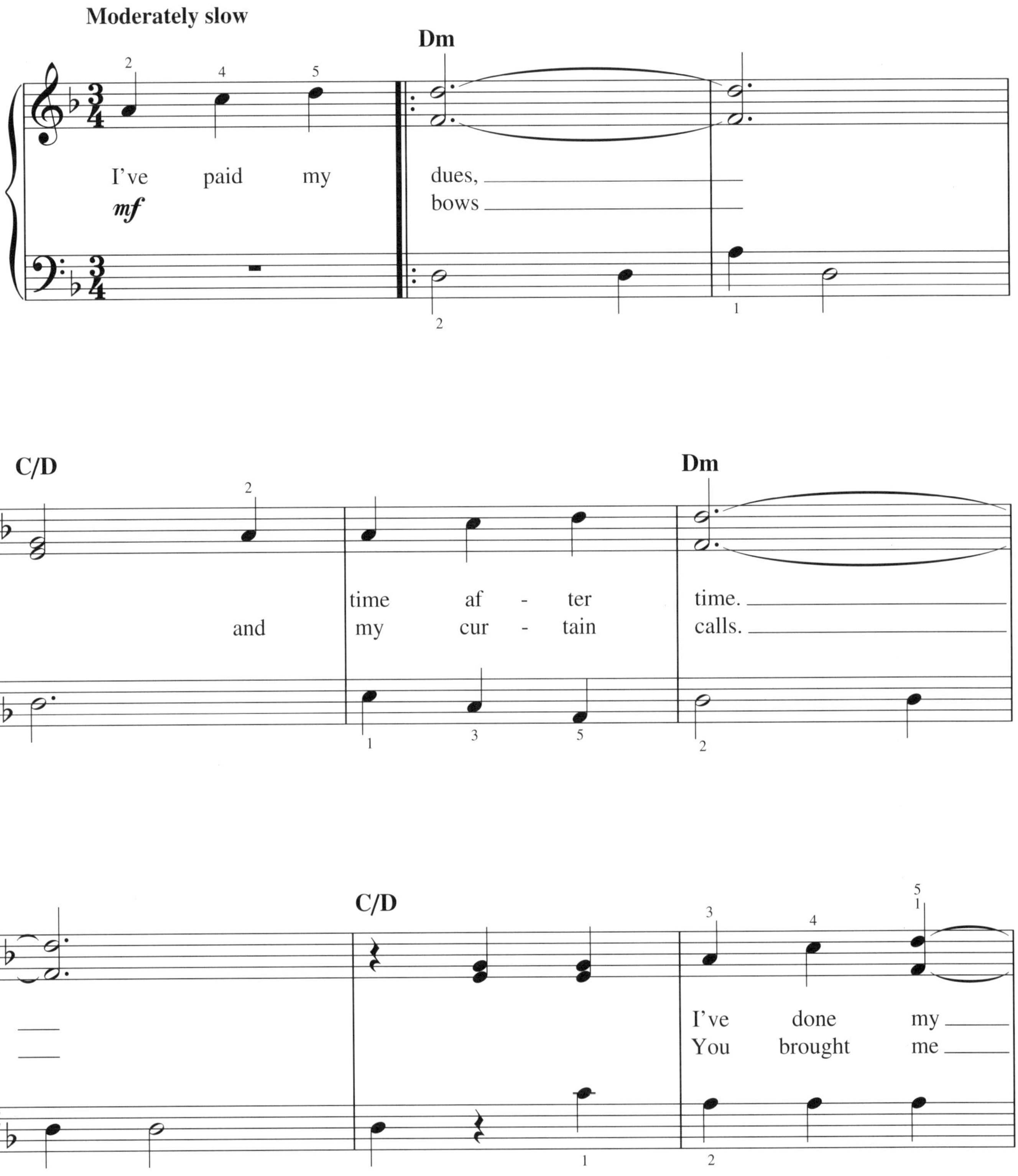

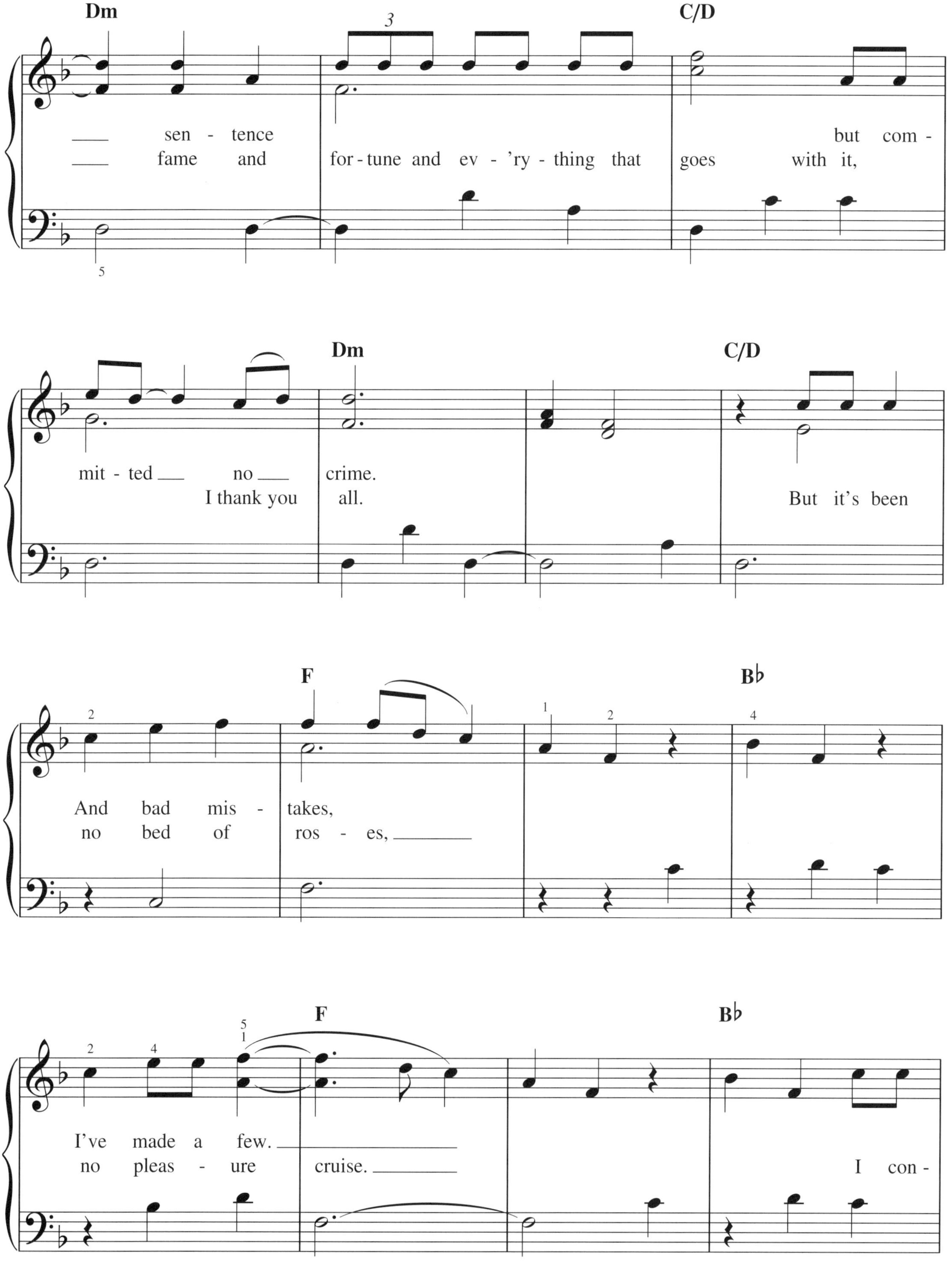
Dm
C/D
sen - tence
but com -
fame and
for - tune and ev - 'ry - thing that
goes with it,
Dm
C/D
mit - ted no
crime.
I thank you
all.
But it's been
F
B♭
And bad mis -
takes,
no bed of
ros - es,
F
B♭
I've made a few.
no pleas - ure
cruise.
I con -

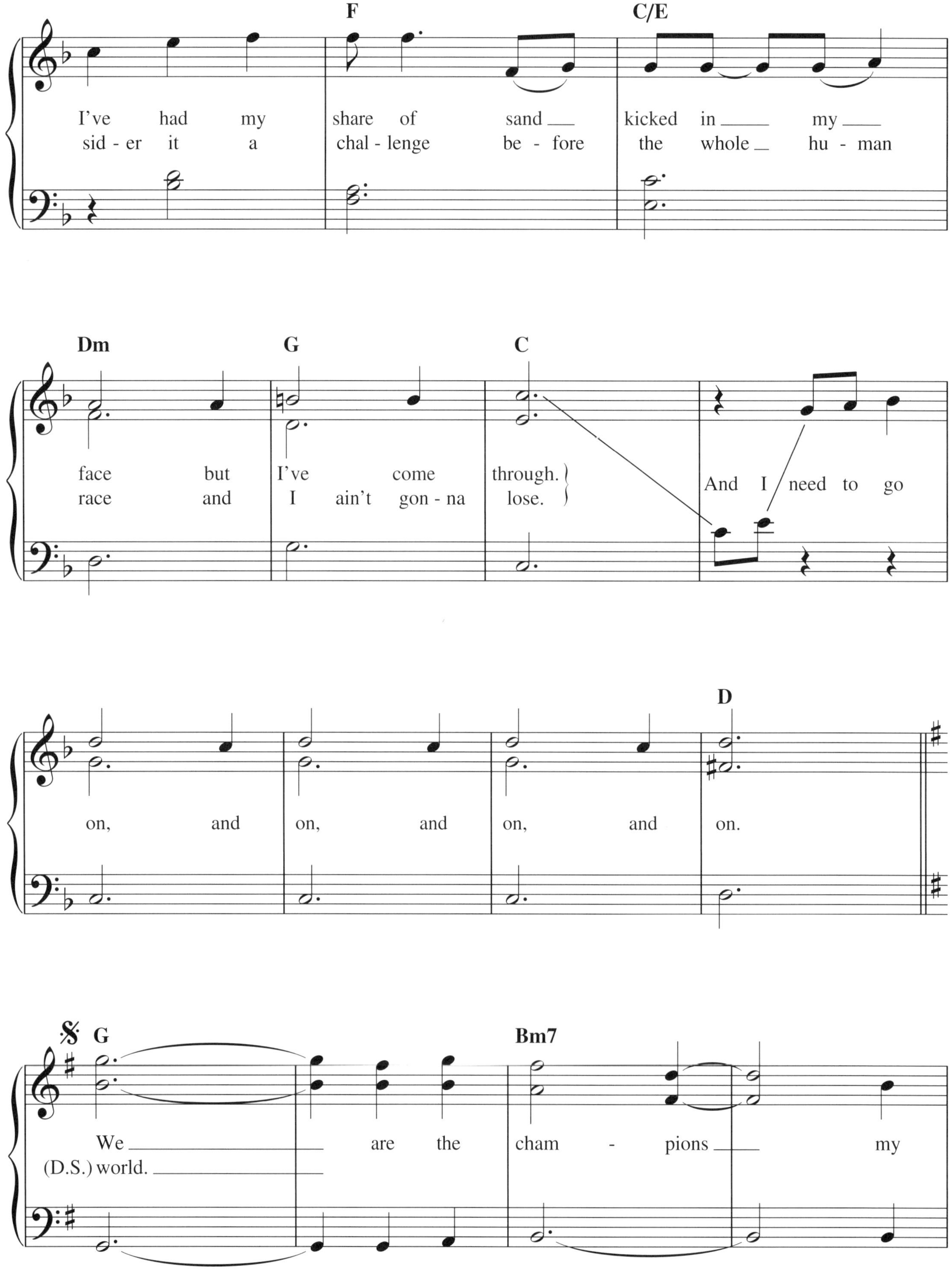
F
C/E
I've had my share of sand kicked in my
sid - er it a chal - lenge be - fore the whole hu - man
Dm
G
C
face but I've come through.
race and I ain't gon - na lose.
And I need to go
on, and on, and on, and on.
D
G
Bm7
We are the cham - pions my
(D.S.) world.

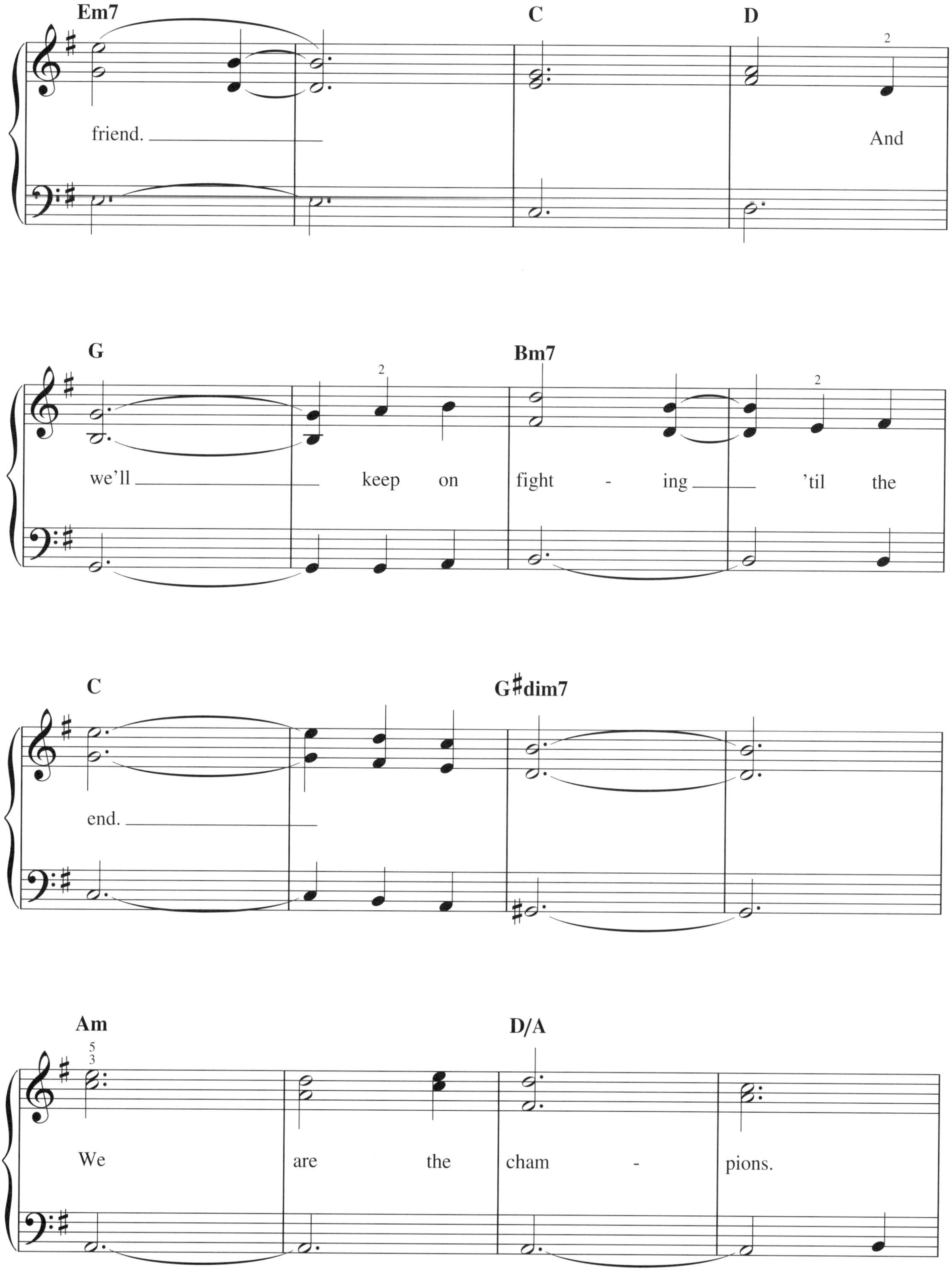
Em7
C
D
2
friend.
And
G
Bm7
2
2
we'll
keep
on
fight
-
ing
'til
the
C
G♯dim7
end.
Am
D/A
5
3
We
are
the
cham
-
pions.

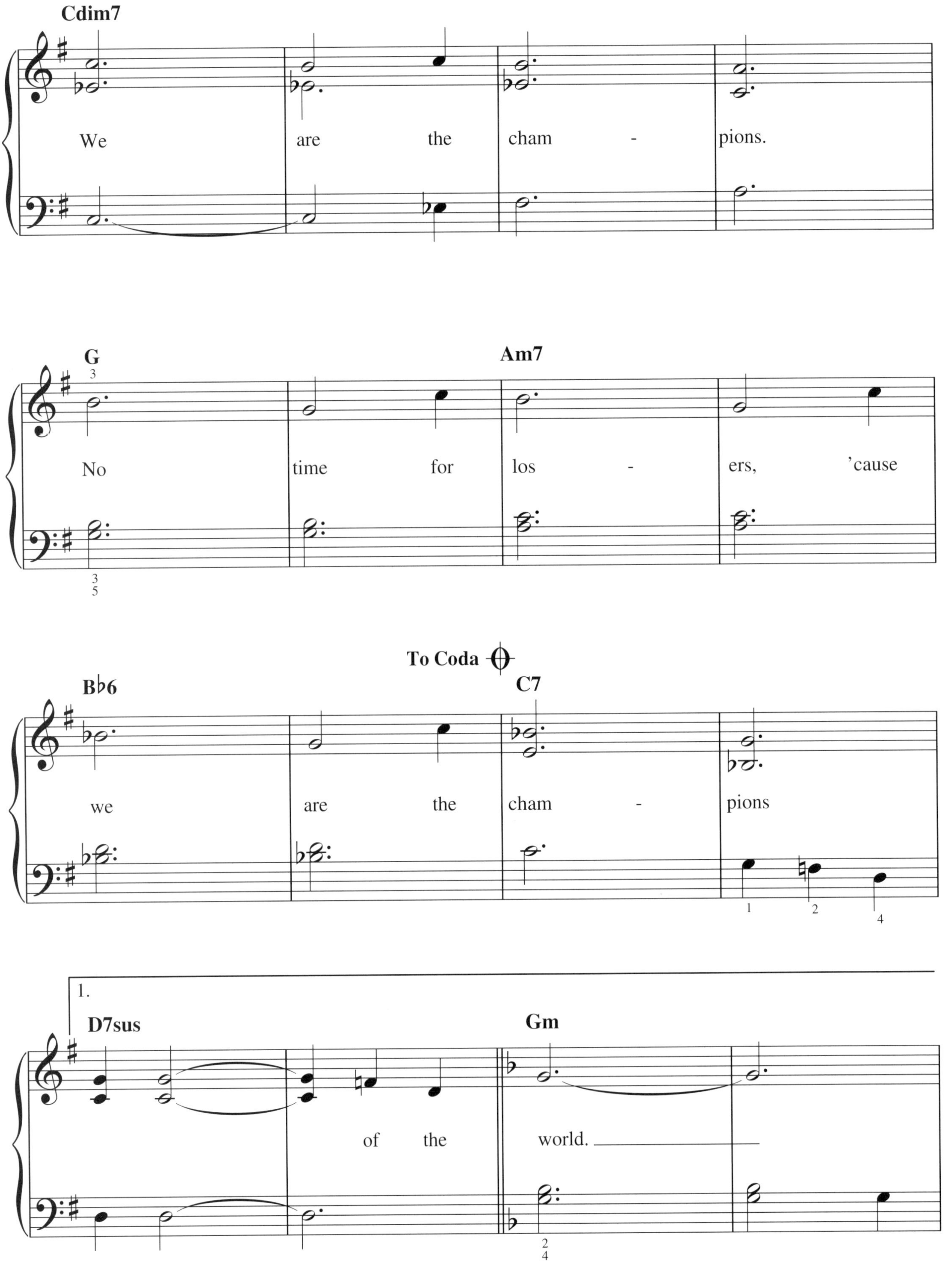
Cdim7
We are the cham - pions.
G
3
Am7
No time for los - ers, 'cause
3
5
To Coda
B♭6
C7
we are the cham - pions
1 2 4
1.
D7sus
Gm
of the world.
2
4

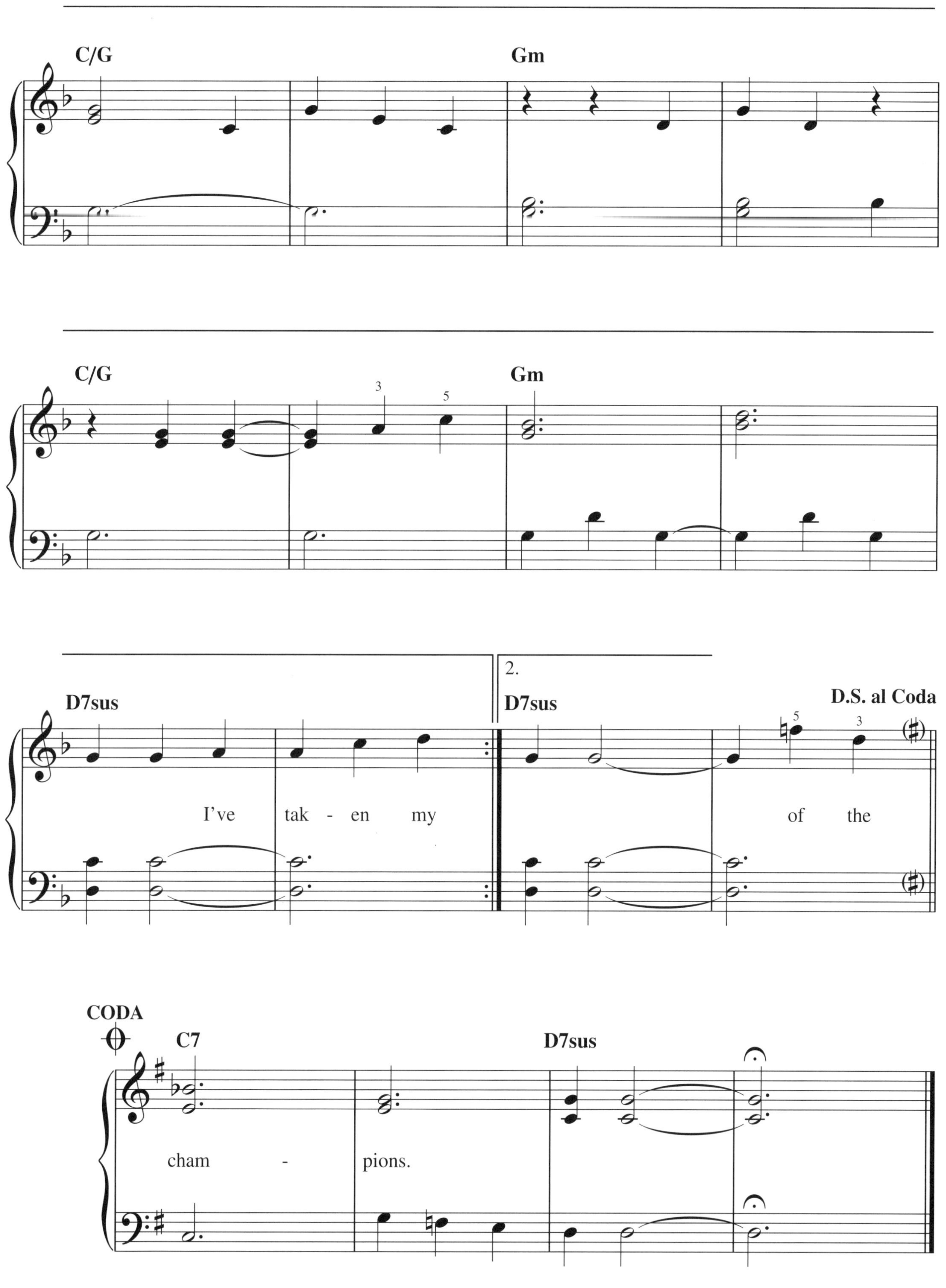
C/G
Gm
C/G
Gm
D7sus
2.
D7sus
D.S. al Coda
I've tak - en my
of the
CODA
C7
D7sus
cham - pions.

You Belong with Me

Words and Music by TAYLOR SWIFT
and LIZ ROSE

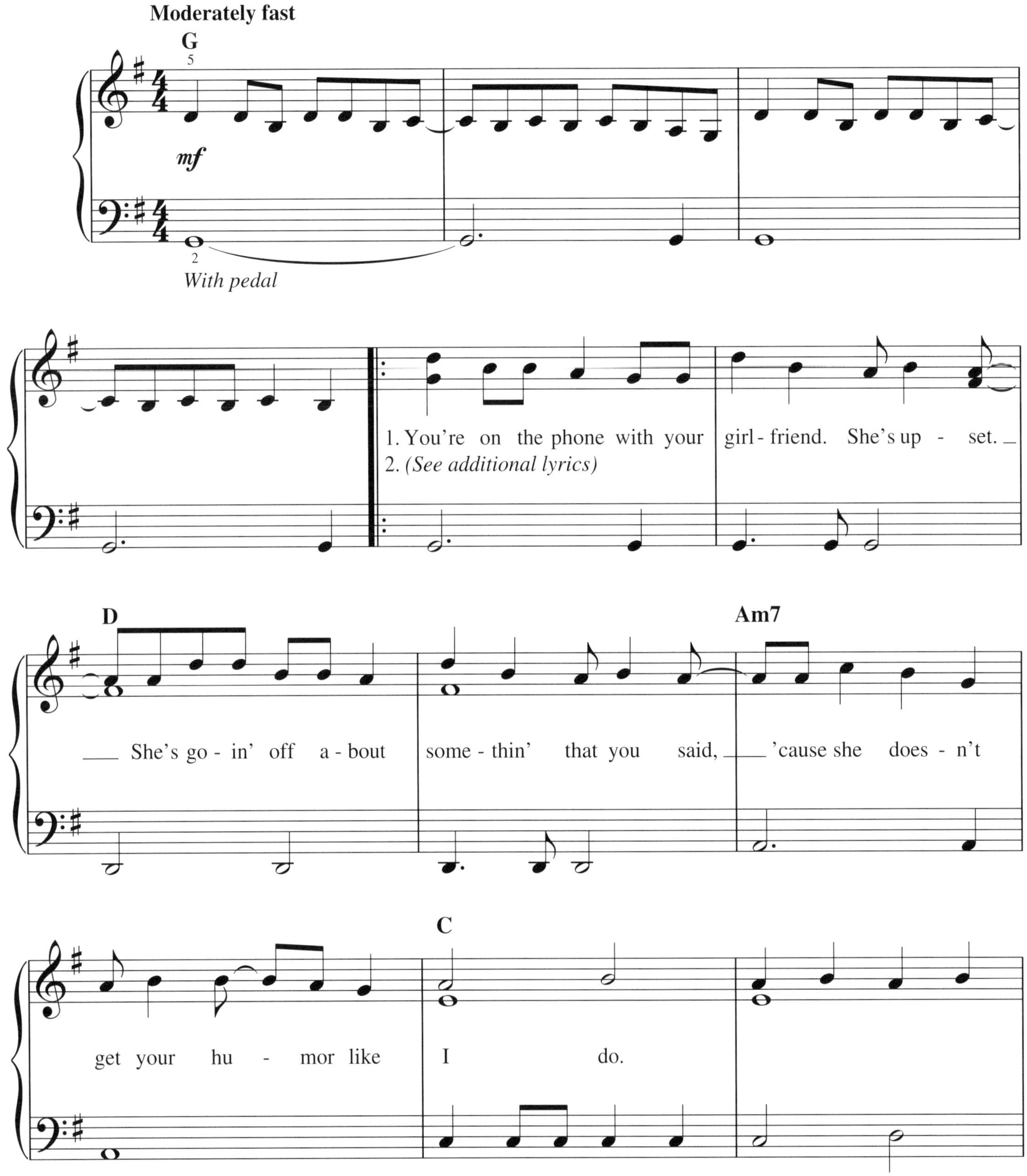

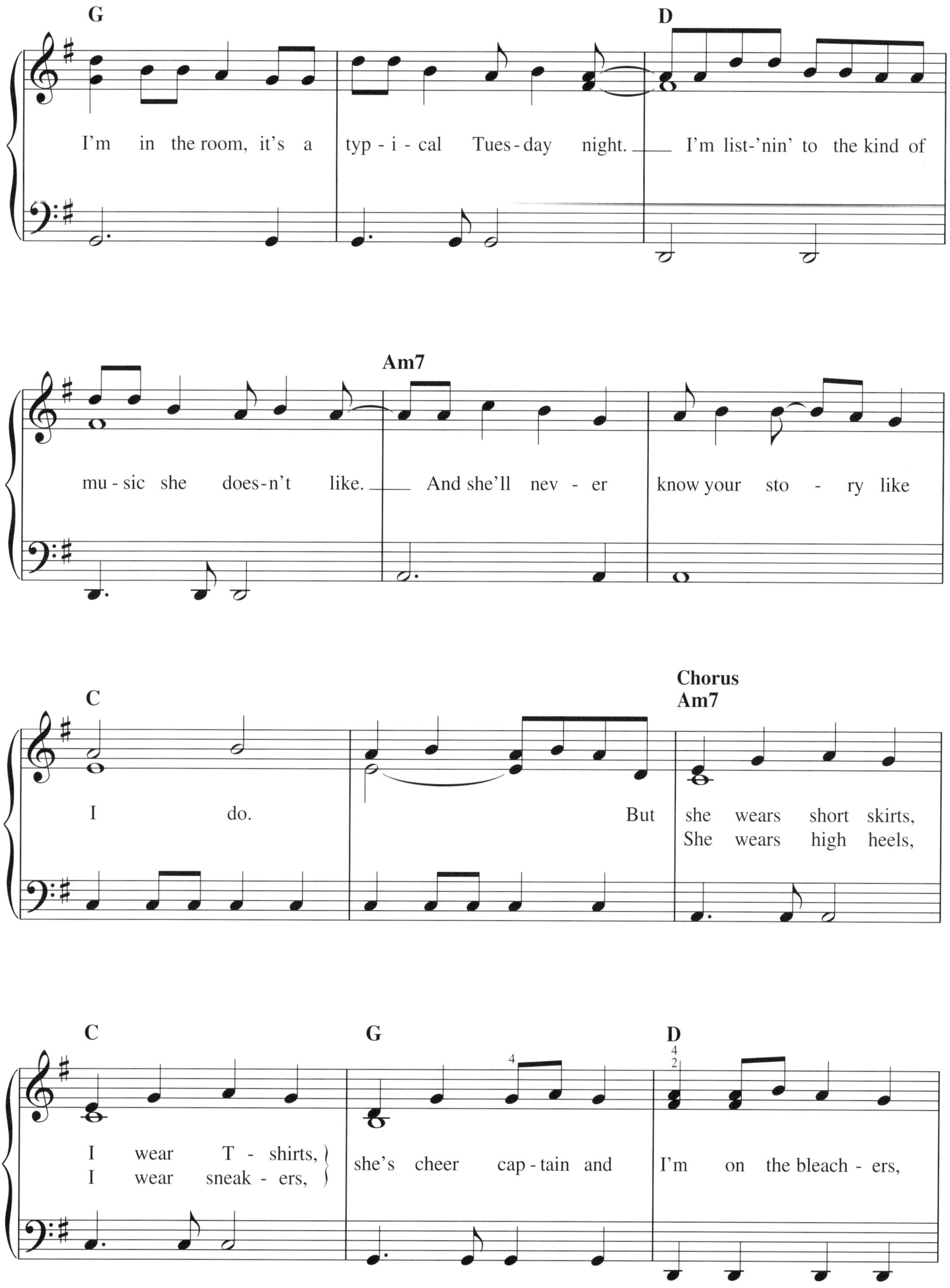
G
D
I'm in the room, it's a typ - i - cal Tues - day night. I'm list-'nin' to the kind of
Am7
mu - sic she does - n't like. And she'll nev - er know your sto - ry like
C
Chorus
Am7
I do. But she wears short skirts,
She wears high heels,
C
G
D
I wear T - shirts,
I wear sneak - ers,
she's cheer cap - tain and I'm on the bleach - ers,

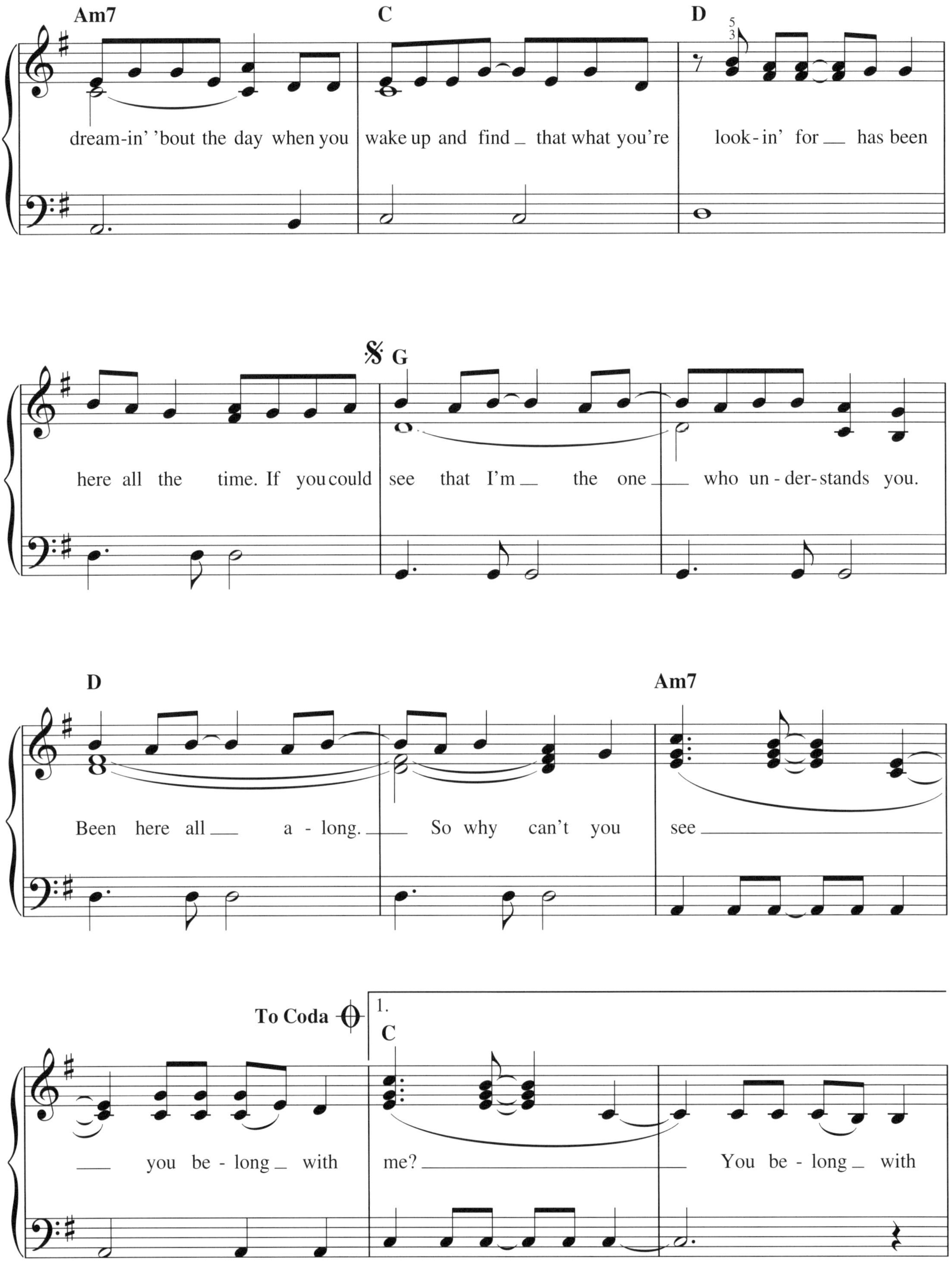
Am7
C
D
dream-in' 'bout the day when you wake up and find _ that what you're look-in' for _ has been
G
here all the time. If you could see that I'm _ the one _ who un-der-stands you.
D
Am7
Been here all _ a - long. _ So why can't you see _
To Coda
1.
C
_ you be - long _ with me? _ You be - long _ with

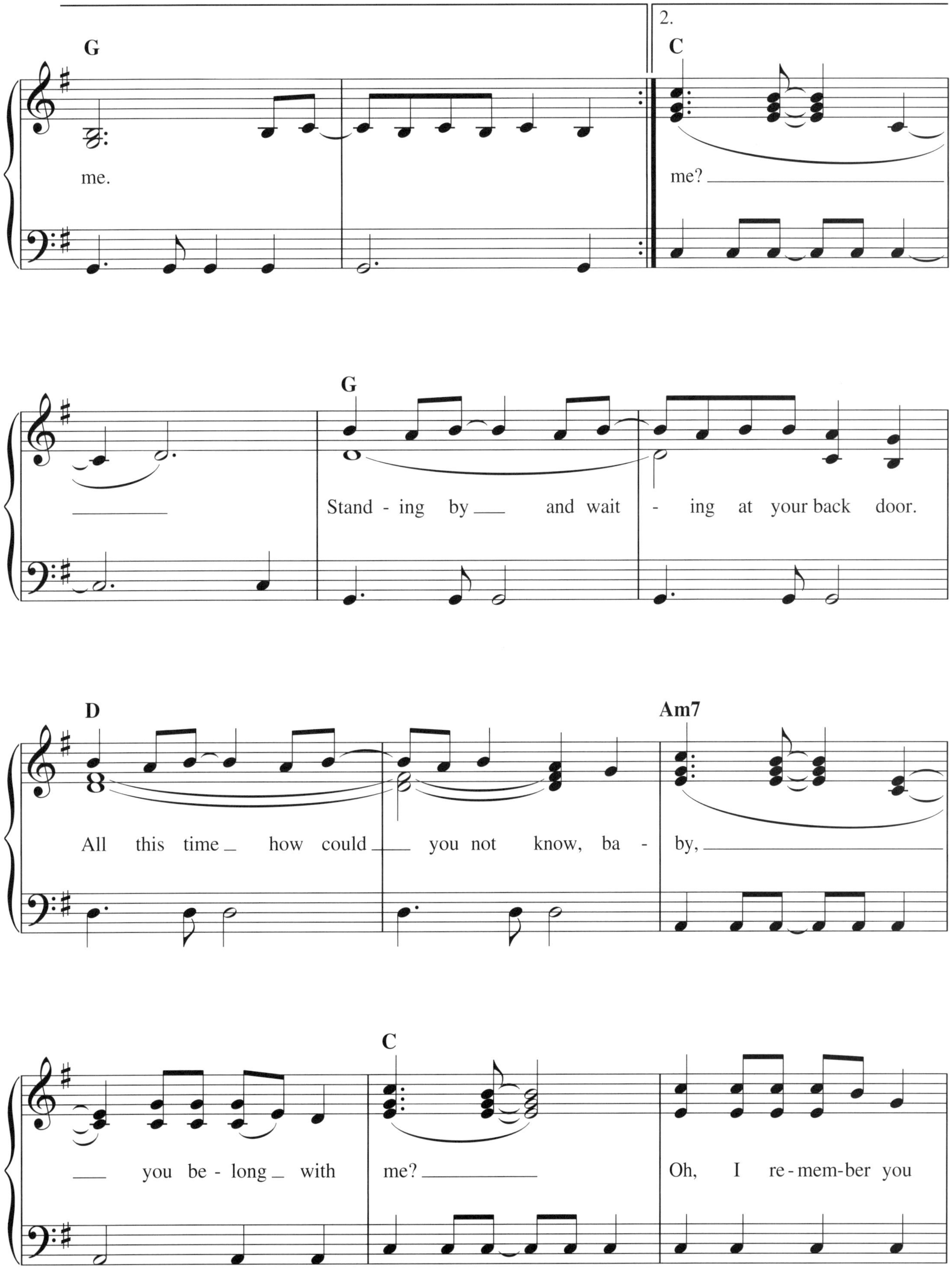
G
me.
2.
C
me?
G
Stand - ing by and wait - ing at your back door.
D
All this time how could you not know, ba - by,
Am7
you be - long with
C
me?
Oh, I re - mem - ber you

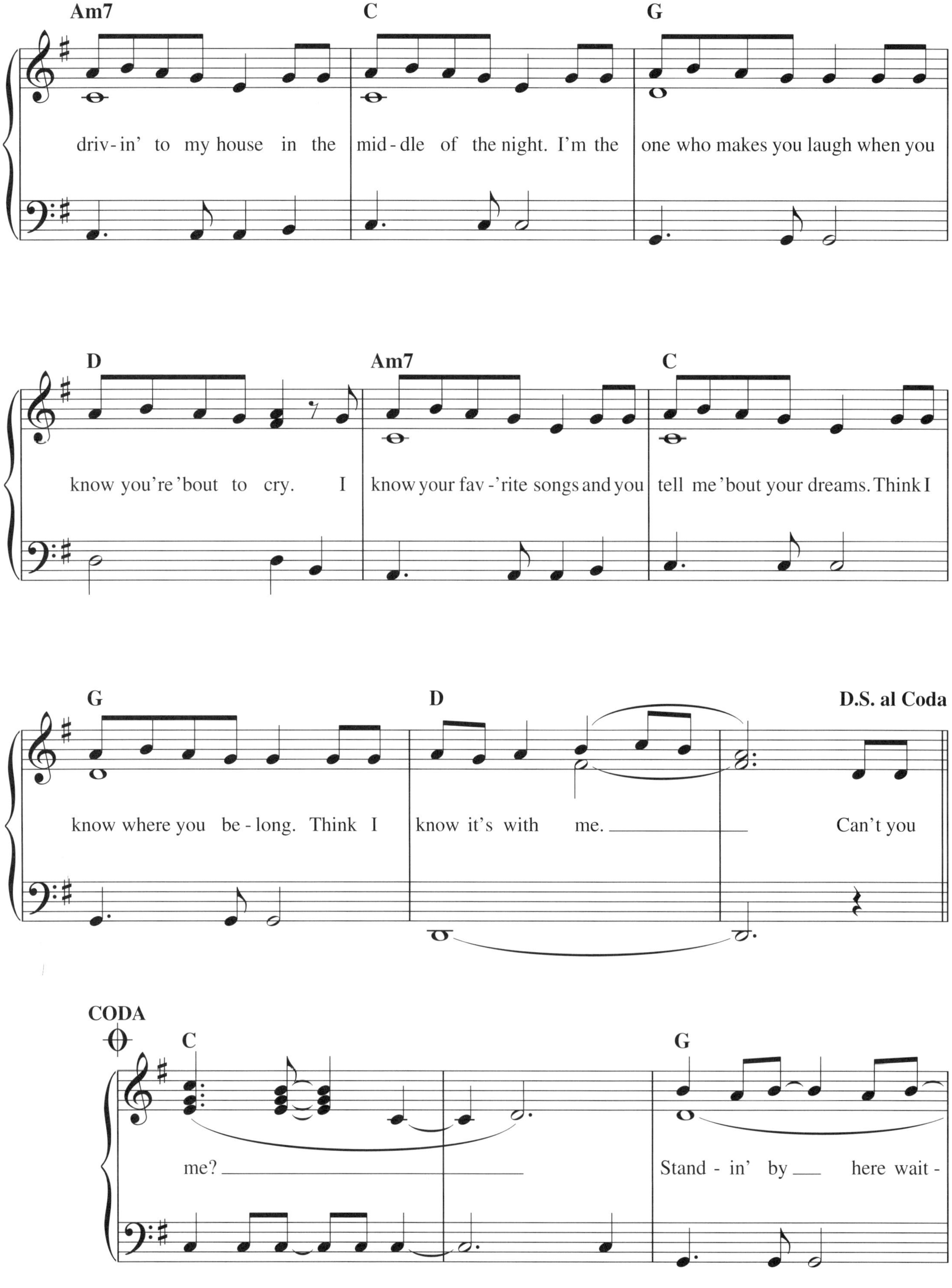
Am7
C
G
driv - in' to my house in the
mid - dle of the night. I'm the
one who makes you laugh when you
D
Am7
C
know you're 'bout to cry. I
know your fav - 'rite songs and you
tell me 'bout your dreams. Think I
G
D
D.S. al Coda
know where you be - long. Think I
know it's with me.
Can't you
CODA
C
G
me?
Stand - in' by here wait -

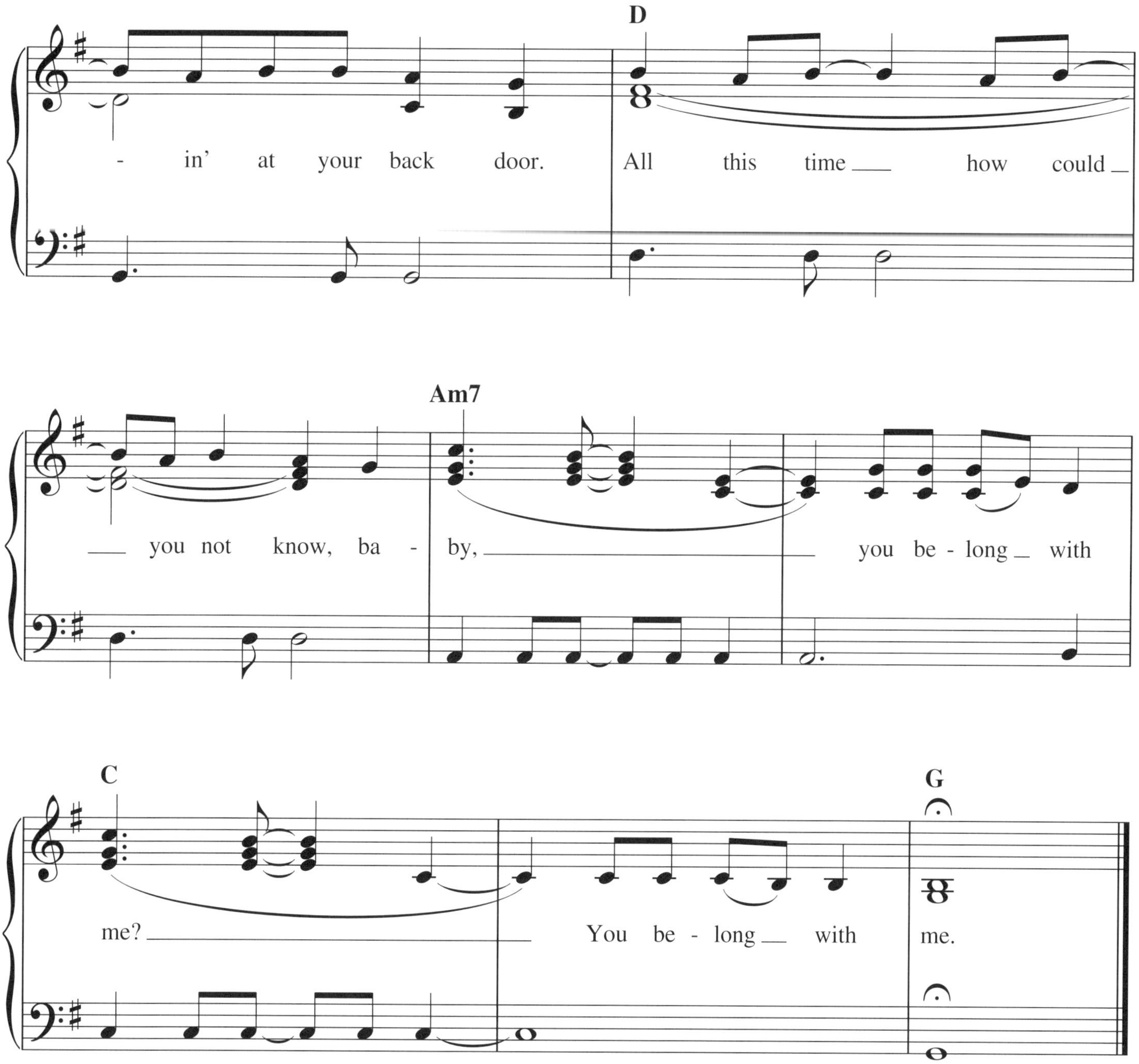
D
- in' at your back door. All this time how could
Am7
you not know, ba - by, you be - long with
C
G
me? You be - long with me.

Additional Lyrics

2. Walkin' the streets with you in your worn out jeans,
I can't help thinkin' this is how it ought to be.
Laughin' on a park bench, thinkin' to myself,
"Hey, isn't this easy?"
And you've got a smile that could light up this whole town.
I haven't seen it in a while since she brought you down.
You say you're fine. I know you better than that.
Hey, what you doin'with a girl like that?
Chorus

You Don't Know Me

Words and Music by CINDY WALKER
and EDDY ARNOLD

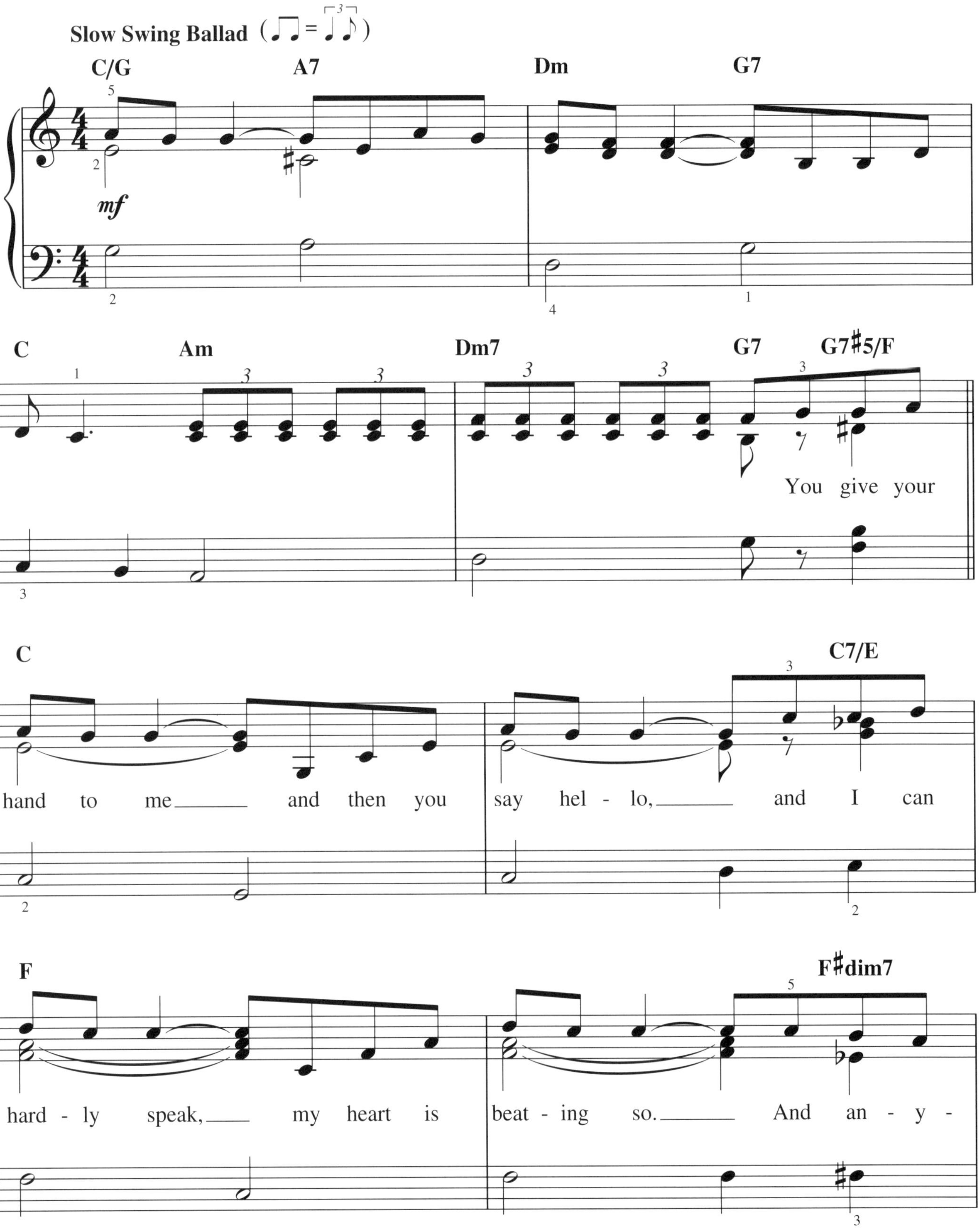

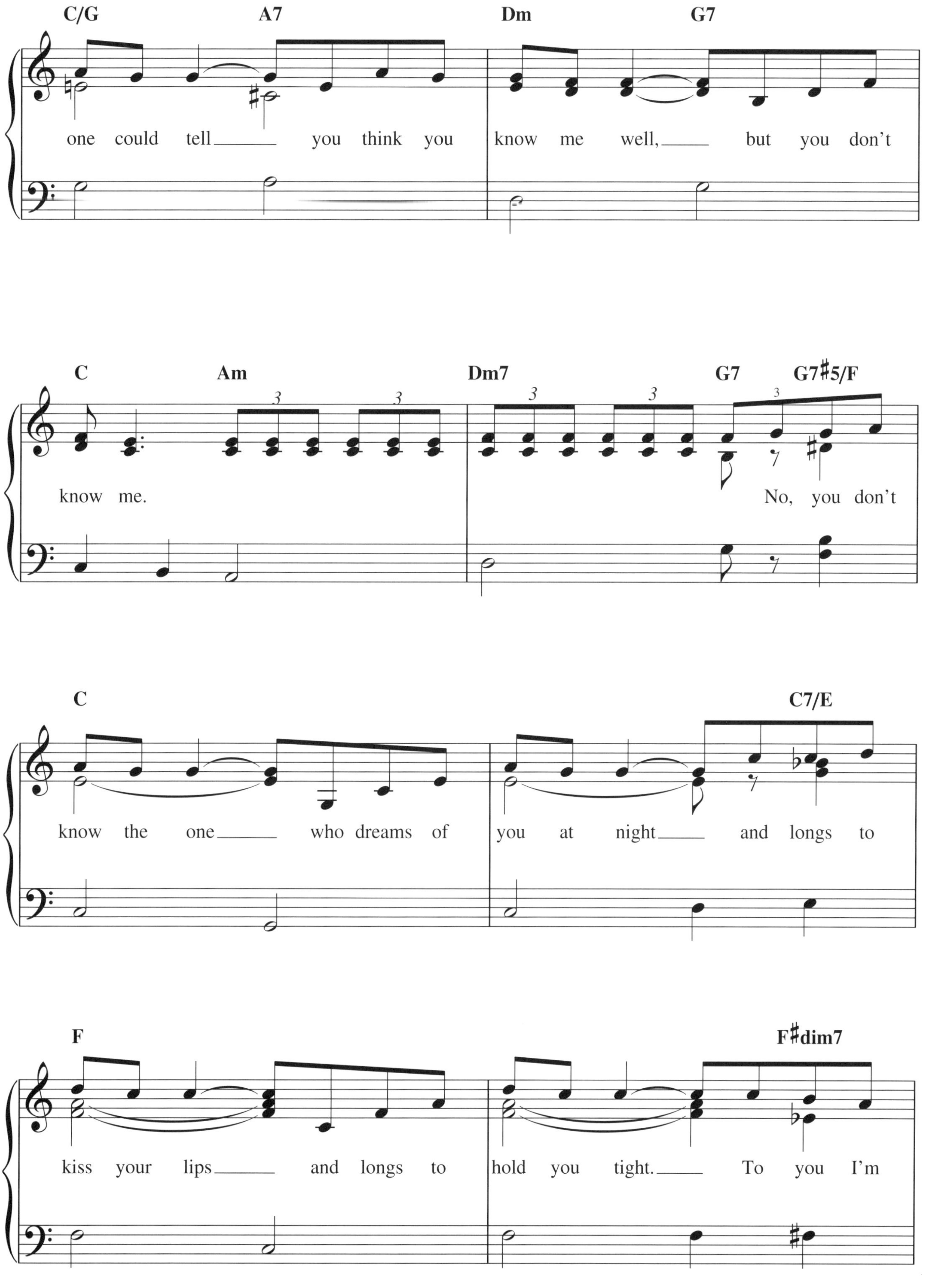
C/G A7 Dm G7
one could tell you think you know me well, but you don't
C Am Dm7 G7 G7♯5/F
know me. No, you don't
C C7/E
know the one who dreams of you at night and longs to
F F♯dim7
kiss your lips and longs to hold you tight. To you I'm

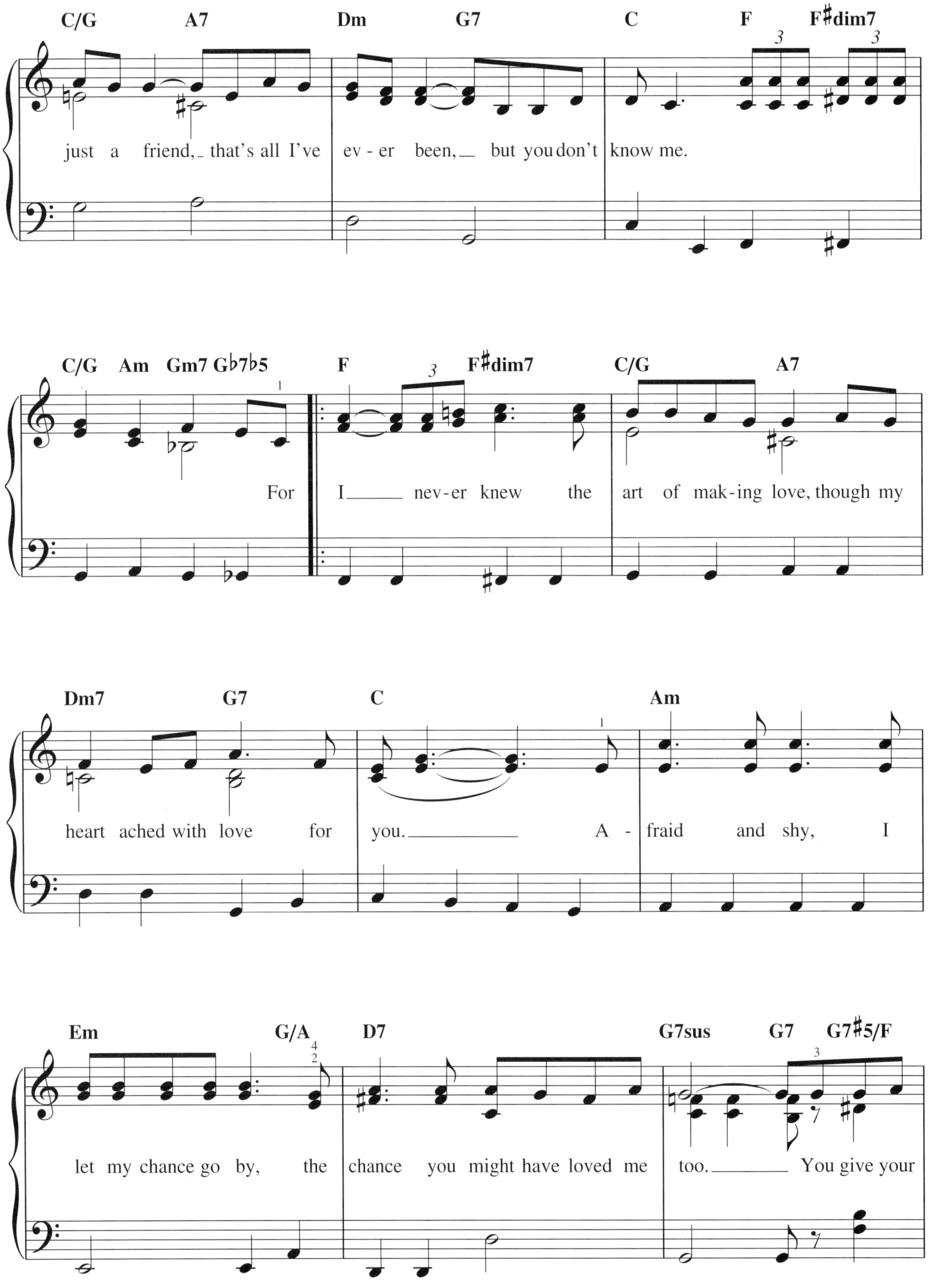
C/G A7 Dm G7 C F F♯dim7
just a friend, that's all I've ev - er been, but you don't know me.
C/G Am Gm7 G♭7♭5 F F♯dim7 C/G A7
For I never knew the art of mak-ing love, though my
Dm7 G7 C Am
heart ached with love for you. A - fraid and shy, I
Em G/A D7 G7sus G7 G7♯5/F
let my chance go by, the chance you might have loved me too. You give your

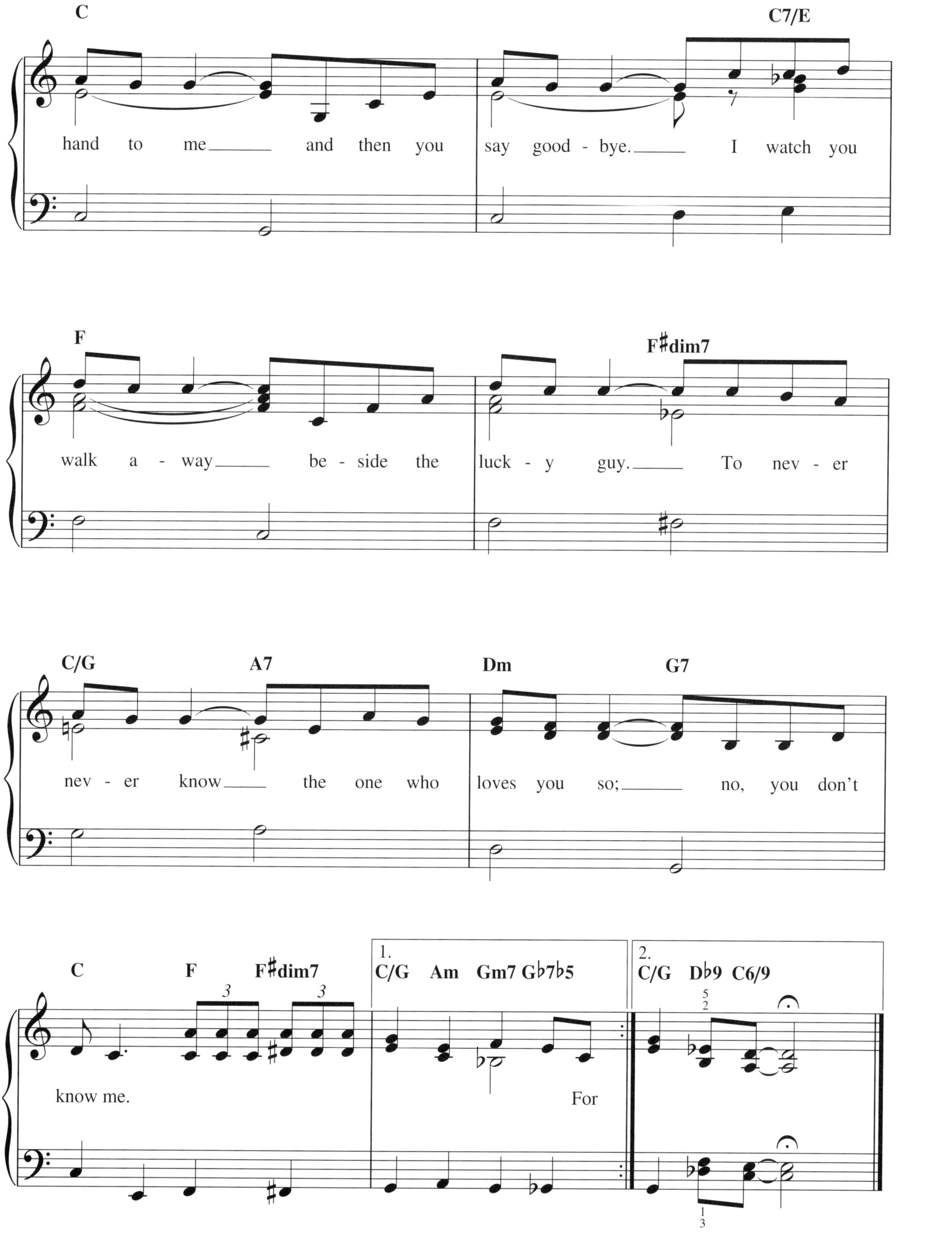
C
C7/E
hand to me___ and then you say good - bye.___ I watch you
F
F♯dim7
walk a - way___ be - side the luck - y guy.___ To nev - er
C/G
A7
Dm
G7
nev - er know___ the one who loves you so;___ no, you don't
C
F
F♯dim7
3
3
1.
C/G Am Gm7 G♭7♭5
2.
C/G D♭9 C6/9
5
2
know me.
For
1
3

Yellow Submarine

Words and Music by JOHN LENNON
and PAUL McCARTNEY

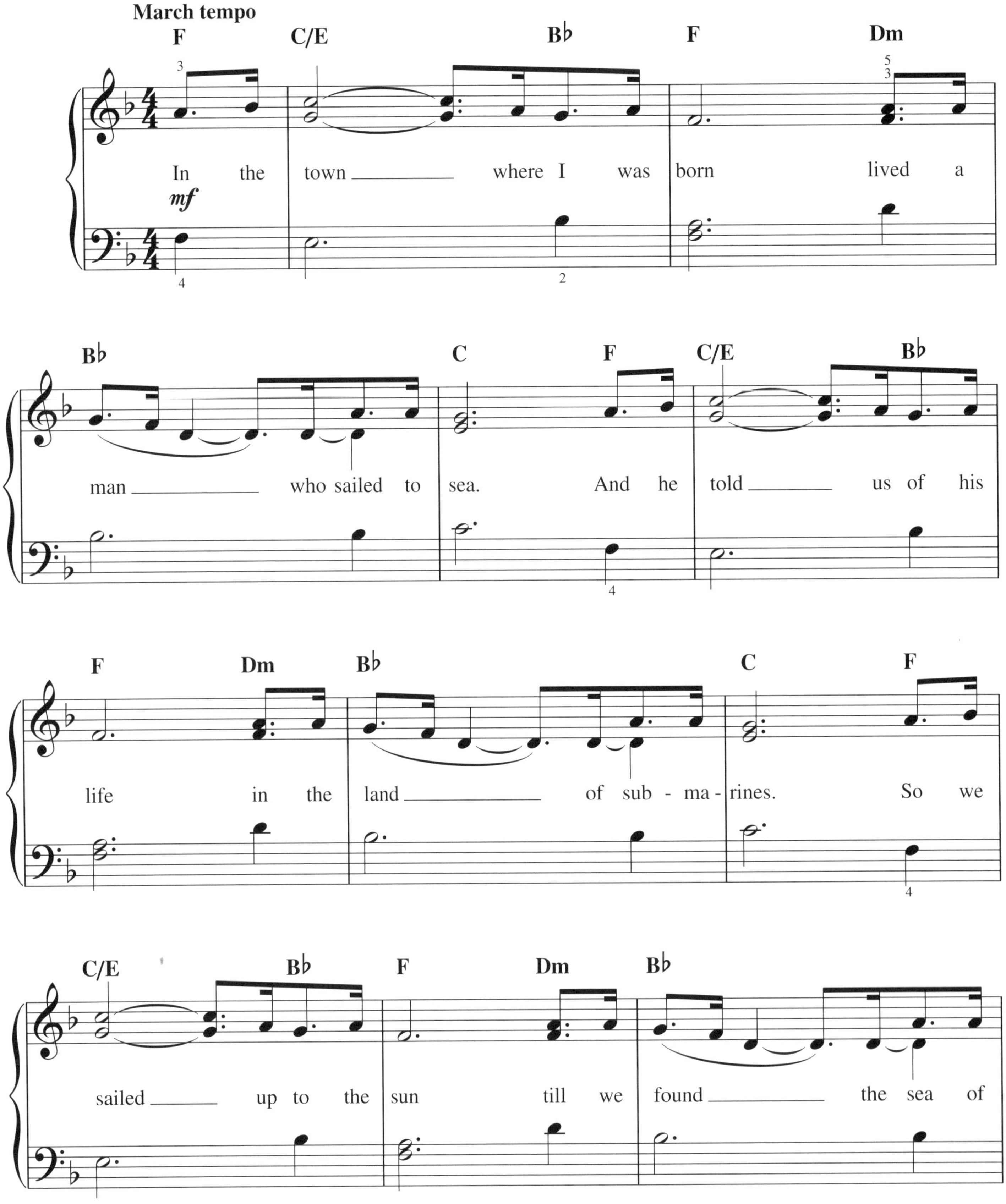
March tempo
F C/E B♭ F Dm
In the town ____ where I was born lived a
mf
B♭ C F C/E B♭
man ____ who sailed to sea. And he told ____ us of his
F Dm B♭ C F
life in the land ____ of sub - ma - rines. So we
C/E B♭ F Dm B♭
sailed ____ up to the sun till we found ____ the sea of

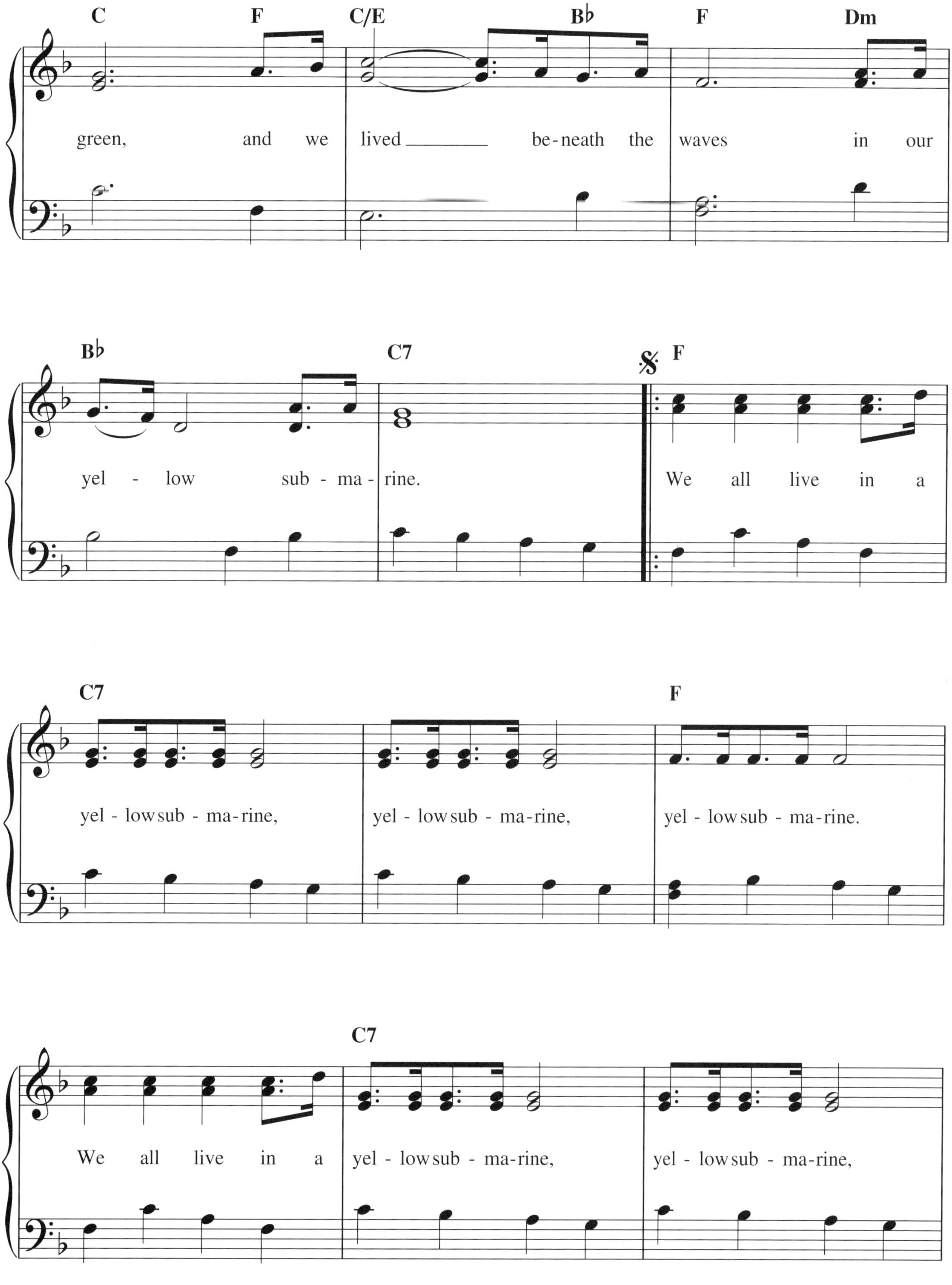
C F C/E B♭ F Dm
green, and we lived ___ be-neath the waves in our
B♭ C7 F
yel - low sub - ma - rine. We all live in a
C7 F
yel - low sub - ma-rine, yel - low sub - ma-rine, yel - low sub - ma-rine.
C7
We all live in a yel - low sub - ma-rine, yel - low sub - ma-rine,

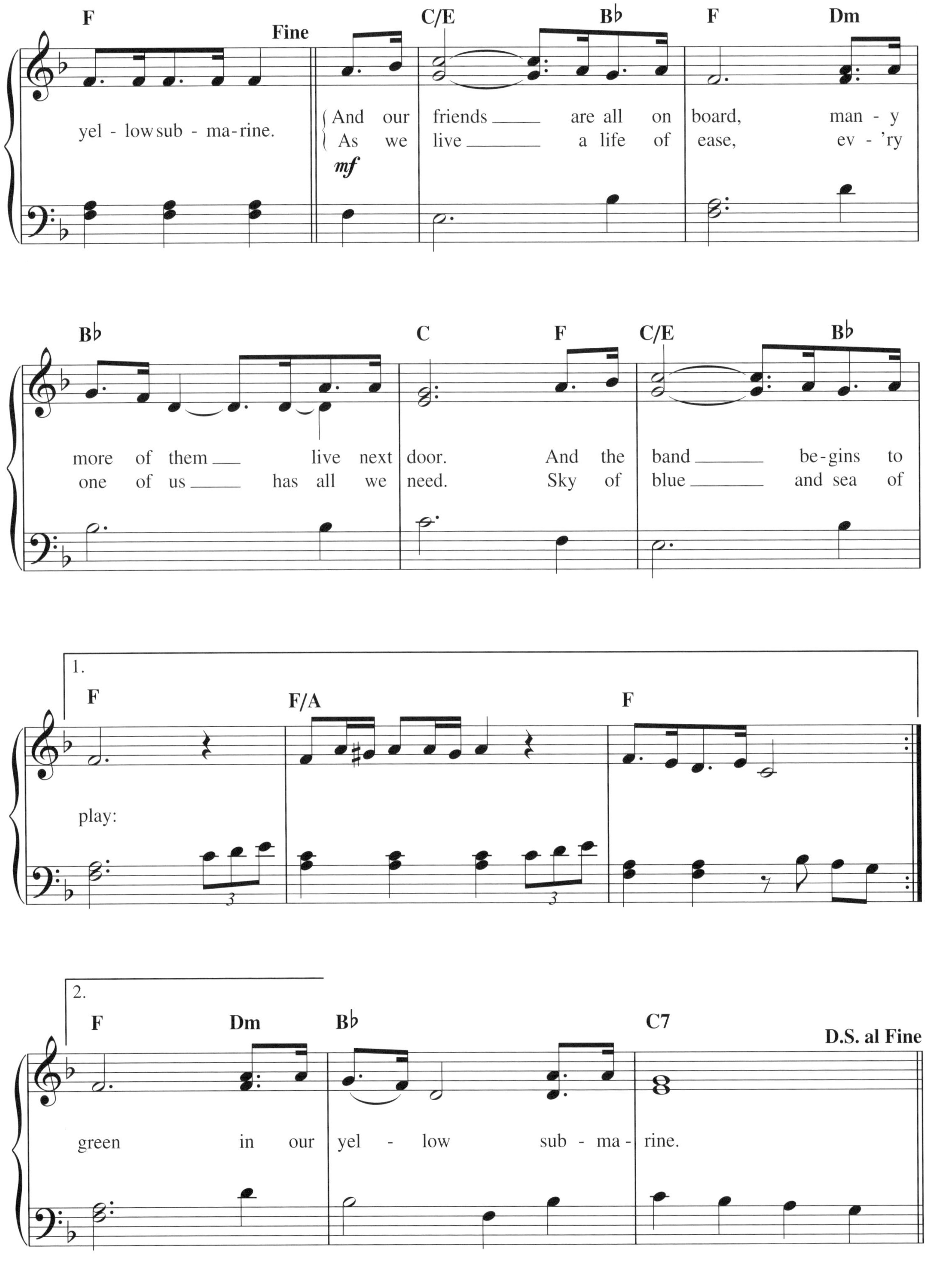
F
Fine
C/E
B♭
F
Dm
yel - low sub - ma-rine.
And our friends are all on board, man - y
As we live a life of ease, ev - 'ry
mf
B♭
C
F
C/E
B♭
more of them live next door. And the band begins to
one of us has all we need. Sky of blue and sea of
1.
F
F/A
F
play:
2.
F
Dm
B♭
C7
D.S. al Fine
green in our yel - low sub - ma - rine.